NATION-
BUILDING &
Citizenship

NATION-BUILDING & Citizenship

Studies of Our Changing Social Order

ENLARGED EDITION

Reinhard BENDIX

WITH A NEW INTRODUCTION AND BIBLIOGRAPHIC ADDENDUM BY

John Bendix

TRANSACTION PUBLISHERS
New Brunswick (U.S.A.) and London (U.K.)

Fifth printing 2007

New material this edition copyright © 1996 by Transaction Publishers. New Brunswick, New Jersey. Enlarged edition originally published in 1977 by University of California Press. Original edition published in 1964 by John Wiley & Sons, Inc. "Tradition and Modernity Reconsidered" included with permission of Mouton & Co., The Hague.

This book is printed on acid-free paper that meets the American National Standard for Permanence of Paper for Printed Library Materials,

Library of Congress Catalog Number: 95-50673
ISBN: 978-1-56000-890-3
Printed in the United States of America

Library of Congress Cataloging-in-Publication Data

Bendix, Richard.
    Nation-building and citizenship: studies of our changing social order / Reinhard Bendix; with a new introduction by John Bendix.—Enl. ed.
        p. cm.
    Includes bibliographical references and index.
    ISBN 1-56000-890-3 (pbk. : alk. paper)
    1. Authority. 2. State, The, I. Title.
HM271.B38   1996   95-50673
306.2—dc20   CIP

For Karen, Erik, and John

CONTENTS

PART THREE

INTRODUCTION TO THE
TRANSACTION EDITION

In 1964, when this book was originally published, 50 new states had emerged and joined the U.N. in the previous twenty years. By 1994, a further 50 new states have achieved sovereignty. Today's entrants to statehood are no less in need of building a national political community than their predecessors were.

While our language of "building" suggests an architectonic metaphor for this process, the present book directs our attention not so much to the community of individuals within the nation as to the relations that are established between individual and state during nation-building. While the development of citizenship and the interplay between tradition and modernity are important in this process of social and political change, the key theme is the examination of authority patterns.

THEMES

What continues to make this book relevant is not only what it has to say directly about past and present nation-building in the cases that are scrutinized, but also what is has to say generally about social and political transformations. Change to the social order comes about in part owing to conflicts between groups, and the past contexts of such conflicts shape issues long afterwards. Social conflicts are not easily reduced only to questions of material interest or the malevolence of elites, nor do they have a predictable trajectory. Nation-building is also not synonymous with creating democracy, even though both take time. Rather, authority relations are transformed through mutations of political institutions as well as of societal interests, through culture and social structures whose nature is driven by ideas and the "half-articulated longings" of individuals.

This book is about how states and civil societies interact in their formation of a new political community, a theme that is as old as the debate between Hegel and Marx and as new as Eastern Europe and Russia in the 1990s. It is a book about the

> varied reactions to having lost one's place in an established order of things and hence of seeking, often desperately, for a new basis of personal and collective self-respect[1]

that is expressed in nationalism, the drive to achieve sovereignty and in the desire for citizenship.

While the methods are historical and comparative, and the argument that all newly independent countries respond both to past models and foreign examples, the central theme of political authority itself deserves some elucidation.[2] The interpretation of authority used here derives from Max Weber's sense that those who exercise rule are rarely satisfied unless convinced they have in some manner earned the right to rule. The ruled look for compensation or reasons for their subordinate position, whether in this world or the next. The consequence of these dual expectations within this hierarchical order is contractual: a legitimation of authority based on social utility, but a limitation imposed through the consent of the ruled.[3]

As Weber himself noted, a legitimate order is guided by the belief in its existence, and it is from this basis in belief that Weber derived his tripartite categorization of authority: traditional, charismatic, and legal-rational. In practice, these forms of authority may overlap, or the beliefs derive from additional sources; in practice, too, the exercise of authority often means tension between following the rules and having individuals act in their own interest.

With the disruption of the established social and political structures in recent centuries brought about by changes in everything from commercialism to scientific and technical discoveries, new claims are made by individuals and groups either for greater political participation or for a greater share in the benefits that have been brought about. The desire for integration in polity and economy is common to both citizenship and nationalism claims, but it is also a function of authority patterns. The legitimation of a divine monarch by his subjects is not the same as the legitimation of an elected Cabinet by citizens; the authority exercised under colonial rule is not the same as native rule after independence; the authority of Communist party rule is not the same as what follows it. The locus of authority and the nature of the relationship of individual to state change each time. Nation-building and the inclusion of new groups into citizenship is a process of finding a new basis for authority in a new polity.

CONTEXTS

The passage of time obscures the context in which a work was originally conceived. Contemporary disputants forget that their own positions came out of examinations and analyses of earlier positions. It is all too easy in the discussion of development and social change to use an anachronistic perspective that finds an older work deficient in its gender, or dependency, or world-systems perspective, even when that very terminology is of later vintage. It makes more sense to try to situate a work within the context of its own time and discourse.

Our perspective has also been affected by where and how newly independent states have been created. In the mid-1960s, new states were primarily in Asia and Africa, with Indian independence in 1947 having a particularly powerful demonstration effect on aspirations elsewhere. Nowhere was this more evident than in sub-Saharan Africa, where in the short period from 1957 to 1964, 25 new countries emerged. The political assessments and economic prospects at the time were optimistic. Still, some colonial powers in Africa proved reluctant to hand over power or end dependent relations, leading to protracted struggles and long independence timetables for countries like Mozambique and Angola.

The states gaining independence in the 1970s and early 1980s were quite different, often small archipelagoes and islands in the Pacific and Indian Oceans and in the Caribbean. While there were valid reasons for granting self-determination, the headiness characteristic of the 1960s was supplanted by concern about the proliferation of microstates, and many of the independence arrangements of the later 1970s were contingent ones. As the colonial vestiges of global empires vanished, new states emerged in a world of economic constraint and globalized commerce, a world in which external political dependence and superpower tensions loomed large. The latest sovereign nations, beginning in the late 1980s, have been the republics of the former Soviet Union.

If one views the developments in conjunction with actions to democratize existing states in the Iberian peninsula, Eastern Europe, South America, and Africa, self-determination resonates differently than in the early 1960s. That is, in an earlier era, political and social change was associated with shaking off foreign and imperialistic rule. Some inhabitants in the new states of the former Soviet Union regard the past rule by ethnic Russians in this older fashion. Colonial rule frequently left behind a legacy of foreign institutional structures, laws, and norms that could be adapted or rejected but could not be ignored. But the more recent sovereign states are emerging in the context of demands to create new or homegrown structures, laws, and norms. Newer states cannot completely ignore what came before, and must make choices of what to adapt and what to reject. My father wrote of the "balancing of contingencies upon which the legitimacy of a political order rests," and it is a viewpoint that has not lost its applicability to the newer versions of state or nation-building we now witness.

One should not forget that gloomier outlooks today about the economic and political prospects of new nations stand in great contrast to the spirit of optimism that prevailed in the late 1950s and early 1960s. National leaders, like Nigeria's Nnamdi Azikiwe, made stirring speeches declaring that

> what remains for us to do now is to dedicate our lives anew to the fascinating task of nation-building. The past is gone with all its bitterness and rancor and recriminations. The future is before us and great events await the leadership of the wise and brave.[4]

Academics spoke of the progress humankind was making in social, economic, and political arenas; economic growth, development, and modernization were the fashionable terms of the day.

Analogies were drawn between the historical emergence of European nation-states and the independence that was being achieved on other continents in the post-World War II era. There was a shared faith between nationalists and social scientists about where things seemed to be headed, and a belief in historical parallels.

Unlike many at the time, my father was troubled by the explicit teleology of much of the discussion, and struck a note of caution about the new faith. To understand the sources of his skepticism, it is useful to sketch some aspects of the intellectual discourse of the day.

The term *nation-building* was used in two political science titles which appeared in 1962 and 1963, one a study of Burma, the other an edited collection arising from a conference panel.[5] That nations needed to be built was not a sudden realization of the later twentieth century, though: d'Azeglio had quipped more than a hundred years earlier that "we have made Italy; now we have to make Italians."[6]

The implication, of course, was that having created a new political entity called the nation (but which more properly should have been called the state), one had to craft a polity out of what had been a relation of dependency. Napoleon stated it clearly in 1800 to the Council of State: "We have finished the romance of the Revolution. Now we must begin its history." The dependency of the past had been that of subjects to their kings and aristocracy; the dependency of the present has been that of distant non-European peoples on European colonial powers. One might venture that the dependencies of the future are still being developed, for sometimes they seem to involve resource or environmental constraints, at other times be bound to economies and global markets, and at still other times seem to be intensely local drives for new kinds of self-sufficiency or self-determination which have as little to do with older state structures as possible.

Max Weber's observation that "time and again we find that the concept 'nation' directs us to political power" is close in spirit to the current work, for it points to the need to examine agency, authority, legitimacy and how citizens are connected to newly formed states.[8] It is easy to forget that

> nation-building is generally a slow process, partly because the new loyalty must in some measure displace some system of old loyalties, tribal or other, and partly because the state is large, vague, impersonal, and often associated in the subject's mind

at least as much with taxes and onerous regulations as with benefits.[9]

In the early 1960s, nation-building was seen as a task that fell to new elites.[10] The term "nation-building" was meant as a shorthand to understand the "discontinuities in tradition, culture, social organization, and material standards" newly independent countries were experiencing.[11] The major "discontinuity" studies that appeared before 1964—Daniel Lerner's *The Passing of Traditional Society* (1958), Rupert Emerson's *From Empire to Nation* (1960), Clifford Geertz, ed., *Old Societies and New States* (1963), Kalman Silvert's *Expectant Peoples* (1963)—pointed to the societal contrasts between tradition and modernity that nation-building implied.

Yet conceptually, analytically disparate processes were being understood under the rubric of nation-building.[12] One contribution came from the economic literature on growth and development; the significant indicator was the accelerating increase in output per head since 1800, attributed to industrialization.[13] Industrialization was seen as a complex process of the substitution of mechanical for animal or human power, intensive use of mineral resources, technological innovation, capital investment, the establishment of factories, and so on. Industrialization processes included mechanization (power), specialization (labor), monetization and accumulation (capital), transportation and distribution (goods), and communication (markets). This structural classification suggested that some nations would be ahead of others in terms of measurable output per head.

Karl Marx's preface to *Das Kapital* had already noted that when some are ahead, others will be behind: "the industrially more developed country presents to the less developed country a picture of the latter's future." Scholars like Leibenstein and Gerschenkron took up this notion, casting it in terms of economic backwardness, to understand and explain what effects such relative position had on growth.[14] Marx, like a number of nineteenth-century German economists (List, Hildebrand, Sombart, Schmoller), was also proposing an evolutionary, stage theory of economic growth.[15]

In the early 1960s, many Western commentators looked less to Marx than to Rostow, whose *Stages of Economic Growth* carried the unsubtle subtitle, *A Non-Communist Manifesto*.[16] Rostow proposed a five phase scheme: traditional society, preconditions for take-off, take-off, drive to maturity, and the age of high mass con-

sumption. Rostow's scheme had the advantage of focusing on ac-
celerated social change, an aspect not always emphasized in stage
theories, and the transition to "self-sustaining" growth stressed how
irreversible the changes were.[17]

A rather different set of impulses and studies came from political scientists, particularly under the auspices of the Social Science
Research Council's Committee on Comparative Politics. The focus was on the idea of political development, and the key figure
was Gabriel Almond. With collaborators, he produced (in rapid
succession) the major programmatic statement in political science
of structure-function theory applied to the non-Western world; a
highly influential, survey-based, comparative study of political
culture; and a new mode of analysis for the subfield of comparative politics.[18] In 1963, the first two edited volumes of the Princeton
series on political development appeared, to be followed by seven
others over the next 15 years.[19] The approach, according to Almond, was to provide codifications of the knowledge at the time
on comparative institutions: communication, bureaucracy, education, political culture, and political parties.[20]

The conceptual scope of political development was all-encompassing. Even in 1966, Pye could find ten meanings associated
with it:[21]

1. the political prerequisite of economic development (Baran,
   Hirschman, Ward);
2. the politics typical of industrial societies (Rostow);
3. political modernization (Coleman, Lipset, Deutsch);
4. the operation of a nation-state (Silvert, Shils);
5. administration and legal development (Weber);
6. mass mobilization and participation (Geertz, Emerson,
   Hoselitz);
7. the building of democracy (Fallers, Eisenstadt, Shils);
8. stability and orderly change (Deutsch, Riggs);
9. mobilization and power (Coleman, Parsons, Almond);
10. one aspect of a multidimensional process of social change
    (Lerner).

From this welter of perspectives, the Comparative Politics
Committee tried to isolate the most fundamental characteristics

of a "development syndrome." They agreed that it was composed of:

    a. an attitude toward equality, as seen in mass participation, universalistic laws, and the recruitment to public office;
    b. political capacity, as measured by government performance in terms of outputs, efficiency, and rationality; and
    c. the differentiation of structures and division of labor in government shown by the functional specificity of roles and the integration of complex structures and processes.

With various nods to Maine, Tönnies, and Weber as precursors, members of the Committee concluded that the process of political development could be seen as encompassing the five crises of identity, legitimacy, penetration, participation, and distribution. The sixth crisis, integration, seen as a resolution of the first five, proved difficult to articulate within the same framework.[22] Indeed, establishing a sequence for the crises that was generalizable proved difficult: the closest approximation was seen in English historical experience, with other European nations following "more chaotic patterns." Rather than adopting a linear, stage sequence, as Rostow had, this framework rested on an implicitly evolutionary theory of turning points, couched in the language of process, transition, and pattern.

The desire for systematic comparison which underlay the analysis of development meant the use of new terminology. The older terms—state, powers, offices, institutions, public opinion, and citizenship training—were eschewed in favor of, respectively, political system, functions, roles, structures, political culture, and political socialization.[23] There was also a universalizing assumption that all societies had structures that performed political functions, and these were conceptualized in terms of inputs and outputs of the political system. Universality permitted comparison between nations, because one had the same basis: if all nations had input functions, then one could ask the same questions in widely different systems, for example, how are interests articulated?[24] Finally, implicit at first but soon made explicit was an emphasis on empirical methodology, particularly surveys, with the goal of developing "plausible, testable hypotheses."[25]

The third approach, and the one closest to *Nation-Building and Citizenship*, came from those social scientists who were interested in the processes of social change. The major impetus came from the Committee for the Comparative Study of New Nations, sponsored by the Carnegie Corporation. The New Nations Committee's genesis came in 1958–59 among a group of resident fellows (Shils, Apter, Fallers, Geertz) at the Center for Advanced Studies in the Behavioral Sciences. They could look to the many new field studies, dissertations, and reflections on India (Weiner, Rudolph, Shils, Harrison, Srinivas) and Africa (Coleman, Sklar, Apter, Zolberg, Carter), and soon on Japan as well (Ward, Lockwood, Scalapino, Levy).

If the Committee on Comparative Politics had its focus on structure and codification, as well as on conferences and edited publications, then the Carnegie-sponsored New Nations Committee's agenda was to research the underlying principles in social and political development of new nations, and to train students in appropriate theories and methods. "Rather than emphasizing area specialization," a 1963 programmatic statement put it, "we prefer to consider certain common experiences that the new nations have entertained, seeking to compare broadly similar historical stages that they share," such as colonialism and the response to it, nationalism.[26] This effort appealed to social anthropologists, historically minded sociologists, economic historians, and to others not primarily engaged in (if at times benefitting from the analysis of) growth statistics or structural-functionalism studies. Behind many of these "new nation" studies lay Weberian inspiration and interpretation.

The key focus was not growth or development but "modernization," summarized by one scholar as a revolutionary, complex, systemic, global, lengthy, phased, homogenizing, irreversible process.[27] The idea of modernization had been linked, by Levy and Black among others, to the use of inanimate sources of power and greater human control over the environment, a development that was assumed to have begun with the rise of science and technology in Europe.[28] As a result, when scholars examined the new nations of the 1960s, they often made analogies to European experience.

Technological change itself was often of less interest than the observable societal concomitants: urbanization, social mobility or the integration of strata in a modernizing sector, the development of secondary associations or of "transitional types" (Lerner), and the behavior of modernizing elites (Shils). Change meant new behavior patterns and modes of thought concerning family relations, the role of government, the importance of education and literacy and so on.[29] If one scholar found the history of political parties, educational and administrative innovation, and a stable geographic base to be the relevant factors, to another it was the consolidation of a modernizing leadership, economic and social transformation and the integration of society.[30]

Free use was made at the time of ideas about growth, political development and modernization by economists, political scientists, and sociologists, and there were many efforts to build bridges across disciplines and approaches. Indeed, it is relevant to the form this book took that my father helped initiate an interdisciplinary Research and Training Group in Comparative Developmental Studies at Berkeley which met regularly at the Institute of Industrial Relations.[31] The group was created "in the belief that intellectual interchange across disciplines is a vital part of regular academic life," and like many faculty seminars at Berkeley, regular meetings were held at which ongoing work was presented and discussed.[32]

In 1964, when my father was chairman, the group included sociologists (Lipset, Smelser, Schurmann), political scientists (Apter, Haas), economists (Galenson, Landes, Leibenstein, Rosovsky), and an anthropologist (Mandelbaum). The major publications by some of the scholars of this group which appeared in the 1960–1965 era— *The First New Nation* and *Political Man* (Lipset), *Ghana in Transition* and *The Politics of Modernization* (Apter), *Labor in Developing Economies* (Galenson), *Beyond the Nation-State* (Haas)—give a sense of the common set of concerns, as well as the kinds of papers which were discussed. The membership of the group fluctuated somewhat over the years,[33] but the relatively close ties between Chicago and Berkeley sociology and anthropology departments (as well as the connection through the Carnegie Committee) meant that Geertz, Fallers, and Shils could be counted as extended members of this intellectual clan.

There was also a second group (co-chaired by Apter and Lipset) which began in 1964 at the Institute of International Studies, its focus more specifically on "Theory and Methods of Comparative

Studies." Its membership was more exclusively comprised of sociologists and political scientists.[34] Various visiting scholars, most importantly Stein Rokkan, who collaborated on the citizenship material in *Nation-Building* (as well as with Lipset on other work), and M.N. Srinavas, also exerted influence on this book. It is also of some importance to the contemporary comparative material that my father received a "Reflective-Year Fellowship" from the Carnegie Corporation which allowed him to spend nine months (1961-62) doing research in India and Japan.

The first preface to *Nation-Building and Citizenship* noted that it seemed worthwhile to "explore in some depth the possibilities of an alternative approach" to the neo-evolutionary orientation many social scientists were taking in their analyses of the underdeveloped areas of the world. My father was not alone in his caution, for even as the frameworks for discussing growth, development, and modernization were articulated, they were found wanting.

At about the same time as Rostow, Hoselitz had proposed an alternate classification of growth (based on Parsonian pattern variables), arguing that "economists have, on the whole, seen little usefulness in the various theories of economic stages," and noting that even Schumpeter considered the use of stages "most primitive."[35] Pye (1963) cautioned that "social thinkers are no longer comfortable with any concept which might suggest a belief in 'progress' or 'stages of civilization,'" and "in a similar mood, Coleman (1965) tells us that the dangers of 'ethnocentrism, teleological bias, and the absence of a single objective measuring rod complicate the conceptualization of 'political development.'"[36] Even the search for the kinds of individual factors favored by structural-functionalists, such as the persistence of competitive party systems, were thwarted by the diversity of the Third World. The process of modernization, if one followed European history, was also a "succession of crises of access" that could "result in a breakdown in national solidarity" due to social displacement, status changes, and discontent with existing institutions.[37]

So while my father was not alone in his skepticism, his responses to the prevailing schools of thought set him apart.[38] He was not enamored of evolutionary parallels, arguing that once a certain kind of social change, such as the French Revolution or the Industrial

Revolution, had occurred, it represented a breakthrough of a kind that could not occur again in the same fashion.[39] He was fond of quoting Heraclitus's observation that it was not possible to step into the same river twice. His view was shaped instead by Weber's notion that the prevailing condition is the persistence of custom. There can be breaks with tradition, which lead to new routinization, and change can also be reversed, but the notion that evolution was directional or that it proceeded from uniform causes were not positions either Weber or my father held.

My father's critique of system and functional analysis was related to this stance, as it derived from his twin belief that Schumpeter had been correct in his observation that "social structures, types and attitudes are coins that do not readily melt" and that "societies are always in transition from past to future." The analytic approaches that made more sense were "before-and-after" perspectives, complemented by taking the demonstration effects of the experience of other countries into account, and bearing in mind that being relatively backward could be a major disadvantage. He objected to using the very terms system and function, for they "take as given what is problematic, namely, the degree of interdependence and of unity that characterizes societies." The abstract terms were taking on greater reality than what they were meant to denote, and seemed a form of the "fallacy of misplaced concreteness" (Whitehead).

The conceptual apparatus of modernization, finally, may be thought of as the central foil for this book, and as such does not need elaboration.[40] But it is appropriate to note my father's later reflections of what he was trying to do. He felt that euphemisms like "developing" or "less developed" were a means of intellectually coping with the vast contrast between rich and destitute countries, for

> it is more comfortable to acknowledge the contrast between rich and poor nations if one can assume that the latter are indeed on their way toward self-sustained economic growth. And this result seems assured if it is assumed that sooner or later every society passes through similar stages of development.[41]

Such a sense of historical inevitability bothered him, for he wanted to

> give back to men of the past the unpredictability of the future and the dignity of acting in the face of uncertainty. In looking back,

we observers tend to deprive the past of the future belonging to it because our knowledge of subsequent events misleads us.

He wanted to take, as he said with reference to Weber, an "anti-utopian view of the social world which is nevertheless open to its possibilities of development." Karl Marx, in the *Eighteenth Brumaire of Louis Bonaparte*, had written that

> Men make their own history, but they do not make it just as they please; they do not make it under circumstances chosen by themselves, but under circumstances directly found, given and transmitted from the past.

Offering a reinterpretation 130 years later, in terms that could equally well be applied to *Nation-Building and Citizenship*, my father asserted instead that

> Men make their own history; but they make it under given conditions, and they become entangled thereby in a fate which is in part the result of other men having made their own history earlier.

NOTES

My thanks to Seymour Martin Lipset, Neil Smelser, Henry Rosovsky, Andrew Janos, Regina Bendix, Gerald Feldman, Noel Farley, and an anonymous referee for their comments and corrections.

1. Reinhard Bendix, *Embattled Reason*, Vol. 1 (New Brunswick, NJ: Transaction Publishers, 1988), p. 211.

2. The following is derived from the entry on "Autorität" contributed to the *Staatslexikon* of the Görres-Gesellschaft (Freiburg: Herder Verlag, 1985), as well as Chapter 9 of *Embattled Reason*, Vol. 1.

3. The quality of the communication, the hierarchical relationship, and the distinction between the authority of the person or that of the office are further aspects of the definition of the term. See "Authority," *International Encyclopedia of the Social Sciences* (New York: Macmillan & Free Press, 1968).

4. From his 1960 Inaugural Address as governor-general, in Larry Diamond, *Class, Ethnicity and Democracy in Nigeria* (Syracuse, NY: Syracuse University Press, 1988), p. 64.

5. Lucian Pye, *Politics, Personality and Nation-Building: Burma's Search for Identity* (Cambridge: MIT Press, 1962), and Karl Deutsch and William Foltz, eds., *Nation-Building* (New York: Atherton Press, 1963). The term was also featured in an article title (*Journal of International Affairs*, 1962), but had been used much earlier in Nicholas Butler's 1930 Cobden lecture, "Nation-Building and Beyond," and by the British colo-

nial secretary Arthur Creech Jones who spoke of "the slow work of nation-building." See his *Labour's Colonial Policy* (London: Fabian Society, 1946).

6. Eric Hobsbawm, *Nations and Nationalism since 1780* (New York:
Cambridge University Press, 1990), p. 44. For more on d'Azeglio, see
Priscilla Robertson, *Revolutions of 1848: A Social History* (New York:
Harper, 1960).

7. Francois Furet and Mona Ozouf, eds., *A Critical Dictionary of the
French Revolution* (Cambridge: Belknap Press, 1989), p. 279.

8. Max Weber, *Economy and Society*, Vol. 1 (New York: Bedminster
Press, 1968), pp. 397–98.

9. J. Roland Pennock, *Democratic Political Theory* (Princeton, NJ:
Princeton University Press, 1979), p. 213.

10. "All the founders of the new states...confront the necessity of
legitimating themselves before their people. They all accept...the task
of organizing and maintaining a modern political apparatus, that is, a
rationally conducted administration, a cadre of leaders in...a party system, and a machinery of public order." See Edward Shils, "On the Comparative Study of the New States," in Clifford Geertz, ed., *Old Societies
and New States* (New York: Free Press, 1963), p. 2.

11. Geertz, *Old Societies*, p. v.

12. Karl Deutsch took the "building" model seriously, suggesting that
the metaphor had implications for the analysis of a new nation's elements,
construction, financing, and whether it was a truly free-standing entity. By
contrast, he saw the "growth" terminology as suggesting an organic set of
stages and "national development" as an integration of building and growth
notions. See Deutsch and Foltz, *Nation-Building*, p. 3.

13. The theoretical groundwork was laid in the interwar years by Harrod
and Domar, modified by Keynes and elegantly reformulated later by
Solow; the empirical data, using Keynes's national income accounting
system, came primarily from Kuznets. Among many others who contributed to the discussion at the time were Heilbroner, Hirschman, Hoselitz,
and Moore.

14. The quote is in Alexander Gerschenkron's *Economic Backward-
ness in Historical Perspective* (New York: Praeger, 1962, p. 6. See also
Harvey Leibenstein, *Economic Backwardness and Economic Growth* (New
York: Wiley, 1957).

15. Ludwig Bendix, Reinhard's lawyer father, studied under Schmoller
but subsequently found Dilthey's teachings more congenial. There is thus
a personal background for the skepticism Reinhard later expressed about
stage theories.

16. Walt Rostow, *The Stages of Economic Growth* (London: Cambridge
University Press, 1960).

17. See Richard Easterlin, "Economic Growth: Overview," in the *International Encyclopedia of the Social Sciences* (New York: Macmillan
& Free Press, 1968). Applications of and variants on Rostow in the mid-
1960s included Organski (*The Stages of Political Development*, 1965),

Black (*The Dynamics of Modernization*, 1966), and Holt and Turner (*The Political Basis of Economic Development*, 1966).

18. Gabriel Almond and James Coleman, eds., *The Politics of the Developing Areas* (Princeton, NJ: Princeton University Press, 1960); Gabriel Almond and Sidney Verba, *The Civic Culture* (Princeton, NJ: Princeton University Press, 1963); Gabriel Almond and G. Bingham Powell, *Comparative Politics: A Developmental Approach* (Boston: Little, Brown, 1966).

19. The first two were Lucien Pye's *Communication and Political Development* and Joseph LaPalombara's *Bureaucracy and Political Development*. They were followed by Robert Ward and Dankwart Rustow, *Political Development in Japan and Turkey* (1964); James Coleman, *Education and Political Development* (1965); Lucian Pye and Sidney Verba, *Political Culture and Political Development* (1965); Joseph LaPalombara and Myron Weiner, *Political Parties and Political Development* (1966); Leonard Binder, *Crises and Sequences in Political Development* (1971); Charles Tilly, *The Formation of National States in Western Europe* (1975); and Raymond Grew, *Crises of Political Development in Europe and the United States* (1978).

20. Gabriel Almond, *A Discipline Divided: Schools and Sects in Political Science* (Newbury Park: Sage, 1990), p. 223.

21. Lucian Pye, *Aspects of Political Development* (Boston: Little, Brown, 1966), pp. 33–45.

22. Pye, *Aspects*, pp. 45–47; 62–67.

23. Almond and Coleman, *Politics of the Developing Areas*, p. 4.

24. Input functions included political socialization and recruitment, interest articulation, interest aggregation, and political communication; output functions were rule making, rule application and rule adjudication. These were derived "from the political systems in which structural specialization and functional differentiation have taken place to the greatest extent," namely, in Western systems. Almond and Coleman, *Politics of the Developing Areas*, pp. 16–17.

25. Almond and Verba, *The Civic Culture*, p. 44.

26. David Apter (then Executive Secretary of the Committee), "Preface," in Clifford Geertz, ed., *Old Societies*, p. vi. The programmatic statement was provided by Edward Shils's contribution to this volume, "On the Comparative Study of the New States."

27. Samuel Huntington, "The Change to Change: Modernization, Development and Politics," *Comparative Politics* (April 1971), pp. 283–322. Some modernization works, such as David Apter's *The Politics of Modernization* (1965), or Cyril Black's *The Dynamics of Modernization* (1966), defy easy disciplinary categorization.

28. For an excellent survey of this and related paradigms, see Andrew Janos, *Politics and Paradigms: Changing Theories of Change in Social Science* (Stanford: Stanford University Press, 1986).

29. Richard Sklar and C.S. Whitaker, *African Politics and Problems in Development* (Boulder: Rienner, 1991), p. 5.

30. Pennock, *Democratic Political Theory*, citing Rustow's *A World of Nations* (1967) and Black's *The Dynamics of Modernization* (1966), p. 214.

31. *Nation-Building and Citizenship* was the first in a series of studies of comparative development published by John Wiley.

32. The quote is from the preface to the first edition of *Nation-Building*. My father particularly cherished this kind of academic fellowship, and he participated in various incarnations of these groups throughout his long career at Berkeley. The sense of belonging, both to a wider academic community and to this particular campus, which they conferred was an important reason why he did not accept offers to teach permanently elsewhere.

33. It included the historian of science Thomas Kuhn and the demographer and sociologist William Petersen, for example.

34. Some of the ideas for the article "Tradition and Modernity Reconsidered," first published in 1967 and included in the second edition of *Nation-Building* (1977), were probably discussed here. This group was transformed in 1966 into the "Scholars' Group," which included other Berkeley faculty (Eugene Hammel, Martin Malia, and later also my father) and was chaired by Neil Smelser; the name was later transformed back to the "Group on Theory and Method in Comparative Studies."

35. See his "Theories of Stages in Economic Growth," in Bert Hoselitz et al., *Sociological Aspects of Economic Growth* (Glencoe: Free Press, 1960).

36. See Almond, *A Discipline Divided*, pp. 227, 229.

37. Kalman Silvert in 1964, cited in Seymour Martin Lipset, *Revolution and Counterrevolution* (New York: Basic Books, 1968), pp. 196-97.

38. And at some odds with contemporaries and colleagues like Eisenstadt; see the articles by Rueschemeyer and Hamilton in Theda Skocpol, ed., *Vision and Method in Historical Sociology* (Cambridge: Cambridge University Press, 1984). For an impressive analysis of the heterodox group of post-WWII historical sociologists to which my father belonged, see Dennis Smith, *The Rise of Historical Sociology* (Philadelphia: Temple University Press, 1991).

39. *Embattled Reason*, Vol. 1, pp. 136-37, 174-75.

40. Those who wish more critical context should consult Dean Tipps, "Modernization Theory and the Comparative Study of Societies: A Critical Perspective," *Comparative Studies in Society and History* XV (March 1973); Anthony D. Smith's "The Religion of Modernization," in his *Theories of Nationalism* (New York: Holmes & Meier, 1983), pp. 42-64 and Alvin So's *Social Change and Development: Modernization, Dependency, and World-System Theories* (Newbury Park, CA: Sage Publication, 1990).

41. Reinhard Bendix, *Force, Fate and Freedom* (Berkeley: University of California Press, 1984), p. 5; subsequent quotes are on pp. 43-49.

NATION-BUILDING
AND CITIZENSHIP

1

STUDIES OF OUR
CHANGING SOCIAL ORDER

Since World War II some 50 former colonial or dependent territories have become independent states in the sense that they have become member states of the United Nations. Now that these countries have been granted sovereignty over their own peoples, it is apparent that independence or sovereignty refer to proximate achievements, even where these terms have a clear legal meaning. Many of these newly independent countries still face the task of building a national political community, and we do not know whether they will succeed. Their efforts may be compared with the nation-building of Western countries during the eighteenth and nineteenth centuries. Ideally we should be able to analyze both processes in the same terms. An earlier generation of social scientists would have had little hesitation in doing so; having confidence in the progress of mankind, they adhered to a theory of social evolution that posited stages through which all societies must pass. Today there is more uncertainty about the ends of social change and more awareness of its costs. Belief in the universality of evolutionary stages has been replaced by the realization that the momentum of past events and the diversity of social structures lead to different paths of development, even where the changes of technology are identical. We have in fact little experience with studies of social change that would encompass the discrepancies of timing and structure between nation-building then and now. Still, the course of events has placed such studies on the agenda of the social sciences once again. As a result, the earlier and simpler theories of evolution are being replaced, however haltingly, by an interest in comparative studies of economic and political modernization. This more differentiated understanding of our changing social order poses an intellectual challenge.

The following studies are offered as an attempt to enhance our understanding of "development" by a re-examination of the European experience. The social and political changes of European societies provided the context in which the concepts of modern sociology were formulated. As we turn today to problems of development in the non-Western world, we employ concepts that have a Western derivation. In so doing, we can proceed in one of two ways: by formulating a new set of categories applying to all societies, or by rethinking the categories familiar to us in view of the transformation and diversity of the Western experience itself. These studies adopt the second alternative in the belief that the insights gained in the past should not be discarded lightly.

PROGRAMMATIC SUMMARY

The common theme of these studies is the analysis of authority relationships. Following an interpretation of public and private authority in Western societies from medieval patterns to those of the modern nation-state, we will contrast these patterns with those characteristic of Russian civilization. This analysis of the European experience is then used as a vantage-point for comparative studies of the preconditions of political modernization in Japan and of current efforts at nation-building in India. The major themes of these studies may be summarized as follows.

1. Western European societies have been transformed from the estate societies of the Middle Ages to the absolutist regimes of the eighteenth century and thence to the class societies of plebiscitarian democracy in the nation-states of the twentieth century. I begin with the type of "public" author-

ity characteristic of the medieval political community. Within this framework I characterize the traditional authority relationships which are an aspect of the rank-order of medieval society. The political and social order of medieval Europe underwent major transformations, ultimately producing the nation-state and a growing equalitarianism. An attempt is made to systematize Alexis de Tocqueville's analysis of this great transformation.

2. Individualistic authority relationships replace the traditional relations between masters and servants. Prompted by the economic opportunities and equalitarian ideas of an emerging industrial society, employers explicitly reject the paternalistic world view, but the same constellation of forces also gives rise to new forms of social protest. One can contrast the protest typical of the medieval political community with the protest typical of Western societies in their era of industrialization and democratization. This is the problem on which Marx focused attention, and it should now be possible to recast his analysis in the perspective of history. Following this reinterpretation of social protest, I focus attention on the extension of citizenship to the lower classes, in order to get at the linkages between changes in authority structure and in social relations. Starting from a condition of society in which the vast majority of the people were considered objects of rule—literally "subjects"—Western societies have steadily moved to a condition in which the rights of citizenship are universal. Where these rights are still withheld, conflict is apparent and often violent.

3. Next I turn to the resulting characteristics of the Western nation-state. By developing a nation-wide system of public authority, governments undergo a process of bureaucratization which is analyzed in contrast with the patrimonial pattern of administration that it supplanted. The analysis of bureaucracy as a self-contained system is then supplemented by an interpretation of policy implementation under conditions of conflicting group pressures, a development that has become an outstanding feature of the modern welfare state.

4. Changes in authority structure and social relations re-

veal broadly comparable patterns in the societies of Western Europe and, *mutatis mutandis,* in their frontier settlements abroad (if we ignore for the moment developments which may be called arrested by comparison, such as those of Spain or Southern Italy). However, there also exists a structural cleavage of long standing within Europe, between West and East. To bring the characteristics of the Western social structure into focus more sharply, it is useful to contrast them with certain features of Russian civilization, and in particular with those aspects of authority and social relations in an industrial setting that are symptomatic of the historically new phenomenon of totalitarianism.

5. Important as studies of Western societies and their structural transformations are, they no longer suffice in a world in which many countries have recently become independent states and in which all underdeveloped countries want to develop. The very fact of differential development calls attention, however, to the preconditions that favor nation-building and industrialization in some countries and not in others. An attempt is made to compare these preconditions for Japan and Prussia. Both of these countries were "late-comers," but both possessed an effective, nation-wide public authority prior to the rapid industrialization of their economies.

6. The assumption of a national authority does not apply to an economically underdeveloped country such as India, even though India is notable for the relative stability of her government since independence. As in other new nations, the success of India's drive toward industrialization is by no means assured, and the creation of a national political community is still at issue. Here we also examine public authority and social relations in a nation-wide context. Historically, as well as in her contemporary setting, India presents a striking contrast to the European experience: the hiatus between her modernizing elite who at present exercises authority and the strength of "communal" ties in the population at large. Examination of that hiatus can lead, however tentatively, to a formulation of some of the alternatives before India today.

The studies just summarized can be understood without the theoretical considerations that are given in the remainder of this chapter. But for those interested it is necessary to state the approach to the study of social change underlying these studies, their specific concern with the problem of authority, and the historical context within which that approach and concern have their place.

THE STUDY OF SOCIAL CHANGE

Like the concepts of other disciplines, sociological concepts should be universally applicable. The concept *division of labor*, for instance, refers to the fact that the labor performed in a collectivity is specialized; the concept is universal because we know of no collectivity without such specialization. Where reference is made to a principle of the division of labor over time—irrespective of the particular individuals performing the labor and of the way labor is subdivided (whether by sex, age, skill, or whatever)—we arrive at one meaning of the term *social organization*. We know of no society that lacks such a principle. It is possible to remain at this level of universal concepts. A whole series of mutually related concepts can be elaborated deductively in an effort to construct a framework of concepts applicable to all societies. But in such attempts the gain in generality is often won at the expense of analytic utility. Efforts in "pure theory" should be subjected to periodic checks to ensure that concepts and empirical evidence can be related one to the other. Universal concepts such as the division of labor require specifications that will bridge the gap between concept and empirical evidence, but such specifications have a limited applicability. Many other concepts of sociohistorical configurations—bureaucracy, estates, social class—are similarly limited. It is more illuminating to learn in what ways the division of labor in one social structure differs from that in another than to reiterate that both structures have a division of labor.

These considerations point to a persistent problem in sociology. Concepts and theories are difficult to relate to empirical findings, while much empirical research is devoid of theoretical significance. Many sociologists deplore this hiatus, but the difficulties persist and tend to reinforce the claims of pure theory on one hand and pure methodology on the other. The following studies attempt to steer a course between this Scylla and Charybdis by relying upon familiar concepts as a base line from which to move forward. Since these concepts have a Western derivation, it is necessary to rethink them in terms of the extent and limits of their applicability. But since they are selected so as to encompass major transformations of society, they may also serve as a framework within which a good many, more detailed empirical studies take on added significance. Such critical use of familiar concepts is adopted here in the belief that the changing social order of Western societies can provide the foundation for studies of social change outside the Western orbit—as long as premature generalizations of a limited experience are avoided.

In this introductory discussion I consider terminological questions as well as certain general assumptions of the conventional approach to the study of social change before formulating the framework to be adopted in the following studies.

Industrialization, modernization, and development are terms frequently used in current discussions of social change. To avoid misunderstanding it is necessary to state how these terms will be used in the following discussion. By *industrialization* I refer to *economic* changes brought about by a technology based on inanimate sources of power as well as on the continuous development of applied scientific research. *Modernization* (sometimes called *social and political development*) refers to all those *social* and *political* changes that accompanied industrialization in many countries of Western civilization. Among these are urbanization, changes in occupational structure, social mobility, development of education—as well as political changes from absolutist institutions to responsible and representative governments, and from a laissez-faire to a modern welfare state. More simply, the two terms refer to the technical-economic and the socio-political changes familiar to us from the recent history of Western Europe. The term *development* may be used where reference is made to related changes in both of these spheres. There is nothing inherently wrong about using the history of Western societies as the basis of what we propose to mean by *development*—as long as the purely nominal character of this definition is understood. The history of industrial societies must certainly be one basis for our definitions in this field. Trouble arises only when it is assumed that these are "real" definitions, that development can mean only what it has come to mean in some Western societies.

The term industrialization and its synonyms or derivatives refer to processes by which a society may change from a preindustrial, or traditional, or underdeveloped to an industrial, or modern, or developed condition. This idea of change suggests, albeit vaguely, that a number of factors are at work such that change with regard to one or several of them will induce changes in one or more dependent variables. Since the idea of such correlated changes culminating in an industrial society is a widely accepted theory of our changing social order, it will be useful to consider it at the outset.

One form of that theory—technological determinism—may be cited here as illustration. Its most consistent formulation is found in the work of Thorstein Veblen. In comparing English economic development with that of Germany and Japan, Veblen modifies the Marxian contention that the industrially more developed country shows the less developed country the image of its own future. Marx had based this conclusion on the argument that England was the "classic ground" of the capitalist mode of production and hence the appropriate illustration of his theoretical ideas, which concerned the "natural laws of capitalist production" that would work "with iron necessity towards inevitable results."[1] In his comparison between England and Ger-

---

[1] See Karl Marx, *Capital* (New York: Modern Library, 1936), p. 13. From the preface to the first edition. Note, incidentally, that Marx employs here the analogy between his procedure and that of

many, Veblen modifies this interpretation by drawing attention to the differences between the two countries. After pointing out that modern technological advance was not made in Germany but borrowed by her from the English-speaking world, Veblen states that:

> Germany combines the results of English experience in the development of modern technology with a state of the other arts of life more nearly equivalent to what prevailed in England before the modern industrial regime came on; so that the German people have been enabled to take up the technological heritage of the English without having paid for it in the habits of thought, the use and wont, induced in the English community by the experience involved in achieving it. Modern technology has come to Germany ready-made, without the cultural consequences which its gradual development and continued use has entailed upon the people whose experience initiated it and determined the course of its development.[2]

Veblen emphasizes especially that in England the "state of the industrial arts" has had time to affect the customs and habits of mind of the people, whereas in such countries as Germany and Japan where industrialization occurred later, ancient ways had been confronted suddenly by the imperatives of a modern technology. This sudden confrontation of the "archaic" and the modern made for an "unstable cultural compound." In contrast to Marx who considered such "transitions" largely in terms of "predicting" their eventual disappearance, Veblen notes the peculiar charac-

---

the physical sciences. Just as the physicist examines phenomena where they occur in their most typical form, so the study of capitalism must use England as its chief illustration.

[2] Thorstein Veblen, *Imperial Germany and the Industrial Revolution* (New York: Viking Press, 1954), pp. 85–86. Originally published in 1915. In the same year Veblen also applied this analysis to Japan. See Thorstein Veblen, "The Opportunity of Japan," *Essays in Our Changing Order* (New York: Viking Press, 1934), esp. p. 252. Veblen's approach, as characterized here, was reformulated and systematized subsequently by William F. Ogburn, *Social Change* (New York: Viking Press, 1932), *passim*, though Ogburn has stated that he was not familiar with Veblen's work when he developed his analysis of social change.

ter of this "transitional phase" in Germany and Japan. He describes the "want of poise" characteristic of German society, which makes for instability but also for "versatility and acceleration of change" as well as for aggression.[3] In the case of Japan, he emphasizes the special strength of the country arising from the combination of modern technology with "feudalistic fealty and chivalric honor."[4] In making such observations (in 1915), Veblen notes that little can be expected in the near future, because *as yet* the new technology has had little effect in inducing new habits of thought. But *in the long run* the "institutional consequences of a workday habituation to any given state of the industrial arts will necessarily . . . be worked out."[5] Thus, Veblen anticipates the transformation in habits of thought as an inevitable consequence of a people's adaptation to modern technology.

Veblen's theory is characteristic of a large class of approaches to the study of development which view the old and the new society in terms that are mutually exclusive. The more there is of modernity, the less there is of tradition —if not now then in the long run. Examples of this approach can be cited beginning, say, with Adam Ferguson's contrast between aristocratic and commercial nations and ending, for the time being, with empirical studies such as Robert Redfield's *Folkculture of Yucatan,* or Talcott Parsons' theory of pattern variables. To be sure, the early nineteenth-century contrasts between tradition and modernity barely disguised a largely ideological reaction to a rising commercial civilization, while later versions are more detached and circumspect. But even where the earlier invidious contrasts between the "golden age" of the past and the modern decay of civilization receive less credence than formerly, it is still difficult to avoid the generalizations implicit in this intellectual legacy. We are so attuned to the idea of a close association among the different elements of "tradition" or

[3] Veblen, *Imperial Germany,* p. 239.
[4] Veblen, *Essays,* p. 251.
[5] See *Imperial Germany,* p. 239. See the comparable prognostication for Japan in *Essays,* pp. 254–255.

"modernity" that wherever we find some evidence of industrialization we look for, and expect to find, those social and political changes which were associated with industrialization in many countries of Western civilization.

Implicit in this approach is the belief that societies will resemble each other increasingly, as they become "fully industrialized." Similarly, economically backward societies will become like the economically advanced countries—if they industrialize successfully. Yet these views, conditional as they are on "full industrialization," have little warrant. The industrial societies of today retain aspects of their traditional social structure that have been combined with economic development in various ways. They are like each other with reference to aspects covered by the adjective "industrial," such as the occupational structure, the urban concentration of the population, and others. Even that assertion is more complex than it appears to be, but it is merely tautological, if all "nonindustrial" aspects of such societies are tacitly eliminated from the comparison. Thus, "industrial society" is not the simple concept it is sometimes assumed to be, the industrialization of economically backward societies is an open question, and the idea of tradition and modernity as mutually exclusive is simply false. The most general experience is that modern, industrial societies retain their several, divergent traditions. It is, therefore, appropriate to consider the phenomenon of "partial development" in positive terms, as Joseph Schumpeter has done.

> Social structures, types and attitudes are coins that do not readily melt. Once they are formed they persist, possibly for centuries, and since different structures and types display different degrees of ability to survive, we almost always find that actual group and national behavior more or less departs from what we should expect it to be if we tried to infer it from the dominant forms of the productive process.[6]

That is, social structures and attitudes persist long after the conditions which gave rise to them have disappeared, and

[6] Joseph Schumpeter, *Capitalism, Socialism, and Democracy* (New York: Harper and Brothers, 1947), pp. 12–13.

this persistence can have positive as well as negative consequences for economic development, as Schumpeter emphasizes.[7] Accordingly, our concept of development must encompass not only the products and by-products of industrialization, but also the various amalgams of tradition and modernity which make all developments "partial."

However, this formulation does not do justice to the case. It may mean no more than that countries coming late to the process will not develop along the lines of Western countries like England or France, Marx and Veblen to the contrary notwithstanding. All countries other than England have been or are "developing" in the sense that they adopt from abroad an already developed technology and various political institutions while retaining their indigenous social structure frequently dubbed "archaic," "feudal," or "traditional." Unless we assume that development once initiated must run its course, we must accept the possibility that the tensions of the social structure induced by a rapid adoption of foreign technology and institutions can be enduring rather than transitory features of a society. Accordingly, our understanding of the changing social order will be seriously deficient, if it is modeled on the idea of an inverse relation between tradition and modernity. Industrialization and its correlates are not simply tantamount to a rise of modernity at the expense of tradition, so that a "fully modern" society lacking all tradition is an abstraction without meaning.

These considerations will be applied to the societies of Western Europe, Russia, Japan, and India which are examined in the following chapters. The development of each reflects this interplay between tradition and modernity. Today, all these societies except India are highly industrialized. All of these societies (including India) also possess relatively viable governments, and this fact sets them apart from "developing" societies marked by political instability. Western Europe, Russia, and Japan have unquestionably under-

[7] *Ibid.*, pp. 135–137. There Schumpeter analyzes the importance of earlier ruling groups for political structures which facilitated economic development by middle-class entrepreneurs.

gone the wholesale transformation of their social structures to which the term "development" refers. India is the only exception in this respect. It, therefore, provides us with an opportunity to examine how far the categories appropriate for the analysis of successful development can be applied meaningfully to a society whose development is uncertain. Such cautious exploration seems indicated as long as the discrepancies to which the phrase "partial development" refers are not assumed to be merely transitory complications. Important as industrialization is as a factor promoting social change, and similar as many of its correlates are, the fact remains that the English, French, German, Russian, or Japanese societies are as distinguishable from each other today as they ever were. Moreover, it is probable that some or many "developing" societies will not "develop" in the sense in which that term can be applied to the industrialized countries of the modern world. To think otherwise is to accept a neo-evolutionist approach which treats the eventual development of all societies (and the universality of processes of change) as a foregone conclusion.

Accordingly, concepts pertaining to industrialization, modernization, and development are concepts of limited applicability. Since so far relatively few societies have developed, our first task is to formulate categories with regard to the transformation of these few societies. Our understanding of "development" derives from this context and employs concepts appropriate to it. As we turn today to the "developing" areas of the non-Western world, we must be on our guard against the bias implicit in that Western derivation.

The source of this bias is not simple provincialism. After all, the degree to which modern social scientists are exploring the four corners of the earth in their quest for social knowledge is probably unique in the history of ideas. There is a cosmopolitan awareness of the diversity of cultures and great tolerance for the unique qualities of each people. Yet this awareness and tolerance are also associated with a scientific spirit that tends to conceive of complex societies as natural systems with defined limits and invariant laws governing an equilibriating process. As a consequence there is a strong tendency to conceive of a social structure and its change over time as a complex of factors that is divisible into independent and dependent variables. The search is on for the discovery of critical independent variables. If we can only discover them, we will have taken the first step toward planning the change of society in the desired direction. Control of critical variables will automatically entail planned change in a host of dependent variables as well. Ultimately, this imagery is derived from the model experiment in which all factors but one are held constant in order to observe the effects that follow when the one factor is varied deliberately and by degrees subject to exact measurement. It is readily admitted, of course, that in the social sciences we are far from approximating this model, but hopefully this deficiency will be overcome in time. Perhaps since every approach makes a priori assumptions, there is good reason to develop inquiries based on these assumptions as far as may be. However, these are not the only possible assumptions.

In particular, studies of social change in complex societies may hold in abeyance the tasks of causal analysis and prediction while concentrating on the preliminary task of ordering the phenomena of change to be analyzed further. Before we can fruitfully ask how social change has come about, or what changes are likely to occur in the future, we should know what changes have occurred, that is, what we want to explain and on what we must base our predictions. Accordingly, the studies assembled in this volume stay closer to the historical evidence than would be possible on the assumption that societies are natural systems, but they attempt conceptualizations of their own that go beyond what many historians (though not all) will find an acceptable level of abstraction. It will be useful to formulate this approach here in general terms. The studies to follow will exemplify it and show its utility and limitations.

As an abstract proposition most social scientists would agree that "order" and "change" must receive equal attention in the analysis of societies. The first term points to the pattern or structure of social life, the second to its fluidity. In practice, it has been difficult to achieve a proper balance in this respect. "Pure theory" and "pure empiricism" are the twin horns of this dilemma. There are those who criticize the insistence on direct observation and exhaustive gathering of facts as "anti-theoretical," as well as those who criticize every concept as an oversimplification and out of touch with social life as it "really" is. What is worse, both criticisms are offered in the name of science, as if that word were a magic wand with which to clear the path to knowledge and be one up on your colleagues. Such fetishism among scholars points to the persistent difficulty of relating concepts and theories to empirical findings, and yet the latter make little sense without them. The study of social change is a striking case in point.

All social structures have a time dimension which exceeds the life-span of any individual. That is, societies retain certain of their characteristics while individuals come and go. But the specification of such enduring (structural) characteristics is a matter of abstraction or inference. Only the behavior of individuals in interaction with others can be observed directly. Of course, such observation of behavior can note changes over time, but the time-span covered is necessarily limited and usually too short to encompass major changes of social structure. It is necessary, therefore, to extend the time-span of observable changes by relying on abstractions from the historical evidence in order to arrive at propositions concerning social change. Such propositions are not generalizations in the ordinary sense. They assert rather that one type of structure has ceased to prevail and another has taken its place. To make such an assertion it is first necessary to "freeze" the fluidity of social life into patterns or structures for purposes of analysis. Obviously, this procedure is hazardous. Wherever possible, an attempt should be made to check the abstractions used in terms of indexes derived from historical documentation or behavioral observation. But it is no argument to say that statements concerning long-run social changes involve abstractions. The only valid criticism is to show that another abstraction than the one proposed is in better accord with the known evidence and provides a more useful tool of analysis.

All studies of social change must use a "before-and-after" model of analysis. The first step is to identify the society or societies to be studied and to make sure that in some definable sense we have the same society after the change as before. This is usually achieved by taking certain geographic, cultural, and historical entities such as countries as givens. Note that this initial step already implies a temporal limitation, since we usually mean, say, by American society, the enduring social structure since the end of the eighteenth century. For certain purposes we might include the colonial period but we surely will exclude the Indian tribes which constituted "American" society before Columbus. Our next step is to formulate a model of the earlier social structure which has since undergone change. By this I mean that we identify that structure in such a way that we can distinguish it from other structures. In doing this, we must be on our guard against the "fallacy of the golden age." It is indispensable to provide a base line of an earlier social structure if we are to study social change. But we must avoid conceiving that change as a falling away from an initial condition which is often idealized unwittingly merely by contrasting it with later structures. Therefore, our model of the initial condition should encompass the range of patterns and, from some standpoint, the assets and liabilities that are compatible with it. The model must allow us to observe that "range" without forcing us to say that the social structure to which it refers has changed already. This usually means, as we shall see later, that a social structure is identified by two (or more) principles of thought and action which are antagonistic and complementary, but not mutually exclusive.[8]

In this way we conceive of the future as uncertain, in the

[8] For a theoretical discussion of this type of concept formation, see Reinhard Bendix and Bennett Berger, "Images of Society and Problems of Concept-Formation in Sociology," in Llewellyn Gross, ed., *Symposium on Sociological Theory* (Evanston: Row, Peterson & Co., 1959), pp. 92–118. Related points are also taken up in Reinhard Bendix, "Concepts and Generalizations in Comparative Sociological Studies," *American Sociological Review*, Vol. 28 (1963), pp. 532–539.

past as well as the present. We do not know where currently observed changes may lead in the long run; hence we must keep the possibility of alternative developments conceptually open. For the present this is relatively easy to do, since we are genuinely uncertain. But the same consideration applies to the past, and here we must be on guard against the "fallacy of retrospective determinism." The task is complicated by our knowledge of the historical outcome, which makes us more knowing than we have a right to be. The fact is that the eventual development of past social structures was uncertain as well. It is, therefore, useful to conceptualize the conflicting tendencies inherent in any complex society. The "unity" of past societies is more often than not an illusion derived from implicit contrasts with the later structure of the same society. But, in fact, feudalism was compatible with strong as well as weak kings; the rule of law is compatible with major changes of emphasis, say, between the rights of the individual property holder and the claims of public convenience and welfare; democratic institutions retain identifiable characteristics even though the nature of parliamentary institutions or political parties has changed greatly. In all such cases the same structure is compatible with much variation. If we comprehend both, we will understand order and change as simultaneous characteristics of society.

One can approach such comprehension by systematically asking questions contrary to the manifest evidence in order to bring out those capacities of the structure which any limited body of evidence tends to omit. By exposing observations at any one time to a wider range of comparison with the past (or with other social structures) than is sometimes customary, we may approach an understanding of social structure and change without at the same time moving too far away from the evidence. In this way we impart a salutary degree of nominalism to the terms we use in referring to social structures.[9] Comparative sociological studies are especially suited

[9] It may be added that in this way we also supplement the observations of participating social actors without losing sight of them entirely. The fact that some social actors are aware not only of their own milieu but of the society in which they live is one

to elucidate such structures, because they increase the "visibility" of one structure by contrasting it with another. Thus, European feudalism can be more sharply defined by comparison, say, with Japanese feudalism, the significance of the Church in Western civilization can be seen more clearly by contrast with civilizations in which a comparable clerical organization did not develop. Such contrasts can help us identify the issues confronting men in their attempts to develop their country along the lines of one pattern or another. And by using this comparative perspective in our analysis of the piecemeal solutions which men have found for the characteristic problems of their society, we can bring into view the historical dimensions of a social structure.

A comment concerning *functionalism* may be added here, albeit without attempting a consideration of the extensive literature on this subject. The idea of society as an interdependent system possessing regularities of its own emerged in the transition from the estate societies of the late medieval period to the equalitarian societies ushered in by the French Revolution. This model is adapted to (and projected from) the new interdependencies that developed with the institution of private property and subsequently with the legal and political extension of individual rights to other areas of social life. Interdependencies with regularities of their own exist in all societies, but unless we propose to develop a set of categories applicable to all such "systems" everywhere and at all times we must fall back upon the construction of more limited models, for example, such types of social structure as "feudalism." Such models are inductive in so far as they are developed by reference to the cluster of attributes brought to prominence by the comparative method, and deductive in so far as they employ the principle of "logical coherence" for the sake of conceptual clarity. If functionalism is merely a term which

---

reason why the social theorist should in my judgment deal with this "theoretical consciousness" as part of his evidence, though he must always remain detached from it in his own work. Social actors not only define their situation, abide by norms, and adhere to values—they also theorize about their society!

emphasizes the scholar's interest in the interdependence of attributes in a given social structure, then the following formulations use a "functional approach." Their purpose is to set up models that are based on logical simplifications of the evidence but that can serve the orderly isolation and analysis of particular clusters of attributes. The "logical coherence" of such models should not be attributed to society, however. If the term "functionalism" is used so as to imply such coherence as an attribute of society, then the typological approach employed here is not a "functional" one.

THEORETICAL PERSPECTIVES

The studies of social change contained in this volume make comparisons and contrasts between similar phenomena in a given society over time, or in several societies. Statements concerning "similarity" require a process of abstraction which allows us systematically to examine men in different times and places and to use their actions as clues to the structure of their societies. To this end the following studies use the distinction between *formally instated authority* typically entailing relations of command and obedience, and customarily or voluntarily established *associations* typically involving relations based on affinities of ideas and interests, or state and society for short.[10] Since my use of this distinction is in-

---

[10] The profusion of more or less overlapping terms is the bane of sociology, and the following discussion is not, I am sorry to say, free of that evil. The distinction between state and society has only limited applicability, presupposing as it does the existence of territorial nation-states. But the distinction between formally instated authority and affinities of interest giving rise to associations among men is found in all societies, and the emphasis here is on this universal. This is the reason why the present discussion relies on Max Weber's work rather than on the otherwise lucid and insightful discussion of Ernest Barker, *Principles of Social and Political Theory* (Oxford: Clarendon Press, 1951), esp. pp. 2–5, 42 ff. The following formulation is based on Reinhard Bendix, *Max Weber, An Intellectual Portrait* (Garden City: Anchor Books, Doubleday & Co., 1962), pp. 473–478.

debted to Max Weber's work, a brief exposition of his approach is appropriate here.

Weber employs two broad criteria for the analysis of *social* actions. One type of action is based on considerations of material advantage irrespective of personal or social obligations (*Vergesellschaftung*). The other type of action is prompted by a sense of solidarity with others—for example, kinship relations, the feeling of affinity among professional colleagues, or the code of conduct observed by members of an aristocracy (*Vergemeinschaftung*). The constant interweaving of economic utility and social affinity in the sense, say, that businessmen develop codes of ethics in their business or devoted parents look to the social and economic advantage in the marriage of their daughter, represents *one* recurrent theme in Weber's work. Indeed, this conceptualization is also a method of analysis. Repeatedly, Weber inquires into the ideas and affinities associated with the apparently most single-minded pursuit of gain and into the economic interests associated with the apparently most other-worldly pursuit of religious salvation. Even then, the approach is limited to social relationships (sometimes referred to as a "coalescence of interests") arising from actions which are construed as a reasoning, emotional, or conventional pursuit of "ideal and material interests."[11]

Men may be guided not only by considerations of utility and affinity, but also by a belief in the existence of a legitimate order of authority. In this way Weber wishes to distinguish between social relations (such as the supply-and-demand relations on a market) that are maintained by the reciprocity of expectations, and others that are maintained through orientation toward an exercise of authority. The latter orientation typically involves a belief in the existence of a legitimate order. Identifiable persons maintain that order through the exercise of authority.

[11] To get at the main outline of Weber's framework, I omit all lesser distinctions, such as the subdivision of reasoning or calculating actions into instrumental and value-oriented behavior, and I use common-sense words in lieu of Weber's complex terminology.

> Action, and especially social actions which involve social relationships, may be governed in the eyes of the participants by the conception that a legitimate order exists.[12]

This order endures as long as the conception of its legitimacy is shared by those who exercise authority and those who are subject to it. In addition, a legitimate order depends upon an organizational structure maintained by the persons who exercise authority and claim legitimacy for this exercise.

> A social relationship will be called a formal organization, where the admission of outsiders is governed by limiting or exclusive rules and where compliance with the regulations [of that organization] is guaranteed by the actions of a chief and, usually, an administrative staff, who are specifically oriented towards the enforcement of these regulations. . . .[13]

The shared conception of a legitimate order and the persons in formal organizations who help to maintain that order through the exercise of authority constitute a network of social relations which differs qualitatively from the social relationships arising out of a "coalescence of interests." In this way actions may arise from the "legitimate order" and affect the pursuit of interests in the society, just as the latter has multiple effects upon the exercise of authority. Throughout his work Weber insists that this interdependence of all social conditions must be recognized, but that at the same time the scholar must make distinctions such as that between a "coalescence of interests" and a "legitimate order" of authority, arbitrary as such distinctions inevitably are.

In one sense the distinction refers to a universal attribute of group life, because the two aspects of association—however

[12] Max Weber, *Wirtschaft und Gesellschaft* (Tübingen: J. C. B. Mohr (Paul Siebeck), 1925), I, p. 16 (cited as Weber, *WuG* hereafter). For a somewhat different translation see Max Weber, *The Theory of Social and Economic Organization* (New York: Oxford University Press, 1947), p. 124.

[13] *WuG*, I, p. 27. For a somewhat different translation see *Theory*, pp. 145–146. Since this translation was published in 1947, the term "formal organization" has become so familiar in the sociological literature and it is so accurate a rendition of Weber's term *Verband* that I prefer to use it rather than "corporate group."

interrelated they are—are not reducible to each other. In all societies there are affinities of interest which arise from relations of kinship, the division of labor, exchanges on the market, and the ubiquitous influence of custom. Such affinities will limit the exercise of authority which would attempt to interfere or destroy those affinities, though admittedly authority can do much in this respect and the limits are always tenuous and changing. But in all societies there also are some individuals designated in some way to discharge the responsibility of maintaining the peace, adjudicating conflicts, and superintending community functions and public works. Certainly, such individuals are involved in social relations and affected by the affinities of interest that characterize these relations. But however pervasive, these involvements will not fully account for the actions constituting the exercise of authority. That exercise requires some element of neutrality, though admittedly such disengagement of the persons in authority is a matter of degree and may become quite nominal. My thesis is that from an analytical standpoint, authority and association constitute interdependent but autonomous spheres of thought and action which coexist in one form or another in all societies. These general considerations provide the basis for formulating the recurrent issues of *legitimation* involved in the exercise of private and public authority.

POLITICAL COMMUNITY AND PUBLIC AUTHORITY

Typically, comparative studies take a single issue which is found in many (conceivably in all) societies and seek to analyze how men in different societies have dealt with that same issue. A few examples will make this point clearer. Max Weber writes on the secular causes and consequences of religious doctrines. We may call the issue with which he is concerned the inner-worldly incentives implicit in religions; this issue is examined in the Western religions, culminating in Puritanism, which are contrasted with the inner-worldly incentives implicit in other religions such as Hinduism or Buddhism. In his *Ancient City,* Fustel de Coulanges writes of the steps by which a consecrated deity of the community generally prevails over the worship of separate deities of family and tribe. Coulanges is concerned with the social (here religious) preconditions of civic unity, which he examines over time and in a comparison between ancient Greek and Roman society. In her *Origins of Totalitarianism*, Hannah Arendt discusses antisemitism in Europe and race relations in South Africa. The author is here concerned with the moral crisis of discrimination. Both those who discriminate and those who are discriminated against, lose or are made to lose their humanity, either because they claim and exploit as virtues what are accidents of birth or because they lose the standards of one community without quite acquiring the standards of another. All these are moral issues, and to neglect them greatly curtails the sociological imagination. Explicit attention to this moral dimension can only enhance the intellectual challenge inherent in sociological concepts.

In these and similar studies a recurrent issue of the human condition is identified in order to examine empirically how men in different societies have encountered that issue. If the emphasis is to be on *men acting* in societies, these studies will have to give full weight not only to the *conditioning* of these actions but in principle also to the fact that men have *acted* in face of the agonizing dilemmas that confront them. To maintain this balanced approach, comparative studies should not only highlight the contrasts existing between different human situations and social structures, but also underscore the inescapable artificiality of conceptual distinctions and the consequent need to move back and forth between the empirical evidence and the benchmark concepts which Max Weber called "ideal types." In this way such studies reveal the network of interrelations which distinguishes one social structure from another.

The common referent of the following studies is the formation and transformation of political communities which today we call nation-states. The central fact of nation-building is the orderly exercise of a nationwide, public authority. The following discussion expands on the abstract distinction between authority and association by analyzing certain recurrent problems in the relations between formally instated officials and the public which is to abide by the rules that are promulgated authoritatively. The purpose is to characterize *the balancing of contingencies upon which the legitimacy of a political order rests.*

Order in a political community can be understood in terms of its opposite—anarchy. Anarchy reigns when each group takes the law into its hands until checked by the momentarily superior force of an opponent. Some subordination of private to public interest and private to public decision is, therefore, the *sine qua non* of a political community. Implicitly more often than explicitly, the members of a political community consent to that subordination in an exchange for certain public rights. While governments vary greatly with regard to the subordination they demand and the rights they acknowledge, the term "political community" may be applied wherever the relations between rulers and ruled involve shared understandings concerning this exchange and hence are based in some measure on agreement.[14]

Both those in high office and the public are affected by whatever shared understandings determine the character of the political community. Ultimately, it is a question of "good will" whether the laws and regulations of political authority are implemented effectively by the officials and sustained by public compliance and initiative.[15] Administrative efficiency and public cooperation are *desiderata* in any country. Everywhere they are in short supply; they wax and wane with circumstances, sentiments, and the efforts made to enhance them. This fluidity is suggested by the phrase "good will." Any exercise of authority depends upon the willingness of officials

[14] For a lucid, modern exposition of this consensual basis of government see Joseph Tussman, *Obligation and the Body Politic* (New York: Oxford University Press, 1960), Chap. 2.

[15] The phrase "good will" refers to a friendly but acquiescent disposition which often borders on or blends with indifference. This willingness to let others proceed is much closer to the accountant's concept of good will as a salable asset arising from the reputation of a business than it is to Kant's "notion of a will which deserves to be highly esteemed for itself and is good without a specific objective."

and the public to respond positively to commands or rules (or at least not too negatively); hence ultimately the official relies on the existence of good will. The single policeman exercising his authority in a crowd of people can suppose, for the most part, that the crowd will allow him to exercise that authority, much as a bank functions effectively as long as the depositors are confident that they can get their checks cashed whenever they want to do so. Effective authority thus depends upon cumulative, individual acts of compliance or confidence. Those in authority proceed on the assumption that the requisite compliance or confidence will be forthcoming; it is only on this basis that the policeman can hope to order a crowd or the bank can invest its funds for long periods. Public good will in these cases consists in the willingness to let the policeman or the bank proceed; and these authorities do so on the assumption that they possess an implicit mandate (or credit) which will become manifest through the public's willingness to let them proceed.

It is hard to discern such an underlying agreement for several reasons. Persons in official positions, in proceeding as if good will is forthcoming, do so presumably because it has been forthcoming in the past. Under ordinary circumstances this expectation turns out to be justified; the requisite, shared understandings are found to exist—though the evidence is indirect. Public compliance and cooperation are similarly implicit. In nontotalitarian countries most citizens have few contacts with public officials. Their private lives are mainly outside the ken of government, and ready compliance with laws or rules further minimizes the occasions for legal and administrative action. Although citizenship *allows* for more active participation, there are only a few instances in which it *requires* positive action—for example, payment of taxes, jury duty, military conscription and service, application for a passport.

But circumstances may not be ordinary. Then the extent and the limits of the implicit agreement are tested, and these intangible foundations of the political community become exposed. Most officials and citizens shy away from such tests. Officials become apprehensive that in exercising their legal authority they may not meet with that minimum of public co-operation which they require in order to do their duty. Since under ordinary circumstances it can be assumed that compliance will be forthcoming once the official's action is initiated, it is only logical to hesitate when extraordinary circumstances put that assumption in doubt.[16] The citizen is in an analogous dilemma. The fewer contacts he has with the government, the less chance there is that his law abidance is put to the test. He knows himself to be ignorant of many laws and rules and he also knows that ignorance does not exempt him from punishment. Again, under ordinary circumstances this knowledge may trouble him only occasionally (e.g., when income-tax returns fall due). But in some critical situations these apprehensions become acute, because easy-going and passive compliance suffices no longer. When the citizen is confronted with policies with which he violently disagrees on moral grounds, ready compliance as the mark of good citizenship becomes a doubtful virtue. Since ethical choices of this kind are usually difficult and often demand great personal sacrifice, most citizens prefer to be saved the pain of standing up and being counted.

Yet there is a positive side to these tests and apprehensions. The very existence of the underlying agreement may be in doubt, if officials are too fearful and fail to exercise their formally constituted authority in critical situations. Certainly, the extent and the limits of that agreement become manifest only as officials take actions the consequences of which are uncertain. Critical situations may be handled successfully: after having taken official initiative, public authorities find that the requisite public cooperation is forthcoming. In such cases prompt action in the face of uncertainty is, indeed, a means of building up shared understandings between the government and its people. But cumulative causation can work both ways. Critical situations successfully handled by public officials will strengthen the political community by increasing

[16] This is presumably one foundation for the rule of thumb according to which judges and administrators tend to confine themselves to the case before them, in terms of its specific attributes, rather than consider its wider policy implications.

everyone's awareness of the shared understandings. Official actions which meet with public defiance reveal the area in which formal authority is out of step with the willingness of the public to comply, and, in addition, raise the specter of a similar discrepancy in other areas that have not yet been tested.

It is too simple, of course, to refer to the "public" in the singular, since there are many publics. A given official action usually involves some publics rather than the "public at large," and any given public is likely to be involved in some of its interests rather than in all. Ever since Rousseau and the French Revolution made the consensus of the "general will" the touchstone of the national political community, it has been apparent that nothing like a nationwide consensus is either possible or necessary. The passive compliance with which citizens ordinarily allow officials to carry out their duties already encompasses substantial disagreements which may be ignored simply because they are not articulated in a politically significant way. Those who argue and grumble when they get traffic tickets do not pose a problem for the regulation of traffic. In the field of political opinion there is evidence of a significant division between those who are politically active and the public at large. The activists show substantial agreement concerning the legal order and the rules of the game, while the public at large shows much dissension and often little support for the rules of the game. But ordinarily such public sentiments are dissipated in small talk. Even where dissension is articulated on a specific issue and poses serious problems for the maintenance of the legal order, it is often combined with consensus on other issues so that there is some leverage for bargaining and pressure tactics. Only the total disloyalty or ostracism of a section of the population is a genuine hazard to the underlying agreement of such a community, though coercion can make a nation-state endure even in the presence of that hazard to its foundations, as South Africa demonstrates.

These examples assume the existence of the nation-state. In the context of the Western experience that assumption tends to be taken for granted, although one must remember that considerable governmental instability is compatible with the nation-state. However, there are many countries which have not succeeded in attaining even a minimum of long-run stability, that is, minimal agreement concerning the rules that are to govern the resolution of conflicts. Under such conditions dissension escalates and tends to prevent effective government. In addition, one should remember that too much agreement is a hazard as well. Nazi Germany, in its later phase, exemplifies a pathology of success rather than failure. The proverbial rule-mindedness of the Germans is certainly a major buttress of public authority, but it was exploited by a criminal regime to ensure the acquiescence, connivance, or cooperation of a whole population in the systematic extermination of the Jews and other peoples designated as undesirable.

HISTORICAL PERSPECTIVES

The exercise of authority will be discussed primarily in relation to changes in the structure of societies since the industrial and democratic revolutions of Western Europe in the eighteenth century. Accordingly, it is necessary to formulate in abstract terms those aspects of the exercise of authority which are specific to the structural transformations of Western societies. As the discussion proceeds and comparisons are added with countries outside the Western orbit, this basic formulation will be modified as this appears appropriate for the particular analytic purposes intended at that point.

Although authority and social relations are *relatively* autonomous spheres of thought and action in all societies, it is probably true that the separation of these "spheres" is greatest in Western societies since the eighteenth century. Already in medieval Europe, the exercise of authority had given rise to the two competing structures of patrimonialism and feudalism: government as an extension of the royal household as against government based on the fealty between landed nobles and their king. This tension between royal authority and the society of estates was a characteristic of medieval political life. A similar duality between state and society has been characteristic of many Western societies since the beginning of the present era in the eighteenth century. A nation-wide market economy emerged, based on the capacity of individuals to enter into legally binding agreements. This legal and economic development occurred at a time when public affairs were in the hands of a privileged few—a restriction which was reduced and eventually eliminated through the extension of the franchise. Both the growth of a market economy and the gradual extension of the franchise gave rise to interest groups and political parties which mobilized people for collective action in the economic and political spheres, thus transforming the social structure of modern society. On the other hand, in the sphere of public authority, access to official positions was gradually separated from kinship ties, property interests, and inherited privileges. As a result, decision-making at the legislative, judicial, and administrative levels became subject to impersonal rules and attained a certain degree of freedom *vis-à-vis* the constellations of interest arising in the society.

These pervasive, structural transformations of Western societies will be examined in more detail (see Chapter 2). They have been accompanied by major changes of intellectual perspective; indeed the social theories that were advanced to interpret these transformations have necessarily been a part of the societies they sought to comprehend. Weber's categoric distinction between legitimate authority and constellations of interests is itself a late outgrowth of our changing social order and intellectual development. In order to use such a distinction as an analytical tool, we must remain aware of its limited applicability, and this is best achieved by understanding its historical context. By learning how men come to think as they do about the societies in which they live, we may acquire the detachment needed to protect us against the unwitting adoption of changing intellectual fashions and against a neglect of the limitations inherent in any theoretical framework. To this end a brief look backward in the history of ideas will be useful.

Medieval European culture was based on the belief in a supreme deity, whereas in modern European culture man and society along with nature are conceived as embodying discoverable laws which are considered the "ultimate reality." As Carl Becker has put it:

> In the thirteenth century the key words would no doubt be God, sin, grace, salvation, heaven and the like; in the nineteenth century, matter, fact, matter-of-fact, evolution, progress. . . . In the eighteenth century the words without which no enlightened person could reach a restful conclusion were nature, natural law, first cause, reason. . . .[17]

The substitution of nature for God indicates the emergence of the modern world view, as this is reflected in literature, for example. Since antiquity "reality" had been represented in a heroic and a satiric-comic mode. The object of this older literature had been a poetic representation of reality as it should be, in terms of ideal contrasts between virtue and vice, between heroes and fools or knaves. These contrasts disappeared only in the naturalistic representations of nineteenth-century literature, since realism left no room for the older, unself-consciously moralistic view of the world. Similarly, premodern historiography consisted in what we would consider a moralistic chronicling of events, an assessment of history in terms of a moral standard accepted as given and unchanging. This perspective extended even to the facts of economic life. For these facts were treated in the context of estate management in which instructions concerning agriculture, for example, occur side by side with advice on the rearing of children, marital relations, the proper management of servants, and so forth. Here the moral approach to human relations was not at all distinguished from economic and technical considerations, because both are considered part of a divinely ordered universe. The common element in these premodern perspectives is the effort to discover "the moral law" which has existed, from the beginning of time, as the central fact of a world created by God.

In this view history consists in the unfolding of the divine law and of man's capacity to understand it and follow its

[17] Carl Becker, *The Heavenly City of the Eighteenth Century Philosophers* (New Haven: Yale University Press, 1932), p. 47.

precepts. To be sure, men cannot fully understand the providential design. But through their thoughts and actions, they reveal a pattern or order of which they feel themselves to be a vehicle or vessel, even though they understand it only dimly. Man's capacity to reason is not questioned, even though his development of that capacity remains forever partial, just as the ends of human action are not in doubt, though in an ultimate sense they remain unknown. One may speak broadly of a premodern world view as long as even the most passionate controversialists do not question the existence of the moral law and the divine ordering of the universe, though it is true that gradually since the Renaissance this world view becomes attenuated.

This long transitional period comes to an end with the emergence of concepts that are basic to modern social science such as economy, society, and the state together with less basic but equally modern ideas such as the public, intellectuals, ideology, and others. Based on a wholly secular conception of man, such as that formulated by Hobbes, concepts such as economy and society refer to a system of interdependence possessing a lawfulness or regularity of its own which must be understood as such rather than by reference to a Divine will. The following examples are given to illustrate how during the eighteenth and early nineteenth century men came to consider this intrinsic lawfulness of society.

In Rousseau's view the social order can be and ought to be based on the general will, an idea which presupposes that the individual acts for the whole community. In such a society, as George Herbert Mead has pointed out, ". . . the citizen can give laws only to the extent that his volitions are an expression of the rights which he recognizes in others . . . [and] which the others recognize in him. . . ."[18] This approach provides a model for a society based on consent so that the power of rule-making can be exercised by and for all. Such consent is directly related to the institution of property. As Mead states:

[18] G. H. Mead, *Movements of Thought in the Nineteenth Century* (Chicago: University of Chicago Press, 1936), p. 21.

If one wills to possess that which is his own so that he has absolute control over it as property, he does so on the assumption that everyone else will possess his own property and exercise absolute control over it. That is, the individual wills his control over his property only in so far as he wills the same sort of control for everyone else over property.[19]

Thus, the idea of a reciprocal recognition of rights specifically presupposes the equality of citizens as property owners. In this model of society equal men assert themselves and easily accept the assertions of others, thus leading to the self-regulation of society. To this day the idea influences our conception of the market and the sociological analysis of reciprocal expectations through which men interact in society.

Two observations may be added with regard to the conception of society as a *natural* order and of the economy as a self-regulating mechanism. In his *Ideas for a Universal History*, Immanuel Kant notes that personal decisions are free and yet part of a pattern of collective behavior with a regularity of its own. The selection of a marriage partner is an entirely personal decision, but in the aggregate marriages conform to an impersonal, statistical pattern.

Individual human beings, each pursuing his own ends according to his inclination and often one against another (and even one entire people against another) unintentionally promote, as if it were their guide, an end of nature which is unknown to them. They thus work to promote that which they would care little for if they knew about it.[20]

Here "nature" is invoked as a regulative principle, a concept somewhere between the traditional idea of the deity and the nineteenth century concept of factual regularity. One may see an analogy between Kant's concept of nature

[19] *Ibid.*, p. 17.
[20] Carl J. Friedrich, ed., *The Philosophy of Kant, Immanuel Kant's Moral and Political Writings* (New York: The Modern Library, 1949), p. 117. In the translation quoted here, the word "rarely" before "unintentionally" does not make sense and does not correspond to anything equivalent in the original; it has, therefore, been omitted.

and the classical economists' idea of men's "propensity to truck, barter, and exchange one thing for another," which enhances the "wealth of nations" if left to itself, thus revealing the workings of what Adam Smith calls the "invisible hand." The economists' model and a positive evaluation of the market with its juxtaposition of individual striving and over-all regularity is strikingly expressed in this passage by Hegel:

> There are certain universal needs such as food, drink, clothing, etc., and it depends entirely on accidental circumstances how these are satisfied. The fertility of the soil varies from place to place, harvests vary from year to year, one man is industrious, another indolent. But this medley of arbitrariness generates universal characteristics by its own working; and this apparently scattered and thoughtless sphere is upheld by a necessity which automatically enters it. To discover this necessary element here is the object of political economy, a science which is a credit to thought because it finds laws for a mass of accidents. . . . The most remarkable thing here is this mutual interlocking of particulars, which is what one would least expect because at first sight everything seems to be given over to the arbitrariness of the individual, and it has a parallel in the solar system which displays to the eye only irregular movements, though its laws may none the less be ascertained.[21]

Accordingly, such concepts as *economy* and *society* represent the recognition of a *natural social order* possessing regularities which can be investigated.

At the same time, social theorists of the eighteenth and nineteenth centuries were aware that this natural social order existed side by side with the *state,* an institutional framework which, in contrast especially to the market, depended upon the subordination of private to public interest. The development of this distinction between society and the state

[21] T. M. Knox, ed., *Hegel's Philosophy of Right* (New York: Oxford University Press, 1942), p. 258. For an analysis of American constitutionalism in terms of its derivation from this basic idea of classical economics see Sheldon Wolin, *Politics and Vision* (Boston: Little, Brown & Co., 1960), pp. 388–393.

has been traced elsewhere.[22] Here it is sufficient to indicate briefly how Weber's categories for the analysis of social relations and the exercise of authority represent a synthesis and development of two major intellectual traditions within the context indicated above.

One of these traditions is that of English empiricism from Hobbes to the Utilitarians, which makes human behavior in its sensory aspects the starting point of analysis. Weber accepts this tradition by acknowledging the basic importance of "material interests," but then modifies it by insisting upon the "ideal interests" involved even in the most single-minded pursuit of gain. If this insistence suggests that he approaches the utilitarian position from the standpoint of German idealism, it must be said also that he approaches the idealization of social solidarity (so prominent in conservative thought during the nineteenth century) from the standpoint of utilitarianism. For by his analysis of the economic interests involved in every relationship based on honor or spiritual ideals, Weber implicitly criticizes writers from Rousseau and de Maistre to Durkheim and Toennies for their praise of the community and social integration.

At the same time Weber recognizes the importance of the problem of integration. He seeks to solve it through an adaptation of Hegel's theoretical synthesis, the second intellectual tradition which greatly influenced him. Hegel had acknowledged that a certain degree of cohesion is achieved in society by the coalescence of interests which occurs through the mechanism of the market. But he insisted that individuals are capable of transcending their private interests, while government officials possess a "consciousness of right and a developed intelligence" which enables them to encourage the fullest development of the citizens. With the sovereign controlling at the top and interest groups exerting influence from the side of the public, the officials are prevented from using their skill and education "as a means to an arbitrary tyranny."[23] Weber develops this Hegelian po-

[22] See the discussion by Ernest Barker, *op. cit.*, pp. 1–88.
[23] See Knox, ed., *op. cit.*, pp. 161, 193, 280. In these passages Hegel combines the idealism of individual freedom with the ideas

sition by giving it a less idealistic interpretation. He believes, like Hegel, that not only the coalescence of interests on the market but cultural norms and conventions produce a degree of social cohesion. In his view individuals frequently transcend their private interests under the pervasive influence of a dominant status group. Like Hegel, Weber believes that social stability depends also on government and the exercise of authority. That exercise remains within bounds to the extent that rulers and ruled share a belief in the existence of a legitimate order. Such a belief may echo Hegel's statements concerning the official's consciousness of right and the individual's transcendance of his private interests, but Weber's analysis constantly emphasizes the materialistic aspect of such idealism. Still, Weber retains Hegel's distinction between "Civil Society" and the "State" by distinguishing the type of consciousness and the type of action appropriate to each. One can say that in his view Civil Society is characterized by the groups formed through the coalescence of material and ideal interests. The State, on the other hand, is based on a shared belief in a legitimate order, and its exercise of authority depends on an administrative organization with imperatives of its own.

Although reference has been made to Max Weber's work, it is well to remember that the broad distinction between authority and association or state and society has been a recurrent theme of social thought until recently. In the utilitarian contrast between the "natural identity" of interests on the market and the "artificial identification of interests" through the agencies of government, in Emile Durkheim's concern not only with the group integration of the individual but also with the use of state authority to protect the individual, or in W. G. Sumner's distinction between "crescive" and "enacted" institutions—we have repeated refer-

of enlightened absolutism by claiming that the free individual and the official of an enlightened absolute king (and thus society and government) stand in a relation of reciprocal support. Weber gives a "materialistic" interpretation of the insights embedded in Hegel's view of state and society in a manner that is analogous to Marx's materialistic interpretation of Hegel's philosophy of history.

ences to these two aspects of human association. There are signs that this tradition has been abandoned: several authors have attempted to show that the distinction between state and society is spurious by interpreting all political phenomena as by-products of the social structure. But is this shift of intellectual prespective a scientific advance, or is it rather an uncritical reflection of our changing social order in which public interests are jeopardized by conflicting group pressures (as they always are) and in which there is a marked decline in the effort to identify public interests?[24] Analysis of the transformation of Western societies can provide a framework for an approach to this question, although a full answer would require other investigations than those attempted in this volume.

[24] For a penetrating analysis animated by this question see Wolin, *op. cit.*, esp. Chaps. 9–10.

PART ONE

The following three chapters formulate benchmarks for analyzing the transformation of Western European societies. Their objective is to state what is meant by the political modernization of these societies. The approach is greatly indebted to the works of Alexis de Tocqueville and Max Weber, two authors often cited as modern classics. If the work of these men is illuminating, as is often asserted, then perhaps we should try to understand why and attempt to develop their analysis further.

Tocqueville analyzes the transformation of Western societies from the "aristocratic nations" of the past to the "democratic nations" of the present and future, covering a time-span of some seven centuries. No one doubts that the feudal order is sharply distinguished from an equalitarian social structure, however much the details of that distinction are subject to dispute. No one doubts that the French Revolution marked a transition despite all equally unquestioned continuities. Moreover, Tocqueville's admittedly speculative fears about a tyranny of the future uses implicitly a "logic of possibilities," which enables him to cope intellectually with contingencies of the future as well as transformations of the past. In this way he makes sure that he is dealing with genuine distinctions between patterns of social relations and political institutions at the beginning and the end of the time-span he chooses to consider. It is the merit of such long-run distinctions that they enable us to conceptualize significant dimensions of the social structure, either within the same civilization over time or between different civilizations. But it also follows that these distinctions will become blurred the more closely we examine social change in a particular setting and in the shorter run. This difficulty can be minimized, even if it cannot be eliminated, by placing the analysis of short-run changes within the framework of the long-run distinctions, for without the latter we are like sailors without stars or compass.

2

PREMODERN STRUCTURES
AND TRANSFORMATIONS OF
WESTERN EUROPEAN SOCIETIES

ASPECTS OF AUTHORITY IN
MEDIEVAL SOCIETY

Medieval Political Life

In turning now to the premodern structures of Western societies, I begin with Max Weber's use of the two concepts of patrimonialism and feudalism. The characterization of medieval political life by means of these concepts schematically presents the approach of a king and then the approach of the landed nobility. The real issues of medieval politics can be understood as conflicts and compromises resulting from these, logically incompatible approaches.

Patrimonialism refers, first of all, to the management of the royal household and the royal domains. This management is in the hands of the king's personal servants, who are maintained as part of the royal household and rewarded for their services at the king's discretion. On this basis patrimonialism develops as a structure of authority with the expansion of royal jurisdiction over territories outside the royal domains, though these may be expanding as well. Expansion in this context always implies increased delegation of authority, or conversely an increased independence of the king's deputies or agents. The men who previously attended the person of the king are charged with increased responsibility, receive greater and more permanent rewards for their service, rise in the world, and thus become less personally dependent upon their royal master.

From the standpoint of patrimonialism, the fundamental issue of medieval politics is the secular and religious position of the king. As the patriarchal master of his household, the lord of his domains, and the ruler of the territories under his jurisdiction, the king possesses absolute secular authority. At the same time he exercises his authority under God, a condition of rule symbolized by the consecration of his succession to the throne. The king performs, therefore, a twofold representative function. As patriarch he has absolute authority over his subjects, but in principle he has also the responsibility to protect his subjects and see to their welfare.[1] As the consecrated ruler under God, the king's authority is likewise absolute, but because of that consecration he is also bound by the divine law which he dare not transgress lest he endanger his immortal soul. Toward his people the ruler is, therefore, the secular representative of God and before God he is the secular representative of his people. This position as an intermediary means that in principle the king cannot deny the moral and religious limitation of his authority without undermining its legitimacy, but that the consecration of that legitimacy also justifies the absolute arbitrariness of his will.

Considered comparatively, these attributes of patrimonial kingship are not at all confined to Western Europe. The combination of the king's arbitrary will and his submission to a "higher law" is a general attribute of "traditional domination," as Max Weber uses that term. In China, for example, the Son of Heaven is responsible for the peace and welfare of

[1] In his concept of "traditional domination," Max Weber emphasizes this double function when he stresses that the king is bound by sacred tradition but that this tradition also legitimizes his absolute arbitrariness. Tocqueville's concept of the aristocratic ruler is rather similar, but perhaps with too little emphasis upon the element of arbitrary authority.

his people. In case of natural calamities a public ceremony is held, in which the Emperor acknowledges that responsibility and blames himself for the deficiencies through which the tranquillity of Heaven has been disturbed. Analogous ideas are found in other civilizations. The attempt to limit the arbitrary will of the supreme ruler by an appeal to the absolute sanctity of a transcendant power is, therefore, a *general* phenomenon. On the other hand, one can distinguish types of patrimonial kingship on the basis of the religious ideas and institutions through which the attempt is made to limit the king's arbitrariness. Western European kingship is distinguished from other types of patrimonial rule by a universal church which pits its organizational power against the absolute claims of secular rulers and, in the name of its transcendant mission, subjects these claims to the juridical conceptions of canon law. This is indeed, as Otto Hintze points out, one world-historical peculiarity of kingship in the Occidental tradition.

From this perspective it is a basic assumption of medieval political life that the personal ruler of a territory is a leader who exercises his authority in the name of God and with the consent of the "people."[2] Because he is the consecrated ruler and represents the whole community, the "people" are obliged to obey his commands; but in turn he is also responsible to the community. This idea of a reciprocal obligation between ruler and ruled was part of an accepted tradition; it can be

[2] The quotation marks refer to the ineradicable ambiguity of this term in medieval society. The "people" were objects of government who took no part in political life. Yet kings and estates frequently couched their rivalries in terms of some reference to the "people" they claimed to represent. In fact, "consent of the people" referred to the secular and clerical notables whose voice was heard in the councils of government. See the discussion of this issue in Otto Gierke, *Political Theories of the Middle Ages* (Boston: Beacon Press, 1958), pp. 37–61. It may be added that this ambiguity is not confined to the Middle Ages, since all government is based in some degree on popular consent and since even in the most democratic form of government the "people" are excluded from political life in greater or lesser degree. These differences of degree, as well as the qualities of consent and participation are all-important, once the typologies are used in specific analyses.

traced back to ancient Roman and Germanic practices, was greatly strengthened by Christian beliefs, but became formal law only very gradually.[3]

These characteristics of medieval kingship are closely related to the political conditions of royal administration. On the basis of the economic resources derived from his domain and, in principle, on the basis of his consecrated claim to legitimate authority, each ruler faces as his major political task the extension of his authority over a territory beyond his domain. In their efforts to solve this task, secular rulers necessarily rely upon those elements of the population which by virtue of their possessions and local authority are in a position to aid the ruler financially and militarily, both in the extension of his territory and the exercise of his rule over its inhabitants. But such aid from local notables can enhance their own power as well as that of the ruler. As a result, secular rulers typically seek to offset the drive toward local autonomy by a whole series of devices designed to increase the personal and material dependence of such notables on the ruler and his immediate entourage.[4] This typical antinomy of the premodern political community in Western Europe becomes manifest with every demand by secular rulers for increased revenue and military service. Local notables typically respond to such demands by exacting further guarantees of their rights, or increases of their existing privileges, by

[3] See Max Weber, *Law in Economy and Society* (Cambridge: Harvard University Press, 1954), Chap. V and *passim*.

[4] In his analysis of traditional domination, Max Weber distinguishes patrimonial from feudal administration, that is, the effort of rulers to extend their authority and retain control by the use of "household officials" or by their "fealty-relationship" with aristocratic notables of independent means. These two devices are by no means mutually exclusive, since "household officials" are usually of noble birth and in territories of any size demand autonomy, while "feudal" notables despite their independence frequently depend upon the ruler for services of various kinds. Contractual obligations as well as elaborate ideologies buttress the various methods of rule under these complementary systems. For an exposition of Weber's approach see Reinhard Bendix, *Max Weber, An Intellectual Portrait* (Garden City: Doubleday and Co., 1960), pp. 334–379.

way of compensating for the greater services demanded of them. The king in turn will resist such tendencies. He may attempt to divide the nobility and thereby weaken their resistance. He may seek allies with whose assistance he can expand the territories under his control and thus buttress his authority. He may seek to expand his administrative and political controls through greater reliance on royal servants. The vicissitudes of such struggles are many; they cannot be considered here.

The point to note is that under medieval conditions the king's power is limited where he finds it necessary or expedient to rely on the landed aristocracy. He may have conquered such nobles in battle and then reinstated them in their possessions provided they pledge their loyalty and service to him. Or territorial lords may have made that pledge of their own accord in return for which they receive what they already possess as grants with the attendant rights and perquisites. Such relations of reciprocal obligation are the basic institution of *feudalism*, which in medieval Europe complement the institution of *patrimonialism*. Writing in the early sixteenth century, Machiavelli already noted the major characteristics of these two competing structures of authority:

> Kingdoms known to history have been governed in two ways: either by a prince and his servants, who, as ministers by his grace and permission, assist in governing the realm; or by a prince and by barons, who hold positions not by favour of the ruler but by antiquity of blood. Such barons have states and subjects of their own who recognize them as their lords, and are naturally attached to them. In those states which are governed by a prince and his servants, the prince possesses more authority, because there is no one in the state regarded as a superior other than himself, and if others are obeyed it is merely as ministers and officials of the prince, and no one regards them with any special affection.[5]

Elements of feudal institutions have been traced back to the Germanic tribes and the conditions of European agriculture

[5] Niccolo Machiavelli, *The Prince and the Discourses* (New York: The Modern Library, 1940), p. 15.

following the decline of the Roman Empire. Relevant for the present discussion is only that eventually individual, self-equipped warriors come to control more or less extensive agricultural holdings of their own. A basic issue of medieval politics is how these separate domains can be combined—one might almost say, federated—into a more or less stable political structure.

From the standpoint of *feudalism* some degree of stability is achieved by means of the reciprocal ties between a ruler and his vassals. The vassal swears an oath of fealty to his ruler and thus acknowledges his obligation to serve him. In return, the ruler grants his vassal a fief, or confirms him in his existing possessions as a fief. Where the feudal element predominates, these grants include a guaranteed "immunity" such that within the territory held in "fief" the vassal is entitled to exercise certain judicial and administrative powers. (When the patrimonial element predominates, such powers either remain part of the royal jurisdiction or separate grants are made of them so that the king divides the powers he finds it necessary or expedient to delegate.) Considered comparatively, this type of authority is, again, a very general phenomenon. Under primitive conditions of communications the ruler who seeks to control a large territory is obliged to delegate the direct exercise of authority to others. These may be former household officials or feudal vassals. Typically, such notables are small territorial rulers in their own right and as such exempt from those obligations which are specifically excluded under the reciprocal understandings of fealty. However, Western European feudalism is characterized in addition by special juridical features and an ideology of "rights." The relations between a ruler and his vassals is consecrated through the affirmation of rights and duties under oath and before God, a practice which presupposes the conception of a transcendant system of justice.[6] Thus, just as the king's

[6] In his analysis of the *feud* as a component of medieval political life, Otto Brunner has shown that lords who defend their rights by force of arms do so in the belief that they are upholding the established order. Indeed, within limits, feuds are conceived in the medieval world as an integral part of politics. See Otto Brunner,

authority is circumscribed in principle by appeals to a higher moral law and by the political and legal powers of the church, so the autonomy of feudal jurisdictions is reinforced by the vassal's consciousness of his "right" and by the way in which the church can employ her secular powers and her canonical authority to protect that right.

The contentions between the patrimonial and the feudal principle of authority result in a system of divided and overlapping jurisdictions (or "immunities"). Each jurisdiction accords positive, public rights which entitle particularly privileged persons and corporate groups to exercise a specific authority and to levy fees or tolls for that exercise. As an aggregate such jurisdictions constitute the political community which may be held together firmly or precariously depending on the momentum of past events, external circumstances, the personal capacity of the participants, and the vicissitudes of the political struggle.[7] Under the ruler's strong or nominal authority the vassals and corporate bodies which owe allegiance to him fight or bargain with him and with each other over the distribution of fiscal and administrative preserves. In this setting politics consists of jurisdictional disputes and their settlement, by force of arms if necessary. Exceptionally strong, personal rulers may succeed in asserting the royal prerogatives and welding the several jurisdictions together, though in the absence of such strength at the center government administration may be little more than a sum total of the component jurisdictions. But even when the political unity of a whole realm is precarious, there is likely to be considerable unity in these jurisdictions.

In principle at least, each man belongs to such a jurisdiction. Depending on his rank he has some choice in the mat-

---

Land und Herrschaft (Vienna: R. M. Rohrer Verlag, 1959), pp. 17–41, 106–110.

[7] From time to time these struggles among patrimonial and feudal powers have a decisive outcome that establishes the pattern of subsequent developments. See the brief sketch of the different patterns in France, England, and Germany in F. L. Ganshof, *Feudalism* (2nd ed., Harper Torchbooks; New York: Harper & Row, 1961), pp. 160–166.

ter; but once he is a vassal to a lord or the member of a guild, his rights and duties are determined for him. He is bound to abide by the rules pertaining to his status lest he impair the privileges of his fellows. Classes in the modern sense do not exist, for the coalescence of interests among the individuals in an estate is based on a collective liability. That is, joint action results from the rights and duties shared by virtue of the laws or edicts pertaining to a group, rather than only from a shared experience of similar economic pressures and social demands. Under these conditions a man can modify the personal or corporate rule to which he is subject only by an appeal to the established rights of his rank or to the personal and, therefore, arbitrary benevolence of his master. In addition, the rights of the group as a whole might be altered in the course of conflicts and adjustments with competing jurisdictions. These principles of the medieval political structure are based, as Max Weber put it, on a system of personal rather than territorial laws:

> The individual carried his *professio juris* with him wherever he went. Law was not a *lex terrae*, as the English law of the King's court became soon after the Norman Conquest, but rather the privilege of the person as a member of a particular group. Yet this principle of "personal law" was no more consistently applied at that time than its opposite principle is today. All volitionally formed associations always strove for the application of the principle of personal law on behalf of the law created by them, but the extent to which they were successful in this respect varied greatly from case to case. At any rate, the result was the coexistence of numerous "law communities," the autonomous jurisdictions of which overlapped, the compulsory, political association being only one such autonomous jurisdiction in so far as it existed at all. . . .[8]

[8] Weber, *Law in Economy and Society*, p. 143. In this connection it should be remembered that the privileges or liberties of medieval society were associated with duties that would appear very onerous to a modern citizen. Also, these individual or collective "privileges" frequently resulted from compulsion rather than a spontaneous drive for freedom, as is vividly described in Albert B. White, *Self-government at the King's Command* (Minneapolis: University of Minnesota Press, 1933). The title itself illuminates the

Accordingly, medieval political life consists in struggles for power among more or less autonomous jurisdictions, whose members share immunities and obligations that are based on an established social hierarchy and on a fealty relation with the secular ruler whose authority has been consecrated by a universal church.

Over the centuries this pattern comes to be replaced by a system of absolutist rule, in which the king exercises certain nationwide powers through his appointed officials, while other important judicial and administrative powers are pre-empted on a hereditary basis by privileged estates and the "constituted bodies" in which they are represented. The variety and fluidity of conditions under these absolutist regimes is as great as under the earlier, patrimonial-feudal structure. For example, the nationwide powers of the king develop much earlier in England than on the Continent, partly as a legacy of the Norman conquest. On the other hand, legal traditions antedating the conquest both in Normandy and in England, the island's immunity from attack, and the relative ease of communications also aid the early growth of "countervailing" powers. None of the Continental countries achieves a similar balance. Their absolutist regimes reveal either a greater destruction of the independent estates and hence a greater administrative effectiveness of royal power, as in France, or an ascendance of many principalities with some internal balance between king and estates but at the expense of over-all political unity, as in Germany. Still, by the eighteenth century, most European societies are characterized by absolutist regimes in which the division of powers between king and oligarchic estates as represented by various "constituted bodies" is at the center of the political struggle.[9]

---

combination of royal power *and* compulsory local autonomy, which was typical of England, but not found to the same extent elsewhere in Europe. Still, the privileges of an estate also had the more ordinary meaning of rights (rather than duties), and this was true to some extent even of the lower social orders. See the discussion of this problem by Herbert Grundmann, "Freiheit als religiöses, politisches und persönliches Postulat im Mittelalter," *Historische Zeitschrift*, CLXXXIII (1957), pp. 23–53.

[9] For a comparative account of this political structure in eight-

The French Revolution with its Napoleonic aftermath destroys this system of established privileges and initiates the mass democracies of the modern world. We can best comprehend this major transformation of the relation between society and the state if we leave the complicated transitional phenomena to one side and focus attention on the contrast between medieval political life and the modern nation-state which emerges in the societies of Western civilization. To do so, it will prove useful first to continue the foregoing discussion by an analysis of traditional authority relations between masters and servants and an interpretation of their relevance for medieval political life.

Traditional Authority Relationships

In his *Principles of Political Economy*, John Stuart Mill gives an idealized image of the traditional, aristocratic ideology:

> . . . the lot of the poor, in all things which affect them collectively, should be regulated *for* them, not *by* them. They should not be required or encouraged to think for themselves, or give to their own reflection or forecast an influential voice in the determination of their destiny. It is the duty of the higher classes to think for them, and to take the responsibility of their lot, as the commander and officers of an army take that of the soldiers composing it. This function the higher classes should prepare themselves to perform conscientiously, and their whole demeanor should impress the poor with a reliance on it, in order that, while yielding passive and active obedience to the rules prescribed for them, they may resign themselves in all other respects to a trustful *insouciance,* and repose under the shadow of their protectors. The relation between rich and poor should be only partially authoritative; it should be amiable, moral and sentimental; affectionate tutelage on the one side, respectful and grateful deference on the other. The rich should be *in loco parentis* to the poor, guiding

eenth century Europe see R. R. Palmer, *The Age of Democratic Revolution* (Princeton: Princeton University Press, 1959), Chap. III and *passim*.

and restraining them like children. Of spontaneous action on their part there should be no need. They should be called on for nothing but to do their day's work, and to be moral and religious. Their morality and religion should be provided for them by their superiors, who should see them properly taught it, and should do all that is necessary to insure their being, in return for labor and attachment, properly fed, clothed, housed, spiritually edified, and innocently amused.[10]

This ideology of the masters does not exist in isolation. In an account which parallels that of Mill, Alexis de Tocqueville points out that in their relationship aristocratic masters and their servants feel strongly identified with each other despite the immense social distance between them. The master's influence upon his servants *is* all-encompassing. From childhood on the servants are accustomed to "the notion of being commanded." Such complete domination and submission has important psychological consequences. Through intimate daily contact with the opinions and habits of their servants, the masters come to look upon them as "an inferior and secondary part" of themselves and "by a last stretch of selfishness" take an interest in their lot. Conversely, the servants complacently invest themselves with the wealth and rank of their masters. To make up for their obscurity and life-long obedience they tend to feed their minds with "borrowed greatness" and by means of this personal identification bridge the personal distance between themselves and their masters. Thus, masters and servants think of each other as an inferior or superior extension of themselves.[11]

It is necessary to accentuate this consensual model of traditional authority relations, because the modern observer tends to see the negative aspects only. Selfish willfulness on one side and manipulating subservience on the other can make a travesty of the master's responsibility and the servant's obedience and respect. But that masters can be sadistic

[10] John Stuart Mill, *Principles of Political Economy* (Boston: Charles C. Little and James Brown, 1848), II, pp. 319–320.

[11] Alexis de Tocqueville, *Democracy in America* (New York: Vintage Books, 1945), II, p. 190. Quoted phrases not otherwise identified are taken from pp. 188–195 of this work.

bullies and servants fawning Iagos does not alter the finished rhetoric of manners and motives which characterizes traditional authority relationships even in their abuses and aberrations. For personal qualities are not enduring enough to alter a rhetoric which for centuries was based on the structure of medieval political life.[12]

This structure involved the delegation and/or appropriation of the functions of government, leading in the same country to absolute authority within the several autonomous jurisdictions and to a politics of fealties, alliances, and feuds between them. Both the right to exercise authority *and* the participation in the struggle over the distribution of rights and obligations are based on hereditary privilege as in the case of noble families, or on an institutional immunity as in the case of the Church or later the municipal corporations. On this general basis the individual enjoys rights and performs duties by virtue of his status, which are defined by heredity (especially at the top and the bottom of the social hierarchy) or by membership in an organization possessing certain immunities or liberties. Except for a handful of the most powerful men (and the personal retainers of the ruler) status involves a mediated relation in the sense that the vast majority of persons do *not* stand in a direct legal or political relationship to the supreme authority of the king.

These conditions of medieval political life also define the position of those who do not enjoy the grant of a fief or of immunities and are thus excluded from the exercise of public rights. Peasants and artisans may, of course, enjoy benefits and they certainly perform duties. But they do so by virtue of their fealty relationship to a lord, or through their membership in an association or corporation possessing a more or less autonomous jurisdiction. In this setting the lower strata of the population are fragmented. Each community of peasants belongs to the jurisdiction of its lord, each group of craftsmen

[12] The link between rhetoric and social structure and the relation of this traditional world view to the history of ideas in Western civilization is the subject of Otto Brunner, *Adeliges Landleben und Europäischer Geist* (Salzburg: Otto Müller Verlag, 1949), esp. pp. 61–138.

to the jurisdiction of its guild and town. Thus, peasants participate in medieval politics only indirectly, usually only when they are called upon as subjects of their lord to aid him in his military struggles. In so far as they are free and possess the right to bear arms, peasants must fight for the jurisdiction of their master, at any rate as long as they remain within the framework of the medieval political structure. The right to bear arms is a coveted privilege, because internal warfare or "civil" strife is an important aspect of that structure. Peasant serfs who do not possess this right are consequently excluded even from this indirect, political participation. And the urban communities (which won autonomous jurisdiction for themselves in a series of struggles during the eleventh and twelfth centuries) gain autonomous jurisdiction because they resort to arms, eventually achieve recognition of their right to do so, and hence participate on equal terms with the church and the nobility in the public life of their society. The great majority of the people do not achieve a comparable recognition; as subjects they are bound up for better or worse with the jurisdictional rights of their lord to whom they are bound in loyalty and service. The traditional rhetoric of authority, which Mill and Tocqueville describe, belongs to this intrajurisdictional and patrimonial relation of masters and servants, of lords and retainers.

In sum, medieval European societies excluded the majority of the people from the exercise of public rights which depends upon grants of immunity. This is tantamount to exclusion from political participation at a time when the authority to exercise governmental functions is indistinguishable from political action. Within this framework social protest takes the form of demanding recognition for a new, autonomous jurisdiction, as in the urban revolutions of the eleventh century. In that case a new urban autonomy is achieved by direct action which curtails or revokes the established privileges of local rulers, but such success depends on the wealth and high rank of the families leading these revolts, as well as on considerable support from the community.

In the absence of such favorable conditions there is no room for social protest within the medieval political structure. Instead, protest through direct action occurs outside the framework of competing jurisdictions. A brief survey of types of social protest such as the following cannot tell us much about medieval politics. But it emphasizes movements outside the traditional political structure and its ideology; hence it provides a needed corrective for the idealization of these traditional patterns. Also, social protest of this kind provides a benchmark that will be useful for the later consideration of social unrest which followed the French Revolution.

In his study of *millenarian movements,* Professor Norman Cohn shows that from the eleventh century onward popular unrest in medieval Europe often involves acceptance of an image of a wholly evil world, as well as a recurrent enthusiastic faith in a new world of perfection in which evil-doers will be destroyed utterly and a flock of true believers will come into a realm of perfect goodness and perfect happiness.[13] Medieval millenarianism completely rejects the existing religious community as defined by the Church and aims at a wholly good world to come. Since the Christian tradition encourages belief in a future fundamentally different from the present, even this radical despair of the present and hope for

[13] See Norman Cohn, *The Pursuit of the Millennium* (Fairlawn: Essential Books, 1957), *passim.* Elsewhere, Professor Cohn defines the syndrome of the millenarian phantasy as follows: "I propose to regard as 'millenarian' any religious movement inspired by the phantasy of a salvation which is to be (1) collective, in the sense that it is to be enjoyed by the faithful as a group, (2) terrestrial, in the sense that it is to be realized on this earth and not in some other worldly heaven, (3) imminent, in the sense that it is to come both soon and suddenly, (4) total, in the sense that it is utterly to transform life on earth, so that the new dispensation will be no mere improvement on the present but perfection itself, and (5) accomplished by agencies which are consciously regarded as supernatural." This last criterion distinguishes all Christian from all modern and secularized millenarian movements. See Norman Cohn, "Medieval Millenarism: Its Bearing on the Comparative History of Millenarian Movements," in *Comparative Studies in Society and History* (Supplement II: The Hague: Mouton Co., 1962), p. 31.

the future can be couched entirely in religious terms.[14] The experience of these "true believers" appears to have involved a fantasy destruction of the powers that be, a psychological withdrawal from all communication with these powers, and a wish-fulfilling belief in the sudden and terrestrial appearances of an age of purity and plenty. Such religious conceptions have political implications, whether or not they are motivated by political goals. For they constitute a religious paraphrase of a people's noncooperation with the ruling powers in their society.[15]

Such noncooperation verges on a second type of social unrest which Professor E. J. Hobsbawm has characterized as *social banditry*. In contrast to millenarian radicalism this is a fundamentally secular and conservative response to physically superior powers, which are conceived of as alien interference with an established way of life that is as yet in-dependent of governmental institutions. On this basis the social bandit finds illicit support among the peasants of his native village, who will condone his outlawry as long as he adheres to their own social code. Since the character of this local support will vary, however, social banditry may take on a more populist or a more conservative slant. The first is symbolized and idealized by Robin Hood, who resists the law and the government, who robs the rich to give to the poor,

[14] It is symptomatic of this completely religious orientation that most leaders of these movements appear to have been men and women who were marginal to the Catholic clergy and to intellectual life, like defrocked priests, laymen who took up the study of theology for one reason or another, and others. And while these movements often coincided with the very mundane social uprisings of medieval Europe, they were not caused by the latter in any simple sense. Cohn suggests that the millenarian prophets and their followers attempted to use these uprisings in order to enlist a large popular following on behalf of their own apocalyptic visions. In other words, social unrest provided the occasion for the spread of millenarian ideas that had existed as an integral part of the Christian tradition for many centuries.

[15] Examples of this "withdrawal" response are analyzed with special reference to Italy and Spain in E. J. Hobsbawm, *Social Bandits and Primitive Rebels* (Glencoe: The Free Press, 1959), pp. 57–92.

and who fuses personal courage and largesse with an implacable ruthlessness that is "justified" by the "evil" of the individuals and powers marked out for extermination. The second consists, in Sicily at least, in a "private government" (*Mafia*) organized with the support of landowners, who use it, albeit at a price, in opposition to the national government in order to support or extend their own dominion over the population.[16] Both the populist and the conservative variations of social banditry represent rejections of the prevailing political community, but their activities differ from simple crime to the extent that the collective support given the outlaws is not itself the product of coercion.[17] As a form of protest against the political community social banditry has declined to the extent that relatively few areas and peoples within Western civilization have remained outside the institutional framework of citizenship.[18]

There is a third type of social unrest, *populist legitimism*,[19] which consists in violent protests against existing conditions for the purpose of setting to right an established order that has been willfully abused by those who exercise immediate authority. Like millenarianism and social banditry, this third type of protest has recurred throughout European history. But unlike the other types, populist legitimism accepts the established political order. Although populist agitation easily becomes infused with millenarian elements, for example, in the peasant wars of sixteenth-century Europe, the two types

[16] See Hobsbawm, *op. cit.*, pp. 13–56 for a telling analysis of social banditry in terms of this distinction between Robin Hood and Mafia.

[17] The distinction is probably impossible to make in practice, especially since criminal activities are frequently rationalized as social banditry of the Robin Hood type.

[18] For an interesting borderline case, see the study by Edmund Wilson, *Apologies to the Iroquois* (New York: Farrar, Straus & Cudahy, 1960). Here a people remain socially outside the dominant culture, but use the legal techniques of the modern state in an attempt to preserve the integrity of this "outside" position.

[19] Hobsbawm's term is convenient and accurate, but his analysis of the phenomena to which the term refers is marred by a schematic Marxist interpretation which characterizes all types of premodern social protest as "primitive."

of unrest are distinct. The peasant rebellions of eighteenth-century Russia are a case in point. The peasants justify their rebellion on the ground that the Tsar's authority has been abused; and if it is proved to them that the Tsar has personally authorized the measures they regard as oppressive, they conclude that such a Tsar must be an imposter. Now, the claims made on behalf of the Tsar's authority had always been that he is a benevolent father who looks out for the welfare of his people. Accordingly, the rebels appeal to the official creed of the Tsarist order, when they interpret their massive deprivations as evidence that the Tsar's authority has been abused. For a rightful Tsar would protect his people against oppression; he would safeguard the just claims even of the lowliest peasant. In this idealized picture of absolute authority the people possess certain basic "rights" vouchsafed to them by their supreme ruler so that scheming officials and illegitimate sovereigns rather than the people willfully violate the established order.[20] Such an appeal to expectations that are justified by ancient custom probably serves to minimize the psychological burden of revolting against a social order that is accepted as legitimate but has become intolerable by specific abuses.[21] In this sense the Russian peasants of the

[20] These conceptions of ancient rights often have an historical foundation despite the wishful thinking which may be involved. See George Vernadsky, *The Mongols and Russia* (New Haven: Yale University Press, 1953), p. 376, for a reference to the historical basis of the claims of the Russian peasants. In England, comparable claims went back to the Elizabethan Poor Law, which acknowledged a communal responsibility for all indigent persons. See the discussion in Sidney and Beatrice Webb, *English Local Government: English Poor Law History* (London: Longmans, Green, 1927), Pt. I, pp. 54 ff. Furthermore, autocratic regimes tend to be sensitive to protests made in terms of the official claims to legitimacy, however ruthlessly the protests themselves are suppressed. Such regimes always make large claims concerning the paternal care of the ruler for "his" subjects. These claims provide a ready basis for dissension within the ruling groups as well as for opposition by the subjects.

[21] This "populist legitimism" should not be idealized. Descriptive accounts of the peasant rebellions in Tsarist Russia make clear the selfish cunning which is invariably a part of "legitimism," though the appeal to "ancient rights" is not the less important for

eighteenth century are an example of a subordinate group which has a stake in the political community, despite the fact that it is excluded from the exercise of public rights.

Of the three types of popular unrest which recurred in Europe prior to the "age of democratic revolution," popular legitimism may be considered a transitional phenomenon. After the sixteenth century the legitimist appeal to ancient rights assumes a new character. For with the rise of absolute monarchies paternalism is transformed from a justification of domestic relations to an ideology of national government. The king becomes less an overlord of a feudal nobility and more the supreme ruler of the nation. Under these conditions a popular appeal to ancient rights suggests on occasion that the autocratic ruler who acts as the "father" of his people can rely on their loyalty in his struggle against the estates. In this sense populist legitimism is a counterpart to the ideology and practices of "enlightened despotism."[22]

---

that reason. See, for example, A. Brückner, "Zur Naturgeschichte der Prätendenten," in *Beiträge zur Kulturgeschichte Russlands im 17. Jahrhundert* (Leipzig: B. Elischer, 1887), p. 30. This type of unrest was not confined to peasants, however. Prior to industrialization many metropolitan centers witnessed the sporadic risings of a "city mob" which aims at immediate concessions by the rich and displays a "municipal patriotism" against foreigners. In important princely residences, especially of Southern Europe, this phenomenon frequently involved a parasitic relationship in which the mob would riot if the ruler did not provide the expected patronage, while it would repay the ruler's largesse with loyalty to king and church. For an illuminating account of this special phenomenon, see Hobsbawm, *op. cit.*, pp. 108–125.

[22] In his *The Idea of Nationalism* (New York: Macmillan, 1951), Chap. 5 and especially pp. 199–220, Hans Kohn has shown that in Western Europe autocratic rule and mercantilist economic policies preceded the rise of nationalism which brought with it the idea of the rights of the people. This sequence suggests that the idea of a political community involving the people as citizens emerged during the eighteenth century not only in opposition to the *ancien régime* but also to some extent as a part of the ideology of autocratic paternalism. See Kurt Von Raumer, "Absoluter Staat, Korporative Libertät, Persönliche Freiheit," *Historische Zeitschrift*, 183 (1957), 55–96, and the case study by Fritz Valjavec, *Die Entstehung der Politischen Strömungen in Deutschland* (Munich: R. Oldenbourg, 1951).

The appeals of populist legitimism and the claim of enlightened despots to be "fathers of their people" and "first servants of the state" are harbingers of equalitarianism and the nation-state in societies marked by hereditary privilege and great differences in rank. Where all people have rights, where all are the subjects of one king, where the king in turn exercises supreme authority over everyone—we get a first intimation of "national citizenship" and one supreme authority over all public affairs which eventually emerge as the distinguishing characteristics of modern Western societies. In the seventeenth and eighteenth centuries this whole development, though not discernible as such, was given special momentum by major economic changes as well as by a revolution of intellectual life which are outside the limits of the present discussion. Instead, I wish to focus attention on those aspects of this "great transformation" which are of special relevance for the exercise of authority, that is, the destruction of the medieval political structure on the one hand, and the crisis in human relations resulting from the spread of equalitarian ideas on the other. Both aspects are the central concern of Tocqueville's life work.

ASPECTS OF AUTHORITY IN THE "GREAT TRANSFORMATION"

The Political Structure

In his famous study of the French Revolution, Tocqueville shows how the *ancien régime* has destroyed the century-old pattern of medieval political life by concentrating power in the hands of the king and his officials and by depriving the various autonomous jurisdictions of their judicial and administrative functions.[23] In pointed contrast to Burke's great

[23] Alexis de Tocqueville, *The Old Regime and the Revolution* (Garden City: Doubleday and Co., 1955), pp. 22–77. For a modern appraisal of the survival of corporate and libertarian elements under the absolutist regimes of the eighteenth century, see Kurt von Raumer, *op. cit.*

polemic against the French Revolution, Tocqueville demonstrates that in France the centralization of royal power and the concomitant decline of corporate jurisdictions have developed too far to make the restoration of these jurisdictions a feasible alternative. The nobility no longer enjoys the rights it had possessed at one time, but its acquiescence in royal absolutism has been "bought" by a retention of financial privileges like tax exemption, a fact which greatly intensifies antiaristocratic sentiment. Through the royal administrative system of the *intendants* the rights of municipal corporations and the independence of the judiciary have been curtailed in the interest of giving the government a free hand in the field of taxation—with the result that the urban *bourgeoisie* is divested of local governmental responsibility and the equitable administration of justice is destroyed. Noblemen thus preserve their pride of place in the absence of commensurate responsibilities, urban merchants ape aristocratic ways while seeking preferential treatment for themselves, and both combine social arrogance with an unmitigated exploitation of the peasants. In lieu of the balancing of group interests in the feudal assemblies of an earlier day, each class is now divided from the others and within itself with the result that "nothing had been left that could obstruct the central government, but, by the same token, nothing could shore it up."[24]

Tocqueville's analysis is concerned explicitly with the problem of the political community under the conditions created by the French Revolution. He maintains that in the medieval societies of Western Europe, the inequality of ranks is a universally accepted condition of social life. In that early political structure the individual enjoys the rights and fulfills the obligations appropriate to his rank; and although the distribution of such rights and duties is greatly affected by the use of force, it is established contractually and consecrated as such.[25] The Old Regime and the French Revolution destroy this system by creating among all citizens a condition of ab-

[24] Tocqueville, *The Old Regime . . .* , p. 137.
[25] *Ibid.*, pp. 15–16.

stract equality, but without providing guarantees for the preservation of freedom. Hence, Tocqueville appeals to his contemporaries that a new community—a new reciprocity of
rights and obligations—must be established, and that this can
be done only if men combine their love of equality and liberty
with their love of order and religion. This admonition arises
from his concern with the weakness and isolation of the individual in relation to government. Because he sees the trend
toward equality as inevitable, Tocqueville is deeply troubled
by the possibility that men who are equal would be able to
agree on nothing but the demand that the central government
assist each of them personally. As a consequence the government would subject ever new aspects of the society to its
central regulation. I cite one version of this argument:

> As in periods of equality no man is compelled to lend his
> assistance to his fellow men, and none has any right to expect
> much support from them, everyone is at once independent and
> powerless. These two conditions, which must never be either
> separately considered or confounded together, inspire the citi-
> zen of a democratic country with very contrary propensities.
> His independence fills him with self-reliance and pride among
> his equals; his debility makes him feel from time to time the
> want of some outward assistance, which he cannot expect from
> any of them, because they are all impotent and unsympathiz-
> ing. In this predicament he naturally turns his eyes to that
> imposing power [of the central government]. . . . Of that
> power his wants and especially his desires continually remind
> him, until he ultimately views it as the sole and necessary
> support of his own weakness.[26]

[26] Alexis de Tocqueville, *Democracy in America* (see footnote
11), II, p. 311. In advancing this thesis Tocqueville refers, for example, to the innovative activities of manufacturers that are characteristic of democratic eras. Such men engage in "novel undertakings without shackling themselves to their fellows," they oppose
in principle all governmental interference with such private concerns, and yet "by an exception of that rule" each of them seeks
public assistance in his private endeavor when it suits his purpose.
Tocqueville concludes that the power of government would of necessity grow, wherever large numbers of mutually independent men
proceed in this manner. See *ibid.*, p. 211, n. 1.

Here is Tocqueville's famous paradox of equality and freedom. Men display an extraordinary independence when they rise in opposition to aristocratic privileges. "But in proportion as equality was . . . established by the aid of freedom, freedom itself was thereby rendered more difficult of attainment."[27] In grappling with this problem, Tocqueville uses as his base point of comparison an earlier society in which men had been compelled to lend assistance to their fellows, because law and custom fixes their common and reciprocal rights and obligations. As this society is destroyed, the danger arises that individualism and central power grow apace. To counteract this threat men must cultivate the "art of associating together" in proportion as the equality of conditions advances, lest their failure to combine for private ends encourage the government to intrude—at the separate request of each—into every phase of social life.[28]

We can learn much from these insights. Tocqueville is surely right in his view that the established system of inequality in medieval society had been characterized by an accepted reciprocity of rights and obligations, and that this system had been destroyed as the *ancien régime* had centralized the functions of government. The French Revolution and its continuing repercussions level old differences in social rank, and the resulting equalitarianism poses critical issues for the maintenance of freedom and political stability. Again, he discerns an important mechanism of centralization when he observes that each man would make his separate request for governmental assistance. In contrast to this tendency as he observes it in France, Tocqueville commends the Americans for their pursuit of private ends by voluntary association, which would help to curtail the centralization of governmental power.

It is necessary, of course, to qualify these insights in view of Tocqueville's tendency to read into modern conditions the patterns of medieval political life. At an earlier time, when landed aristocrats protect their liberties or privileges by resisting the encroachments of royal power, the centralization of that power appears as an unequivocal curtailment of such

27 *Ibid.*, p. 333.
28 *Ibid.*, pp. 114–132.

liberties. Today, however, centralization is an important bulwark of all *civil* liberties, though by the same token government can infringe upon these liberties more effectively than
before, as Tocqueville repeatedly emphasizes. The collective
pursuit of private ends, on the other hand, is not necessarily
incompatible with an increase of central government, because
today voluntary associations frequently demand more rather
than less government action in contrast to the medieval estates whose effort to extend their jurisdictions was often synonymous with resistance to administrative interference from
the outside. Durkheim clearly perceives this positive aspect
of modern government and, correspondingly, the dangers implicit in group control over the individual.

> It is the State that has rescued the child from patriarchal domi-
> nation and from family tyranny; it is the State that has freed
> the citizen from feudal groups and later from communal
> groups; it is the State that has liberated the craftsman and his
> master from guild tyranny. . . .
> [The State] must even permeate all those secondary groups
> of family, trade and professional association, Church, regional
> areas and so on . . . which tend . . . to absorb the personality
> of their members. It must do this, in order to prevent this
> absorption and free these individuals, and so as to remind
> these partial societies that they are not alone and that there
> is a right that stands above their own rights.[29]

Important as these qualifications are, they should not make
us overlook the reason why Tocqueville's interpretation of
the "great transformation" is illuminating.[30] By contrasting
an earlier condition of political life, the transformation
brought about by the *ancien régime*, the new condition of
equality ushered in by the French Revolution, and the possibility of a new tyranny in the future—Tocqueville is concerned

[29] Emile Durkheim, *Professional Ethics and Civic Morals* (Glencoe: The Free Press, 1958), pp. 64–65.

[30] A fuller critical appraisal of Tocqueville's facts and interpretations is contained in the essay by George W. Pierson, *Tocqueville in America* (Garden City: Anchor Books, Doubleday and
Co., 1959), pp. 430–477, though Pierson slights Tocqueville's theoretical contribution which is emphasized above.

with "speculative truths" as he calls them. This simplification of different social structures enables him to bring out the major contrasts among them, and these are not invalidated by the short-run and more deductive analyses that went astray. As I see it, Tocqueville's work becomes intellectually most useful, if we attempt to develop within his over-all framework a set of categories that may enable us to handle the transition to the modern political community and some of the outstanding problems, which he discerns, in closer relation to the evidence as we know it today. Fortunately, a systematization of Tocqueville's own analysis of "domestic government" in its transition to the "age of equality" can provide us with a first step in this direction.

Crisis in the Relation of Masters and Servants

In Tocqueville's view the facts and the ideals of the traditional relation between aristocratic masters and their servants are destroyed by the spread of equalitarian ideas. As the social distance between masters and servants decreases, the points of personal disagreement between them sharply increase. In the "secret persuasion of his mind" the master continues to think of himself as superior, though he no longer dares to say so, and his authority over the servant is consequently timid. But the master's authority is also harsh, because he has abandoned the responsibilities of paternalism while retaining its privileges. The servant, on the other hand, rebels in his heart against a subordination to which he has subjected himself and from which he derives actual profit. "An imperfect phantom of equality" haunts his mind and he does not at once perceive "whether the equality to which he is entitled is to be found within or without the pale of domestic service." Obedience is no longer a divine obligation and is not yet perceived as a contractual obligation. The servant consents to serve because this is to his advantage; however, he blushes to obey because where all men are equal subordination is degrading. Under these circumstances the servants,

. . . are not sure that they ought not themselves to be masters, and they are inclined to consider him who orders them as an unjust usurper of their own rights.

Then it is that the dwelling of every citizen offers a spectacle somewhat analogous to the gloomy aspect of political society. A secret and internal warfare is going on there between powers ever rivals and suspicious of each other: the master is ill-natured and weak, the servant ill-natured and intractable; the one constantly attempts to evade by unfair restrictions his obligation to protect and to remunerate, the other his obligation to obey. The reins of domestic government dangle between them, to be snatched at by one or the other. The lines that divide authority from oppression, liberty from license, and right from might are to their eyes so jumbled together and confused that no one knows exactly what he is or what he may be or what he ought to be. Such a condition is not democracy, but revolution.[31]

Tocqueville analyzes this revolution in "domestic government" in the context of his contrast between revolutionary France and democratic America.[32] The reactions of a hypothetical servant to the idea of equality symbolize for him the unsettled conditions of French society in the nineteenth century. In his view France would have to approximate the conditions of settled equality in the United States, if she is to overcome her revolutionary fever and combine liberty with order. In America, servants regard their masters as equals despite the manifest differences in wealth and status; in lieu of personal loyalty the servants acknowledge the obligations of contract. In France, on the other hand, servants display neither loyalty nor a sense of contractual obligation. Economic need rather than an unalterably inferior status forces them to be subordinates.[33] But in the absence of a sense of contractual obligations servants regard their continued sub-

[31] Tocqueville, *Democracy in America*, II, 195. In the preceding paragraph I have reordered Tocqueville's unexcelled phrasing in order to bring out his central thesis.

[32] See Tocqueville's letter to M. de Kergorlay, dated October 19, 1843, in Alexis de Tocqueville, *Memoirs, Letters and Remains* (Boston: Ticknor & Fields, 1862), I, pp. 341–342.

[33] Tocqueville, *Democracy in America*, II, 190–195.

ordination as a blemish on their character (at least initially), while the availability of other opportunities makes them careless of pleasing and impatient of control. Thus the dominant concern of Tocqueville's servant is the consciousness of a position with claims and rights that are not acknowledged by the powers that be. Legally, the servant is the equal of his master, economically the servant is a subordinate—a discrepancy which creates a "confused and imperfect phantom of equality." The question arises why there should be any difference between the equality which the individual enjoys as a citizen and the inequality to which he is forced to submit himself in his economic capacity. The distinction between the public character of the law and the private character of economic pursuits is easily blurred when such ambiguity serves the interest of the servant. Hence, the protest against economic subordination quickly assumes a political character, as the servants "consider him who orders them an unjust usurper of their own rights."[34]

It may be noted that Tocqueville attributes the crisis of "domestic government" to the spread of equalitarian ideas by men of letters. He maintains that in eighteenth-century France this diffusion was facilitated by a gradual increase of economic prosperity rather than poverty.[35] But although the

[34] *Ibid.*, p. 195.

[35] This, it seems to me, is the issue in the debate concerning the proper interpretation of the industrial revolution in England. T. S. Ashton has shown that there was a slow secular improvement in living standards. See the contributions by Ashton and Hutt in F. A. Hayek, ed., *Capitalism and the Historians* (Chicago: University of Chicago Press, 1954). Although the level of living standards in the early nineteenth century is still a subject for scholarly debate, the point here is that a slow improvement after long deprivations is precisely the condition singled out by Tocqueville as a major cause of revolution. This possibility is neglected in the famous studies of the Hammonds which tend to equate all deprivation with increasing misery, although they also show much sympathetic understanding of the psychology of social unrest. Other observers agree with Tocqueville on this point. See the telling statement by Frederick Douglass, the early spokesman of American Negro slaves: "Beat and cuff your slave, keep him hungry and spiritless, and he will follow the chain of his master like a dog; but

diffusion of equalitarian ideas and their inherent revolutionary potential appear inevitable to him, the actual development depends on a nation's "moral and intellectual qualities given by nature and education." In contrast to Marx, Tocqueville does not attempt to predict the final outcome of the tendencies he discerns or to explain away ideas by reference to some ultimate determinant like the organization of production. He seeks to account for the frame of mind in which servants reject the "rules of the game" on which the established society is founded. To do this he formulates a theory of crisis in the relations of masters and servants: (1) in an earlier condition the socially inferior person possesses a recognized status, which is reflected in the sense of "borrowed greatness" among the servants of aristocratic masters; (2) in the crisis of transition the masters retain their privileges but no longer perform their functions, while the servants retain their obligations but perceive new opportunities; (3) in consequence the servants consider that the traditional claims of their status have been abrogated unilaterally and/or that they are now entitled to an equality of rights with all other social ranks since in his capacity as a citizen every man is the equal of every other.

Tocqueville's theory of crisis in "domestic government" refers to the master's evasion of "his obligation to protect and to remunerate," but then gives special attention to the ideas of equality which elicit and shape the lower-class protest that initiates the "age of democratic revolution." Both perspectives will be examined in Chapter 3 together with an analysis of the extension of citizenship.

---

feed and clothe him well,—work him moderately—surround him with physical comfort,—and dreams of freedom intrude. Give him a *bad* master, and he aspires to a *good* master, give him a good master, and he wishes to become his own master," quoted in Kenneth Stampp, *The Peculiar Institution* (New York: A. A. Knopf, 1956), p. 89. See also Eric Hoffer, *The True Believer* (New York: Harper, 1951), pp. 25–29. However, this view was relatively rare compared with that of the theory of revolution as a result of increasing misery, which was a commonplace in Europe from the seventeenth century on. See the study by Robert Michels, *Die Verelendungstheorie* (Leipzig: Alfred Kröner, 1928).

3

TRANSFORMATIONS OF WESTERN
EUROPEAN SOCIETIES SINCE
THE EIGHTEENTH CENTURY

Tocqueville carries his analysis forward to the beginning of
the "age of equality." He characterizes the impact of equalitarian ideas on the relations between masters and servants and
analyzes the resulting crisis in human relations. Writing in the
1830's, he speculates about the future, especially in his brilliant comparison between the settled conditions of equality in
America and the unsettled conditions in France. Today, we
can look upon these speculations, as well as those of Karl
Marx, from the vantage point of a later time. Without the
effort of these men to discern the outlines of the future we
would lack guidelines for a critical analysis.

We saw that medieval political life depends on the link between hereditary or spiritual rank in society, control over land
as the principal economic resource, and the exercise of public
authority. All those whose rank or status excludes them from
access to control over land are thereby excluded from any
direct participation in public affairs. Rights and liberties are
extended to groups, corporations, estates rather than to individual subjects; representation in judicial and legislative
bodies is channeled through traditionally privileged estates.
Within this framework no immediate rights are accorded to
subjects in positions of economic dependence such as tenants,
journeymen, workers, and servants: at best they are classified

under the household of their master and represented through him and his estate. This system is broken up by the twin revolutions of the West—the political and the industrial—which lead to the eventual recognition of the rights of citizenship for all adults, including those in positions of economic dependence.

The following analysis begins with the crisis in "domestic government" analyzed by Tocqueville. From that crisis a new pattern of class relations emerges, replacing the earlier traditional one by an individualistic authority relationship. New forms of unrest arise from this new pattern of class relations, involving the idea of equal rights for all citizens. An attempt is made to reinterpret the radicalization of the lower classes in the course of English industrialization. Against this background the process of nation-building is examined in terms of a comparative analysis of the rights of citizenship. In the emerging nation-states of Western Europe the critical political problem was whether and to what extent social protest would be accommodated through the extension of citizenship to the lower classes.

CLASS RELATIONS IN AN AGE OF CONTRACT

Individualistic Authority Relationships

The reciprocity of social relations falls into patterns because men orient themselves toward the expectation of others and every action of "the other" limits the range of possible responses. Authority means that the few in command have a wide choice of options. Conversely, subordination means that the many who follow orders have their range of choice curtailed. But the options of the few are limited, even when the power at their command is overwhelming. One of these limits is that even the most drastic subordination leaves some choices to those who obey. Tacit noncooperation can be varied, subtle, and more important than overt protest. Subordinates make judgments, leading to degrees of cooperation or noncooperation that are important variables in every established pattern of authority.

The traditional ideology which defends the privileges of the aristocracy in the name of its responsibilities must be seen in this light. Tocqueville emphasizes the positive aspects of the social relations which correspond to this world view. However willful and evasive individual lords were, it is reasonable to assume that for a time the sense and practice of aristocratic responsibility for their inferiors were relatively high, just as the loyalty and obedience of subordinates were genuine. Indeed, without some responsibility on one side and some loyalty on the other, it would be meaningless to say that traditional authority relations were disrupted. It is best to consider the traditional pattern as partly a behavior pattern and partly an ideal in view of the violent conflicts which also characterize medieval society. Ideals are essential in this connection because they affect the orientation even of those who fail to live up to them. Traditional authority relations remain intact as long as the actions and beliefs which deviate from this pattern as well as those which sustain it do not undermine the basic reciprocity of expectations.

To say that a crisis of transition sets in when men consciously question previously accepted agreements and conventions, does not help us to distinguish this questioning from the continual adjustments of rights and obligations which occur while traditional authority relations remain "intact." Such adjustments involve modifications of detail which turn into a questioning of basic assumptions only if they should cumulate. Usually, the contemporary observer is barred from recognizing this distinction. He can see a crisis (no age is without its Cassandras), but he cannot tell whether it is *the* crisis and where it will lead. In his analysis of traditional authority relations in decline, Tocqueville observes that the masters increasingly evade their responsibility "to protect and to remunerate" but retain their customary privileges as an inalienable right. This process extends over centuries, during which the actual rejection of responsibility is thoroughly obscured by the traditional ideology. When does this discrepancy between the rights and responsibilities of the masters become manifest?

Ideas concerning the position of the poor do not provide the best clue in this respect. Throughout the centuries the poor are taught the duty to labor and the virtue of being satisfied with the station to which God has called them. Condemnation of their indolence and dissipation are a constant theme, but these failings are considered ineradicable—a token of low social rank. Human quality and social responsibility are believed to go together. The low station and quality of the poor also exempt them from responsibility; not much can be demanded of them. On the other hand, high rank also means great responsibility. Even where traditional practices are abandoned, it is easy to continue the convenient pretext that the rich and powerful treat the laboring poor as parents treat their children. Throughout much of the nineteenth century paternalism retains its appeal; a deeply ingrained view is not readily destroyed. It is all the more striking, therefore, that in the early phase of English industrialization the responsibility of protecting the poor against the hazards of life is rejected explicitly. The contrast with paternalism makes this rejection of upper-class responsibility a visibly new phenomenon.

During the last half of the eighteenth century a number of clergymen, writers, and political economists begin to reject the "responsibility of the rich" as a pious fraud. The dislocations of the industrial revolution with their cruel effects upon masses of people lead to or call for new interpretations of the cause of poverty. Three of these interpretations are cited here. Though closely linked one with the other, they represent more or less separable themes of English social thought when, toward the end of the eighteenth century, traditional charity and the old poor-law legislation as a means of helping the indigent become controversial issues.[1]

One approach sees the cause of poverty in the very effort to relieve distress. The poor are not inclined to exert them-

[1] The details need not concern us here. For fuller discussion and citations see my study *Work and Authority in Industry* (New York: John Wiley & Sons, 1956), pp. 73 ff.

selves; they lack the pride, honor, and ambition of their betters. Previously this observation supported the view that the poor must be guided; now it supports the view that charity only destroys incentive and hence intensifies poverty. Indolence increases where provision is made to succor the poor; dire necessity is the most natural motive of labor, for it exerts unremitting pressure on the poor. "The slave must be compelled to work; but the freeman should be left to his own judgment and discretion."[2] Here the accent is on the supposition that the rich cannot help the poor, even if they would, and further that the lower orders must depend upon themselves. Rejection of upper-class responsibility goes hand in hand with the demand that the poor should be self-dependent.

In the second approach the pernicious efforts of charity are linked with the market theory of labor. Hunger must be permitted to do its work so that laborers are compelled to exert themselves. Otherwise they will reduce their efforts and destroy their only safeguard against starvation. Here labor is viewed as a commodity like any other, its wage being determined by the demand for this commodity rather than the need of the laborer or his ability to survive. The only relevant question is what the labor is worth to the employer. For the employer is subject to the same necessities of supply and demand as the laborer. This means in the long run that he cannot pay him more than he offers without jeopardizing his enterprise, and hence that the interests of capital and labor are identical. The market theory means that the employer cannot act irresponsibly without damaging his own interest and that the laborer has no safeguard but exertion and no guarantee against starvation.

The third approach, specifically identified with the work of Malthus, relates this market theory of labor to the theory of population. Instead of asserting a harmony of interest between rich and poor, Malthus acknowledges the inevitability of periodic and acute distress. He attributes this phenomenon to the tendency of population to increase faster than the means of subsistence, a law of nature which the upper classes

[2] Statement of Rev. Townsend quoted in *ibid.*, p. 74.

are powerless to alter. Malthus states that poverty is inescapable and a necessary stimulus to labor, that charity and poor relief only increase indolence and improvidence, that the higher classes are not and cannot be responsible for the lot of the poor. But in terms of the present context he also adds an important idea. If it is a law of nature for the poor to increase their numbers beyond the available food supply, it is the responsibility of the higher classes to understand this law and instruct the lower orders accordingly. Improvidence may be a natural tendency, but it also results from ignorance and lack of moral restraint, and these failings can be combated through education.

Education, then, is the keynote of the new, entrepreneurial ideology, since employers no longer possess the all-encompassing personal authority of the aristocratic master. Much reliance is placed on such impersonal forces as economic necessity and the pressure of population on resources —much more reliance than was the case when the master exercised an entirely personal domination over his household. Even so, employers must deal with the management of men, and early in the nineteenth century complaints are heard concerning the increasing personal distance which makes such management difficult, especially on the old, paternalistic basis. With the spread of equalitarian ideas the emphasis on social rank declines; the gulf between the classes widens, as Tocqueville observes, and the personal influence of employers declines. Accordingly, reliance is placed not only on impersonal economic forces but also on the impersonal influence of ideas and education. It is in this context that free-lance propagandists such as Samuel Smiles formulate the new entrepreneurial ideology with its emphasis on the "immense amount of influence" which employers possess, if they would approach their workers "with sympathy and confidence" and "actively aid [them] in the formation of prudent habits."[3] Henceforth entrepreneurial ideologies consist of thematic combinations of the following three elements: (1) the paternalistic element, modeled after the traditional household in which personal

[3] Quoted in *ibid.,* p. 112.

domination of the master over his family and servants is the keynote; (2) the impersonal element, modeled after the market conception of the classical economists in which the anonymous pressure of supply and demand, of the struggle for survival, forces the workers to do the bidding of their employers; and (3) the educational element, modeled after the classroom, the psychological laboratory, or the therapeutic session in which instruction, incentives and penalties, or indirect, motivational inducements are used to discipline the workers and prompt them to intensify their efforts.

For the course of Western European industrialization we can posit a sequence leading first to a decline of the paternalistic and a rise of the impersonal element and subsequently a declining reliance on market forces and an increasing reliance on educational devices. The sequence applies most closely to the English and American development, though even here it is a rough approximation. For paternalism always includes an educational element, reliance on market forces has often been adumbrated in a paternalistic manner, and the educational dimension is compatible with an impersonal as well as a personal approach. Different cultural antecedents as well as the changing organizational structure of economic enterprises have much to do with varying emphases among managerial ideologies such as those of the United States, Germany, and Japan.[4]

The political dimension of these ideologies is of special moment, however. In an emerging nation-state which has destroyed the earlier fragmentation of public authority, agencies of the national government afford employers of labor legal protection for their rights of property. These rights are part of a broad egalitarian trend which also finds expression in the praise of frugal habits and hard work, qualities that enable every man to acquire property and status. At the impersonal level of ideological appeals this approach produces certain typical paradoxes that are of political significance.

[4] *Ibid.*, Chap. 5; Heinz Hartmann, *Authority and Organization in German Management* (Princeton: Princeton University Press, 1959), *passim;* and James G. Abegglen, *The Japanese Factory* (Glencoe: The Free Press, 1958).

Individualistic interpretations of the authority relationship do not remain confined to the enterprise. The idea of an impersonal market which will induce workers to offer their services and work diligently calls for policies that will facilitate the operation of that market. Moreover, recourse to ideological appeals and educational methods suggest that impersonal incentives are insufficient. Entrepreneurs also seek to inculcate the desired habits and motives. But by encouraging the self-dependence of the workers, they run the risk that such individualism will eventuate in social and political protest rather than cooperation and compliance.

For the praise of good habits and hard work lends itself to invidious judgments of a very provocative type. The good and honest worker is a model to be followed as distinguished from the lazy and improvident one, whose deficiencies are broadcast for the benefit of all who will listen and as a warning that invites contempt and condemnation. The public manner in which these "collective attributes" are discussed makes them into a political issue. The moral division of the lower classes into diligent and improvident poor not only challenges the complacency of the idle, but also jeopardizes the self-respect of those who remain poor despite the most strenuous efforts. That self-respect is jeopardized still further when economic success is interpreted as a synonym of virtue and failure as a sign of moral turpitude. In a context of widening agitation such judgments help to make the civic position of the lower orders into a national political issue. The individualist interpretation of authority relations in industry appears from this standpoint as an effort to deny the rights of citizenship to those who are unsuccessful economically, an approach that can arouse a new sense of right on the part of the lower classes and lead to groping efforts to define the position of these classes in the national political community. Just as Tocqueville focuses attention on a transition in domestic relations, marked by a change in the terms of commands and obedience, so the following discussion will focus attention on a transition in group relations on the national level, marked by changing ideas concerning the rights and obligations of the lower classes.

Lower-Class Unrest Becomes Political: England

When political developments are attributed to economic determinants, the changing position of the lower classes and the emergence of national citizenship appear as by-products of industrialization. This line of interpretation develops at the end of the eighteenth century. It appears plausible in the sense that the revolutions in the United States and France "reflect the rise of the bourgeoisie," while the industrial revolution in England leads to the political mobilization of an emerging industrial work force. Greatly simplified as these statements are, they refer to historical phenomena rather than general principles. Yet it is in the light of these *historical* phenomena that *all* political events were first construed as more or less direct by-products of social and economic processes.[5] Today we know that elsewhere political revolutions have occurred in the absence of an economically strong and politically articulate middle class, or perhaps because of that absence, as in Russia or Japan. Again, the political mobilization of the lower classes has occurred as a prelude to industrialization, rather than as a result of it, as, for example, in the United States. Thus, although changes in the economic and political spheres are closely related, their influences work in both directions. Hence we get little guidance if we tacitly accept Western Europe and especially England as our model. It is true that there democratic ideas originated under circumstances in which socio-economic changes had a massive impact upon the political structure, but these ideas have spread around the world ever since in the absence of similar circumstances. National citizenship and modern industrialism have been combined with a variety of social structures; hence we should recognize democratization and industrialization as *two*

[5] To some extent modern social and economic theories still reflect the historical situation in which they were first developed, but a century and a half later it should be possible to guard against this bias.

processes, each distinct from the other, however intimately they have been related on occasion.

The two processes have been closely linked in England. For a long time the English development has served as a model for an understanding of economic growth in relation to political modernization—perhaps simply because England was the first country to develop a modern industry. Just for these reasons it may be well to show that even in England it is possible to distinguish the political element in the midst of economic change. We saw that prior to the eighteenth century the lower classes might try to wring concessions from the ruling powers by a "legitimist" posture mixed with violence; or that they might compensate for their exclusion from the exercise of public rights by millenarian fantasies and banditry. Different forms of lower-class protest became possible, however, after enlightened despotism and the philosophers of the Enlightenment had formulated the principle of equal rights for all men. The spread of this idea was certainly facilitated by industrialization, a fact which was recognized early:

> Of the working men, at least in the more advanced countries of Europe, it may be pronounced certain that the patriarchal or paternal system of government is one to which they will not again be subject. That question was decided, when they were taught to read, and allowed access to newspapers and political tracts; when dissenting preachers were suffered to go among them, and appeal to their faculties and feelings in opposition to the creeds professed and countenanced by their superiors; when they were brought together in numbers, to work socially under the same roof; when railways enabled them to shift from place to place, and change their patrons and employers as easily as their coats; when they were encouraged to seek a share in the government, by means of the electoral franchise.[6]

[6] John Stuart Mill, *Principles of Political Economy*, II, pp. 322–323. Mill's statement is cited here as an exceptionally clear formulation of what was apparently a common topic of conversation. See the illuminating survey of the growing consciousness of class relations by Asa Briggs, "The Language of 'Class' in Early Nineteenth Century England," in Asa Briggs and John Saville, eds., *Essays in Labour History in Memory of G. D. H. Cole* (London: Macmillan, 1960), pp. 43–73.

In this statement Mill describes a relatively industrialized country, and his references to dissenting preachers and the electoral franchise point to conditions that are more or less peculiar to England at this time. But he also notes several factors which have been rather generally associated with the recruitment of an industrial work force: the literacy of workers, the spread of printed matter among them, physical concentration of work, increased geographic mobility, and the depersonalization of the employment relationship. Mill's descriptive account may be considered equivalent to Mannheim's statement that "modern industrial society"—by physically and intellectually mobilizing the people—"stirs into action those classes which formerly only played a passive part in political life."[7]

Under the influence of ideas of equality this mobilization of lower-class protest comes to be oriented, broadly speaking, toward realizing full participation in the existing political community or establishing a national political community in which such participation would be possible. This consideration may be applied initially to some of the popular disturbances in early nineteenth-century England. For Marx these disturbances are similar to the sporadic rebellions in which for several centuries peasants and artisans have destroyed machines as the most immediate instruments of their oppression.[8] Later writers have shown that this violence was directed against bankers or money-lenders as much as against machines, and that despite their obvious agitation the workers of early nineteenth-century England show a most surprising respect for property not directly connected with their distress. By distinguishing in practice between looting and a "justified" destruction of property, the workers may be said to have

[7] This is Karl Mannheim's definition of "fundamental democratization," which is compatible with different forms of government, not only with "democracy." The definition is useful, however, because it highlights the emergence of a national political community in which all adults regardless of class are citizens and hence participants. See Karl Mannheim, *Man and Society in an Age of Reconstruction* (New York: Harcourt, Brace, 1941), p. 44.

[8] See Karl Marx, *Capital* (New York: Modern Library, 1936), pp. 466–478 for his survey and interpretation of such rebellions.

engaged in "collective bargaining by riot" at a time when combinations were prohibited by law.[9] Such evidence is compatible with the idea that the workers who engage in violence desire at the same time to demonstrate their respectability. They are face to face with a manifest legal inequity; they are prevented from combining for peaceful collective bargaining, while combinations of employers are tolerated or even encouraged. Hence, "collective bargaining by riot" easily accompanies the demand for civil rights which has been denied despite acceptance of formal equality before the law.[10]

Although very inarticulate at first, the appeal against legal inequities involves a new dimension of social unrest. To get at the relative novelty of this experience we have to rely on the circumstantial evidence of the period. In the late eighteenth and through the nineteenth centuries the civic position of the common people became a subject of national debate in Europe. For decades elementary education and the franchise are debated in terms of whether an increase in literacy or of voting rights among the people would work as an antidote to revolutionary propaganda or as a dangerous incentive to insubordination.[11] It is difficult to know what sentiments

[9] The phrase has been coined by E. J. Hobsbawm, "The Machine Breakers," *Past and Present*, I (1952), 57–70. Evidence concerning the distinction between looting and such disturbances as the famous Luddite riots is analyzed in Frank O. Darvall, *Popular Disturbances and Public Order in Regency England* (London: Oxford University Press, 1934), pp. 314–315 and *passim*.

[10] Note in this respect Marx's emphasis upon the way in which combinations of workers and employers stimulated each other and the reference in the text below to the awareness of this inequity among English magistrates. A study of industrial and agrarian disputes in Japan suggests that much the same mechanism operates in a very different cultural setting. See the comment that "an increasing number of tenant farmers became convinced of the need for political action, when they learned how often court verdicts, which were based on existing laws, went against them," in George O. Totten, "Labor and Agrarian Disputes in Japan Following World War I," *Economic Development and Cultural Change*, IX (October 1960), pt. II, 194.

[11] Similar questions were raised with regard to universal conscription, since arms in the hands of the common people were considered a revolutionary threat. A case study of the conscription

such debates arouse among the people themselves. Faced with the inequity of their legal position and a public debate over their civic reliability, there is naturally much vacillation. The people seem to alternate between insistence on ancient rights and violent uprisings against the most apparent causes of oppression; protestations of respectability and cries for bloody revolution; proposals for specific reforms and utopian schemes of bewildering variety. But such a diversity of manifestations can have a common core in the transitional experience which Tocqueville characterizes:

> . . . there is almost always a time when men's minds fluctuate between the aristocratic notion of subjection and the democratic notion of obedience. Obedience then loses its moral importance in the eyes of him who obeys; he no longer considers it as a species of divine obligation, and he does not yet view it under its purely human aspects; it has to him no character of sanctity or justice, and he submits to it as to a degrading but profitable condition.[12]

In England, at the political level, this ambivalence is resolved as the idea gains acceptance that the people's rights as citizens have been denied unjustly because as working people they have rights by virtue of their contribution to the nation's wealth.

There are several reasons for accepting the plausibility of this interpretation, even though it may be impossible to prove. One such reason is that legal inequity and the public debate over the people's civic unreliability represent a cumulative denial of their respectability which occurs just when industrialization and the spread of equalitarian ideas stirs "into

---

issue and its significance for the development of class relations in Germany is Gerhard Ritter, *Staatskunst und Kriegshandwerk* (Munich: R. Oldenbourg, 1954), pp. 60–158 and *passim*. See also the related discussion in Katherine Chorley, *Armies and the Art of Revolution* (London: Faber & Faber, 1943), pp. 87–107, 160–183. The related debates on literacy are analyzed in detail with reference to the English experience in M. G. Jones, *The Charity School Movement* (Cambridge: Cambridge University Press, 1938), *passim*.

[12] Tocqueville, *Democracy in America*, II, 194–195.

action those classes which formerly only played a passive part in political life" (Mannheim). On occasion this denial of respectability is tantamount to a denial of the right to existence, as in this passage from Thomas Malthus, which became a notorious object of socialist attacks.

> A man who is born into a world already possessed, if he cannot get subsistence from his parents on whom he has a just demand, and if the society does not want his labour, has no claim of right to the smallest portion of food, and, in fact, has no business to be where he is. At Nature's mighty feast there is no vacant cover for him. She tells him to be gone, and will quickly execute her own orders.[13]

Extreme statements such as this or Burke's reference to the "swinish multitude" were made by intellectuals and may not have been widely known. However, haughtiness and fear were widespread in middle-class circles, and it is reasonable to expect a growing sensitivity among the people, however inarticulate, in response to this public questioning of their respectability.

Contemporary observers frequently commented on the popular reaction. These observers are often remote from working-class life, partisans in the debate concerning the "lower classes," and divided among themselves. Their biases are many, but partisanship can sensitize as well as distort understanding. In England such different observers as Thomas Carlyle, William Cobbett, Benjamin Disraeli, and Harriett Martineau comment on the feeling of injustice among the workers, on their loss of self-respect, on the personal abuse which the rulers of society heap upon them, on the Chartist movement as the common people's expression of outrage at the denial of their civil rights, and on the workers' feeling of being an "outcast order" in their own country.[14] Such a civic

---

[13] Thomas Malthus, *An Essay on the Principle of Population* (2nd ed.; London: J. Johnson, 1803), p. 531. This passage was modified in the later editions of the Essay.

[14] See the chapter "Rights and Mights" in Thomas Carlyle, *Chartism* (Chicago: Belford, Clarke, 1890), pp. 30–39; G. D. H. and Margaret Cole, eds., *The Opinions of William Cobbett* (London: Cobbett, 1944), pp. 86–87, 123–124, 207, and *passim; Hans-*

disaffection of the people was regarded with grave concern by prominent spokesmen in many European societies. In retrospect this concern appears justified in the sense that the position of the "people" as citizens was indeed at issue.[15]

The implicit or explicit denial of the people's civic respectability is countered rather naturally by an insistence on people's rights which must not be abrogated. That insistence is founded first on a sense of righteous indignation at the idea that labor which is "the Cornerstone upon which civilized society is built" is "offered less . . . than will support the family of a sober and orderly man in decency and comfort."[16] This conception of a "right to subsistence" with its traditional overtones, the idea of "labor's right to the whole product," and the belief that each able-bodied worker has a

---

ard's *Parliamentary Debates*, Vol. XLIX (1839), cols. 246–247; and R. K. Webb, *The British Working Class Reader* (London: Allen & Unwin, 1955), p. 96 for the sources of these statements. Also relevant here is the famous simile of the "two nations between whom there is no intercourse and no sympathy; who are as ignorant of each other's habits, thoughts and feelings, as if they were dwellers in different zones, or inhabitants of different planets, who are formed by a different breeding, are fed by a different food, are ordered by different manners, and are not governed by the same laws." This passage occurs in Benjamin Disraeli's novel *Sybil* (Baltimore: Penguin Books, 1954), p. 73.

[15] For a survey of propagandistic efforts to counteract this "civic disaffection" in England, see R. K. Webb, *op. cit., passim,* and Reinhard Bendix, *Work and Authority in Industry*, pp. 60–73.

[16] The quoted phrase is from a Manchester handbill of 1818 reprinted in J. L. and Barbara Hammond, *The Town Labourer* (London: Longmans, Green, 1925), pp. 306–308. In Tocqueville's paradigm this idea may be said to fall midway between the belief in "ancient rights" that have been wrongfully abrogated and the claim that the servants themselves should be the masters. Note also the analysis by von Stein who states that the antagonism between workers and employers "arises from the belief in the rights and worth of the individual workers, on one hand, and from the knowledge that under present conditions of machine production the wages of the worker will not be commensurate with his claims as an individual." See Lorenz von Stein, "Der Begriff der Arbeit und die Prinzipien des Arbeitslohnes in ihrem Verhältnisse zum Sozialismus und Communismus," *Zeitschrift für die gesamte Staatswissenschaft,* III (1846), 263.

"right to labor" are the three inherent or natural rights put in opposition to the contractually acquired rights that alone are recognized by the prevailing legal system.[17] Although the theoretical elaborations of these concepts in the socialist literature do not reveal the thinking of the ordinary man, it is plausible to assume that the common theme of these theories expresses the strivings of the workingman in the nation-state.[18]

In England, lower-class protests appear to aim at establishing the citizenship of the workers. Those who contribute to the wealth and welfare of their country have a right to be heard in its national councils and are entitled to a status that commands respect. In England, these demands never reach the revolutionary pitch that develops rather frequently on the Continent, although occasionally violent outbursts disrupt English society as well. If the political modernization of England for all its conflicts occurred in a relatively continuous and peaceful manner, then one reason is perhaps that throughout much of the nineteenth century England was the leader in industrialization and overseas expansion. English workers could claim their rightful place in the political community of the leading nation of the world.[19] Within that favorable

[17] For a detailed exposition of these conceptions of natural rights in socialist thought and of their incompatibility with the law of property, see Anton Menger, *The Right to the Whole Produce of Labour* (London: Macmillan, 1899), *passim*.

[18] Presumably, Marx's use of the labor theory of value had its great moral impact on the basis of these conceptions of "natural rights," as analyzed by Menger.

[19] Engels considered the two phenomena causally linked, as in his comment to Marx that the "bourgeoisification of the English proletariat" was in a sense "quite natural in a nation that exploited the whole world." See his letter to Marx of October 7, 1858, in Karl Marx and Friedrich Engels, *Ausgewählte Briefe* (Berlin: Dietz Verlag, 1953), pp. 131–132. Yet, this interpretation ignores the historical legacies which prompt a "national reciprocity of rights and obligations" despite the threat of revolutionary ideas and the strains of rapid economic change. The coincidence of England's favored position and her favorable legacies for effecting this political "incorporation" of the "fourth estate" has been discussed so far only in bits and pieces. See J. L. Hammond, "The Industrial Revolution and Discontent," *The Economic History Review*, II

context the national debate concerning the proper status of the lower classes is carried on in the traditional language of religion. Certainly, English workers are greatly disillusioned with the established Church and with religious appeals which all too often are thinly disguised apologies for the established order. Nevertheless, doctrinaire atheism is rare, and English working-class leaders often couch their demands in Biblical or quasi-Biblical language.[20] Thus, England's prominence as a world power and a common religious background may have facilitated the civic incorporation of the workers, even though the new national balance of rights and duties was not accomplished easily.

An example from the field of industrial relations illustrates the niceties of this English transition to a modern political

(1930), 227–228; Henri de Man, *The Psychology of Socialism* (New York: Henry Holt, 1927), pp. 39–41, with regard to the role of injured self-respect in English radical protest; and Selig Perlman, *A Theory of the Labor Movement* (New York: Augustus Kelley, 1949), p. 291, who emphasizes the special significance of the franchise issue.

[20] Some evidence of the relation between religious revivalism and working-class protest is discussed in my *Work and Authority in Industry*, pp. 60–73, but the issue is controversial. In his *Social Bandits and Primitive Rebels*, pp. 126–149, Hobsbawm questions that the religious movements among workers diminished their radicalism. In his *Churches and the Working Classes in Victorian England* (London: Routledge and Kegan Paul, 1963), K. S. Inglis assembles a mass of evidence which suggests that English workers were markedly indifferent towards religious observances throughout the nineteenth century. But even Inglis admits (*ibid.*, 329–332) that atheism was rare among English workers (though pronounced among their fellows on the Continent), and that large numbers of working-class children attended Sunday schools. Such an admission may well be critical, however, since the question is not whether English workers were true believers, but whether they continued to use religious ideas in their "quest for respectability." Religious ideas are not necessarily less important when they become associated with secular concerns. See the analysis of secularity and religion in the American context by S. M. Lipset, *The First New Nation* (New York: Basic Books, 1963), pp. 151–159, and of the exacerbation of class-relations in the absence of a viable religious language by Guenther Roth, *The Social Democrats in Imperial Germany* (New York: The Bedminster Press, 1963), *passim*.

community. At first glance, the legal prohibition of trade unions in the early nineteenth century looks like brute suppression. "Workingmen's combinations" are said to curtail the employer's as well as the worker's formal legal rights. However, in their survey of early trade unionism, the Webbs conclude that the inefficient organization of the police, the absence of effective public prosecution, and the inaction of the employers were responsible for the widespread occurrence of illegal combinations despite this unequivocal legal prohibition.[21]

More recently, a publication of documents on the early trade unions has revealed why neither employers nor government officials would resort to all the legal remedies open to them. Apparently, the employers wished the government to institute proceedings against illegal combinations. An opinion of the Attorney General, sent to the Home Secretary in 1804, is of special interest in this respect. The opinion sets forth details of the great evil of combinations among workmen throughout the country, combinations said to be clearly illegal and liable to prosecution. But if the government were to initiate the prosecution in the case under consideration, then applications for similar actions on the part of the government can be anticipated from every other trade, since "combinations exist in almost every trade in the kingdom."

> It will lead to an opinion that it is not the business of the masters of the trade who feel the injury to prosecute, but that it is the business of Government. . . . It must be admitted indeed that the offence has grown to such height and such an extent as to make it very discouraging for any individual to institute a prosecution—as the persons whom he would prosecute would be supported at their trial and during their imprisonment by the contributions of their confederates, and his own shop would probably be deserted by his workmen. But then it is clear that it is owing to the inertness and timidity of the masters that the conspiracy has reached this height, and it may well be feared that this inertness will be rather increased than diminished by the interference of Government.

[21] Sidney and Beatrice Webb, *The History of Trade Unionism* (New York: Longmans, Green & Co., 1926), p. 74.

. . . When they once think the punishment of such offences to be the business of Government, they will think it also the business of Government to procure the evidence, and not theirs to give it, so that the future detection and prosecution of such offences would probably be rendered more difficult. Besides . . . the impartiality of Government would be awkwardly situated, if, after undertaking a prosecution at the instance of the masters against the conspiracy of the journeymen, they were to be applied to on the part of the journeymen to prosecute the same masters for a conspiracy against their men.[22]

This opinion is instructive, even though its judiciousness cannot be considered representative.

Whatever their partiality toward the employers, the magistrates are responsible for maintaining law and order. This task is complicated time and again by the reluctance of employers to make use of the law prohibiting combinations, by their repeated attempts to induce the government to do it for them, by their tendency to connive in these combinations when it suits their purpose, and finally by their tendency to reject all responsibility for the consequences of their own actions in the belief that ultimately the government will maintain law and order and protect their interests. It is not surprising that the magistrates are often highly critical of the employers, holding that the latter act with little discretion, that they can well afford to pay higher wages, and that the complaints of the workers are justified even though their combinations are illegal. Sometimes the magistrates even act as informal mediators in disputes between employers and their workers in the interest of maintaining the peace.[23] Thus, neither the partiality of the magistrates nor the principle of a hands-off policy nor the employers' evident opportunism is tantamount to suppression, even though in practice little is done to meet the workers' complaints except on terms calcu-

[22] A. Aspinall, ed., *The Early English Trade Unions, Documents from the Home Office Papers in the Public Record Office* (London: Batchworth Press, 1949), pp. 90–92.

[23] For examples of these several aspects, see *ibid.*, pp. 116, 126, 168–169, 192–193, 216–219, 229, 234–235, 237–238, 242, 259–260, 272, 283, and so on.

lated to injure their status as self-respecting members of the community.

In this period of transition Tocqueville sees a major revolutionary threat. The master continues to expect servility, but rejects responsibility for his servants, while the latter claim equal rights and become intractable. At the societal level the English case approximates this model. Many early English entrepreneurs certainly reject all responsibility for their employees and yet expect them to obey; they reject all governmental interference with management, though they seek to charge government with responsibility for any untoward public consequences of their own acts.[24] Government officials support the entrepreneurs in many cases because they are profoundly concerned with unrest and truculence. But having said this, several reservations must be added. There are some manufacturers who acknowledge the traditional obligations of a ruling class. Among some magistrates the principle of noninterference by government is adhered to by a detached and critical attitude, even in the first decades of the nineteenth century. Finally, the demand for equality of the developing working class is cast in a more or less conservative mold in the sense that on balance it adds up to a quest for public acceptance of equal citizenship. In other words, English society proved itself capable of accommodating the lower class as an equal participant in the national political community, though even in England this development involved a prolonged struggle and the full implications of equality as we understand them today evolved only gradually.

[24] On this basis even staunch ideological spokesmen for *laissez-faire* were actively engaged in the extension of governmental controls. For details see Marion Bowley, *Nassau Senior and Classical Economics* (London: Allen & Unwin, 1937), pp. 237–281; S. E. Finer, *The Life and Times of Edwin Chadwick* (London: Methuen, 1952), *passim;* J. B. Brebner, "Laissez-faire and State Intervention in 19th Century Britain," *Journal of Economic History*, VIII (Supplement 1948), 59–73.

Theoretical Implications

The preceding discussion is confined to developments in England. Industrialization can be initiated only once; after that its techniques are borrowed; no other country that has since embarked on the process can start where England started in the eighteenth century. England is the exception rather than the model. For a time England possessed a near monopoly on the most advanced techniques of industrial production, and other countries borrowed from her. For the better part of the nineteenth century England stood in the forefront in that she combined industrial wth political pre-eminence. In retrospect we know that as a result of these and related conditions she possessed a national political community in which the rising "fourth estate" was eventually permitted to participate through a gradual redefinition of rights and obligations rather than as a consequence of war or revolution. But an understanding of as singular a case as this is important in the comparative study of social and political change, for indirectly it may point to what many of the other "cases" have in common.

As we compare industrial latecomers with England and democratic latecomers with France, we can ask: what happens when a country does not possess a viable political community or if the community which it possesses is so "backward" in comparison with democratically and industrially advanced countries that it must be reconstituted before the demand for "full citizenship" becomes meaningful at all? It is not a novel idea to suggest that lower-class protest may progress from a demand for full citizenship within the prevailing political community to a demand for a change of this community in order to make full citizenship possible. But although this idea is compatible with Marx's theory of an advance from machine breaking to political action, it should be noted that I emphasize the alienation from the political community rather than the alienation which results from "creative dissatisfactions," as Marx does. This shift of emphasis helps us to see together two mass movements of the nineteenth century—socialism and nationalism—in contrast to Marx who explains the first while ignoring the second. There is a very close link between socialist and nationalist agitation in that both aim in different ways at the political integration of the masses previously excluded from participation. This link is obscured by the Marxist separation of these movements and by the fact that England's pre-eminence as a world power made it unnecessary for the English lower class to demand a national political community to which it could belong in self-respect.[25] Yet, the exceptional development of England has served social theorists for a century as the model which other countries are expected to follow.

The approach here proposed is not a mere reversal of the Marxist theory. Marx looks upon social movements of the nineteenth century as protests against psychic and material deprivations that cumulate as a result of the capitalist process; he sees in the masses a fundamental craving for creative satisfactions in a good society. I interpret these protest movements as *political* and define their character in terms of the contrast between a premodern and a modern political community. When this view is taken, the eighteenth century appears as a major hiatus in Western European history. Prior

[25] See the following statement from a speech of the Chartist leader Hartwell, delivered in 1837: "It seems to me to be an anomaly that in a country where the arts and sciences have been raised to such height, chiefly by the industry, skill and labours of the artisan . . . only one adult male in seven should have a vote, that in such a country the working classes should be excluded from the pale of political life." Quoted in M. Beer, *A History of British Socialism* (London: Allen & Unwin, 1948), II, pp. 25–26. It is instructive to contrast this statement with that by the Italian nationalist leader Mazzini: "Without Country you have neither name, token, voice, nor rights. . . . Do not beguile yourselves with the hope of emancipation from unjust social conditions if you do not first conquer a Country for yourselves. . . . Do not be led away by the idea of improving your material conditions without first solving the national question. . . . Today . . . you are not the working class of Italy; you are only fractions of that class. . . . Your emancipation can have no practical beginning until a National Government [is founded]." See Joseph Mazzini, *The Duties of Man and Other Essays* (New York: E. P. Dutton, 1912), pp. 53–54.

to that time the masses of the people were entirely barred from the exercise of public rights; since then they have become citizens and in this sense participants in the political community. The "age of democratic revolution" extends from that time to the present. During this period some societies have universalized citizenship peacefully, while others have been unable to do so and have consequently suffered various types of revolutionary upheavals. So conceived, the problem of the lower classes in a modern nation-state consists in the political process through which at the level of the national community the reciprocity of rights and duties is gradually extended and redefined. It is quite true that this process has been affected at every turn by forces emanating from the structure of society. But it is here maintained that the distribution and redistribution of rights and duties are not mere by-products of such forces, that they are vitally affected by the international position of the country, by conceptions of what the proper distribution in the national community ought to be, and by the give and take of the political struggle.[26]

My thesis is in keeping with Tocqueville's stress on the reciprocity of rights and obligations as the hallmark of a political community. In Europe the rising awareness of the working class expresses above all an experience of *political alienation*, that is, a sense of not having a recognized position in the civic community or of not having a civic community in which to participate. Because popular political participation

[26] This approach differs from Marxism which treats politics and government as variables dependent upon the changing organization of production, without coming to grips either with the relative autonomy of governmental actions or the continuous existence of national political communities. It also differs from the sociological approach to politics and formal institutions which construes the first as mere by-products of interactions among individuals and the second as the "outward shell" inside which these interactions provide the clue to a realistic understanding of social life. See a critical analysis of this reductionism in Wolin, *op. cit.*, Chaps. 9 and 10. An alternative approach which emphasizes the partial autonomy as well as the interdependence of government and society is contained in the work of Max Weber, as discussed above on pp. 18–21.

has become possible for the first time in European history, lower-class protest against the social order relies (at least initially) on prevailing codes of behavior and hence reflects a conservative cast of mind, even where it leads to violence against persons and property.[27] Rather than engage in a millenarian quest for a new social order, the recently politicized masses protest against their second-class citizenship, demanding the right of participation on terms of equality in the political community of the nation-state.[28] If this is a correct assessment of the impulses and half-articulated longings characteristic of much popular agitation among lower classes in Western Europe, then we have a clue to the decline of socialism. For the civic position of these classes is no longer a pre-eminent issue in societies in which the equality of citizenship has been institutionalized successfully.

The following section of this chapter traces this institutionalization on a comparative basis.

THE EXTENSION OF CITIZENSHIP TO THE LOWER CLASSES[29]

Elements of Citizenship

In the nation-state each citizen stands in a direct relation to the sovereign authority of the country in contrast with the

[27] See in this connection Engels' expression of disgust with regard to the ingrained "respectability" of English workers and their leaders in his letter to Sorge of December 7, 1889, in *Ausgewählte Briefe,* p. 495.

[28] The perspective presented above has been developed by a number of my former students. The study by Guenther Roth of "Working-Class Isolation and National Integration" in Imperial Germany was cited earlier. See also Gaston Rimlinger, "The Legitimation of Protest: A Comparative Study in Labor History," *Comparative Studies in Society and History,* II (April 1960), pp. 329–343, by the same author, "Social Security, Incentives and Controls in the U.S. and the U.S.S.R.," *loc. cit.,* IV (November 1961), pp. 104–124, and Samuel Surace, *The Status Evolution of Italian Workers, 1860–1914* (Ph.D. Dissertation, Department of Sociology, University of California, Berkeley, 1962).

[29] The following section was written jointly with Dr. Stein Rok-

medieval polity in which that direct relation is enjoyed only by the great men of the realm. Therefore, a core element of nation-building is the codification of the rights and duties of all adults who are classified as citizens. The question is how exclusively or inclusively citizenship is defined. Some notable exceptions aside, citizenship at first excludes all socially and economically dependent persons. In the course of the nineteenth century this massive restriction is gradually reduced until eventually all adults are classified as citizens. In Western Europe this extension of national citizenship is set apart from the rest of the world by the common traditions of the *Ständestaat*.[30] The gradual integration of the national community since the French Revolution reflects these traditions wherever the extension of citizenship is discussed in terms of the "fourth estate," that is, in terms of extending the principle of *functional representation* to those previously excluded from citizenship. On the other hand, the French Revolution also advanced the *plebiscitarian principle*. According to this principle all powers intervening between the individual and the state must be destroyed (such as estates, cor-

---

kan, Christian Michelsen Institute, Bergen, Norway. I have adapted the original essay in keeping with the purposes of this volume. Subsequent formulations will emphasize the classificatory sense in which the term "lower classes" is used. The question is left open which sections of the "lower classes" develop a capacity for concerted action and under what circumstances. Although in some measure a response to protest or the result of anticipating protest, the extension of citizenship occurred with reference to broadly and abstractly defined groups such as all adults over 21, or women or adults having specified property holdings, fulfilling certain residence requirements, etc. Such groups encompass many people other than those who have few possessions, low income, little prestige, and who because of these disabilities are conventionally understood to "belong" to the lower classes. The reference here is to the larger, classificatory group of all those (including the "lower classes") who were excluded from any direct or indirect participation in the political decision-making processes of the community.

[30] So much so that the historian Otto Hintze denies the *indigenous* development of constitutionalism anywhere else. See his "Weltgeschichtliche Vorbedingungen der Repräsentativverfassung," in *Staat und Verfassung* (Göttingen: Vandenhoeck & Ruprecht, 1962), pp. 140–185.

porations, etc.), so that all citizens as individuals possess equal rights before the sovereign, national authority.[31]

A word should be added concerning the two adjectives "functional" and "plebiscitarian." The phrase "functional representation" derives from the medieval political structure in which it is deemed proper, for example, that the elders or grand master of a guild represent it in a municipal assembly. Here function refers generically to any kind of activity considered appropriate for an estate. Used more broadly, the term "function" designates *group-specific activities or rights and duties.* As such it encompasses both, observations of behavior and ethical mandates of what is thought proper. The latter imply very different theories of society, however. In medieval society the rank and proper functions of the constituent groups are fixed in a hierarchical order. In modern Western societies this older view has been superseded by concepts of group function which presuppose the ideal of equality, except where medieval connotations linger on. The term "plebiscite" refers to the *direct vote on an important public issue by all qualified electors* of a community. The broader the community, the more minimal the qualifications stipulated for the electors, and hence the larger the number of persons standing in a direct relationship to public authority, the more will the plebiscitarian principle conflict with the functional. The specific meaning of both principles varies naturally with the definitions of group-specific activities and the extent and qualifications of community membership.

Various accommodations between the functional and plebiscitarian principle have characterized the sequence of enactments and codifications through which citizenship became national in many countries of Western Europe. To

---

[31] These two models have been analyzed in terms of the distinction between the representative and the plebiscitarian principle by Ernst Fraenkel, *Die Repräsentative und die Plebiszitäre Komponente im Demokratischen Verfassungsstaat* (Heft 219–220 of Recht und Staat; Tübingen: J. C. B. Mohr, 1958). The ideology of plebiscitarianism is documented in J. L. Talmon, *The Origins of Totalitarian Democracy* (New York: Frederick A. Praeger, 1960).

examine this development comparatively the several rights of citizenship must be distinguished and analyzed. In his study of *Citizenship and Social Class,* T. H. Marshall formulates a threefold typology of rights:

> —*civil* rights such as "liberty of person, freedom of speech, thought and faith, the right to own property and to conclude valid contracts, and the right to justice";
> —*political* rights such as the franchise and the right of access to public office;
> —*social* rights ranging from "the right to a modicum of economic welfare and security to the right to share to the full in the social heritage and to live the life of a civilized being according to the standards prevailing in the society."[32]

Four sets of public institutions correspond to these three types of rights:

> the *courts,* for the safeguarding of civil rights and, specifically, for the protection of all rights extended to the less articulate members of the national community;
> the local and national *representative bodies* as avenues of access to participation in public decision-making and legislation;
> the *social services,* to ensure some minimum of protection against poverty, sickness, and other misfortunes, and the *schools,* to make it possible for all members of the community to receive at least the basic elements of an education.

Initially, these rights of citizenship emerge with the establishment of equal rights under the law. The individual is free to conclude valid contracts, to acquire, and dispose of, property. Legal equality advances at the expense of legal protection of inherited privileges. Each man now possesses the right to act as an independent unit; however, the law only defines his legal capacity, but is silent on his ability to use it. In addition, civil rights are extended to illegitimate children, foreigners, and Jews; the principle of legal equality

[32] The essay referred to has been reprinted in T. H. Marshall, *Class, Citizenship and Social Development* (Garden City, New York: Doubleday & Co., Inc., 1964), pp. 71–72. The following discussion is greatly indebted to Professor Marshall's analysis.

helps to eliminate hereditary servitude, equalize the status of husband and wife, circumscribe the extent of parental power, facilitate divorce, and legalize civil marriage.[33] Accordingly, the extension of civil rights benefits the inarticulate sections of the population, giving a positive libertarian meaning to the legal recognition of individuality.

Still, this gain of legal equality stands side by side with the fact of social and economic inequality. Tocqueville and others point out that in medieval society many dependent persons were protected in some measure against the harshness of life by custom and paternal benevolence, albeit at the price of personal subservience. The new freedom of the wage contract quickly destroyed whatever protection of that kind had existed.[34] For a time at least, no new protections are instituted in place of the old; hence class prejudice and economic inequalities readily exclude the vast majority of the lower class from the enjoyment of their legal rights. The right of the individual to assert and defend his basic civil freedoms on terms of equality with others and by due process of law is *formal* in the sense that legal powers are guaranteed in the absence of any attempt to assist the individual in his use of these powers. As Anton Menger observed in 1899: "Our codes of private law do not contain a single clause which assigns to the individual even such goods and services as are indispensable to the maintenance of his existence."[35]

[33] See R. H. Graveson, *Status in the Common Law* (London: The Athlone Press, 1953), pp. 14–32. For details of these legal developments in Germany, Austria, Switzerland, and France, see J. W. Hedemann, *Die Fortschritte des Zivilrechts im 19. Jahrhundert* (Berlin: Carl Heymanns Verlag, 1910 and 1935), two volumes. A brief survey of the background and extent of these developments in Europe is contained in Hans Thieme, *Das Naturrecht und die europäische Privatrechtsgeschichte* (Basel: Halbing and Lichtenhahn, 1954). A more extended treatment is contained in Franz Wieacker, *Privatrechtsgeschichte der Neuzeit* (Göttingen: Vandenhoeck & Ruprecht, 1952), esp. pp. 197–216 and *passim*.

[34] Alexis de Tocqueville, *Democracy in America* (New York: Vintage Books, 1954), II, pp. 187–190.

[35] Anton Menger, *The Right to the Whole Product of Labor* (London: Macmillan and Co., 1899), pp. 3–4.

In this sense the equality of citizenship and the inequalities of social class develop together.

The juxtaposition of legal equality and social and economic inequalities inspired the great political debates which accompany the nation-building of nineteenth-century Europe. These debates turn on the types and degrees of inequality or insecurity that should be considered intolerable and the methods that should be used to alleviate them. The spokesmen of a consistent *laissez-faire* position seek to answer this question within the framework of formal civil rights. Having won legal recognition for the exercise of individual rights, they insist that to remain legitimate the government must abide by the rule of law. It is consistent with this position that in most European countries the first Factory Acts seek to protect women and children, who at the time are not considered citizens in the sense of legal equality.[36] By the same criterion all adult males are citizens because they have the power to engage in the economic struggle and take care of themselves. Accordingly, they are excluded from any legitimate claim to protection. In this way formally guaranteed rights benefit the fortunate and more fitfully those who are legally defined as unequal, while the whole burden of rapid economic change falls upon the "laboring poor" and thus provides a basis for agitation at an early time.

[36] Ideological equalitarianism as well as an interest in breaking down familial restrictions upon the freedom of economic action were presumably the reason why protection was first extended to these most inarticulate sections of the "lower class." For a critical analysis of the German Civil Code of 1888 exclusively in terms of the economic interests its provisions would serve, see Anton Menger, *Das bürgerliche Recht und die besitzlosen Volksklassen* (Tübingen: H. Laupp'sche Buchhandlung, 1908). The book was originally published in 1890. This perspective omits the self-sustaining interest in formal legality which is the work of legal professionals and leads to the prolonged conflict between legal positivism and the doctrine of natural law. See in this respect the analysis of Max Weber, *Law in Economy and Society* (Cambridge: Harvard University Press, 1954), pp. 284–321. See also the illuminating discussion of this point in Fr. Darmstaedter, *Die Grenzen der Wirksamkeit des Rechtsstaates* (Heidelberg: Carl Winters Universitätsbuchhandlung, 1930), pp. 52–84.

This agitation is political from the beginning. One of the earliest results of the legislative protection of freedom of contract is the legislative prohibition of trade unions. But where legislative means are used both to protect the individual's freedom of contract and deny the lower classes the rights needed to avail themselves of the same freedom (i.e., the right of association), the attacks upon inequality necessarily broaden. Equality is no longer sought through freedom of contract alone, but through the establishment of social and political rights as well. The nation-states of Western Europe can look back on longer or shorter histories of legislative actions and administrative decisions which have increased the equality of subjects from the different strata of the population in terms of their legal capacity and their legal status.[37] For each nation-state and for each set of institutions we can pinpoint chronologies of the public measures taken and trace the sequences of pressures and counterpressures, bargains and maneuvers, behind each extension of rights beyond the strata of the traditionally privileged. The extension of various rights to the lower classes constitutes a development characteristic of each country. A detailed consideration of each such development would note the considerable degree to which legal enactments are denied or violated in practice. It would thus emphasize how the issue of the civic position of the lower classes was faced or evaded in each country, what policy alternatives were under consideration, and by what successive steps the rights of citizenship were extended eventually. A full analysis could illuminate each step along the way, but it would also obscure the over-all process of nation-building.

For taken together, the developments of the several Euro-

[37] When all adult citizens are equal before the law and free to cast their vote, the exercise of these rights depends upon a person's ability and willingness to use the legal powers to which he is entitled. On the other hand, the legal status of the citizens involves rights and duties which cannot be voluntarily changed without intervention by the State. A discussion of the conceptual distinction between capacity as "the legal power of doing" and status as "the legal state of being" is contained in Graveson, *op. cit.,* pp. 55–57.

pean countries also constitute the transformation from the estate societies of the eighteenth to the welfare state of the twentieth centuries. A comparative study of this transformation from the standpoint of national citizenship will inevitably appear abstract if juxtaposed with the specific chronology and detailed analysis of successive legislative enactments in each country. However, such a study will have the advantage of emphasizing the truth that, considered cumulatively and in the long run, legislative enactments have extended the rights of citizenship to the lower classes and thus represent a genuinely comparable process in nineteenth- and twentieth-century Europe.

The following discussion is limited to one aspect of Western European nation-building: *the entry of the lower classes into the arena of national politics.* Only those policies are considered which have immediate relevance for lower-class movements seeking to enter national politics.[38] The decisions on the *right to form associations* and on the *right to receive a minimum of formal education* are basic, for these rights set the stage for the entry of the lower classes and condition the strategies and activities of lower-class movements once they are formally allowed to take part in politics. Next, the actual *rights of participation* are analyzed in terms of the extension of the *franchise* and the provisions for the *secrecy of the vote.* Considered together, the extension of these rights is indicative of what may be called the civic incorporation of the lower classes.

A Basic Civil Right:
The Right of Association and Combination

Civil rights are essential to a competitive market economy in that "they give to each man, as part of his *individual* status, the power to engage as an *independent* unit in the economic

[38] Accordingly, only incidental consideration is given to the initial and the terminal phases in this process of change: the breakup of estate-societies through the extension of civil rights and the final codification and implementation of welfare rights in our modern, "mass-consumption" societies.

struggle."[39] By taking cognizance only of persons who possess the means to protect themselves, the law in effect accords civil rights to those who own property or have assured sources of income. All others stand condemned by their failure in the economic struggle according to the prevailing views of the early nineteenth century. The abstract principle of equality underlying the legal and ideological recognition of the *independent* individual is often the direct cause of greatly accentuated inequalities. In the present context the most relevant illustration of this consequence is the law's insistence that the wage contract is a contract between equals, that employer and worker are equally capable of safeguarding their interests. On the basis of this formal legal equality, workers in many European countries were denied the *right to combine* for the sake of bargaining with their employers.

However, this denial of the right to combine raised conceptual and political difficulties from the beginning. Civil rights refer not only to the rights of property and contract but also to freedom of speech, thought, and faith which include the freedom to join with others in the pursuit of legitimate private ends. Such freedoms are based on the *right of association*—an accepted legal principle in several European countries (France, England, Belgium, Netherlands) which nevertheless decided to prohibit the workers' *right to combine*. It was held that conditions of work must be fixed by agreements freely arrived at between individual and individual.[40] Such legal prohibitions were distinguished, however, from the right to form religious or political associations in so far as associations not specifically prohibited by law were legal. Accordingly, enactments singled out workmen of various descriptions by special regulations in order to "uphold" the principle of formal equality before the law.

[39] Marshall, *op. cit.,* p. 87. Italics added.

[40] See statement by Le Chapelier, author of the French act prohibiting trade unions of July 1791, as quoted in International Labour Office, *Freedom of Associations* (ILO Studies and Reports, Series A, No. 28; London: P. S. King & Son, 1928), p. 11. Further references to this five-volume work will be given in the form *ILO Report,* with the number and pages cited.

The distinction between association and combination was not made in all countries, however. To understand this contrast we must recall the traditional approach to the master-servant relationship which was similar in many European countries. Statutory enactments had been used to regulate the relations between masters and servants and to control the tendency of masters and journeymen to combine in the interest of raising prices or wages. Such regulation increased in importance as guild organizations declined, though governmental regulations were often made ineffective by the new problems arising from a quickening economic development. Efforts to cope with these new problems could take several forms.

The government could attempt to use an extension of the traditional devices. This approach worked temporarily in England but gave way to the distinction between associations which were allowed and workers' combinations which were prohibited. In the Scandinavian countries and Switzerland the traditional policies proved more successful. These countries remained predominantly agricultural until well into the nineteenth century. They experienced a remarkable proliferation of religious, cultural, economic, and political associations which followed the breakdown of the estate society. Except for a few cases of violent conflicts, their governments did little or nothing either to restrict or to legalize these activities. There were differences here also in the various efforts to cope with the mounting unruliness of journeymen and agricultural workers. But none of these countries went as far as England in enacting special prohibitory legislation designed to stamp out rather than curb combinations of workingmen. In this traditional setting with its estate ideology such a prohibition would have violated the widely accepted right of association.

Such reservations did not prevail in Prussia and Austria, where by the end of the eighteenth century conventional absolutist controls over journeymen's associations were extended to a general prohibition of all "secret assemblies" as in the Prussian Civil Code of 1794. This prohibition was directed principally against Free Masons and other early forms of quasi-political organizations, which were springing up in response to the ideas and events of the French Revolution (such legislation was used against workingmen's combinations as well). A specific prohibition of the latter occurred in Prussia only in the 1840's, although in Austria it had occurred already in 1803. This absolutist approach may be considered together with analogous policies elsewhere which had much the same general effect on workingmen's combinations. In Italy and Spain restrictions of associational activity were traditional and local and hardly required specific legislative enactments to ensure their implementation. In France, on the other hand, the plebiscitarian tradition of direct state-citizen relations led to the promulgation of the famous *Loi Le Chapelier* in 1791, and this tendency to restrain all associations was further strengthened under Napoleon. Here was ample evidence that absolutism and plebiscitarian rule are mutually compatible.

Finally, in England, the early invidious distinction between associations and combinations proved difficult to maintain in the long run. The right of association permitted political agitation through which the prohibition of trade unions could be opposed. Although the Act of 1824 repealing the anti-combination laws was not effective, its early passage is evidence of opposition to the harsh prosecution of workingmen's combinations. We have seen that these repressive measures need to be balanced against others in which violations went unpunished, because employers would not lodge complaints and magistrates would not act in˙the absence of a complaint.

When the decline of the guild system together with the increasing pace of economic development suggested the need for new regulations of master-servant relations and of journeymen's associations, the several Western European countries responded with three broadly distinguishable types of policies. The Scandinavian and Swiss type continued the traditional organization of crafts into the modern period, preserving the right of association at the same time that they extended the statutory regulation of master-servant relations and journeymen's associations to cope with the new problems. In modified form this variant represents the medieval concept of liberty as a privilege, a concept which certainly allows for a statutory reinforcement of existing arrangements. The second, absolutist type is exemplified by the Prussian prohibition first of journeymen's associations, then of all secret assemblies, and finally of the newly formed workingmen's combinations—in keeping with the policy of enlightened absolutism which seeks to regulate all phases of social and economic life. This type represents a major break with the tradition of liberty as a corporate privilege in so far as the king destroys all powers intervening between himself and his subjects, though this destruction could be just as thoroughgoing under plebiscitarian auspices. Finally, the liberal policy exemplified by England went from the earlier regulation of guilds and the master-servant relationship to a policy which combined the specific prohibition of workingmen's combinations with the preservation of the right of association in other respects. Thus, liberalism with its invidious distinction between association and combination represents a halfway mark between the preservation of the right of association (as this was understood in the premodern social structure of Europe) and the complete denial of the right of association which was an outgrowth of absolutist and plebiscitarian opposition to the independent powers of estates and corporations.

Countries of the first type are characterized by relatively insignificant histories of repression, while countries of the other two types suppressed workingmen's combinations by outright prohibition or severe statutory regulations for periods ranging from 75 to 120 years. We can compare countries in terms of this interval between the first decisive measures taken to repress tendencies toward workingmen's combinations and the final decision to accept trade unions. In Denmark, for example, that interval comprised 49 years, in England 76 years, and in Prussia/Germany either 105 or 124 years, depending on whether we consider 1899 or 1918 as the date most appropriate for the legal recognition of trade unions. But the dating of such intervals is problematic. The early acts of repression inevitably blurred the distinction between a mere extension of traditional regulations and a novel and harsher prohibition which singled out the newly developing working class. It is also difficult to date the final legalization of trade unions precisely, since in most cases such legalization occurred gradually. However, these difficulties of dating do not invalidate the rough, threefold typology of the policies which have guided the extension of the right of association to the lower classes in Western Europe.

The legal right to form associations combines the plebiscitarian with the functional principle. Whenever *all* citizens possess this right, we have an instance of plebiscitarianism in the formal sense that everyone enjoys the same legal capacity to act. However, in practice only some groups of citizens take advantage of the opportunity, while a large majority remain "unorganized." Thus, in the developing nation-states of Western Europe private associations exemplify the functional principle of representation on the basis of common interests, in contrast with the medieval estates that collectively enjoyed the privilege of exercising certain public rights in return for a common legal liability. It was recognized early that organizations based on common economic interests would perpetuate or re-establish corporate principles analogous to those of the medieval period.[41] In his argument against mutual benefit societies, Le Chapelier expresses this view in his 1791 speech before the Constituent Assembly to which reference was made earlier:

> The bodies in question have the avowed object of procuring relief for workers in the same occupation who fall sick or become unemployed. But let there be no mistake about this. It is for the nation and for public officials on its behalf to supply work to those who need it for their livelihood and to succour the sick. . . . It should not be permissible for citizens in certain occupations to meet together in defence of their pretended common interests. There must be no more guilds in the State, but only the individual interest of each citizen and the general interest. No one shall be allowed to arouse in any citizen any kind of intermediate interest and

41 We do not go into the question of the continuity or discontinuity between medieval and modern corporations, a problem treated at length in the writings of Figgis, Gierke, Maitland, and others.

to separate him from the public weal through the medium of corporate interests.[42]

This radically plebiscitarian position which does not tolerate the organization of any "intermediate interest" is difficult to maintain consistently. For the individualistic tendencies of the economic sphere, which are partly responsible for this position, are likewise responsible for legal developments which undermine it. A growing exchange economy with its rapid diversification of transactions gives rise to the question how the legal significance of each transaction can be determined unambiguously. In part, this question is answered by attributing "legal personality" to organizations such as business firms and hence by separating the legal spheres of the stockholders and officials from the legal sphere of the organization itself.[43] Incorporation establishes the separate legal liability of the organization and thus limits the liability of its individual members or agents. Although "lim-

[42] Quoted in *ILO Report,* No. 29, p. 89. Le Chapelier's statement reflects the principle enunciated by Rousseau: "If, when the people, sufficiently informed, deliberated, there was to be no communication among them, from the grand total of trifling differences the general will would always result, and their resolutions be always good. But when cabals and partial associations are formed at the expense of the great association, the will of each such association, though *general* with regard to its members, is *private* with regard to the State: it can then be said no longer that there are as many voters as men, but only as many as there are associations. By this means the differences being less numerous, they produce a result less general. Finally, when one of these associations becomes so large that it prevails over all the rest, you have no longer the sum of many opinions dissenting in a small degree from each other, but one great dictating dissentient; from the moment there is no longer a general will, and the predominating opinion is only an individual one. It is therefore of the utmost importance for obtaining the expression of the general will, that no partial society should be formed in the State, and that every citizen should speak his opinion entirely from himself. . . ." See Jean Jacques Rousseau, *The Social Contract* (New York: Hafner Publishing Company, 1957), pp. 26–27.

[43] Weber, *Law in Economy and Society,* pp. 156–157 ff. The editors have added references to the extensive literature in this field.

ited liability" was denounced for a time as an infringement of individual responsibility, massive interests were served by this new device and objections based on the concept of obligation were quickly overcome. Incorporation is a most important breach in the strictly plebiscitarian position. It represents a first limitation of that radical individualism which stands for strictly formal equality before the law and against the formation of "intermediate interests."

Marshall states that in the field of civil rights "the movement has been . . . not from the representation of communities to that of individuals [as in the history of parliament], but from the representation of individuals to that of communities."[44] The device of incorporation and the related principle of limited liability make it possible for an economic enterprise to take risks and maximize economic assets on behalf and for the benefit of individual shareholders. Through its officials the enterprise performs a representative function in the sense that it makes decisions and assumes responsibilities for the collectivity of its investors, which is frequently composed of other corporate groups as well as of individuals. Through much of the nineteenth century this representative function of the corporation was confined to economic goals. However, such concepts as "corporate trusteeship," the development of public relations, and direct political participation by many large corporations suggest that in recent decades this earlier restriction has been abandoned—a development whose significance for citizenship still needs to be explored.

These considerations provide useful background for an understanding of the special position of trade unions. As Marshall points out, trade unions:

> . . . did not seek or obtain incorporation. They can, therefore, exercise vital civil rights collectively on behalf of their members without formal collective responsibility, while the individual responsibility of workers in relation to contract is largely unenforceable. . . .[45]

44 Marshall, *op. cit.*, p. 94.
45 *Ibid.*, p. 93. The following discussion is based on Marshall's analysis on pp. 93–94, but our emphasis differs somewhat.

If we take the prohibition or severe restriction of combinations as our starting point, then the development of trade unions also exemplifies the movement of civil rights from the representation of individuals to that of communities. This collective representation of the economic interests of the members arises from the inability of workers to safeguard their interest individually. Trade unions seek to raise the economic status of their members. The workers organize in order to attain that level of economic reward to which they feel entitled—a level which in practice depends on the capacity to organize and to bargain for "what the traffic will bear." These practical achievements of trade unions have a far-reaching effect upon the status of workers as citizens. For through trade unions and collective bargaining the right to combine is used to assert "basic claims to the elements of social justice."[46] In this way the extension of citizenship to the lower classes is given the very special meaning that as citizens the members of these classes are "entitled" to a certain standard of well-being, in return for which they are only obliged to discharge the ordinary duties of citizenship.

The legalization of trade unions is an instance of enabling legislation. It *permits* members of the lower classes to organize and thus obtain an equality of bargaining power which a previously imposed, formal legal equality has denied them. But to achieve this end it becomes necessary, as we saw, to discriminate in favor of "combinations" by allowing them legal exemptions without which the disadvantaged groups are unable to organize effectively. In other words, civil rights are used here to enable the lower classes to participate more effectively than would otherwise be the case in the economic and political struggle over the distribution of the national income.

However, many members of the lower classes either do not avail themselves of the opportunities afforded them by the law or are prevented from doing so by the exclusivist or neo-corporatist devices of established trade unions. Hence, *in effect* legal opportunities have turned into privileges avail-

[46] *Ibid.*, p. 94.

able to workers who are willing and able to organize in order to advance their economic interests. Such privileges are buttressed, in turn, by legal, extralegal, and illegal devices to make union membership obligatory or nonmembership very costly. Thus, the right to combine turns out to be a "privilege of those organized in trade unions." In a sense this is a measure of the weakness of corporatist tendencies in modern Western societies, since the same right more generally applied would mean that every adult belongs to an organization representing his occupation. Instead, the right to combine has given rise to a "corporatist enclave." The very effectiveness of exclusive practices by trade unions makes membership quasi-obligatory, however beneficial, and unwittingly it is often related to the failure of drives for new members. In this way the right to combine can be used to enforce claims to a share of income and benefits at the expense of the unorganized and the consumers. This exceptional position of *some* trade unions has not altered the *principle* that civil rights are permissive rather than obligatory, though it may be said to have infringed upon it. This permissiveness of civil rights needs special emphasis in the present context because of the contrast with the second element of citizenship, *social* rights, to which we now turn.

A Basic Social Right: The Right to an Elementary Education

The right to an elementary education is similar to the "right to combine." As long as masses of the population are deprived of elementary education, access to educational facilities appears as a precondition without which all other rights under the law remain of no avail to the uneducated. To provide the rudiments of education to the illiterate appears as an act of liberation. Nonetheless, social rights are distinctive in that they do not usually permit the individual to decide whether or not to avail himself of their advantages. Like the legislative regulation of working conditions for women and children, compulsory insurance against industrial accidents, and similar welfare measures, the right to an elementary education is indistinguishable from the duty to attend school. In all Western societies elementary education has become a duty of citizenship, perhaps the earliest example of a prescribed minimum enforced by all the powers of the modern state. Two attributes of elementary education make it into an element of citizenship: the government has authority over it, and the parents of all children in a certain age group (usually from 6 to 10 or 12) are required by law to see to it that their children attend school.

Social rights as an attribute of citizenship may be considered benefits which compensate the individual for his consent to be governed under the rules and by the agents of his national political community.[47] It is important to note the element of agreement or consensus which is at the root of the *direct relationship between the central organs of the nation-state and each member of the community.* But in now turning to a consideration of social rights, we find that this plebiscitarian principle of equality before the sovereign nation-state involves duties as well as rights. Each eligible individual is *obliged* to participate in the services provided by the state. It is somewhat awkward to use the term "plebiscitarian" for this obligatory aspect of citizenship as well. Yet there is a family resemblance between the right of all citizens to participate (through the franchise) in the decision-making processes of government and the duty of all parents to see to it that their children in the designated age groups attend school. In the fully developed welfare state citizens as voters decide to provide the services in which citizens as parents of school children are then obliged to participate. The right to vote is permissive, whereas the benefits of school attendance are obligatory. But both are principles of equality which establish a direct relationship between the central organs of the nation-state and each member of the community, and this direct relationship is the specific meaning of *national* citizenship.

It may be useful to reiterate the major distinctions at this point. There is first the distinction between an indirect and

[47] This formulation is indebted to the perceptive analysis by Joseph Tussman, *Obligation and the Body Politic* (New York: Oxford University Press, 1960), Chap. II.

a direct relation between the nation-state and the citizen. We have discussed the *indirect* relationship in the preceding section in connection with the *rights to association* and the *right to combine*. Although these civil rights are in principle available to all, in practice they are claimed by classes of persons who share certain social and economic attributes. Thus, group (or functional) representation is of continued importance even after the earlier, medieval principle of privileged jurisdictions has been replaced by equality before the law. In now turning to the *direct* relationship between the nation-state and the citizen, we consider *social* rights before we turn to the discussion of *political* rights. The extension of social rights with its emphasis upon obligation may leave privilege intact and broadens the duties and benefits of the people without necessarily encouraging their social mobilization, whereas the extension of the franchise unequivocally destroys privilege and enlarges the active participation of the people in public affairs.

There is clear indication that on the Continent the *principle* of an elementary education for the lower classes emerged as a by-product of enlightened absolutism. In Denmark, for example, Frederick IV established elementary schools on his own domains as early as 1721 and provided them with sufficient resources and a permanently employed teaching staff. Attempts to follow through with this policy failed, because the landed proprietors evaded their responsibility for the employment and remuneration of teachers by imposing charges for teacher salaries on the peasants who could ill afford them. Following the principal measures alleviating the obligations imposed on the peasants (1787–88), Frederick VI proceeded to establish a new organization of elementary schools which has remained the basis of national education in Denmark since 1814.

This Danish development may be compared with the corresponding development in Prussia, where the program of a system of national education also developed early. The profoundly conservative purpose of this program is not in doubt. In 1737, a basic Prussian school law was issued with the commentary that it had grieved the king to see youth living and growing up in darkness and thereby suffering damage both temporally and to their eternal souls. On this occasion the king donated a sum to facilitate the employment of capable teachers, and for several decades thereafter the Prussian kings and their officials promoted the scheme on the basis of such incidental appropriations. By 1763 an ordinance was issued regulating school affairs for the entire monarchy and including provisions for disciplinary measures against teachers who neglect their duties, thus at least envisaging a regular administration of the schools. At the same time efforts were made to alleviate the teacher shortage by earmarking special funds for this purpose. These measures encountered difficulties, because parents were reluctant to send their children to school and local bodies would not assume their share of the financial responsibility. In 1794, the schools (together with the universities) were declared institutions of the state, and in the ensuing years the whole system of national education became part of the national liberation movement against Napoleon. Although some officials publicly expressed doubts concerning the usefulness of literacy for the ordinary man, military defeat and patriotic enthusiasm generally removed such doubts. Official declarations demanded that all subjects without exception should be provided with useful knowledge; national education would raise the moral, religious, and patriotic spirit of the people.[48] In all probability national education became acceptable to the conservative rulers of Prussia on the ground that it would help to instill loyalty for king and country in the masses of the population. It is well to remember, however, that in the field of military recruitment the same effort to mobilize the people in the wars of liberation led to great controversies and provoked a very strong reaction among ultra-conservatives, once the immediate danger was passed.[49] Thus, enlightened absolutism may be

---

[48] The preceding two paragraphs are based on A. Petersilie, *Das Öffentliche Unterrichtswesen* (Vol. III of Hand- und Lehrbuch der Staatswissenschaften; Leipzig: C. L. Hirschfeld, 1897), I, pp. 158–166, 203–204, and *passim*.

[49] For details see the excellent study by Gerhard Ritter, *Staats-*

considered the reluctant or equivocal pioneer of extending social rights to the people. Absolutist rule endorses the principle that nothing should intervene between the king and his people, and hence that the king out of his own free will distributes benefits among them. But absolutism naturally insists that the people are the king's subjects; it rejects the idea of rights and duties derived from and owed to the sovereign authority of the nation-state.[50]

The ideas of national citizenship and a sovereign national authority are basic concepts of liberalism. They have special relevance for education, because in Europe teaching had been in the hands of the clergy for centuries. Accordingly, the schools were under clerical rather than political authority so that pupils to receive an education are subject to this special jurisdiction. This clerical control is destroyed, where absolutist rulers or the nation-state assume authority over the schools. In Lutheran Prussia such secular control over education could be imposed without difficulty. When ministers of the church as well as teachers are subject to the sovereign authority of the king, it is easy to recruit the ministers into the teaching profession. But when, as in France, the Catholic clergy is under an authority separate from that of the state, the establishment of a national system of edu-

---

kunst und Kriegshandwerk (Munich: R. Oldenbourg, 1959), I, Chaps. 4 and 5.

[50] The significance of absolutist regimes for elementary education varied with the prevailing religious beliefs of the country. In Austria, elementary education was organized by the government as early as 1805, with the clergy acting as the supervisory agent of the state. In Catholic countries with less religious unity than Austria such an approach did not prove possible; in France, for example, the traditional Catholic claim to superintend education was challenged in the 1760's with the suppression of the Jesuits and the endorsement of a nationally organized system of lay education. (See p. 110.) Again, in countries with Protestant state churches (Prussia, Denmark, Norway, and Sweden) little or no conflict developed as the unity of church and state in the person of the monarch allowed for the ultimate authority of government over elementary education, with ministers of the church acting in this field as agents of the monarch or (later) of a ministry for education and ecclesiastical affairs.

cation and hence of a direct relationship between each citizen and the government becomes incompatible with the existing system. In his *Essai d'education nationale,* published in 1763, La Chalotais opposes the clergy's control of education by demanding that the teaching of letters and science should be in the hands of a secular profession. After observing that distinguished men of letters are laymen rather than clerics, and that "idle priests" overrun the cities while the country is deprived of clergy, La Chalotais continues:

> To teach letters and sciences, we must have persons who make of them a profession. The clergy cannot take it in bad part that we should not, generally speaking, include ecclesiastics in this class. I am not so unjust as to exclude them from it. I acknowledge with pleasure that there are several . . . who are very learned and very capable of teaching. . . . But I protest against the exclusion of laymen. I claim the right to demand for the Nation an education that will depend upon the State alone; because it belongs essentially to it, because every nation has an inalienable and imprescriptible right to instruct its members, and finally because the children of the State should be educated by members of the State.[51]

The statement parallels the plebiscitarian principle enunciated by Le Chapelier which was quoted earlier.[52] Where Le Chapelier had argued against mutual benefit societies on the ground that no "intermediate interest" should be allowed to separate any citizen from the "public weal through the medium of corporate interests," La Chalotais here echoes the same idea in his argument against the clergy. There must be a profession of teachers which is entirely at the disposal of the state, in order to implement a program of instruction in which nothing intervenes between the "children of the State" and the teachers who are members and servants of the state.

At a later time the principle of a national system of ele-

[51] See La Chalotais, "Essay on National Education," in F. de la Fontainerie, ed., *French Liberalism and Education in the Eighteenth Century* (New York: McGraw-Hill Book Company, 1932), pp. 52–53.

[52] See page 101.

mentary education also became acceptable to the emerging industrial work force. Among laborers the desire to become educated was strong, partly to better their chances in life, partly to see to it that the children had a better chance than their parents, and partly in order to give additional weight to the political claims made on behalf of the working class. If this desire led to voluntary efforts to provide educational facilities for workers, as it did notably in England and Germany, such action was largely a response to the fact that no other facilities were available to them. Once these facilities became available, voluntary efforts in the field of workers' education declined (though they did not cease), another indication of the relative weakness of corporatist tendencies.

It is probable, therefore, that systems of national education develop as widely as they do, because the demand for elementary education cuts across the spectrum of political beliefs. It is sustained by conservatives who fear the people's inherent unruliness which must be curbed by instruction in the fundamentals of religion and thus instill loyalty to king and country. Liberals argue that the nation-state demands a citizenry educated by organs of the state. And populist spokesmen claim that the masses of the people who help to create the wealth of the country should share in the amenities of civilization.

Compulsory elementary education becomes a major controversial issue, however, when governmental authority in this field comes into conflict with organized religion. Traditionally, the Catholic Church regards teaching as one of its inherent powers, with the work of instruction being conducted by the religious orders. In this view the *corporate* principle is paramount in so far as the Church administers man's "spiritual estate" and in this realm possesses the exclusive right and duty of *representation*. This principle was challenged during the eighteenth century in France, and conflict over clerical or lay control of education has lasted to this day. Similar conflicts have also persisted in Protestant countries in which the population is sharply divided over religious issues. That is, a national system of elementary education has been opposed wherever the Church or various religious denominations have insisted upon interposing their own educational facilities between their adherents and the state. Thus, such countries as England, Belgium, and the Netherlands have been the scene of protracted struggles over the question whether or under what conditions the national government should be permitted to give assistance or exercise authority in the field of elementary education. In England, for example, voluntary contributions in aid of education amounted, in 1858, to double the amount of support provided by the government. Since 1870 a new system of state schools has been developed, not as a substitute for the schools based on voluntary contributions, but in addition to them. Thus, until well into the modern period local and voluntary efforts preserve elements of "functional representation," despite the steady growth of a national (plebiscitarian) system of education.[53] Perhaps the most outstanding example of the corporate or representative principle in education is provided by the Netherlands with its three separate school systems: one Catholic, one Calvinist, and one secular-humanist. The significant fact here is that all three systems are financed by the government and all three are based on the principle of obligatory attendance, thus neatly combining the plebiscitarian principle in finance with the representative principle in the organizational and substantive control over the educational process.

Political Rights: The Franchise and the Secret Vote

This strain between estate orientation and nation orientation in the determination of policy is even more apparent in the debates and enactments concerning *rights of political participation:* the right to serve as a representative, the right to vote

[53] See the historical sketch of the English educational development in Ernest Barker, *The Development of the Public Services in Western Europe* (New York: Oxford University Press, 1944), pp. 85–93 and the comparative account by Robert Ulich, *The Education of Nations* (Cambridge: Harvard University Press, 1961), *passim.*

for representatives, and the right of independent choice among alternatives.

The basic condition for the development toward universal rights of participation was the *unification of the national system of representation.* In the late Middle Ages the principle of territorial representation had on the Continent increasingly given way to a system of representation by *estates:* each estate sent its separate representatives to deliberate at the center of territorial authority and each had its separate assembly.[54] Only in England was the original system of territorial representation retained: the House of Commons was not an assembly of the burgher estates but a body of legislators representing the constituent localities of the realm, the counties and the boroughs. The greater openness of English society made it possible to keep up the territorial channels of representation, and this, in turn, set the stage for a much smoother transition to a unified regime of equalitarian democracy.[55]

Regardless of the principle of representation in these *anciens régimes,* only the economically independent heads of households could take part in public life. This participation was a right they derived not from their membership in any national community but from their ownership of territory and capital or from their status within legally defined functional corporations such as the nobility, the church, or the guilds of merchants or artisans. There was no representation of individuals: the members of the assemblies represented

[54] The primary authority on the history of corporate estates and their representation is still Otto von Gierke, *Das deutsche Genossenschaftsrecht* (Berlin: Weidmann, 1868), I, pp. 534–581.

[55] This question of territorial vs. functional representation is at the heart of the debate over the reasons for the survival of Parliament during the age of absolutism. Otto Hintze has stressed the historical continuities between medieval and modern forms of representation and has argued that the two-chamber polities beyond the reach of the Carolingian Empire offered the best basis for the development of pluralist, parliamentary rule. See his "Typologie der ständischen Verfassungen des Abendlandes," *Staat und Verfassung,* pp. 120–139.

recognized stakes in the system, whether in the form of property holdings or in the form of professional privileges.

The French Revolution brought about a fundamental change in the conception of representation: the basic unit was no longer the household, the property, or the corporation, but the *individual citizen;* and representation was no longer channeled through separate functional bodies but through a *unified national assembly* of legislators. The law of August 11, 1792, went so far as to give the franchise to all French males over 21 who were not servants, paupers, or *vagabonds,* and the Constitution of 1793 did not even exclude paupers if they had resided more than six months in the *canton.* The Restoration did not bring back representation by estates: instead the *régime censitaire* introduced an abstract monetary criterion which cut decisively across the earlier criteria of ascribed status.

A new phase in this development opened up with the Revolution of 1848 and the rapid spread of movements for representative democracy through most of Europe. Napoleon III demonstrated the possibilities of plebiscitarian rule, and leaders of the established elites became increasingly torn between their fears of the consequences of rapid extensions of the suffrage to the lower classes and their fascination with the possibilities of strengthening the powers of the nation-state through the mobilization of the working class in its service.[56] These conflicts of strategy produced a great variety of transitional compromises in the different countries. The starting points for these developments were the provisions of the *Ständestaat* and the postrevolutionary *régime censitaire,* and the end points were the promulgations of universal adult suffrage. But the steps taken and the paths chosen from the

[56] See H. Gollwitzer, "Der Cäsarismus Napoleons III im Widerhall der öffentlichen Meinung Deutschlands," *Historische Zeitschrift,* Vol. 152 (1952), 23–76. In a number of countries the demands for universal manhood suffrage became intimately tied in with the need for universal *conscription.* In Sweden the principal argument for the breakup of the four-estate *Riksdag* was the need for a strengthening of national defense. In the Swedish suffrage debates, the slogan "one man, one vote, one gun" reflects this tie up between franchise and military recruitment.

one point to the other varied markedly from country to country and reflected basic differences in the dominant values and character of each social structure.[57]

We may conveniently distinguish five major sets of criteria used in limiting the franchise during this transitional period: (1) traditional *estate* criteria: restriction of franchise to heads of households within each of the established status groups as defined by law; (2) *régime censitaire:* restrictions based on the value of land or capital or on the amounts of yearly taxes on property and/or income; (3) *régime capacitaire:* restrictions by literacy, formal education, or appointment to public office; (4) *household responsibility* criteria: restrictions to heads of households occupying own dwellings of a minimum given volume or lodged in premises for a given minimum rent; (5) *residence* criteria: restrictions to citizens registered as residents either in the local community, the constituency, or the national territory for a given minimum of months or years.

The Norwegian Constitution of 1814 provides a good example of an early compromise between estate criteria, the *régime censitaire* and the *principe capacitaire*. The franchise was given to four categories of citizens: two of these, the *burghers* of incorporated cities and the *peasants* (freeholders and leaseholders), corresponded to the old estates; a third, applicable only in cities and towns, was defined by ownership of real estate of a given minimum value; and the fourth was simply made up of all officials of the national government. This system gave a clear numerical majority to the farmers, but as a political precaution the interests of the burghers and officials were protected through inequalities in the distribution of mandates between urban and rural constituencies.[58] The simplicity of the social structure made the Norwegian

[57] The details of these developments have been set out in such compendia as Georg Meyer, *Das parlamentarische Wahlrecht* (Berlin: Haering, 1901), and Karl Braunias, *Das parlamentarische Wahlrecht* (Berlin: de Gruyter, 1932), Vol. 2.

[58] See Stein Rokkan, "Geography, Region and Social Class: Cross-Cutting Cleavages in Norwegian Politics," in S. M. Lipset and Stein Rokkan, eds., *Party Systems and Voter Alignments* (New York: The Free Press of Glencoe, forthcoming).

compromise a straightforward one: the age-old division between peasant and burgher estates corresponded to an established administrative division into rural districts and chartered towns, and the only class of voters explicitly placed above this territorial-functional division was the king's officials, the effective rulers of the nation for several decades to come.

Much more complex compromises had to be devised in multinational polities such as Austria. In the old Habsburg territories the typical *Landtag* had consisted of four *curiae:* the nobles, the knights, the prelates, and the representatives of cities and markets. The *Februarpatent* of 1861 kept the division into four *curiae,* but transformed the estate criteria into criteria of *interest representation.* The nobles and the knights were succeeded by a *curia* of the largest landowners. The ecclesiastical estate was broadened into a *curia* of *Virilstimmen* representing universities as well as dioceses. The burgher estate was no longer exclusively represented by spokesmen for cities and markets, but also through the *chambers of commerce and the professions:* this was the first recognition of a corporatist principle which was to become of central importance in the ideological debates in Austria in the twentieth century. To these three was added a *peasant* division: this was new in the national system; direct peasant representation of the type so well known in the Nordic countries had only existed in Tyrol and Vorarlberg. The most interesting feature of the Austrian sequence of compromises was the handling of the lower classes so far excluded from participation in the politics of the nation. True to their tradition of functional representation, the Austrian statesmen did not admit these new citizens *on a par* with the already enfranchised, but placed them in a new, a fifth *curia, die allgemeine Wählerklasse.* This, however, was only a transitional measure: eleven years later even the Austrian *Abgeordnetenhaus* fell in with the trend toward equalitarian mass democracy and was transformed into a unified national assembly based on universal manhood suffrage.[59]

[59] A useful account of these developments in Austria is found in

The rise of commercial and industrial capitalism favored the spread of the *régime censitaire*. The ideological basis was Benjamin Constant's argument that the affairs of the national community must be left to those with "real stakes" in it through the possession of land or through investments in business. The *principe capacitaire* was essentially an extension of this criterion: the franchise was accorded not only to those who own land or have invested in business but also to those who have acquired a direct interest in the maintenance of the polity through their investments in professional skills and their appointment to positions of public trust. The implicit notion is that only such citizens can form rational judgments of the policies to be pursued by the government. A Norwegian authority on constitutional law links the two elements together in his statement: "Suffrage . . . should be reserved to the citizens who have *judgment* enough to understand who would prove the best representatives, and *independence* enough to stick to their conviction in this matter."[60]

This question of criteria of intellectual independence was at the heart of the struggles between liberals and conservatives over the organization of the suffrage. Liberals favored the *régime censitaire* and feared the possibilities of electoral manipulation inherent in the extension of the suffrage to the economically dependent. Conservatives, once they recognized the importance of the vote as a basis of local power, tended to favor the enfranchisement of the "lower orders": they had good reason to expect that, at least on the patriarchal estates in the countryside, those in positions of dependence would naturally vote for the local notables. This conflict reached a climax in the discussions at the German National Assembly

---

Ludwig Boyer, *Wahlrecht in Österreich* (Vienna, 1961), pp. 80–85. It is interesting to compare the Austrian mixture of medieval estate-orientation and modern corporatism with the Russian provisions for the *Duma* in 1906; see Max Weber's detailed analysis in "Russlands Übergang zum Scheinkonstitutionalismus" *Gesammelte Politische Schriften* (Tübingen: J. C. B. Mohr, 1958), pp. 66–126.

[60] T. H. Aschehoug, *Norges nuverende Statsforfatning* (Christiania: Aschehoug, 1875), Vol. I, p. 280.

in Frankfurt in 1848–49. The Constitutional Commission had recommended that the franchise should be restricted to all *independent* citizens, and this term was at first interpreted to exclude all servants and all wage earners. This interpretation met with violent protests in the Assembly. There was general agreement that subjects who received public assistance or were in bankruptcy were not independent and should be excluded from the franchise, but there was extensive disagreement on the rights of servants and workers. The left claimed full rights for the lower classes and was only moderately opposed by the conservatives. The result was the promulgation of universal manhood suffrage. As it happened, this law could not be enforced at the time: it took another 17 years until Bismarck was able to make it the basis for the organization of the *Reichstag* of the North German Federation. The Prussian Chancellor had already had the experience of a system of universal suffrage, but a markedly unequal one—the Prussian system of three-class suffrage introduced by royal decree in 1849. Under that system the "lower orders" had been given the right to vote, but the weight of their votes was infinitesimal in comparison with those of the middle classes and the landowners. This system had obviously served to bolster the power of the *Gutsbesitzer*, particularly east of the Elbe: the law had simply multiplied by n the number of votes at their disposal, since they counted on being able to control without much difficulty the behavior of their dependents and their workers at the polls.[61] Bismarck detested the three-class system for its emphasis on abstract monetary criteria and its many injustices, but he was convinced that a change to equal suffrage for all men would not affect the

[61] For a recent detailed account see Th. Nipperdey, *Die Organisation der deutschen Parteien vor 1918* (Düsseldorf: Droste, 1961), Chap. V. For a parallel with conditions in the similarly structured rural areas of Brazil, see the chapter by Emilio Willems in Arnold Rose, ed., *The Institutions of Advanced Societies* (Minneapolis: University of Minnesota Press, 1958), p. 552: "The main functions *of suffrage was that of preserving* the existing power structure. Within the traditional pattern, suffrage added opportunities for displaying and reinforcing feudal loyalty. At the same time, it reinforced and legalized the political status of the landowner."

power structure in the countryside: on the contrary it would strengthen even further the landed interests against the financial. Generally, in the countryside the extensions of the suffrage tended to strengthen the conservative forces.[62]

There was much more uncertainty about the consequences of an extended suffrage for the politics of the urban areas. The emergence and growth of a class of *wage earners outside the immediate household* of the employer raised new problems for the definition of political citizenship. In the established socio-economic terminology their status was one of dependence, but it was not evident that they would inevitably follow their employers politically. The crucial battles in the development toward universal suffrage concerned the status of these emerging strata within the political community. A great variety of transitional compromises were debated and several were actually tried out. The basic strategy was to underscore the structural differentiations within the wage-earning strata. Some varieties of *régime censitaire* in fact admitted the better paid wage workers, particularly if they had houses of their own.[63] The householder and lodger franchise in Britain similarly served to integrate the better-off working class within the system and to keep out only the "real proletariat," migrants and marginal workers without established local ties. The retention of residence requirements has served similar functions even after the disappearance of all economic qualifications for suffrage: these restrictions are adhered to most stubbornly in the provisions for local elections.

Another set of strategies in this battle to control the onrush of mass democracy comprises the institutions of *weighted suffrage* and *plural votes*. The crudest examples are no doubt

[62] See D. C. Moore, "The Other Face of Reform," *Victorian Studies*, V (September 1961), pp. 7–34 and G. Kitson Clark, *The Making of Victorian England* (London: Methuen, 1962), especially Chap. VII.

[63] A special tax census taken in Norway in 1876 indicates that more than one-quarter of the urban workers who were on the tax rolls were enfranchised under the system adopted in 1814: by contrast only 3 per cent of the workers in the rural areas had been given the vote. See Statistisk Centralbureau ser. C. No. 14, 1877, pp. 340–341.

the Austrian *Kurien* and the Prussian three-class system:
universal suffrage is granted, but the weights of the votes
given to the lower classes are infinitesimal in comparison
with those of the established landed or financial elite. The
most innocuous system of plural voting is perhaps the British
provision for extra votes for university graduates and for
owners of business premises in different constituencies. Sociologically the most interesting is the Belgian system of plural
voting devised in 1893: universal manhood suffrage is introduced, but extra votes are given not only on *capacitaire*
criteria but also to *pères de famille* upon reaching the re-
spectable age of 35. The basic motive is clearly to underscore
structural differentiations within the lower strata and to exclude from the system the elements least committed to the
established social order.

Closely related to these strategies is the stubborn resistance
to changes in the delimitation of constituencies. Rapid urbanization produces glaring inequalities even under conditions of formally equal universal suffrage. The injustices of
the Prussian districting provisions were the object of acrimo-
nious debate for decades. The extreme solution adopted
in the Weimar Republic—the establishment of a unitary system of proportional representation for the entire Reich—
no doubt gives every voter the same abstract chance to influence the distribution of seats, but at the same time brings to
the fore the inherent difficulties of such standardization across
localities of very different structure. The continued over-
representation of rural areas in the United States is another
example.

The entry of the lower classes into the political arena also
raises a series of problems for the *administration of elections*.
Sociologically the most interesting issue is the safeguarding of
the *independence of the individual electoral decision*. The
defenders of estate traditions and the *régime censitaire* argue
that economically dependent subjects cannot be expected to
form independent political judgments and would, if enfranchised, corrupt the system through the sale of votes and
through violent intimidation. Corrupt practices were, of
course, widespread in many countries long before the exten-

sion of the suffrage, but the enfranchisement of large sections of the lower classes generally provides added incentive to reforms in the administration and control of elections. The secrecy of the ballot is a central problem in this debate.[64]

The traditional notion was that the vote was a public act and only to be entrusted to men who could openly stand by their opinions. The Prussian system of oral voting was defended in these terms, but was maintained for so long largely because it proved an easy way of controlling the votes of farm laborers.

The secret ballot essentially appeals to the liberal urban mentality: it fits as another element into the anonymous, privatized culture of the city, described by Georg Simmel. The decisive factor, however, is the emergence of the lower-class vote as a factor in national politics and the need to neutralize the threatening working-class organizations: the provisions for secrecy isolate the dependent worker not only from his superiors but also from his peers. Given the state of electoral statistics, it is very difficult to determine with any exactitude the effects of secrecy on the actual behavior of workers at the polls. But it seems inherently likely, given a minimum amount of cross-class communications, that secrecy helps to reduce the likelihood of a polarization of political life on the basis of social class.

In this respect the secret ballot represents the national and plebiscitarian principle of civic integration, in contrast to working-class organizations which exemplify the principle of functional representation. That is, the claims of trade unions and labor parties which seek recognition for the rights of the *fourth estate* are counterbalanced by the claims of the *national* community and its spokesmen. The provision for secret voting puts the individual before a personal choice and makes him at least temporarily independent of his immediate environment: in the voting booth he can be a national citizen. The provisions for secret voting make it possible for the in-

[64] A recent one-nation account of the development of standards for the control of elections is Cornelius O'Leary, *The Elimination of Corrupt Practices in British Elections, 1868–1911* (Oxford: Clarendon Press, 1962).

articulate rank and file to escape the pressure for political partisanship and at the same time put the onus of political visibility on the activists within the working-class movement. In sociological terms we can say, therefore, that the national electoral system opens up channels for the expression of secret loyalties while the political struggle makes it necessary for the party activist to publicize his views and expose himself to censure where he deviates from the "establishment."[65]

CONCLUDING CONSIDERATIONS

The extension of citizenship to the lower classes of Western Europe can be viewed from several complementary points of view. In terms of the comparison between the medieval and the modern political structure the discussion exemplifies the simultaneous trends toward equality and a nationwide, governmental authority. The constitution of a modern nation-state is typically the fountainhead of the rights of citizenship, and these rights are a token of nationwide equality. Politics itself has become nationwide, and the "lower classes" now have the opportunity of active participation.

The preceding discussion has stressed the over-all similarity of the Western European experience, arising from the common legacies of European feudalism. The estate assemblies and parliaments of the eighteenth century provide the immediate background for the development of modern parliaments and for the conception of a right to representation which was gradually extended to previously unrepresented sections of the population. This extension has two, more or

[65] Some socialist parties try to counteract these effects of secret voting by establishing intimate ties with trade unions. Note in this respect the controversy over the political levy paid by members of British trade unions as discussed in Martin Harrison, *Trade Unions and the Labour Party since 1945* (London: Allen & Unwin, 1960), Chap. 1. Trade union members who wish to be excused from payment hand a "contracting-out" form to their branch secretary, but although the payment is nominal and the procedure simple, controversy has been intense, in part because "contracting-out" is a public act which indirectly jeopardizes the secrecy of the ballot.

less disparate, elements. According to the plebiscitarian idea, all adult individuals must have equal rights under a national government; according to the functional idea, the differential affiliation of individuals with others is taken as given and some form of group representation is accepted. The two ideas reflect the hiatus between state and society in an age of equality. When the extension of legal, political, and social rights becomes a principle of state policy, abstract criteria must be used to implement these rights. Hence, there are recurrent attempts to define in what respects all persons must henceforth be considered equal. However, the society continues to be marked by great inequalities. Hence, all adults who would take advantage of their legal, political, and social rights naturally associate with one another in order to advance their claims as effectively as possible, and such associations reflect (or even intensify) the inequalities of the social structure. The preceding discussion has shown that the relations between the plebiscitarian and functional ideas are frequently paradoxical.

Formal equality before the law at first benefits only those whose social and economic independence enables them to take advantage of their legal rights. Efforts to correct *this* inequality take many forms, among them regulations which enable members of the lower classes to avail themselves of the right of association for the representation of their economic interests. However, these regulations in turn do not reach those individuals or groups who will not or cannot take advantage of the right of association. Accordingly, equality before the law unwittingly divides a population in a new way. Further legal provisions attempt to deal with remaining inequalities or cope with newly emerging ones, for example, the institution of the public defender where the defendant is unable to take advantage of his right to counsel, or efforts to protect the rights of shareholders who are unable to do so under existing legislation. As yet there are only debates concerning the best ways of protecting members of trade unions against possible violations of their individual rights by the organization which represents their economic interests. The principle of formal legal equality may be called "plebiscitarian" in the sense that the state directly establishes each individual's "legal capacity." In addition, special provisions seek to reduce in various ways the unequal chances of individuals to use their rights under the law. In the latter case the rule-making authorities "represent" the interests of those who do not or cannot use their legal powers.

The right and duty to receive an *elementary education* may be considered another way of equalizing the capacity of all citizens to avail themselves of the rights to which they are entitled. Although elementary education provides only a minimal facility in this respect, it is perhaps the most universally approximated implementation of national citizenship, all other rights being either more permissive or selective in character. As such, public elementary education exemplifies the plebiscitarian component of the nation-state, since school attendance is not only incumbent upon all children of a certain age group but also depends on the financial contribution of all taxpayers.[66] But here again, formally instituted equalities give rise to or are the occasion for new types of inequalities. Those concerned with teaching and the organization of schools join together because of common professional and economic interests. These specialists in education often develop organizations with entrenched opinions concerning education. As such, teachers as a group confront parents as individuals, just as they confront the state with the influence of their organization in all matters affecting their interests. More indirectly, public elementary education helps to articulate, however inadvertently, the existing residential divisions within the community, since children will be assigned to schools closest to their area of residence and the school population will reflect the social characteristics of residential areas. Efforts to counteract these consequences of

[66] Children attending elementary school are more numerous than taxpayers since school attendance allows for no exemptions as does the tax system. Indeed, even the children of resident aliens are subject to this requirement, but this may be considered an administrative convenience, a welfare measure, a preparation of potential citizens, and so on rather than a matter concerning the principle of national citizenship.

the functional principle such as the Parent-Teacher Associations and the reassignment of children among different school districts as in the United States are examples of plebiscitarianism within the system of public education. In addition, there is the prolonged resistance of denominational groups against public education as such, to which reference was made earlier. The plebiscitarian principle is resisted since the agencies of the church or the denominations, by controlling the curriculum, seek to represent the special religious and cultural interests of parents as members of their respective congregations. Religious groups thus use the right of association to implement their special concerns in the field of education, though they differ widely in terms of whether and to what extent they rely financially on tax support or on assessments of their congregations.

With regard to the *franchise* the conflicts between the plebiscitarian and the representative principles may be divided into the two phases of a variously restricted and a universal right to vote. The restrictions we have reviewed are typically administrative criteria to which functional significance is imputed. When the right to vote is made dependent upon a certain level of income, tax payment, property ownership, or education, it is assumed that those who meet minimum standards in these respects also share social and political views compatible with the established social order. It is also assumed that the representatives elected from these strata of the population will be notables capable of thinking and acting in terms of the whole community. This legal recognition of the representative principle is in large part abandoned once the right to vote has become universal. Yet the plebiscitarian principle of the right to direct participation by all adults as eligible voters is quite compatible with an acceptance of group differences and various indirect forms of functional representation. The electoral process itself is greatly influenced by the social differentiation of the voting public, and it is supplemented at many points by other influences on policy formation, many of them depending on special interest groups. Social differentiation and interest groups result in modifications of the plebiscitarian principle and in new inequalities which may in turn provoke countermeasures in order to protect the plebiscitarian principle of equality of all adults as eligible voters.

Accordingly, the extension of citizenship to the lower classes involves at many levels an institutionalization of abstract criteria of equality which give rise both to new inequalities and new measures to deal with these ancillary consequences. The system of representative institutions characteristic of the Western European tradition remains intact as long as this tension between the plebiscitarian idea and the idea of group-representation endures, as long as the contradiction between abstract criteria of equality and the old as well as new inequalities of the social condition is mitigated by ever new and ever partial compromises. The system is destroyed when, as in the totalitarian systems of recent history, these partial resolutions are abandoned in the interest of implementing the plebiscitarian principle alone under the aegis of a one-party state.

4

ADMINISTRATIVE AUTHORITY IN
THE NATION-STATE

The patrimonial-feudal structure of medieval political life, the "great transformation" of public authority in the imme- diate premodern period, individualistic as contrasted with traditional authority relationships, social protest in the mod- ern as contrasted with protest in the medieval period, the elements of national citizenship and their gradual extension to previously excluded sections of the population—all these are concepts of limited applicability. The social structures and behavior patterns to which they refer prevail for a time that exceeds the lifespan of the individuals involved. None- theless they are of limited duration, and this implies a period of emergence and decline. Concepts appropriate to such structures can only designate the cluster of attributes by which they may be identified; they cannot also encompass the ebb and flow of these attributes over time.

The concept "nation-state" is another case in point. It refers to attributes of public authority which are most un- equivocal when contrasted with the attributes of medieval political life. In the medieval conception the king not only rules over a territory as a private domain, he also owns the judicial and administrative functions of government and hence can dispose of them as if they were pieces of property. In theory the king retains ultimate authority even over those lands, and rights to the exercise of authority, which he has granted to a vassal in perpetuity. The fiction of royal sovereignty is maintained by the ruler through formal re-instatement of successive heirs in the titles and rights of their forefathers. In practice the vassal often treats the lands and rights granted him as if these are a property to which his family has a hereditary claim. Thus, governmental authority is as much linked to family as to property. The ruler and his vassals claim a prescriptive right to the exercise of authority, not for themselves as individuals but as members of families in which that title inheres by virtue of royal or aristocratic lineage. Edmund Burke's dictum concerning society as a partnership applies to this context. "As the ends of such a partnership cannot be obtained in many generations, it becomes a partnership not only between those who are living, but between those who are living, those who are dead, and those who are to be born."[1] In the medieval conception the "building block" of the social order is the family of hereditary privilege, whose stability over time is the foundation of right and of authority, while the rank-order of society and its transmission through inheritance regulates the relations among such families and between them and the supreme ruler.

The modern nation-state presupposes that this link between governmental authority and inherited privilege in the hands of families of notables is broken. Access to important political and administrative posts in the governments of nation-states can be facilitated by wealth and high social position through their effect on social contacts and educational opportunities. But facility of access is not the same as the prerogative which aristocratic families in medieval politics claim by virtue of their "antiquity of blood," to use Machiavelli's phrase. For the decisive criterion of the Western nation-state is the substantial separation between the social structure and the exercise of judicial and administrative functions. Major functions of government such as the adjudication of legal disputes, the collection of revenue, the control of currency, military recruitment, the organization of the postal system, the construction of public facilities, and others have

[1] Edmund Burke, *Reflections on the Revolution in France* (Gateway Editions, Inc.; Chicago: Henry Regnery Co., 1955), p. 140.

been removed from the political struggle in the sense that they cannot be appropriated on a hereditary basis by privileged estates and on this basis parceled out among competing jurisdictions. Politics ceases to be a struggle over the distribution of sovereign powers whenever the orderly dominion over a territory and its inhabitants is conceived to be the function of one and the same community—the nation-state.[2] Instead, politics becomes a struggle over the distribution of the national product and over the policies and the administrative implementation which affect that distribution. One unquestioned corollary of this emergence of the nation-state is the development of a body of officials, whose recruitment and policy execution were separated gradually from the previously existing involvement of officials with kinship loyalties, hereditary privileges, and property interests.[3] The following discussion examines this process of bureaucratization and then turns to an analysis of selected aspects of the relation between administrators and the public in the modern nation-state.

BUREAUCRATIZATION

One attribute of all government is the implementation of commands through an administrative staff. The appointment of officials and their manner of implementing commands differentiate one type of political structure from another. Since the base point of the preceding discussion is the medieval political structure of Western Europe, we can best characterize the process of bureaucratization by means of a systematic contrast with the patrimonial type of government.

[2] See Max Weber, *Law in Economy and Society* (trans. and ed. by Max Rheinstein and E. A. Shils; Cambridge: Harvard University Press, 1954), p. 338 and *passim*. See also Max Weber, *The Theory of Social and Economic Organization* (New York: Oxford University Press, 1947), p. 156.

[3] A comparative study of administrative history, in which this process of separation is traced since the middle of the seventeenth century, is contained in Ernest Barker, *The Development of Public Services in Western Europe, 1660–1930* (New York: Oxford University Press, 1944).

The patrimonial ruler or chief is related to his personal subordinates and officials in the following manner:

1. Through arbitrary decisions of the moment the ruler grants powers to his officials, or commissions them to perform set tasks; in principle he is free to alter these grants or commissions as it suits him.

2. "The question who shall decide a matter—which of his officials or the chief himself—. . . is treated . . . [either] traditionally, on the basis of the authority of particular received legal norms or precedents, [or] entirely on the basis of the arbitrary decisions of the chief."

3. ". . . Household officials and favourites are very often recruited on a purely patrimonial basis from among the slaves or serfs of the chief. If the recruitment has been extra-patrimonial [i.e., outside the ruler's personal household domain], they have tended to be holders of benefices which he has granted as an act of grace without being bound by any formal rule."

4. Qualification for office depends entirely upon the ruler's personal judgment of quality among his household officials, retainers or favorites.

5. "Household officials and favourites are usually supported and equipped in the household of the chief and from his personal stores. Generally, their exclusion from the lord's own table means the creation of benefices . . ." and hence a weakening of patrimonial rule as here defined.

6. Through abrupt changes in appointment and a series of other arbitrary acts the ruler makes every effort to prevent the identification of any one household official or favorite with the office he occupies at a given time.

7. The ruler himself, or his official and favorites who act in his name, conduct the affairs of government when and if they consider it appropriate, i.e., either upon payment of a fee or as a unilateral act of grace.[4]

[4] The quoted passages are taken from Max Weber, *The Theory of Social and Economic Organization*, pp. 343, 344, and 345. The remaining characteristics of patrimonial rule are extracted from Max Weber, *Wirtschaft und Gesellschaft* (Tübingen: J. C. B. Mohr, 1925), II, pp. 679–723. Related discussions are found in Max

Government is considered a mere extension of the ruler's private domain. We saw that under patrimonialism arbitrary personal rule is considered legitimate on the basis of immemorial and sanctified tradition. But tradition does not legitimize disregard of the sanctions which consecrate and authenticate tradition. Repeatedly, the patrimonial ruler confronts the task of balancing one principle against another. This consideration applies to all the conditions enumerated above: the delegation of authority, the basis of recruitment and remuneration, qualification for office, obedience of subordinates to the ruler or the relative independence of their position, and finally the degree to which ruler and officials treat official business as an act of personal indulgence or the performance of that duty which tradition makes incumbent upon them. In these respects neither personal arbitrariness nor adherence to sanctified precedent can be dispensed with. For if arbitrariness comes to prevail, patrimonialism gives way to tyranny; if established rights eliminate the arbitrary will of the ruler, patrimonialism gives way to feudalism or a large realm disintegrates into smaller patrimonial domains. Patrimonial rule will endure as long as these eventualities are avoided, but it is also true that *within* this framework arbitrary rule or adherence to sanctified tradition can become dominant.

Weber's characterization of patrimonial rule subsumes a great diversity of historical events, and the paired concepts of sanctified arbitrariness and sanctified precedent provide an interpretive device for an analysis of social change. But every concrete exercise of authority by a historical ruler is, by the same token, an instance in a series of events which reveals a pattern only when viewed in retrospect and over the long run. Although the conceptualization of that pattern enables the analyst to approach any specific case with a knowledge of the "principles of action" which are at issue, that knowledge is inevitably removed from the ambiguities and compromises by which men of action thread their way between opposing principles. It is necessary, therefore, to

Weber's *Religion of China* (Glencoe: The Free Press, 1951), pp. 33–104.

emphasize the dilemmas intrinsic in benchmark concepts like patrimonial administration, in order to reduce the gap between concept and behavior. On the other hand, as we learn how to assess the price of every line of action, the avoidable and unavoidable drawbacks it entails for the attainment of its own ends, we also reduce that gap from the side of behavioral analysis. Parallel considerations apply to the system of administration under the rule of law.

In the modern nation-state of the Western type governmental administration is characterized by an orientation toward legal and administrative regulations. Since Weber's definition of bureaucracy parallels the points just cited regarding patrimonial administration, I repeat it here in abbreviated form. A bureaucracy tends to be characterized by: (1) defined rights and duties, which are prescribed in written regulations; (2) authority relations between positions which are ordered systematically; (3) appointment and promotion which are regulated and are based on contractual agreement; (4) technical training (or experience) as a formal condition of employment; (5) fixed monetary salaries; (6) a strict separation of office and incumbent in the sense that the employee does not own the "means of administration" and cannot appropriate the position; (7) administrative work as a full-time occupation.[5]

Each of these characteristics stands for a condition of employment in modern government administration. The process of bureaucratization may be interpreted as the manifold, cumulative, and more or less successful imposition of these employment conditions since the nineteenth century. The problems of management arising from this process can be characterized in a general way by contrasting each bureaucratic condition of employment with its nonbureaucratic or antibureaucratic counterpart.

The endeavor to define rights and duties in accordance

[5] H. H. Gerth and C. W. Mills, eds., *From Max Weber: Essays in Sociology* (New York: Oxford University Press, 1946), pp. 196–198. The following discussion is based on my book, *Work and Authority in Industry* (New York: John Wiley & Sons, 1956), pp. 244–248.

with formal (impersonal) criteria will encounter persistent attempts to interpret them in a manner the individual concerned regards as advantageous to himself.

The systematic ordering of authority relationships will be opposed, though often quite unwittingly, by attempts to subject these relationships to informal bargaining by using favors of various kinds.

Similar personal considerations may also affect the appointment and promotion of employees, even when there is outward compliance with the rules.

Technical training as a condition of employment is perhaps least subject to such practices, though even here personal relationships and subjective interpretations may modify what otherwise would be a purely formal adherence to this condition. I think of such factors as the preference of hiring officials for applicants who have certain personal characteristics as well as the required technical competence. Subjective evaluation also enters into the weighting of a candidate's experience, professional standing, and so on.

Similar considerations apply to fixed monetary salaries. Although salary scales can be readily fixed and administered, appointment and promotion are subject to bargaining and personal influence, as is the whole system of job classification without which a salary scale is meaningless. In addition, there are continual efforts at supplementing any given salary scale by various fringe benefits which are not as readily systematized as the scale itself, and hence permit the maneuvering which the scale seeks to eliminate.

The strict separation between official and incumbent, between the position and the employee, is an ideal condition which is rarely achieved in practice, especially with regard to salaried employees and skilled workers. Incumbents endow their work performance with personal qualities that range from dispensable idiosyncrasies to untransferable and often indispensable skills, so that some measure of identification of the employee with his position is unavoidable. Under modern conditions of employment the individual cannot appropriate his position in the sense in which, say, in the British government during the eighteenth century administrative offices were a form of private property a family could pass on from one generation to the next. But the safeguards against dismissal established in modern government under the slogan of "job security" have endowed employment with a quasi-proprietary character which is more or less incompatible with the strict separation between the job and the employee.

Although the idea of work as a full-time occupation is generally accepted, the intensity of work is subject to disputes and interpretations. "Full-time" is unambiguous as contrasted with part-time or avocational work. But the amount of work done in a full-time occupation continues to be a most controversial condition of employment, which employers seek to regularize by the use of incentives and penalties and which workers interpret in their own way by the practice of output restriction. In this way bureaucratization is an ongoing process, in which those in authority subject the conditions of employment to an impersonal systematization, while the employees seek to modify the implementation of the rules in a manner they consider advantageous to themselves. We may say that employees continue to "bargain" silently over the rules governing their employment, long after they have signed the contract which ostensibly precludes such further "bargaining." On the other hand, those in authority endeavor to maximize the predictable performance of employees by the strategic use of penalties, incentives, and ideological appeals.

Within the administrative context these conflicting strategies replicate what Weber considers the basic characteristics of legal domination. In so far as "love, hatred, and every purely personal . . . feeling [is excluded] from the execution of official tasks," modern government approximates the ideal type of the bureaucracy under legal domination.[6] But such approximation is a human and hence a conditional achievement. The tendencies toward an impersonal administration of rules arise from the basic beliefs in accordance with

[6] See this conditional formulation in Weber, *Law in Economy and Society*, p. 351.

which laws are regarded as legitimate, if they have been enacted by the proper authorities on the basis of procedures having the sanction of law. In modern society legislators, lawyers, judges, administrative tribunals, and others are concerned with working out the rules and procedures that are to govern the recurrent transactions among individuals and groups. Impersonal administration provides an indispensable buttress of regularity, detachment, calculability, and all the other positive attributes of order, but these gains are inextricably linked with a studied disregard of person and circumstance and hence of considerations of equity.

Accordingly, as Weber shows in his sociology of law, advance in "formal rationality" has been and continues to be circumscribed at many points by the concern of interested parties, and indeed the rule-makers themselves, with principles of equity. A belief in legality means first and foremost that certain formal procedures must be obeyed if the enactment or execution of a law is to be considered legal. But while legal rule-making tends to eliminate the idiosyncrasies of personal rule in the interest of developing a consistent body of rules that is the same for everyone, it also militates against the exercise of judgment in the individual case. Yet attention to rules for these reasons may engender an interest in rule-making for its own sake—just as too much regard for equity in the individual case can jeopardize the integrity of the rule-making process. Hence, the rule of law endures as long as piecemeal solutions for these conflicting imperatives are found and neither the concern with equity nor with the formal attributes of rule-making is allowed to predominate. The basic and anguishing dilemma of form and substance in law can be alleviated, but never resolved, for the structure of legal domination retains its distinguishing features only as long as this dilemma is perpetuated.

The conflicting imperatives of "formal and substantive rationality" extend even into the relatively simple rules governing public administration, for it appears that the implementation of such rules is beset by certain incompatibilities inherent in the structure of hierarchical organizations. The problem of communication is a case in point. The hierarchy of ranks indispensable in large organizations involves a formally unambiguous order of authority. All subordinates receive their orders from superiors, who by definition know more about the policy of the organization and its "proper" execution than those whom they command. Yet their superior knowledge is limited or circumscribed by the fact that their high rank within the organization removes them automatically from day-to-day experience with its operational problems. In the parlance of organization theory, this is called the problem of two-way communication. But, as Florence has pointed out, the information which should come up the line of authority from those who are in daily touch with operational problems "tends to be neglected for the very reason that it comes from a subordinate."[7] It should be emphasized that the reason for such neglect is not necessarily the ill-will of superiors or the ineptitude of subordinates. It is rather that the hierarchy of ranks involves different levels of information so that subordinates are not in a good position to judge what aspects of day-to-day operation are of special interest to their superiors. Nor is it possible for superiors to spell this out in too much detail, for this would interfere with the very delegation of responsibility which large-scale organizations make necessary. Hence, subordinates are left to judge in some measure what their superiors want or ought to know. Since the subordinate's performance is evaluated in part by his manner of keeping the superior informed, the information he supplies is likely to be an amalgam of the necessary, the frivolous, and the self-serving. Superiors and subordinates deal daily with this and similar problems, and solve them as best they can in the light of circumstances and with the organizational skills at hand. Study and research may well improve such solutions, but they cannot, it seems to me, eliminate the dilemmas inherent in rule-abiding behavior and hierarchical organizations.[8]

[7] P. Sargant Florence, *The Logic of British and American Industry* (London: Routledge and Kegan Paul, Ltd., 1953), p. 153.

[8] In his book, *Administrative Behavior* (New York: Macmillan Co., 1948), pp. 20–44, Simon has shown how such dilemmas have led to administrative theories which are as contradictory as prov-

The preceding discussion of patrimonial and bureaucratic administration shows that benchmark concepts of social structures can encompass a range of historical experience. A given type of administration will retain its character as long as rulers and officials achieve some balance between that type's conflicting imperatives. The analytic task is to identify these imperatives and hence the issues or conflicts whose repeated resolutions define and redefine the attributes of the type. To avoid the reification of the type, that is, the fallacy of attributing to a social structure a concreteness it does not possess, we must see these "attributes" as objects of action by specific groups.

The discussion also exemplifies an approach to social change which allows for transformations from one type to another. For example, the dependence of patrimonial officials upon the household of the ruler contrasts with the impersonal fixation of monetary salaries of bureaucratic officials. As the ruler's domain becomes more extensive, the number of household officials grows, as does the difficulty of maintaining them in the household. Accordingly, benefices and hence relative independence from the household increasingly take the place of the earlier arrangement. The ruler's officials will seek to make their benefices hereditary, while the ruler will attempt to reclaim the benefice as his own upon termination of service

---

erbs. Administrative efficiency requires specialization. Again, specialization requires clear criteria for a division of labor, but these criteria overlap or conflict with one another and hence call for coordination that is often incompatible with specialization. The contention that such dilemmas are ineradicable and hence that judgments are indispensable, is quite compatible with the endeavor to put managerial decision making on a more scientific basis. The substitution of machine methods for manual operations is obviously an ongoing process that has greatly curtailed some areas of discretion, though such methods also create new opportunities for discretionary judgment. But although organizational changes (including those based on prior research) curtail and reallocate the areas in which discretion is possible or desired, they cannot, as I see it, eliminate the exercise of judgment. At any rate, Professor Simon's contradictory administrative proverbs are likely to continue, as long as the operation of hierarchical organizations requires such judgments.

or the death of the incumbent. This conflict will be fought out in terms of the personal arbitrariness and respect for tradition which are the characteristics of patrimonial rule. When the officials succeed in making themselves personally independent, they have taken the first step away from the complete identification of ruler and government. Note, however, that this first step consists in the complete identification of government with many rulers; hence it remains well within the framework of patrimonial government. In Western Europe this framework prevailed for many centuries, but it was gradually undermined from within, as the performance of governmental functions declined in effectiveness with the commercialization of offices.

Eventually, the idea of government office as a type of personal and inheritable property was superseded by the complete separation between office and incumbent with remuneration now taking the form of regular salary payments in lieu of the earlier dependence of the incumbent on the ruler's household and on income from the performance of official functions. It is true that this new principle, like the earlier one, is subject to considerable variations. Although salary scales are fixed and officials possess no proprietary rights in their positions, these conditions of administrative service are subjected to bargaining and personal influence. Such factors as fringe benefits and personal indispensability can modify the salary scale and the separation of office and incumbent, often to a considerable extent. The balance struck will depend on the conflicting efforts of those who administer the salary scale and supervise the conditions of employment, as against those who use bargaining and influence to maximize their advantages. If the former were completely successful, they would codify fringe benefits and employment conditions so minutely as to minimize bargaining and personal influence. If the bargainers were completely successful, they would undo the formal conditions of modern administration and re-establish personal decision-making on questions of remuneration and employment. The extent to which this patrimonial alternative has become impossible is a true measure of the degree to which the bureaucratic type of administration has become the prevailing pattern. But bargaining and influence continue to affect the conditions of administrative work, and to this extent the prevailing bureaucratic pattern is subject to gradual alteration. Whether these alterations are mutually countervailing and hence preserve the identity of bureaucracy, whether they cumulate in one or another direction and give rise to "neo-patrimonial" or "neo-feudal" patterns, or whether entirely new types of administration emerge—all this is subject to empirical investigation. The following discussion is relevant for such an investigation in that it relates Weber's ideal type of bureaucratic organization to two critical problems of public administration in a Western nation-state.

PUBLIC ADMINISTRATION AND SOCIAL STRUCTURE

In the second part of the epilogue with which he concludes his novel *War and Peace,* Leo Tolstoy describes the root metaphor of hierarchic organizations. As men unite for common action, the largest number of them take a direct share in the action, while a smaller number take a less direct share. The commander-in-chief never takes part directly, but instead makes general arrangements for the combined action. For Tolstoy a perfectly shaped cone represents the model of any hierarchic organization.[9]

In his ideal type of an administrative staff under legal authority, Max Weber refers to the same model when he emphasizes the *monocratic* type in which a "chief" exercises *supreme authority over the whole administrative staff.* However, in his specification of the attributes which distinguish bureaucratic from patrimonial administration, he focuses primary attention on *intraorganizational authority relations. By ordering and facilitating the faithful implementation of commands, authority insulates officials from influences which would interfere with that implementation.* We have therefore

[9] Leo Tolstoy, *War and Peace* (New York: The Modern Library, n.d.), pp. 1128–1129 and *passim.*

two critical variables. One refers to the nature of the authority exercised *over* an administrative staff, the other to the organizational conditioning and insulation of that staff which affects its implementation of commands. Both aspects are equally important for the exercise of public authority in the Western nation-state, but I shall here concentrate on the second.

At the level of public-personnel policy, government officials are now recruited irrespective of their kinship loyalties, while privileges of hereditary estates exist no longer. The safeguards against outright appropriation and direct involvement with family and property interests are supplemented by the several conditions of public employment in which Weber sees the distinguishing characteristics of a modern bureaucracy. Taken together, these conditions are to ensure that no extraorganizational influences will interfere with the implementation of commands as this passes down the hierarchy from the decision-making level at the top to the executive official "on the firing line." In this way the exercise of administrative functions is to be insulated effectively from the surrounding social structure. Ideal-typically, the bureaucratic hierarchy is a structure of its own: basic policy decisions are arrived at prior to and clearly distinguished from their administrative implementation; officials are so conditioned as to confine themselves willingly and with technical competence to that implementation; and the public complies with the resulting rules and does not attempt to influence their formulation or execution. Yet these assumptions can only be approximated.[10] Several conditions impinge on the hierarchy as a whole: the structure of supreme authority (which, as Weber saw, is frequently *not* monocratic), the bureaucratic culture

[10] Weber himself offers a behavioral analysis in his political writings, especially in his analysis of the bureaucratic problem in Imperial Germany under Bismarck. See his *Gesammelte Politische Schriften* (Tübingen: J. C. B. Mohr (Paul Siebeck), 1958), pp. 299 ff. We do not know how he would have developed the relation between the ideal-typical and the behavioral level of analysis, had he lived to complete his sociology of the state.

pattern which forms the prevailing outlook of public officials, and the contacts between administrators and the public.[11]

Accordingly, the *assumptions* of Weber's model (rather than the attributes which make up the model) will be modified in the following discussion in order to approach a fuller understanding of administrative authority in the modern nation-state. The discussion will focus on two critical issues: the legal and political position of civil servants, and certain typical problems in the relation between administrators and the public.

Authority and the Bureaucratic Culture Pattern

The emergence of the nation-state is accompanied by the growth of a large-scale governmental structure, staffed by officials who, on entering public employment must accept the conditions of employment laid down by public authority. In the absence of hereditary privileges and with the decline of extended kinship groups, public employees accept these conditions readily enough. But with the universalization of citizenship, traced in the preceding chapter, a question arises. Should public employees be permitted to retain all the rights of the private citizen, or should certain special restrictions be imposed on them in view of their responsibilities and powers as public officials? Typically, three answers have been given to these questions. At one extreme is the view that the two roles are entirely compatible so that the public official enjoys the full rights of the private citizen whenever he acts in that latter capacity. This view may be called *democratic plebiscitarianism* in that it treats all citizens alike and does not permit the special status of the official to infringe upon the universal rights of citizenship. At the other extreme is the view that civil servants are above all servants of the state and hence that public employment implies positive political support for

[11] My first attempt to formulate structural preconditions of bureaucratic behavior is contained in Reinhard Bendix, *Higher Civil Servants in American Society* (University of Colorado Series, *Studies in Sociology*, No. 1; Boulder: University of Colorado Press, 1949), Chap. I.

the government in power. This view may be called *autocratic* or *totalitarian plebiscitarianism* whenever that same demand of complete allegiance is made of all the citizens; rights of citizenship are nullified whenever they interfere with this overriding allegiance so that under these circumstances there is again no difference between the ordinary citizen and the public official. Between these extremes is the position which urges upon all public employees and especially those in positions of responsibility the ideal of political neutrality. Here, public officials are deliberately set apart from all private citizens. Either informally or through special legislation they are asked to accept special restrictions upon their expression of political views and their participation in political activities in order to safeguard the impartiality of governmental administration as well as public confidence in that impartiality. In the Western democracies the view is widespread that public officials must surrender some of their rights as citizens because governmental employment involves a public trust which could be jeopardized by an injudicious use of those rights. In the terms of the preceding discussion this approach exemplifies the *functional principle* in the sense that public officials are recognized as an occupation possessing *particular* rights and duties. Hence, with reference to public employment, the plebiscitarian principle of universal rights of citizenship is rejected.[12] The discussion immediately following will be restricted to the third approach just mentioned. Its purpose is to show the impact of the authority structure and the bureaucratic culture pattern on the effort to define the legal and political position of public officials in the United States and in Germany.[13]

[12] For a brief survey exemplifying these three approaches with reference to France under the Third Republic, Nazi Germany and Fascist Italy, and Great Britain, see Thomas I. Emerson and David M. Helfield, "Loyalty among Government Employees," *Yale Law Journal*, Vol. 58 (1948), pp. 120–133.

[13] The following discussion is greatly indebted to Ernst Fraenkel, "Freiheit und Politisches Betätigungsrecht der Beamten in Deutschland und den USA," in *Veritas, Iustitia, Libertas* (Festschrift in Honor of the Bi-Centenary of Columbia University transmitted by the Freie Universität Berlin and the Hochschule für Politik; Berlin: Colloquium Verlag, 1953), pp. 60–90.

In the American setting suspicion toward public officials goes back to the beginning of independence. Among the complaints of the colonies against the "repeated injuries and usurpations" of the king of Great Britain is the declaration that "He has erected a multitude of new offices, and sent hither swarms of officers to harass our people and eat out their substance."[14] The Virginia Bill of Rights of 1776, as well as the corresponding declaration of rights for Massachusetts, Pennsylvania, and other states, put the top officials of the executive branch of government on the same footing as the legislative with reference to the principle of rotation. Appointed as well as elected officials should be returned to private life at fixed intervals, both as a safeguard against the abuse of power and as a means whereby they can participate once again in the cares and deprivations of the people. Thus, government administration should reflect the will of the people directly, and government officials are literally servants of the public. On the basis of his observations in 1831, Tocqueville noted that in the United States government is considered a necessary evil, any "ostensible semblance of authority" needlessly offensive, and that "public officers themselves are well aware that the superiority over their fellow citizens which they derive from their authority, they enjoy only on condition of putting themselves on a level with the whole community by their manners."[15] When men in public office are not at all distinguished from the general population, rotation in office is seen as a guarantee that no invidious distinctions can be introduced in the future, while men from all ranks of the population are considered equally qualified to hold public office.[16] This anti-bureaucratic sentiment has remained a potent influence

[14] Quoted in Carl L. Becker, *The Declaration of Independence* (New York: Vintage Books, 1958), p. 12.

[15] Alexis de Tocqueville, *Democracy in America* (New York: Vintage Books, 1954), I, pp. 214–215.

[16] See James Bryce, *The American Commonwealth* (Chicago: Charles H. Sergel & Co., 1891), II, pp. 127–128. The importance of these views is not diminished by the finding that the spoils system was not as extensive under Andrew Jackson as had been supposed. See S. M. Lipset, *The First New Nation* (New York: Basic Books, Inc., 1963), pp. 101–102.

upon American public administration, even after the Civil Service Reform of 1883 abolished the spoils system and introduced certain legal safeguards into the rules government public employment.

Ernst Fraenkel cites two decisions exemplifying this pervasive attitude. In the case of *Butler* v. *Pennsylvania* (51, U.S. 1850), plaintiffs argued that their appointment to a position in the State government was based on contract protected under Article 1, Sect. 10 of the Constitution, which forbids the states to pass laws "impairing the obligations of contracts." But in the opinion of the Court,

> appointment to, and the tenure of an office created for the public use, . . . do not come within the import of the term contracts, or, in other words, the vested, private personal rights thereby intended to be protected. They [appointment to, and tenure in, public office] are functions appropriate to that class of powers and obligations by which governments are enabled, and are called upon, to foster and promote the general good: functions therefore which governments cannot be presumed to have surrendered. . . .

A century later, in *Bailey* v. *Richardson* (182 f. 2d., 1951), the Court upheld the right of the government to dismiss an employee of whose loyalty it was not completely convinced. In the opinion supporting this judgment the Court also commented on the nature and legal status of public employment:

> The due process clause does not apply to the holding of a Government office. . . . Government employment is subject to many restrictions upon otherwise unrestricted individual rights in respect to activities, property ownership, etc. . . . So in the present case, if Miss Bailey had no constitutional right to her office, and the executive officers had power to dismiss her, the fact that she was injured in the process of dismissal neither invalidates her dismissal nor gives her a right to redress. . . . These harsh rules which run counter to every known precept of fairness to the private individual have always been held necessary as a matter of public policy, public interest, and the unimpeded performance of the public business.

Thus, since positions in the civil service do not depend upon the rights of contract protected under the Constitution, termination of public employment does not deprive the incumbent of any rights in view of the overriding importance of the public business.[17]

Such separate and discriminatory treatment of public officials was not applied in the political sphere, at least at the beginning. Article 1, Section 6 of the Constitution declares that no person be allowed to hold an appointive and elective office at one and the same time. In principle, this prohibition circumscribed the permissible political activities of federal employees. As Thomas Jefferson pointed out in 1801, the separation of powers makes it "improper for officers depending on the Executive . . . to control or influence the free exercise of the elective right" so that electioneering by public officials is "deemed inconsistent with the spirit of the Constitution."[18] But this interpretation was not heeded, political activities by federal employees were generally accepted as a part of the spoils system, and only the constitutional provision itself was obeyed. However, this generally lenient attitude changed following the Civil Service Reform of 1883. In a directive of 1886 President Cleveland forbade federal employees to engage in "obtrusive partisanship," pointing out that "the proprieties of official place will also prevent their assuming the active conduct of political campaigns." Twenty years later the same principle was formalized by Theodore Roosevelt and incorporated in the Civil Service Rules that remained in force until 1939, when the Hatch Act extended the same rules to all federal employees as well as to certain employees of state and local governments.[19] Since then the Civil Service Commission has implemented these restraints by a

[17] See Fraenkel, *op. cit.*, pp. 84–85. See also my discussion of American civil servants as an "underprivileged group" in *Higher Civil Servants in American Society*, pp. 100 ff.

[18] Quoted in Joseph M. Friedman and Tobias G. Klinger, "The Hatch Act: Regulation by Administrative Action of Political Activities of Government Employees," *The Federal Bar Journal*, VII (October 1945), p. 6.

[19] See Milton J. Esmein, "The Hatch Act—a reappraisal," *Yale Law Journal*, Vol. 60 (June 1951), p. 988 for the source of the directives of Presidents Cleveland and Roosevelt.

detailed specification of the political activities in which federal employees may engage as well as those which are proscribed.[20]

The several opinions expressed in the case of *United Public Workers* v. *Mitchell* [330, U.S. 75 (1947)] reveal the underlying logic of such specifications. In this instance a federal employee had been dismissed for his active participation in the political campaign. In his minority opinion Mr. Justice Black held that the Hatch Act curtails the constitutionally guaranteed freedom of millions of public officials who are prevented from contributing their arguments and suggestions to the free discussion of public issues. Employees of the government are thus made into second-class citizens, mere spectators of the discussions which result in policies concerning the public welfare. This consideration is based on the plebiscitarian view which accords the same rights and duties to all citizens irrespective of their status in the community. In part this view is shared by Mr. Justice Douglas, who considers it unconstitutional to curtail the political activities of ordinary public employees. However, Justice Douglas concurs with the majority of the Court when he expresses the fear that civil servants in administrative positions could jeopardize the smooth functioning of the executive branch of government, if they were allowed to engage in political activities without restraint. Here the "functional principle" is adduced in support of special rules for the particular status of the civil servant in a responsible position. In the majority opinion of the Court this same consideration is applied still more broadly so that the "functional principle" predominates. Writing for the majority, Mr. Justice Reed states that two dangers would arise if public officials could double as party functionaries. The principal danger for administrative officials is that partisan activities would interfere with the performance of their public duties; for the great majority of ordinary, public employees, partisan activities could strengthen the hold of the party in power and thus give rise to tendencies favoring a one-party state. Accordingly, the Hatch Act serves as a safeguard against

[20] See *ibid.*, pp. 990–991, for a listing of political activities under these two headings.

the political contamination of the civil service as well as against the possibility of a bureaucratic manipulation of party politics—a major effort to ensure the separation of politics and administration.

Efforts to achieve such a separation have not characterized the development of the German civil service. In the American case the initial and dominant experience was the colonial opposition to the "swarms of officers" sent from England. In the Prussian case the initial experience was the emergence of highly educated public officials to a position of great influence and relative political independence after protracted struggles against arbitrary, personal rule. Recruited in considerable part outside Prussia these officials were loyal to the monarch rather than the Prussian nobility. While in the royal service they received seminoble privileges and a hereditary title of nobility if they attained high rank. The contrast between this emerging bureaucratic nobility and the subordinate position of American public officials mentioned earlier could not be more striking:

> The policy of ennoblement in Prussia, whether inadvertently or by design, helped to fix the social identity and the loyalties of the civil bureaucracy as a distinctive status group within the remodeled upper class. As such, it was detached and alienated from the common and inferior people. It was imbued with the hierarchical and corporative ideals of the superior class of the preabsolutist past which had been intimately blended with the authoritarian outlook and the arrogant habits of militaristic *Herrenmenschen.* In the execution of their orders, the commissars were apt to act like commanding officers in their own right and accustomed to bending the lower orders to their will.[21]

Until the death of Frederick II (1786) these autocratic officials were at the same time "royal servants" in the literal sense. But under the influence of the Enlightenment and with the weakening of autocratic rule these educated men became increasingly restive in their subservient position. The subse-

[21] Hans Rosenberg, *Bureaucracy, Aristocracy and Autocracy* (Cambridge: Harvard University Press, 1958), p. 142.

quent decline of Prussia and her defeat at the hands of Napoleon in 1806 provided them with opportunities for administrative and social reforms. Thus, the idea of enlightened, technically competent rule by highly placed governmental officials was associated in Prussia with the endeavor to curb the arbitrary rule of a royal autocrat and with the promotion of reforms in opposition to the established privileges of the nobility.[22]

This is the setting in which early German liberalism supported the idea that civil servants must be protected against arbitrary disciplinary measures and unjustified dismissals. In the first half of the nineteenth century, liberal spokesmen advocated the constitutional protection of the rights of civil servants in order to offset the earlier subservience of officials to the monarch. Once officials enjoy the legal protection of their position, they are able to protect the public against arbitrary edicts of the monarch or unlawful actions of privileged groups. Accordingly, in contrast to the American constitution, the early German constitutions contained provisions guaranteeing the legal regulation of public employment. A civil servant can be dismissed from his position, or his salary can be reduced, only on the basis of a proper adjudication of his case. The same liberal orientation also gave rise to the view that civil servants should be permitted to serve as members of parliament. This view found support in the experience of South-German legislative assemblies (*Landtage*) before 1848. Delegates whose civil-service position was secure on the basis of constitutional guarantees, proved themselves independent of the ruling government and determined defenders of the constitution.[23] Even in Prussia there had been significant in-

[22] This brief resume is based on Otto Hintze, *Geist und Epochen der preussischen Geschichte* (Leipzig: Koehler & Amelang, 1943), especially pp. 25–33, 537 ff., 566 ff.

[23] Fraenkel, *op. cit.*, pp. 87–89. Taking together all delegates who are considered public officials in Germany, a survey shows that from one-fifth to more than one-half of the representatives in successive legislative assemblies have been civil servants. Their proportion has declined from a high of 55% of all delegates in the Paulskirche of 1848. Since then the proportion of civil servants among Reichstag representatives has been 47% in 1871, 38% in

stances prior to 1848 in which officials voiced their independent judgment at the risk of instant dismissal. And in the absence of representative institutions some top officials interpreted such independence as playing the role of a constitutional opposition in an absolutist state.

These are the circumstances under which the political orientation and activities of civil servants became a general issue. The complete political freedom of public officials appeared desirable to liberal spokesmen, as long as these officials opposed arbitrary, monarchical rule and contributed to the growth of parliamentary institutions—tendencies which naturally aroused apprehension among conservatives. These positions were reversed in the years following the revolution of 1848, whenever high officials of liberal persuasion found themselves confronted by staunchly conservative subordinates who opposed constitutional government. The result was a compromise. Previous legislation had legitimized the dismissal of civil servants in cases of moral turpitude. In 1852 a new disciplinary regulation was added according to which ministers have the power to place officials in a position of temporary retirement (*einstweiligen Ruhestand*) at half-pay, but without any further abridgment of their legally guaranteed rights. This power is not limited by procedural safeguards and it extends to a specified group of high civil servants who came to be known as "political officials" in the 1880's. Although details have been modified from time to time, this compromise of 1852 has remained in force ever since. It appears to uphold the legal or constitutional protection of the civil service with its freedom of political expression and participation, as well as safeguard the efficiency of government.[24]

1887, 25% in 1912, and 21% in 1930. This includes university professors, teachers and superintendents of secondary schools, army officers, clergymen, as well as civil servants. For further details see Karl Demeter, "Die soziale Schichtung des deutschen Parlaments seit 1848," *Vierteljahrsschrift für Sozial-und Wirtschaftsgeschichte*, Vol. 39 (1952), p. 13 and *passim*. After World War II the proportion of civil servants in the parliamentary bodies of the Federal Republic rose once again, initially because of a lack of suitable candidates for elective office.

[24] See Fritz Hartung, "Studien zur Geschichte der preussischen

Experience with this compromise solution has been very mixed. In the nineteenth century German governments would employ public officials in electoral campaigns as well as call upon them for an active defense of policies in parliament and elsewhere. Before 1914 these attempts were by no means always successful, since higher civil servants—among them those designated as "political officials"—often defended the rule of law against what they considered political expediency. In retrospect we can see that such independence was facilitated by the conservative outlook of the officials; their quarrels with a conservative government were conflicts among like-minded men, rather than between opposed, ideological camps. After 1918 the situation changed when ministers of the Weimar Republic found themselves confronted by staunchly conservative public officials who opposed a constitutional regime. Accordingly, the device of "temporary retirement" was used to replace recalcitrant officials by others more acceptable to the party in power, thus undermining the independence of the civil service and furthering its partisanship rather than its neutrality. After 1933 political endorsement of the regime was made a positive requirement of public employment.[25] These vicissitudes have not affected the prevailing outlook, however.

To this day public officials are allowed to double as legislators and party spokesmen, although many arguments favoring a prohibition of this practice have been brought forward in the course of the German debates on this issue.[26] How-

---

Verwaltung," in *Staatsbildende Kräfte der Neuzeit* (Berlin: Duncker & Humblot, 1961), pp. 248–254. In the pages following Hartung gives a detailed account of policies concerning "political officials" in the period 1848–1918.

[25] Evidence for the political independence of civil servants prior to 1914 is cited by Hartung, *op. cit.*, who seems however to underestimate (on pp. 273–275) the degree to which high public officials were obliged to "toe the line" politically during the Weimar Republic. For a survey of this latter problem see Theodor Eschenburg, *Der Beamte in Partei und Parlament* (Frankfurt: Alfred Metzner Verlag, 1952), Chaps. 2–3.

[26] See Werner Weber, "Parlamentarische Unvereinbarkeiten," *Archiv des öffentlichen Rechts*, Vol. 58 (1930), pp. 208 ff. for a

ever, the policy which allows officials to serve in parliament remains associated not only with the belief in political liberties for all citizens irrespective of their status, but more specifically with the idea that the legally protected independence of civil servants must not be impaired since it is a buttress of the rule of law. Similarly, maintenance of the legal order remains identified with a civil service, whose members are appointed for life, protected against changes of positions which do not represent the exact career equivalent of the previous office, protected against arbitrary dismissal or removal from the service (except in cases of "temporary retirement"), and entitled to an adequate subsistence for themselves and their families.[27] In the American setting these conditions have hardly even been approximated, and further the improved status of the American civil servant has not brought with it anything like the prestige, security, and supporting ideology of the German civil service.

The implications of this difference became evident when at the end of World War II the American Military Government sought to apply the precepts of the Hatch Act to the reorganization of the German civil service. In the view of German observers this attempt appeared motivated by American suspicion of the German civil service as a survival of an absolutist tradition, animated by reactionary political attitudes, cumbersome and antiquated in its procedures, and enjoying excessive economic and social privileges owing to the special trust characterizing the relation between government and its officials.[28] But these considerations are not considered applicable to a system based on codified law, which in contrast to the com-

---

comprehensive comparative analysis of the arguments advanced and the relevant legislation.

[27] See Klaus Kroeger, "'Parteipolitische Meinungsäusserungen' der Beamten," *Archiv des öffentlichen Rechts*, Vol. 88 (June 1963), p. 134 for the relevant legal citations. This article contains on pp. 121–147 a full, if turgid, restatement of the views characterized above. There are indications that this view is shared widely by the German public. See Brian Chapman, *The Profession of Government* (London: George Allen & Unwin, 1959), pp. 308–310.

[28] Ernst Kern, "Berufsbeamtentum und Politik," *Archiv des öffentlichen Rechts*, Vol. 77 (1951/52), p. 108.

mon law greatly limits the discretion of the judge or the official. In the American case dangers arise where officials become involved in partisan activities, because they are allowed considerable discretion in their public duties and "obtrusive partisanship" can easily distort their exercise of discretion. But in the German case officials are bound by legal norms; the expertise and impartiality of their public actions must be safeguarded by the conditions of employment which ensure their security and independence. In this view the privileged employment conditions of German civil servants are a guarantee of their independence from extraneous pressures arising from political parties and interest groups; as long as that independence is ensured, it makes little difference whether a few judges and civil servants serve for a time as elected representatives and participate in parliamentary deliberations. The important thing is to protect the expertise of the official and prevent the intrusion of politics into the administrative process—both important safeguards of the rule of law.[29]

This conventional defense of the German civil service has been challenged by those who favor that special restrictions be placed on the political activities of public officials.[30] When civil servants serve as parliamentary delegates, they help enact and supervise the execution of laws, thus leading to a bureaucratization of parliament. It is just as much of an abuse if political parties put their top functionaries in civil-service positions. Both the legislative and the executive branch of government are harmed if either is made into a mere extension of the other. One writer states that political neutralization of the civil service can only enhance the integrity of the

[29] I follow here the argument advanced in *ibid.*, pp. 109–110. The same volume of the *Archiv* contains a rebuttal by Otto Kuester (on pp. 364–366) in which the author argues against the special legal position of civil servants as no longer justified today, but no reference is made to the special problem of political activities by civil servants.

[30] A survey of opinions and of several proposals for remedial legislation are contained in Eschenburg, *op. cit.*, pp. 59–77. The author examines the implications of political activities by civil servants with numerous examples from the German context in Chapter 4 of this work.

state. But in thus favoring the clear separation between politics and administration, he also adds a consideration which reveals the basic difference between the German and the American institutional structure. Political neutralization will

> presumably strengthen the inner homogeneity of the [German] civil service. But then the question arises whether this is really in accord with the intentions of the [American] military government. For they are concerned in the first place to eliminate the "caste-like segregation" of the privileged civil service (*Beamtenstand*). The political neutralization of the officialdom could prove to be a genuine privilege, however, even though the denial of elective office to the civil servant constitutes a diminution of his rights as a citizen. For this neutralization also precludes the possibility that the officialdom is pervaded by forces outside its own province (*"berufsfremde" Kräfte*).[31]

When a traditional position of special privilege exists, political neutralization may only intensify the social and psychological distance between officials and the public which the reforms are supposed to reduce. This is in contrast with the American case, where similar measures reinforce the "second-class citizenship" of public officials. The German context thus tends to transform the meaning of political neutrality, as Ernst Fraenkel points out.[32] For the prohibition to engage in partisan activities may mean in effect that the German civil servant is enjoined to display a pointed emphasis on the neutrality of his position and the special obligations arising from its legal privileges. Accordingly, public officials often claim a special trust and authority as functionaries of the state. In their eyes the prohibition of partisan activities can be tantamount to an authoritative depreciation of politics as such and hence "justifies" the idea of executive immunity from the parliamentary controls that "only" reflect partisanship.

[31] "Beamte als Abgeordnete," *Archiv des öffentlichen Rechts*, Vol. 75 (1949), pp. 108–109. There are other opinions, of course. See, for example, Eschenburg, *op. cit.*, p. 67 where neutralization is considered a potential danger, because in the absence of political participation civil servants would be politically ignorant or uncertain and might again fall victim to "wrong tendencies."

[32] See Fraenkel, *op. cit.*, p. 80.

The German word for the obligations of the public officials is, characteristically, *Treuepflicht*, or duty of faithful service, recalling an earlier condition when civil servants were personal servants of the monarch. Under the influence of political romanticism this idea was transformed into the official's special duty to the state and this in turn was interpreted to mean that he was the special guardian of the *Staatsinteresse*, which could mean anything from power politics to public welfare. Against this background it is not surprising that restraint on the political activities of these "public guardians" could appear to some as the elimination from politics of the one group which was explicitly identified with the public and the national interest.

The preceding discussion has focused attention on the political activities of public officials in relation to their social and legal status. Such officials are separated from involvement with kinship loyalties, hereditary privileges, and property interests by the conditions of their recruitment, while the relations of authority among them are stipulated in impersonal terms. But once this is achieved, it becomes necessary to guard these impersonal criteria of public employment against *new* forms of influence. Restraints imposed on the political activities of civil servants are one example of such a safeguard. The insulation of officials from the influences of partisan politics becomes a common attribute of the nation-state, where the separation of government from society is instituted under conditions of a modern system of plebiscitarian parties. But each nation-state is also affected by the momentum of past events peculiar to itself. The same idea of curtailing the political activities of public officials may have contrasting repercussions, as in the German and the American social structures. Without attention to the divergent bureaucratic culture patterns, we cannot understand the significance for each society of bureaucracy as an ideal type of administration under the rule of law.[33]

The exclusion of civil servants from direct participation in

[33] A fuller analysis of bureaucracy from a similar perspective is contained in Michel Crozier's *The Bureaucratic Phenomenon* (Chicago: University of Chicago Press, 1964).

"obtrusive partisanship" is, however, only one side of the problem delineated earlier. Even when politics and administration are distinguished clearly, it remains an open question how much the administrative process can be insulated from influences or pressures affecting the implementation of policies.

Administrators and the Public

THE PLEBISCITARIAN SETTING. Modern, Western societies are characterized by national political communities. They exemplify the modern duality between government and society: a nationwide jurisdiction with administrative authority in the hands of a functionally defined group of officials on the one hand, and formally equal participation in public affairs by all citizens on the other.[34] As stated earlier, politics under these circumstances ceases to be a struggle over the distribution of sovereign powers and becomes instead a struggle over the distribution of the national product and over the principles guiding governmental administration. With the universalization of citizenship, demands on the government and hence governmental activities expand greatly. This growth of plebiscitarianism is reflected in the development of political parties into mass organizations. Parliaments become transformed from a body of deliberating notables who represent or claim to represent the public at large, to a body of professional politicians who are identified with a political party and represent its constituency. In the field of public employment earlier restrictions based on family background and social standing are gradually replaced by reliance on training and educational qualifications as the sole criterion of selection. With these changes goes a major transformation of public life

[34] Polities organized on the federal principle present special problems, of course, but they do not invalidate this general characterization. Usually, constitutional provisions see to the division of powers between the federal center and state or provincial and local authorities, with certain nationwide authorities remaining with the center. Although complex disputes occur with reference to this division, any major alteration requires constitutional amendments and these are relatively infrequent.

arising from the development of the mass media and the gradual but pervasive encroachment of publicity on spheres previously considered confidential and privileged.[35]

The use of the term "plebiscitarianism" with regard to public officials is an equivocal matter. In the electoral context the term means that all citizens as individuals possess the right to vote and to stand for elections. To establish these rights, corporate powers—Le Chapelier's "intermediate interests"— were destroyed. This anticorporatist legacy helps to explain that until recently Western constitutions have not provided for the existence of political parties, for these were considered new corporate powers intervening between individuals and the nation-state. The same legacy helps to explain those instances in which all distinctions between civil servants and other citizens are denied. Examples are the American spoils system, Lenin's contention that every literate person is qualified for public employment in view of the increasing simplicity of government, or the contention of the French civil service unions that public officials should have full political freedom when not formally serving the government. Yet, in practice leveling has aimed less at abolishing the special status of officials than at eliminating privileged access to public employ-

[35] A brief summary can do no more than point to the complex transformation from a politics of notables with its emphasis on functional representation to a politics of plebiscitarian parties. See the analysis of this transformation on a comparative basis in Gerhard Leibholz, *Strukturprobleme der modernen Demokratie* (Karlsruhe: Verlag C. F. Mueller, 1958), pp. 78 ff. See also the brilliant analysis by Jürgen Habermas, *Strukturwandel der Öffentlichkeit* (Neuwied: Hermann Luchterhand, 1962), *passim*, who examines especially the cultural and social-psychological consequences of the "universalization" of political life. With regard to the American development this transformation occurred much earlier than on the Continent or in England, and as the author notes American political parties do not exercise a discipline over elected representatives that is at all comparable to that exercised by European parties. Thus, although the politician as notable disappeared earlier in the United States than in Europe, some aspects of a politics of notables linger on here, because some individual politicians succeed in building safe constituencies of their own which enable them to defy the leadership of their own party, a phenomenon that is familiar where it has a more general, regional basis as in the South.

ment. That issue has become less important when privileges have diminished and formal rules govern recruitment procedures and the rights and duties of civil servants.

Access to *influence upon the administrative process* is a problem of increasing importance, however. As rights are universalized and governmental activities proliferate, it is less problematic that the uneducated citizen is barred from public employment because he cannot qualify, than that he may not possess the aptitudes and attitudes needed to obtain reasoned consideration of his case by the public authorities. Such individuals are aided in their dealings with the government when their disadvantages are recognized. We should not gloss over the tragic incongruities between human concerns and administrative procedure, but the direct confrontation between individuals and officials characterizes only a fraction of the relations between administrators and the public. The latter is composed of discrete individuals only when the citizen requires public assistance, acts in his capacity as a voter, and so on. When citizens desire to influence policy at any level, as they have a right to do, they often combine their demands with those of others, whether the object is to have a party win an election, intercede with individual representatives, or modify the implementation of policy through contact with an administrative agency.

Interest groups have proliferated along with the increase and diversification of governmental activities. In dealing with large-scale government, there is safety as well as advantage in numbers and collective action. It is useful to summarize these developments of the "public" in a series of propositions. With reference to the citizen as an individual possessing the freedom to conclude contracts and the right to vote, we can adopt Sir Henry Maine's famous formulation:

> It is Contract which replaces by degrees those forms of reciprocity in rights and duties which have their origin in the Family. Starting, as from one terminus of history, from a condition of society in which all the relations of Persons are summed up in the relations of Family, we seem to have stead-

ily moved towards a phase of social order in which all these relations arise from the free agreement of Individuals.[36]

This formulation must be altered if we refer to the citizen as an individual in need who is entitled to public assistance. In that case public authority recognizes his social right to a minimum subsistence. We may adapt Maine's formulation accordingly:

> Starting as from one terminus of history, from a condition of society in which all the relations of persons arise from the free agreement of individuals, we seem to have steadily moved towards a phase of social order in which social, political and economic inequalities that affect the legal capacity of individuals have become of sufficient public concern so as to lead to a corrective redistribution of the rights and duties of citizenship by means of legislation and administration.

Such "corrective redistribution" through government exemplifies the increase of governmental activities generally, since these effect a redistribution of rights and duties, even if this is not their explicit purpose. Interest groups or political parties are formed and become active both as causes and consequences of this proliferation of government. We can, therefore, rephrase the preceding proposition as follows:

> Starting as from one terminus of history, from a condition of society in which the reciprocity of rights and duties has its origin in the free agreement of individuals, we seem to have steadily moved towards a phase of social order in which that reciprocity has its origin in the relations of persons arising from actions of government. As a result citizens organize in order to modify to their advantage the rights and duties which are affected by actions of public authorities.

Thus, governmental activities which develop in response to public demands, in turn encourage the formation of groups based on the principles of common interest and "organizability" rather than "inherited privilege."

[36] Henry Maine, *Ancient Law* (Everyman's Library; New York: E. P. Dutton, 1931), p. 99.

REPRESENTATION BY ORGANIZED INTERESTS.[37] The proliferation of organized interests has given rise to a proliferation of terms "grappling" with this phenomenon. Interest groups, lobbies, pressure groups, invisible government, neo-feudalism, power concentrations, anarchy of particularized interests, infiltration of government, countervailing powers, veto groups —these are some of the phrases which have come into use. Their very number suggests both the concern and the intellectual uncertainty with which these organized interests are regarded. In the present context I only wish to comment briefly on two aspects of this very complex problem: the over-all significance of organized interests for the "neutral administrator" and for the sociopolitical theory of groups in the nation-state.

We saw earlier that Weber's ideal type of bureaucracy assumed the existence of effective (monocratic) authority over the administrative staff and clear separation between policy decisions at the top and policy execution below. In his political analyses Weber also commented on the tendency of high German officials to make political decisions under the guise of a concern with purely technical, administrative problems—a tendency which complicated the already difficult task of effective supervision by parliamentary bodies. In Germany this problem was especially acute because of the strength of the bureaucracy and the great weakness of political parties and of parliament. Weber's political preoccupation with these questions overshadowed his own concern with their generic significance. The fact is that with the proliferation of governmental functions "secrecy" of the administrative process is a by-product of complexity more often than it is the result of a strong-willed and entrenched officialdom. Also, parliamentary supervision of administrative acts declines in coverage if not in skill and vigor, even when political parties and parliamentary institutions are strong and widely accepted. Under these circumstances administrators become concerned with policy

[37] This phrase is taken from the title of Joseph Kaiser, *Die Repräsentation organisierter Interessen* (Berlin: Duncker & Humblot, 1956). Despite a rather corporatist interpretation this is the most comprehensive, comparative analysis so far.

and exercise discretionary judgments, probably more so than formerly, because the "chain of command" has lengthened and responsible public officials in the best sense can no longer meet their responsibilities without such concern and such judgments.[38]

Policies often allow administrators to decide among alternative courses of action, and they do not wish to act arbitrarily. "Administrative responsibility" may take the form of consulting with the organized interests most directly concerned. Here responsibility comes to mean responsiveness to the "public." This may mean no more than the administrator's sense of what the public wants or needs, but such estimates shade off into ideas of what public wants ought to be. This is treacherous ground which many administrators will avoid or would avoid if they knew they were treading on it. There is the risk of adverse repercussions from the public and the legislature, if the official's estimate is drastically wrong. Accordingly, administrators look for support of the discretionary judgments which broadly drawn policy directives and the organizational complexity of government oblige them to make.

They find such support in the opinions and expert advice which organized interests are only too willing to provide. At this point there is a noteworthy interaction between "state" and "society." In a comprehensive study of *Government by Committee*, K. C. Wheare states with reference to English practices:

> It is sometimes the case that it is only after hearing the interested parties and bringing them together to hear each other and perhaps to negotiate a little with each other, that a Department can obtain the guidance it needs. With govern-

[38] Incidental but telling evidence for this point is the discrepancy of the case load handled by the court system as compared with administrative adjudication. "In any one year the [American] Veterans Administration adjudicates in its formal procedural realm (the Board of Veterans Appeals) almost half the number of cases adjudicated by the entire federal court system. But informal adjudication handled by the VA in a year amounts to more than thirty times the number of cases adjudicated by the federal court system." See Peter Woll, *Administrative Law* (Berkeley: University of California Press, 1963), p. 7.

ments committed to planning and the control of economic life, it is essential to obtain the cooperation of those affected by Government policy.[39]

In a parallel discussion of American conditions we learn that advisory committees are rarely established for the purpose of detached counseling alone. Persons serving on such committees typically expect to remain in contact with the policy-making processes of the program on which they have been consulted and "this extension of the relationship far beyond the point of actual advice dovetails neatly with the administrator's real but unspoken purpose of strengthening and validating his program and its support."[40] In emphasizing this quest for support, the author acknowledges the conciliating function of the administrator who "has taken up the task of broker to the various claims where the legislator left off."[41]

There is evidence, on the other hand, that negotiation or consultation with public authorities has major effects upon the organized interests themselves. In a revealing letter Professor Arnold Brecht has explained that the formal obligation of German ministries to consult only with representatives of federations of interest groups (the so-called peak associations) originated after 1918, when every citizen or local association addressed their demands or wishes personally or in writing to the ministries and the Reichs-Chancellery. The purpose of this ruling was not to give privileged recognition to the federations, but to prevent the inundation of the government. Thus, entirely procedural considerations and the concern for efficiency had the effect of encouraging the federations to articulate various local demands before contacting the government. No sinister purpose or conspiratorial theory need be invoked here. It is an especially clear instance in which entirely

[39] K. C. Wheare, *Government by Committee* (Oxford: Clarendon Press, 1955), p. 53.

[40] Mort Grant, "The Technology of Advisory Committees," in Carl Friedrich and Seymour Harris, eds., *Public Policy* (Yearbook of the Graduate School of Public Administration, Harvard University; Cambridge: Harvard University Press, 1960), Vol. X, p. 94.

[41] *Ibid.* Note also the similar emphasis in the analyses by Norton Long, *The Polity* (Chicago: Rand McNally & Co., 1962), Chap. 4.

formal considerations can increase the power of federated groups and their key functionaries and thus have a major effect on the structure of organized interests.[42]

Consultation with organized interests becomes itself an article of policy. In the words of the Haldane Committee on the Machinery of Government:

> The preservation of the full responsibility of Ministers for executive action will not, in our opinion, ensure that the course of administration which they adopt will secure and retain public confidence, unless it is recognized as an obligation upon departments to avail themselves of the advice and assistance of advisory bodies so constituted as to make available the knowledge and experience of all sections of the community affected by the activities of the Department.[43]

According to K. C. Wheare, consultation between public officials and organized interests is considered a recognized part of the British Constitution. The recent PEP (Political and Economic Planning) report states explicitly that "the object of having committees with advisory status but great independent authority is to detach administrative work from the main Government machine."[44] This statement is not considered incongruous because in theory ultimate control remains with the minister. And in England public officials and functionaries of organized interests have a similar social background and apparently a tacit understanding of the proprieties of their

[42] Brecht's letter is quoted in Wilhelm Hennis, "Verfassungsordnung und Verbandseinfluss," *Politische Vierteljahrschrift*, II (1961), p. 28.

[43] Quoted in Political and Economic Planning (PEP), *Advisory Committees in British Government* (London: Allen & Unwin, 1960), p. 6.

[44] See Wheare, *op. cit.*, p. 32 and PEP Report, *op. cit.*, p. 16. Advisory committees are, of course, only one of many contacts between public officials and organized interests. An account of the range and variety of contacts between officials and individual citizens as well as organized groups is contained in Report of the Committee on Intermediaries, Cmd. 7904 (London: H.M.S.O., 1950). In a country of 53 million people the agencies reviewed handle in excess of 19 million applications annually (*ibid.*, p. 8).

relationship, which helps them to distinguish issues of policy from issues of administration.[45]

Elsewhere the same tendencies appear in different form. The Constitution of the Federal Republic of Germany does not recognize the existence of organized interests. However, the manuals of procedure (*Geschäftsordnungen*) of the principal ministries formally provide for the consultation of major associations in the initial preparation of legislative proposals by the federal government. Advisory committees are another recognized device for channeling the reciprocal influences between officials and associations. In addition, Chancellor Adenauer personally received top functionaries of major organized interests, thereby violating the formal procedures of the federal government. This type of "chancellor-democracy" not only militates against ministerial responsibility in the executive but also jeopardizes the constitutional functions of parliament.[46]

In the United States matters of organization and procedure in the executive branch are recognized by the courts as falling within the province of administrative discretion. Thus, the procedure of administrative tribunals, executive appointments of administrative officers, and the functioning of advisory committees may in several ways take into account the representations of organized interests. When law-making powers have been delegated to private groups, the courts have insisted that ultimate responsibility remains in the hands of public officials, though in practice this has meant that the resulting administrative acts are based on consensus between group interests and the formally responsible public officials.[47] Thus,

[45] See, for example, Sir Raymond Street, "Government Consultation with Industry," *Public Administration*, Vol. 37 (1959), p. 7 and S. E. Finer, "The Individual Responsibility of Ministers," *Public Administration*, Vol. 34 (1956), pp. 377 ff. See also Henry Ehrmann's and Norman Chester's remarks in Henry Ehrmann, ed., *Interest Groups on Four Continents* (Pittsburgh: University of Pittsburgh Press, 1958), pp. 6–7, 285, and *passim*.

[46] See the excellent discussion of these points by Wilhelm Hennis, *op. cit.*, pp. 23–35.

[47] See Avery Leiserson, *Administrative Regulation* (Chicago: University of Chicago Press, 1942), Chap. 9 and *passim*. See also

frequent and intimate contact between public officials and organized interests is an accepted part of the administrative process. In this context the legal regulation of "conflicts of interests" seeks to insulate administrators from influences which would interfere with their implementation of policy directives.

Several principles appear to have guided this regulation.[48] The basic rule against bribery is concerned with cases in which private persons through payment to an official seek to influence an official act, and in which in return the official permits himself to be so influenced. Under the "conflict-of-interest" laws additional principles have been developed which deal with the official's conduct in his public as well as his private capacity. With reference to the first transactions are considered unacceptable whenever an official participates in public actions that significantly affect his personal economic interests. In addition, it is unacceptable to have private sources transfer economic values to public officials, even when such transfers do not constitute bribery. Here the principle is that public officials should not accept any transfer of economic values from a private source, which is at the discretion of the latter. Such transfers are acceptable only if they are pursuant to an enforceable contract or property right of the official. In other words, the conduct of public business is to be insulated against the danger that a public official becomes subservient to private interests. Other principles relate to officials acting in their private capacity. Officials should not appear in a government forum in their private capacity or have dealings in matters in which the government is a party. As a matter of principle officials are not to step out of their official positions in order to assist private interests in their transactions with the government. The same prohibition applies also in the

the very useful survey by the same author, "Interest Groups in Administration," in Fritz Morstein-Marx, ed., *Elements of Public Administration* (New York: Prentice-Hall, Inc., 1946), pp. 314–338.

[48] My discussion is based on Roswell B. Perkins, "The New Federal Conflict-of-Interest Law," *Harvard Law Review,* Vol. 76 (April 1963), pp. 1113–1169.

case of former officials, although here it tends to be confined to a limited period of time following the termination of public employment as well as by the degree of connection between the matter in hand and the past responsibilities of the former official. Finally, there is the principle that public officials should not be allowed to use for personal gain confidential information acquired in their official capacities; in this area only piecemeal regulation has been attempted so far because it is difficult to distinguish in a general way between the legitimate and illegitimate use of acquired experience. The foregoing principles in "conflict-of-interest" legislation are so many efforts, then, to guard the impersonal criteria of public employment against the new forms of influence arising from the proliferation of organized interests.

THEORETICAL IMPLICATIONS.   Having briefly analyzed the significance of organized interests for the "neutral administrator," we must bring the discussion back to the structural changes of Western societies considered in the preceding chapters. The simultaneous development of a nationwide authority, a corps of public officials formally insulated from "extraneous" influences, and the plebiscitarian tendencies in the political realm are accompanied by the development of functionally defined, organized interests. The efforts of public officials to obtain support, information and guidance from the relevant "publics" are matched point for point by the efforts of organized interests to influence government actions so as to benefit their members or clients.[49] It may be considered a corollary of nationwide authority, on one hand, and the proliferation of interests organized to influence that authority,

[49] To my knowledge we have no comprehensive comparative study of the degree to which these "publics" are organized. By way of illustration it is useful, however, to cite S. E. Finer's estimates for England. According to Finer 90% of all farmers belong to the National Farmers' Union, 80% of all directors to the Institute of Directors, 85% of all manufacturing firms to the Federation of British Industries, 85% of all doctors to the British Medical Association, 80% of all teachers to the National Union of Teachers, but only 48% of the labor force to various trade unions. See S. E. Finer, "Interest Groups and the Political Process in Great Britain," in Ehrmann, *op. cit.*, pp. 118–124.

on the other, that in Western nation-states consensus is high at this national level. In these political communities no one questions seriously that functions like taxation, conscription, law enforcement, the conduct of foreign affairs, and others belong to (or must be delegated by) the central government, even though the specific implementation of most of these functions is in dispute.[50]

Yet this high degree of national consensus is paradoxical. National political communities are characterized by the continuous exercise of central authority. Continuity is ensured by the depersonalization of governmental administration so that it has become a matter of little moment in all but a few, key-posts, which individuals are appointed. Continuity is also ensured by the national consensus on the essential functions of government. Accordingly, a national government of the modern type represents a more or less autonomous principle of decision-making and administrative implementation.[51] Even for a group-theorist like Emile Durkheim it was the state which alone under modern conditions could guarantee

[50] Admittedly, these matters are in flux, and significant differences exist within Western civilization. Still, no one can doubt the instances in which this fundamental assumption is questioned, as in the American civil war, the widespread opposition to constitutional government in Germany during the Weimar Republic, or more recently in the conflict between the national government in France and the French army stationed in Algeria. Such extreme cases aside, consensus on the national functions of government, or what E. A. Shils calls the "civil disposition," is compatible with a highly developed separation of powers and the proliferation of competition and conflict. See the general analysis in cultural terms by E. A. Shils, "The Theory of Mass Society," *Diogenes,* Vol. 39 (1962), pp. 45–66, and the institutional analysis of the American political system by Henry Ehrmann, "Funktionswandel der demokratischen Institutionen in den USA," in Richard Löwenthal, ed., *Die Demokratie im Wandel der Gesellschaft* (Berlin: Colloquium Verlag, 1963), pp. 29–55.

[51] Neither medieval political life nor the absolutist regimes of the eighteenth century nor yet many of the "developing areas" of the modern world knew or know a government of this type, because adjudication and administration were and are decentralized, personal, intermittent, and subject to a fee for each governmental service.

the "moral existence" of the individual. The state can have this effect, because it is "an organ distinct from the rest of society."[52] Presumably the people accept the over-all jurisdiction of the state, because they believe in the orderly achievement and revision of an over-all reciprocity of rights and duties. We can say that this belief is expressed in the claims which individuals and organized interests make upon the state. But if it be true that consensus is high with regard to the institutions which can satisfy these claims, it is also true that the multitude and diversity of claims may make any consistent policy impossible. Indeed even the interest in formulating such policies may weaken when *any* identification of "public welfare" is bound to work to the detriment of some interests. A high degree of consensus at the national level may, therefore, be quite compatible with a decreasing ability to reach agreement on questions of national policies. Except in emergencies consensus at the national level possesses, therefore, an impersonal quality which does not satisfy the persistent craving for fraternity or fellow feeling.

Nor is that craving satisfied at other levels of group formation. Indeed, the development of a nationwide consensus has been accompanied by a decline of social solidarity. Classes, status groups, and formal associations arise from the coalescence of "ideal and material interests." Yet none of them involves a consensus comparable to the acceptance by all citizens of the idea that the national government possesses sovereign authority. This is not a new issue. Social and political theorists have deplored and criticized the loss of social solidarity from the very beginning of the modern political community. When writers like Tocqueville and Durkheim stress the importance of "secondary groups," they do so in the belief that such groups can counteract both the isolation of each man from his fellows *and* the centralization of government. Yet much of this analysis remains at a level where considerations of policy and an element of nostalgia merge

[52] Emile Durkheim, *Professional Ethics and Civic Morals* (Glencoe: The Free Press, 1958), pp. 64, 82.

with considerations of fact, especially in the ever-recurring, invidious contrasts between tradition and modernity.[53]

Despite the eminent names associated with it, we should discard this intellectual legacy. The "great transformation" leading to the modern political community makes the decline of social solidarity inevitable. No association based on a coalescence of interests or on ethnic and religious affiliation can recapture the intense reciprocity of rights and duties that was peculiar to the "autonomous jurisdictions" of an estate society. The reason is that in these "jurisdictions," or "law communities" (*Rechtsgemeinschaften*) as Max Weber called them, each individual is involved in a "mutual aid" society which protects his rights only if he fulfills his duties. This great cohesion within social ranks exacted a heavy price in personal subordination. Above all it was a counterpart to the very loose integration of a multiplicity of jurisdictions at the "national" political level. In this respect the absolutist regimes achieved a greater integration through centralized royal administration and the people's loyalty to the king, although the privileges appropriated by Church and aristocracy also subjected the ordinary man to the autocratic rule of his local master. Where such privileges replaced the "law communities" of an earlier day, the privileged groups achieved considerable social cohesion, but the people were deprived of what legal and customary protection they had enjoyed, and hence excluded even from their former, passive participation in the reciprocity of rights and obligations.[54] Modern political communities have achieved a greater centralization of government than either the medieval or the absolutist political systems, and this achievement has been preceded, accompanied, or followed by the participation of all adult citizens in

[53] For a survey of this line of thought, see Robert A. Nisbet, *The Quest for Community* (New York: Oxford University Press, 1953).

[54] Tocqueville tends to obscure this distinction by identifying this reciprocity in the earlier estate societies of medieval Europe with the later symbiosis of absolutist rule and aristocratic privilege, though he is quick to point out how absolutism tended to undermine the aristocratic position.

political life (on the basis of the formal equality of the franchise). But one price of these achievements is the diminished solidarity of all "secondary groups."

This "price" is a by-product of the separation between society and government in the modern political community. Whereas solidarity had been based on the individual's participation in a "law community" or on his membership in a privileged status group possessing certain governmental prerogatives, it must arise now from the social and economic stratification of society aided by the equality of all adult citizens before the law and in the electoral process.

> In the legal systems of the older type all law appeared as the privilege of particular individuals or objects or of particular constellations of individuals or objects. Such a point of view had, of course, to be opposed by that in which the state appears as the all embracing coercive institution. . . . The revolutionary period of the 18th century produced a type of legislation which sought to extirpate every form of associational autonomy and legal particularism. . . . This was effected by two arrangements: the first is the formal, universally accessible, closely limited, and legally regulated autonomy of association which may be created by anyone wishing to do so; the other consists in the grant to everyone of the power to create law of his own by means of engaging in private legal transactions of certain kinds.[55]

On this basis joint actions and exchange relations can exclude governmental control without thereby encroaching upon the sovereign authority of government. Though the governmental performance of administrative tasks may be affected in detail, individual and collective actions need not detract from the continuous functioning of the national political community. In the societies of Western civilization we should accept, therefore, the existence of a hiatus between the forces making for social solidarity or conflict independently of government and forces accounting for the continuous exercise of authority in the national political community.

What has been said concerning the political community of

[55] Weber, *Law in Economy and Society*, pp. 145–146.

the modern Western nation-state is true in terms of a then-and-now contrast. Compared with the multiplicity of largely autonomous jurisdictions, more or less loosely held together by the sacrosanct authority of the king and the fealty owed to him by his vassals, the modern nation-state represents a structure of authority possessing sovereign functions that can no longer be appropriated and inherited as attributes of the rights of ownership. Then-and-now comparisons between medieval and modern political life will bring the enduring features of the nation-state into the foreground, but by highlighting the contrasts they will also diminish the relevance of the resulting concepts for an understanding of behavior. Though the characteristics of the nation-state have remained, they have been combined with changes of structure and behavior such as those analyzed above with reference to bureaucratic culture patterns and the relations between administrators and the public.

SUMMARY

This chapter has analyzed the transformations of Western European societies from the side of public authority, supplementing the earlier analysis of social relations in the context of changing political structures.

The first part of the chapter exemplifies the use of concepts of limited applicability. In studies of change we usually define social structures by a list of attributes which distinguish one from another. Such definitions are indispensable benchmarks which enable us to state in summary form that a change such as that from patrimonial to bureaucratic administration has occurred. Yet each structure possesses a degree of flexibility which a mere listing of its distinctive attributes tends to obscure. This element of flexibility can be analyzed, however, if each attribute is conceived as an issue over which men contend with one another and on which after a time they arrive at temporary agreements. Historians deal with these contentions and agreements as sequences of events, while sociologists analyze their common denominator or pattern. For patrimonial administration this common denominator is the tension between the sanctioned arbitrariness of the supreme ruler and the inviolability of tradition. For bureaucracy it is the tension between the equity sought by universally applicable rules and the equity sought by giving attention to the particularities of the case to be decided. We have seen that these characteristic tensions are reflected in the conditions of employment which distinguish bureaucratic from patrimonial administration.

Emphasis on this distinction is supplemented in the second part of the chapter by analyses which take the nation-state and its bureaucracy as given rather than emerging. The hallmark of both is the destruction of inherited privilege, leading to a nationwide jurisdiction. Administration of that jurisdiction is in the hands of officials whose work is insulated from kinship loyalties and property interests. But such insulation is unequivocal only if considered in contrast to patrimonial administration. It is a much more conditional achievement if the context of bureaucracy itself is considered. Then it is seen that a country's past affects the legal and political position of civil servants so that a given attribute of bureaucracy—like political neutrality—can have quite different implications as in Germany and the United States.

This contextual analysis of bureaucracy also reveals changes in the relations between state and society. Increasing access to public employment and to influence upon the administrative implementation of policies are a counterpart to the extension of citizenship. Where all adults enjoy the rights of citizenship, access to public employment will be unrestricted except for educational qualifications. Similarly, the growth of plebiscitarian politics will give rise to a proliferation of attempts to influence the administration and to a regularization of contacts between administrators and the "public." These developments reveal the conditions under which national allegiance grows at the expense of group solidarity. In Western societies "organized interests" have formed in great numbers on the impersonal basis of common interests. They have been encouraged by the right to form associations, by the administrative use of group representation, by the great resources available at the national level, and by the degree to which politics has become a struggle over the distribution of the national product. Accordingly, attention is focused at the governmental and national level, while group feeling or fraternity are on the wane despite the growth of "organized interests."

These developments of Western societies provide a useful vantage-point for the comparative studies to follow. It will be seen that each of them deals with the problem of public authority in relation to the group-forming tendencies arising in the social structure.

PART TWO

The transformation of Western European societies analyzed earlier gives one meaning to the term "modernization." In now turning to countries outside the Western European orbit, I shall explore other meanings of the same term. Since the countries selected for comparison are Russia, Japan, and India, it is inevitable that the following discussion lacks continuity. These countries are as different from each other as they are from Western Europe; no attempt is made to achieve an artificial unity of presentation. Instead, I shall consider the modernization of each country in terms of a separate comparison with the Western European experience. Each of these comparisons will have a distinct purpose. The comparison between Russia and Western Europe delineates the distinctively Russian development of private and public authority as a basis for defining the organizational structure of a totalitarian regime. Next, the preconditions of development in Japan will be compared, not with Western Europe generally but specifically with those of Prussia. Here the purpose is to analyze the critical importance of a ruling group—its social characteristics and political decisions—for the blend of tradition and modernity that is achieved in the development of a country. Finally, consideration will be given to India's community development movement as a clue to the structure of her emerging, political community. Here the purpose is to analyze the relations between central, governmental authority and the local community. Comparison with Western Europe shows these relations to be problematic throughout; but they are especially acute in India which is only beginning the process of nation building.

5

PRIVATE AND PUBLIC AUTHORITY IN WESTERN EUROPE AND RUSSIA

GUIDING CONSIDERATIONS

The Soviet system of domination has inherited an important political tradition of Western Europe. Absolutist rule and the French Revolution opposed the existence of *pouvoirs intermédiaires*. Nothing should intervene in the relations between the absolute monarch and his subjects or between the nation and its citizens. In his *Origins of Totalitarian Democracy*, Professor Talmon has shown that this plebiscitarian principle was developed into an all-embracing ideology during the second half of the eighteenth century. One may say that ideologically plebiscitarianism has come to prevail in Western European societies, with the exception of a country like Spain. By its diffusion around the world, this ideology has fostered the demand for independence and "popular government" everywhere.

We have seen that in practice plebiscitarianism has had to contend throughout with the principle of functional representation. Based originally on a severely restricted franchise, representative institutions (parliaments, local assemblies, etc.) involved originally a politics of notables. These *Honoratioren* —in Weber's terminology—considered participation in public affairs a natural prerogative of their position in the community and claimed to speak for that community as a whole. With the expansion of the franchise the basis of representation broadened, though even under conditions of a universal franchise much public apathy remains, leading to a natural prevalence of the politically active sections of the population. Moreover, the expanding franchise brings more of the existing differentiation of society into the political arena, mobilizes additional claimants for public consideration, and may eventuate in rights and duties which have a differentiating rather than universalizing effect on the population. Also, organized interests often develop at the expense of unorganized or "unorganizable" sections of the population. Finally, as the plebiscitarian principle of equal rights is applied to a socially differentiated society, the people are categorized by public authority. Such categorization is universalist (e.g., all children of school age, all unemployed, all persons of voting age) and seeks to make political and social rights available to all who come within the category. Although the plebiscitarian intention is to increase equality of status, its implementation occurs through discrimination in favor of the disadvantaged and thus unwittingly strengthens the functional principle of group-specific rights and duties.

The distinguishing characteristic of Soviet totalitarianism is that organizationally and ideologically it does not wish to tolerate these breaches of the plebiscitarian principle. Under the Soviet system every individual is alike in sharing the overriding obligation to the cause of the proletarian revolution and the national community which embodies that cause. His service to that cause is rated by the rank he achieves in the organizations of the ruling party. All *pouvoirs intermédiaires* are destroyed as autonomous centers of action; they are "coordinated" through the Party as the single, exclusive representative body of the people as a whole, while all unorganizable sections of the population are identified as the criminal elements of the society. As Karl Marx put it in his critique of the Gotha Program: "Freedom consists in converting the state from an organ superimposed upon society into one completely subordinate to it."[1] Society, it turns out, is embodied by the Party.

---

[1] See Lewis Feuer, ed., *Basic Writings on Politics and Philosophy, Karl Marx and Friedrich Engels* (Garden City: Anchor Books, 1959), p. 126.

Although the Soviet system of domination has received plebiscitarian impulses from the Western tradition at the ideological level, its organizational implementation of these ideas represents a new historical phenomenon. On the basis of modern technology, through the organization of the ruling, totalitarian party, and by the whole gamut of material incentives and modern as well as ancient devices of tyranny, this system has achieved rapid economic growth. In this respect, as well as in its atomization of civil society, it differs fundamentally from the patrimonial despotism of the ancient and oriental world.

This assertion is meaningful only within specific limits. To date, the principles of totalitarian rule are exemplified most clearly by the Soviet system. These principles implement the plebiscitarian ideology by effectively suppressing the organization of interests arising from the differentiation of the social structure. State and society lose their distinction, when the social is absorbed by the political rank-order. We saw earlier that this distinction arose when the centralized government of a modern state came to be juxtaposed with a national citizenry in an internally differentiated society—a new historical phenomenon as compared with the structure of medieval political life. Thus, if the emergence of monarchical absolutism and plebiscitarian nationalism reveal the limited applicability of the concept "state" in the past, then the Soviet system of domination reveals the limited applicability of the "state-society" distinction in the present.

The novelty of this system is reduced if it is considered within the context of Russian civilization. In the words of Merle Fainsod, Bolshevism is "an indigenous, authoritarian response to the environment of Tsarist absolutism which nurtured it."[2] As we trace these antecedents in the Russian past, we discover a differentiation between Western and Eastern Europe which goes back to the direct and indirect effects of Mongol rule (1240–1452). There are parallels with Western European conditions prior to that period, but the Mongols destroyed the earlier independence of landed aristocrats and

[2] Merle Fainsod, *How Russia is Ruled* (Cambridge: Harvard University Press, 1955), p. 4.

municipalities though allowing both leeway enough to fight each other. As Mongol rule declined and the struggle against it favored a temporary internal unity, the Grand Dukes of Moscow achieved ascendancy over their rivals, eventually attaining a supremacy which equaled or exceeded that of the Mongols. During two centuries prior to the industrialization and democratization of Western Europe, the Russian Tsars succeeded in subordinating all ranks of society to their autocratic commands. The aristocracy was obliged to render military service, being compensated for their submission by the possibility of attaining rank at Court, the serfdom of their peasants, and the right to a completely autocratic rule over their estates.[3] City merchants were commercial agents of the Tsar, handicrafts remained backward, with some few exceptions independent, municipal institutions were suppressed— and the major burden of this system fell upon the servile peasantry. The symbol of this social structure was the liability to corporal punishment of *all* sections of the population on one hand, and the legendary sanctification of many Tsars as a retrospective legitimation toward the end of their reigns on the other.[4] Russian aristocrats incurred more and more personal obligations than their Western European peers. Russian cities achieved no municipal autonomy comparable to that achieved in the urban revolutions of the eleventh century in the Rhineland, Northeastern France, and the Low Countries. The sanctification of Tsarist rule is symbolic of the absence in Russian civilization of that conflict between church and secular authority which in Western Europe provided one basis

[3] The two centuries mentioned above may be dated from the definitive destruction of boyar independence (the so-called *oprichnina* under Ivan IV) in 1565 to the exemption of the aristocracy from its service obligation under Paul III in 1762.

[4] Some repercussions of Mongol rule are discussed in my book *Work and Authority in Industry* (New York: John Wiley, 1956), pp. 117–128. A comparison between urban developments in Western and Eastern Europe is contained in Otto Brunner, *Neue Wege der Sozialgeschichte* (Göttingen: Vandenhoeck & Ruprecht, 1956), pp. 80–115. The legitimation of Tsarist rule in contrast to Western European kingship is analyzed in Michael Cherniavsky, *Tsar and People* (New Haven: Yale University Press, 1961), pp. 1–100.

for the development of representative institutions. These attributes of the Russian social structure indicate a subordination of society to the autocratic ruler, which, albeit in significantly altered form, has lasted to the present day.

Yet, mention of this old, cultural division between Western and Eastern Europe should not be allowed to obscure the fact that in the modern era, roughly from the reign of Catherine II (1762–96), Russia has come under the cultural influence of Western Europe, more so probably than at any other time since the Mongol conquest in the thirteenth century.[5] A good case can be made for considering the Bolshevist movement and the Soviet system a direct heir of the eighteenth-century Enlightenment, especially at the ideological level, as long as it is added that these ideas were combined with the cultural and political traditions of Russian autocracy just mentioned. The task here is to analyze the resulting structure of private and public authority in order to characterize the novelty of this historical phenomenon more specifically. To do so within reasonable compass and in the context of the preceding discussion, I shall concentrate on the cultural preconditions of sustained work effort and administrative rationality in Western and Eastern Europe. This topical delimitation requires a brief explanation.

The exercise of private authority is adumbrated by ideologies whenever reliance is not placed exclusively on the strength of the few. Briefly put, such ideologies are an amalgam of in-group rationalizations, cultural conditioning, and the quest for legitimation. They are also part of the manipulative and educational effort by which the few seek to make their subordinates do their bidding. Manipulation and education by the few become less important when the many are more or less ready to comply with commands and to execute instructions with judgment and a sustained work effort. I shall be concerned with the reciprocity of trust or distrust by the few

---

[5] One can date the inception of increasing influence earlier, from the reign of Peter I (1689–1725), but the beginning of liberalizing tendencies within the Tsarist autocracy as a result of ideas from above dates more clearly from the 1762 edict, mentioned above.

and good will or passive resistance by the many as these have developed in Western and Eastern Europe.

Somewhat analogous considerations apply to the exercise of public authority. Administrative implementation of public edicts is rational when it is characterized by an orientation toward norms and thus permits relatively stable expectations with regard to the conduct of official business. Such rationality presupposes that the norms governing the conduct of public business stay put for reasonable lengths of time—an assumption which cannot be made when the highest authority refuses to be bound by norms or considers its own will the only norm compatible with the claim to absolute authority. In analyzing the Soviet system of domination, I shall be concerned with the organizational consequences of normative instability in the exercise of public authority.[6]

PRIVATE AUTHORITY AND WORK HABITS

In Western Europe work habits were strongly influenced by the Protestant ethic. Although the direction of this influence is amply documented, Max Weber's original essay on this theme leaves unspecified how religious ideas influence the conduct of individuals. His later sociology of religion makes this influence of ideas on conduct still more problematic, since he emphasizes the great emotional, social, and intellectual distance between religious leaders and the mass of the people. Nevertheless, Weber does not neglect this ques-

[6] In keeping with the intentions of this comparative analysis my formulations will be ideal-typical. They are designed to characterize the problematics of a totalitarian regime in one respect at least, rather than to analyze specific solutions. On the empirical side my own work in this field consists of a case study of industrial relations and specifically of managerial ideologies in East Germany. Since my purpose here is typological, I abstract from the specific conditions of this satellite country on the basis of a reading knowledge of Soviet conditions. The original paper was presented before a symposium on the Soviet economy, meeting in Berkeley, California in 1958. The proceedings of the symposium have been published by Gregory Grossman, ed., *Value and Plan* (Berkeley: University of California Press, 1960).

tion. In his essay on the Protestant sects he points out that sectarian religions provide sanctions as well as incentives designed to inculcate methodical work habits. Through social pressure the individual is forced to conform to the standards of the community:

> The member of the sect had to have qualities of a certain kind in order to enter the community circle. . . . In order to hold his own in this circle, the member had to *prove* repeatedly that he was endowed with these qualities. . . . For, like his bliss in the beyond, his whole social existence in the here and now depended upon his "proving" himself. . . .
>
> According to all experience there is no stronger means of breeding traits than through the necessity of holding one's own in the circle of one's associates.[7]

Weber does not investigate the diffusion of the ideas which were inculcated in this manner. He states only that they had retained their influence long after the conditions of their origin had disappeared. Today, "the idea of duty in one's calling prowls about in our lives like the ghost of dead religious beliefs."[8] One can summarize Weber's contention by stating that he attributes to the ideas expressed in Puritan preaching the spirit of sober zeal and rationality which he finds characteristic of capitalist economic activities. He looks to the social pressure of the sectarian community for the "mechanism" of internalization; and he believes that once launched these ideas attain a momentum of their own, owing to their affinity with economic activities and to their secularized diffusion in all phases of modern culture.

The managerial ideologies discussed in Chapter 3 are a special instance of this diffusion. Their emphasis on the virtues of hard work and the systematic ordering of daily activities provides a code of conduct quite apart from religious belief. Weber refers to the significance of this code for the development of economic entrepreneurship. However,

[7] Max Weber, *Essays in Sociology* (New York: Oxford University Press, 1946), p. 320.

[8] Max Weber, *The Protestant Ethic and the Spirit of Capitalism* (New York: Scribner, 1930), p. 182.

this creed acquires a new dimension when it is applied to the lower classes, as it was in England during the nineteenth century and in attenuated form in other Western societies. Prior to the industrial revolution the ancient precept of man's duty to labor had been associated with his low station in life; since then it has been associated with man's responsibility for his fate in this world—at least until the latter-day development of the welfare state. People of the lower classes are admonished with evangelical zeal to exert themselves in order to better their condition; if they fail, it is their failure and not God's inscrutable decree. Today, this secular extension and perversion of the Protestant ethic may be considered old-fashioned; at the time it was often denounced as the hypocrisy of men who would misuse religion to buttress the social order despite its manifest flaws. Still, it was an unprecedented extension of equality to exhort masses of people to depend upon their own efforts, and a good many contemporaries feared the "monstrous" idea that ordinary people would consider themselves on equal terms with their betters. We have seen that the drive toward equality developed in many other ways as well. But for the exercise of private authority in many Western societies it is significant that the managerial theory of a self-dependent laboring class helped to neutralize and transform the ancient distrust with which ruling groups have regarded the masses of the people.

For a time the early English entrepreneurs could neglect the problem of organizing their work force. There was little active interest in managerial skills or a managerial ideology, in so far as managerial responsibility and the risks of failure fell to the lot of subcontractors who frequently relied on traditional authority relationships. However, the problems of labor-management came to the fore whenever the organization of production involved the concentration of all work operations within the enterprise and depended to some extent on an *internalized* ethic of work performance on the part of unskilled as well as skilled workers. Under the conditions of factory production such an ethic involves a number of variables. Workers must be willing to do the work assigned with a steady intensity. They must have a positive interest in accuracy and exercise reasonable care in the handling of tools and machinery. And they must be willing to comply with general rules as well as specific orders in a manner which strikes a reasonable balance between the extremes of blind obedience and capricious unpredictability. Moreover, under conditions of factory production the intensity of work, its accuracy, and the careful treatment of tools and machinery cannot remain the attributes of an individual's performance. These qualities of work must be coordinated with the production schedule, and this coordination depends to some extent on the good judgment of each worker as he complies with general rules and specific instructions. Probably, this ethic of work performance developed among the masses of English workers out of the combined legacies of craftsmanship, the Puritan ethic, and the rising ideology of individual striving and success—*prior to the growth of modern large-scale industry.*

The significance and the timing of this Western European background are appreciated best by considering the contrast with the development in Tsarist and Soviet Russia. Under autocratic rule the total depravity of workers and serfs seems to have been an article of faith. An ethic of work performance is not expected of the laboring masses; it is assumed, rather, that they owe the utmost exertions to their masters and that they need to be punished severely if they fail in their obligations. An English engineer who supervised various construction projects in Russia during the early eighteenth century suggested that at least the best among the peasant serfs should be given some small monetary reward. He reports that this suggestion was rejected indignantly with the comment that the peasants would do their duty or they would be beaten until they did.[9] Workers and serfs will act as they ought to act, because they fear what will befall them if they do not. Ideological appeals in this setting exclusively stress the sacred duty of submission. In advising the police on how the peasants

[9] John Perry, "The State of Russia," in Peter Putnam, ed., *Seven Britons in Imperial Russia* (Princeton: Princeton University Press, 1952), p. 61.

can be quieted, a spokesman of the Orthodox Church states in 1839:

> ". . . in their instructions to the people [the clergy] should remind them how sacred is the duty of submitting to the authorities, and above all to the Highest authority; how necessary is a trusting and united respect for the government, which of course knows better than private persons what is the good of all, and cannot but wish the well-being of its subjects; and how dangerous is credulous acceptance of injudicious or ill-intentioned advice, from which proceed folly and disorders. . . ."[10]

The distinctive feature of such appeals is the emphasis upon submission to the government as the principal rule of conduct. Subordination to this own lord or employer is, therefore, only a token of the worker's submission to the highest authority, an idea expressed with classic simplicity in the following address of an aristocratic landowner to his peasants:

> I am your master, and my master is the Emperor. The Emperor can issue his commands to me, and I must obey him; but he issues no commands to you. I am the Emperor upon my estate; I am your God in this world, and I have to answer for you to the God above.[11]

Thus, the exercise of private authority uses a political interpretation in order to ensure compliance with its commands, an approach which precludes ideological appeals concerned with the inculcation of work habits.

Comparison with England highlights these characteristics of autocratic rule. The assumption that the laboring poor are depraved was probably as widespread in England as in Russia in the eighteenth and early nineteenth centuries. Complete submission to the higher classes and the government is demanded there also without equivocation. A real concern

[10] Statement of the Metropolitan Filaret of Moscow quoted in John S. Curtiss, *Church and State in Russia* (New York: Columbia University Press, 1940), p. 30.

[11] Quoted in Baron von Haxthausen, *The Russian Empire, Its People, Institutions, and Resources* (London: Chapman & Hall, 1856), I, p. 335.

with the attitudes of workers only arises as it does in Russia when the people show signs of rebelliousness. Nevertheless, these similarities are superficial. In England the depravity of the poor is rarely mentioned without reference to the good qualities which every self-respecting man can develop, and even the demands for submission are still couched in terms which make submission synonymous with ideal qualities of work and conduct.[12] Little distinction is made between submission to the authority of government and the work performance expected of the ideal laborer. Hard work is already a token of good citizenship. In Tsarist Russia these assumptions do not apply. By relying on fear and coercion, employers fail to appeal to the conscience or self-esteem of the workers; there is little or no idealization of an internalized ethic of work performance. The demand for unquestioning submission is a duty made sacred by reference to God and Tsar, but it is not related to any other aspect of personal conduct. In this setting landowners and employers act autocratically in turn, probably because their own self-esteem depends upon an exercise of private authority patterned after that of the Tsar and his officials. And the latter are concerned with the conduct of the people only in so far as the maintenance of public order makes that concern imperative. To go beyond this concern and set a pattern for the *education* of the people lies outside the established routine of autocratic rule, for which unconditional submission to the Tsar's supreme authority is an unquestioned axiom.

Under these circumstances an ethic of work performance does not become a managerial problem in Russia until after the revolution of 1917, when industrialization has become synonymous with the development of large-scale enterprises.

[12] The polemical literature in this field, above all the passionate diatribes of Marx and his followers, always reserve their strongest invectives for the hypocrisy of employers, who admonish starving workers to work hard, live frugally, and be content with their lot. Yet the contrast with Tsarist Russia suggests that this moralizing approach differs significantly from a demand for submission as such.

It is instructive to read Lenin's reflections on this problem, written in 1918:

> The Russian is a bad worker compared with workers of the advanced countries. Nor could it be otherwise under the Tsarist regime and in view of the tenacity of the remnants of serfdom. The task that the Soviet government must set the people in all its scope is—learn to work. The Taylor system, the last word of capitalism in this respect, like all capitalist progress, is a combination of subtle brutality of bourgeois exploitation and a number of its greatest scientific achievements in the field of analyzing mechanical motions during work, the elimination of superfluous and awkward motions, the working out of correct methods of work, the introduction of the best systems of accounting and control, etc. The Soviet Republic must at all costs adopt all that is valuable in the achievements of science and technology in this field. The possibility of building socialism will be determined solely by our success in combining the Soviet government and the Soviet organization of administration with the modern achievements of capitalism.[13]

When Lenin speaks of adopting the Taylor system without its capitalist abuses, or when Alexander Blok writes a poem in praise of "Communist Americanism," they are clearly borrowing techniques and ideas associated with Western industrialization and derived in part from the Puritan heritage. But diffusion is only a small part of the story. During the 1920's Russia experienced an "outbreak" of technocratic zeal comparable in some ways to the enthusiasm for inventions in mid-eighteenth-century England. As an example of this type of evidence, I refer to Fülöp-Miller's *The Mind and Face of Bolshevism*, in which the author surveys the technocratic zeal of the 1920's as it found expression in poetry, drama, novels, and films, in demonstrations, billboards, and other public displays, in the slogans of pamphleteers and in

[13] V. I. Lenin, *Selected Works* (New York: International Publishers, n.d.), VII, pp. 332–333. At the same time Lenin inveighs against the "Left-Wing Childishness and Petty Bourgeois Mentality" of those who fear that labor-discipline will restore capitalism, alienate the workers, diminish their initiative and thereby jeopardize productivity. See *ibid.*, VII, pp. 351–378.

theoretical discussions. The revolutionary grandiloquence is well expressed in a declaration of the Central Labor Institute, founded in 1920 by A. K. Gastev, a poet as well as an industrial engineer.

> The cultural level of the masses is low, yet they believe themselves close to a turning-point in history. Their spirit is growth, they await great determining gestures, they dream of great men, who are leaders, they anticipate the advent of gigantic technical powers. Europe and America are guarding established traditions, while Eastern Europe witnesses a spring-flood of an incomparable love of life, an unlimited belief in progress. The land of tremendous rivers, unruly hurricanes, steppes without limit, which is peopled by pilgrims and pioneers, will give birth to an unusual patriotism and will call into life courageous men of daring deeds and accomplishments. . . .[14]

The passage expresses the revolutionary fervor of the period and links its technocratic ideals with nationalism. But by itself this enthusiastic language has nothing to do with the inculcation of work habits. The spirit expressed in Gastev's proclamation is zealous, but hardly sober.

This second element of an internalized ethic of work comes to the fore as the product of organization. Gastev's institute was discontinued, probably because his "bourgeois" methods of analyzing bodily movements after the manner of Taylor and Gilbreth could only be made the basis of individual instruction and efficiency ratings as in the West. However, at about the same time a mass campaign to inculcate methodical work habits is launched by the Red Army and then applied to offices and enterprises. Small groups are organized in order to fight "for the proper use and economy of time." Under the impetus of activists these groups are organized in the *Time League,* whose members are obliged to keep a card on which they record their daily activities. Each member is further obligated to protest against and to report every waste of time he encounters. Here is the text of a leaflet

[14] Quoted in Franziska Baumgarten, *Arbeitswissenschaft und Psychotechnik in Russland* (Munich: R. Oldenbourg, 1924), p. 13. My translation.

with which the *Time League* sought to eliminate the "organizational illiteracy" of the Russian people:

TIME   SYSTEM   ENERGY

What do these words mean?

Time:

    Measure your time, control it!

    Do everything on time! exactly, on the minute!

    Save time, make time count, work fast!

    Divide your time correctly, time for work and time for leisure!

System:

    Everything according to plan, according to system!

    A notebook for the system. Order in your place of work!

    Each must work according to plan.

Energy:

    Pursue your goal stubbornly!

    Try hard. Don't retreat after failures!

    Always finish what you have started!

    Communist Americanism, realism and vigilance![15]

To "make time count," to use leisure so as to work better afterward, to be orderly and work according to plan, to show perseverance in the face of reverses—these are the familiar admonitions of Puritan divines in seventeenth-century England. Even the device of a daily record is similar to the diaries which Puritan divines commended to their parishioners as a means of making sure that their time was not spent in activities harmful to the soul.[16] In this initial period

[15] Quoted in *ibid.*, pp. 111–112. The phrase "Communist Americanism" reflects the enthusiasm for technology in the early 1920's, when America was the symbol of technical advance. The shift towards the goal of emulating and surpassing Western technical achievements probably began during the first years of Hitler's regime in Germany. See Klaus Mehnert, *Stalin vs. Marx* (London: G. Allen & Unwin, 1952), *passim*.

[16] Whether the work habits which resulted from these campaigns actually became more rational is another question. The Stakhanovite campaigns, beginning in the 1930's, would indicate that they did not. The fact that Stakhanovism is still an important incentive method does not necessarily mean, on the other hand, that no improvement in the direction of more rational work habits has occurred, although Stakhanovism by itself is the opposite of a

the methods used to inculcate work habits of steady intensity are closely similar to the examinations of conscience, the daily scrutiny of conduct, and the public disclosure and discussion of individual failings characteristic of the sectarian community. Perhaps, the pedagogical techniques of A. S. Makarenko reflected as well as influenced these early methods of agitation. Makarenko's emphasis on the precedence of collective goals over individual values together with his skillful manipulation of shame and guilt within the adolescent peer group as a means of inculcating discipline and work habits are reminiscent of the collectivism and techniques of social control in the sect, both at their best and their worst.[17]

Several striking differences between the Western European and the Russian "case" must now be noted. First, there is an important difference in background. The Puritan revolution occurred in line with many correlated developments favoring sustained and systematic work habits; it was a manifestation of ethical rationalism that had its roots in the Old Testament prophets and the message of Jesus. As far as I know, the Russian revolution has no comparably favorable background,

---

steady work effort. The fact that this type of special purpose campaign is endemic in the Soviet system does not rule out the possibility of a cumulative development of an internalized ethic. The tactics of evasion which have been studied intensively at the managerial level, may be used at the level of the workers as a means of making a steady intensity of work possible despite the Stakhanovite campaigns. My guess is that this would depend on an acceptance of the industrialization drive as a national cause, and if so that acceptance might well be a partial result of the Stakhanovite movement. For evidence of a rejection of both and hence of a barely disguised hostility between workers and "activists" of any kind see my *Work and Authority in Industry*, pp. 400 ff.

[17] See A. S. Makarenko, *Ausgewählte Pädagogishe Schriften* (Berlin: Volk and Wissen, 1953), pp. 25–45, 77–89, and the interesting study of Makarenko's work as a whole in Frederic Lilge, *A. S. Makarenko, An Analysis of His Educational Ideas in the Context of Soviet Society* (University of California Publications in Education, Vol. 15, No. 1; Berkeley and Los Angeles: University of California Press, 1958). It may be added that Makarenko explicitly used the mutual dependence and the solidarity of the military unit as his model.

though a recent study suggests that the zeal of the 1920's had deep roots in an anti-Western Messianic tradition.[18] Second, there is a difference in timing. In Western Europe the Puritan ethic of work developed and became diffused (in secularized form) two centuries before this ethic was utilized in rationalizing the methods of work performance and the organizational structure of the modern enterprise. In Russia an ethic of work and industrialization developed simultaneously, whether we take as the beginning date the rapid development of railroads in the 1880's or the revolution of 1917. Presumably, this difference in timing meant that at the level of work performance economic rationality was firmly established in Western Europe long before the modern requirements of industrial organization emerged; and even then more than a century intervened between Adam Smith and Frederick Taylor. In Russia, on the other hand, the development of industry coincided directly with the demand for a rational organization of work. Third, there is a major difference of ideas between a secular utopia linked to invidious contrasts between Mother Russia and a universal enemy on the one hand, and a transcendental conception of God's relationship to a community of believers on the other. The many ramifications of this point need not be considered in the present context. Fourth, there is a major difference between an inculcation of work habits which occurs through interaction among members of a religious community and diffuses from there, and a comparable inculcation which occurs throughout the nation (rather than within the community) and through the organized drive of a totalitarian party.

All of these differences have a bearing on another aspect of economic rationality which I would like to call "the stability of expectations." In the Western European experience

---

[18] Emanuel Sarkisyanz, *Russland und der Messianismus des Orients* (Tübingen: J. C. B. Mohr, 1955). As a layman in this field I can only record my impression that the author's very interesting emphasis may have led him to underestimate the influence on Russian revolutionary thought of the European enlightenment, especially the idea of progress through science. This is my reason for referring to the "technocratic ideals" of the 1920's.

men increased the zeal (intensity) and rationality (method) of their work effort, while in their economic transactions and in relation to government they came to know what to expect, at least in certain respects. But the study of totalitarian government is teaching us today that men may also increase the zeal and rationality of their work effort while they are systematically led to distrust one another and in certain respects are deliberately prevented from knowing what to expect. I now turn to a closer examination of this contrast.

PUBLIC AUTHORITY AND THE STABILITY OF EXPECTATIONS

In his study of economic rationality, Max Weber buttresses his assertions concerning Puritanism with a series of related studies. These deal with the ethical rationalism of the Old Testament prophets, with the decline of kinship ties in urban communities due to the equality of citizens as Christian believers and as armed defenders of their city, and with the emergence of legal and administrative rationality in the Catholic Church, the absolute monarchies, and the legal profession of Western Europe. All these developments have in common that they tend to promote *stable expectations* in economic transactions. Following Weber, I shall relate this important aspect of economic rationality first to the Protestant ethic and then to the system of legal domination which emerged with the development of absolute monarchy.

Puritanism places major emphasis upon a double aspect of man's unremitting service to God. To prove worthy of the gifts and opportunities which God has placed at man's disposal, he must not permit anything to interfere with the productive use of his time; thus, all emotional ties are a danger to man's immortal soul for they easily divert him from God's service. This inner-worldly asceticism, as Weber calls it, results in a profound depersonalization of family and neighborhood, for it demands that man treat his next of kin and his associates with sober detachment, lest his love for them or their love for him jeopardize the work to which God has called him. And this emotional detachment within the community also reduces the emotional distance between its members and all persons who are strangers to the community. For hatred is as dangerous to the soul as love, and where the relation to one's associates is detached, it becomes difficult to distinguish it from one's relations with strangers which are similarly detached. Subsequently this detachment often gave rise to a calculating approach in all human relationships, but originally this attitude had a profoundly ethical basis. Implicit in the Puritan ethic is the demand that man should order *all* his personal relationships with the same detachment so that he may be single-minded in attending to the purpose of life which transcends all mundane concerns. The significance of this orientation for economic rationality may be summarized in Weber's words:

> Originally, two opposite attitudes toward the pursuit of gain exist in combination. Internally, there is attachment to tradition and to the pietistic relations of fellow members of tribe, clan, and house-community, with the exclusion of the unrestricted quest of gain within the circle of those bound together by religious ties; externally, there is absolutely unrestricted play of the gain spirit in economic relations, every foreigner being originally an enemy in relation to whom no ethical restrictions apply; that is, the ethics of internal and external relations are categorically distinct. The course of development involves on the one hand the bringing in of calculation into the traditional brotherhood, displacing the old religious relationship. As soon as accountability is established within the family community, and economic relations are no longer strictly communistic, there is an end of the naive piety and its repression of the economic impulse. This side of the development is especially characteristic of the West. At the same time there is a tempering of the unrestricted quest of gain with the adoption of the economic principle into the internal economy. The result is a regulated economic life with the economic impulse functioning within bounds.[19]

Thus, interpersonal reliability is buttressed by diminishing both the emotional involvement among the true believers

[19] Max Weber, *General Economic History* (London: Allen & Unwin, n.d.), p. 356.

within the community and the emotional distance between them and persons on the outside. This proved to be an essential element in economic transactions in that it furthered the development of mutual trust among men who sought and recognized in each other the same criteria of trustworthiness. The built-in secularization of the Puritan ethic (which John Wesley noted when he says that piety produces riches, and riches a decline of religion) leads on the positive side to established norms of economic conduct, albeit at the price of personal detachment and of a tendency toward calculation in human relations.[20]

These unanticipated and secularized consequences of Puritanism are not, however, the only and perhaps not the most important foundation for the development of stable expectations in economic transactions. In his sociology of law and in his study of domination, Weber demonstrates that certain legal and administrative developments have favored this aspect of rationalism in Western culture. Under a traditional system of domination stable expectations in economic affairs cannot develop readily. We have seen that the belief in sacred norms which sustains this system is typically combined with the endorsement of paternal authority which is essentially arbitrary. The irrationality of personal arbitrariness in government is matched by the irrationality of a legal system which consists of many autonomous jurisdictions whose conflicts have to be resolved by compromise or forced settlement in the absence of a nationally valid and codified body

[20] In Weber's eyes this tendency to obliterate the distinction between the in-group and out-group in economic affairs is associated with the decline of kinship ties and the religious equality of Christian believers in the cities of Western Europe. He contrasts this development especially with the persistent communalism of the Oriental cities, their taboo against commercialism among insiders and their "no-holds-barred" attitude toward the exploitation of outsiders. See Max Weber, *Wirtschaft und Gesellschaft* (Tübingen: J. C. B. Mohr, 1925), II, pp. 528–544. More recently, Benjamin Nelson has shown that this transition from a double to a single standard of economic ethic is intimately related to the whole history of Christian universalism. See his *The Idea of Usury, From Tribal Brotherhood to Universal Otherhood* (Princeton: Princeton University Press, 1949).

of laws. Weber shows that stable expectations become possible when the development of legal procedure and administrative organization gradually brings about an orientation toward abstract norms which are regarded as valid. Part of this development has been discussed earlier, but it will stand us in good stead if I summarize here the essential elements of Weber's definition of legal domination in the modern state.

Such a system of domination exists when the political community is characterized by a legal order subject to change by legislation and possessing binding authority over all citizens within its area of jurisdiction. Binding authority under law means that all use of force within the body politic is regarded as legitimate only if it is either permitted or prescribed by the legally constituted government, that is, if it is in accordance with enacted statute or legal precedent. An administrative apparatus conducts official business in accordance with legislative regulation. This means that the persons who occupy positions of authority are not personal rulers, but superiors who temporarily occupy an office by virtue of which they possess limited authority. As a result the officials are appointed to their positions on the basis of contracts, their loyalty is enlisted in order to ensure the faithful execution of their official duties, and their work is rewarded by a regular salary and by prospects of regular advancement in a lifetime career.[21] Conscious orientation toward abstract norms and the depersonalization of the exercise of authority tend to increase the stability of expectation under the rule of law.

The contrast of the Russian development with that of Western Europe is very great. In Russia there is no analogue for the gradual diffusion of the mutual trust which originated in Weber's view in the autonomous urban communities and the Protestant sects but eventually encompassed many indi-

[21] This list of attributes is a paraphrased synopsis of several enumerations in which Weber discusses the modern state, the legal order, administration under the rule of law, and the social position of officials. See Max Weber, *The Theory of Social and Economic Organization* (New York: Oxford University Press, 1947), pp. 154, 156, 329–336; and Max Weber, *Essays in Sociology*, pp. 198–204. See also the earlier discussion of bureaucratization in Chapter 4.

viduals previously regarded as aliens or outsiders. The Tsarist rulers destroyed the autonomy of the urban community (with one or two important exceptions) and suppressed sectarian groups, even if they did not extirpate them. For centuries the Russian aristocracy was divided into rival kinship groups. Competition for social rank bestowed at the court and through governmental office militated against the emergence of a cohesive status group of landed notables.[22] In the absence of group autonomy representative institutions and an effective rule of law did not develop. Although in Western Europe the legal order was strengthened through codification during the nineteenth century, Russian attempts in this direction failed. Instead, autocratic rule helped to perpetuate a government of rival administrative cliques and prevent the development of a bureaucracy in the terms discussed previously. These allusions must suffice as a reminder of the historical background which in Russia accounts for the absence of stable expectations and of legal and administrative rationality. Yet, despite the absence of these elements, there is a possibility of rationality under a totalitarian regime. Since Weber's work contains the most extensive analysis of the cultural conditions favoring rationality in Western Europe, it seems worthwhile to test the utility of his approach by using it as a framework for this typological analysis of totalitarian government in the Soviet Union. In order to do this, it is necessary to spell out his analysis of bureaucracy with regard to the problem of power.

An ideally functioning bureaucracy represents the most efficient method of solving large-scale organizational tasks. But the conditions of efficiency can also be conditions which lead to a subversion of the rule of law, and hence to the transformation of bureaucracy from an organization implementing directives into a decision-making body. Most important in this respect is the knowledge of the official. This knowledge is technical, so far as appointments depend on educational qualifications, and it is specifically administrative

22 The classic work by Leroy-Beaulieu is perhaps still the best analysis of the relation between the Russian aristocracy and the Tsarist court and government.

so far as organizational know-how is acquired through day-to-day experience with the minutiae of administration. Under modern conditions the only alternative to administration by officials who possess such knowledge is administration by dilettantes. And this alternative is ruled out wherever the expert performance of administrative functions is indispensable for the promotion of that order and welfare which is regarded as mandatory by the decision-making powers. Thus, the technical and organizational knowledge of the official is a sign of his indispensability and hence of his power, unless he is controlled by persons who possess not only the authority to supervise him but also the knowledge to do so effectively. The latter condition is especially important in Weber's view. Officials tend to buttress their superiority as technical and organizational experts by treating official business as confidential, thus securing their work against outside inspection and control. This tendency toward secrecy becomes imperative wherever the power interests of an organization are at stake in its contest with hostile organizations, for concealment may improve the chances of success. But the tendency prevails even when this justification does not apply: every bureaucracy will conceal its knowledge and operation unless it is forced to disclose its conduct of affairs. If need be, it will simulate the existence of hostile interests in order to justify such concealment. Such practices subvert the rule of law, because an administration which cannot be inspected and controlled will tend to become a law unto itself.[23]

Weber's discussion of this issue is concerned with the task of establishing effective parliamentary control over the bureaucracy. He confronted a situation in which the autocratic monarchs of Russia and Germany, though exercising supreme authority, were in fact in the hands of uncontrolled bureaucratic cliques or powerful chancellors. To create or restore a system of legal domination in that situation, a parliamentary regime was required whose enactments reflect the positive ideas of gifted political leaders, constellations of interest in

[23] These points are discussed in Max Weber, *Theory*, p. 339; *Essays in Sociology*, pp. 232–235; and *Gesammelte Politische Schriften* (Tübingen: J. C. B. Mohr, 1958), pp. 339 ff.

the population, and the minimal consensus needed for a viable system of government. Since in Germany a functioning and highly qualified bureaucracy existed, it was principally a question of establishing political control over it so that the officials would execute policy rather than determine it. The bureaucracy "is easily made to work for anybody who knows how to gain control over it."[24] For this prediction to be accurate, a good many assumptions are needed relating to the incorruptibility of officials, their sense of duty, and their commitment to the rule of law—attitudes strongly buttressed by a highly developed consciousness of rank. When these assumptions apply, government officials represent a bulwark of the norms enacted into law or incorporated in administrative regulations so that even major shifts in political leadership are compatible with stable norms and expectations for reasonable lengths of time.[25]

In a totalitarian regime the problem of political control is essentially different. Even if we assume that the officials are highly qualified, incorruptible, and prompted by a high sense of duty, we cannot assume that their commitment to the rule of law will ensure stable norms and expectations, since laws and regulations will change rapidly in keeping with the revolutionary rationale of the Party. Like all bureaucracies the officials of such a regime will practice the arts of concealment, but the Party cannot be satisfied with establishing control over the apparatus at the top only, because it wishes to do more than supervise the functioning of that apparatus. The following pages describe what I conceive to be the principles of totalitarian rule. Given the forced

[24] Weber, *Essays in Sociology*, p. 229. The special circumstances which make sense of these assumptions and inferences are described briefly in Theodor Eschenburg, *Herrschaft der Verbände?* (second edition; Stuttgart: Deutsche Verlags-Anstalt, 1963), p. 14. A comprehensive presentation of Weber's political analyses is contained in Wolfgang Mommsen, *Max Weber und die Deutsche Politik, 1890–1920* (Tübingen: J. C. B. Mohr, 1959), *passim*.

[25] An outstanding example is the praise which former Prime Minister Clement Attlee bestowed on the British officials whose liberal or conservative leanings did not diminish the loyalty of their service to the labor government.

pace and frequent changes of policy which have characterized the process of industrialization in the Soviet Union,
these principles are reflected in an exercise of public authority organizationally adapted to the instability of norms and
expectations.

Under totalitarian rule every organized activity is thought
to be politically significant and is subjected in principle to
two interlocking hierarchies of authority. One of these hierarchies is always the Party; the other varies with the field of
activity. The operation of these hierarchies may be analyzed
here in terms of a hypothetical factory. One hierarchy of
authority extends from the Presidium (or Polit-bureau) of
the Party through the successive levels of the planning authorities of government down to the director of the individual enterprise. The director has to follow the detailed plans
issued to him by the superordinated planning agencies,
though as Professor Berliner has shown, he will take a hand
whenever possible in the formulation of these plans in order
to facilitate the successful operation of the enterprise.[26]
Within the limits stipulated by the economic plan the director has absolute authority over the enterprise. An official
textbook of industrial organization states that "the Director
of the factory . . . is the agent of the Soviet State. He determines the ways and means by which the enterprise can fulfill
the tasks set for it by the economic plan."[27]

The other hierarchy of authority also descends from the
Presidium of the Party, but then goes through the Party sec-
retariats at the several geographic levels down to the Party
secretary in the factory. The basic organizational unit of the
Party consists of rank and file members recruited among the
employees of the factory, but here we need only be concerned with the leaders of the Party cell, that is, its activists
and the Party secretary who is a full-time appointee of the
higher Party authorities. Although these local Party leaders

[26] See Joseph S. Berliner, *Factory and Manager in the USSR*
(Cambridge: Harvard University Press, 1957), Chap. 14.
[27] S. E. Kamenizer, *Organisation und Planung des sozialistischen
Industriebetriebes* (Berlin: Verlag Die Wirtschaft, 1953), p. 110.
My translation.

must follow the specific directives issued by the Party, their general functions are described as a regular aspect of industrial organization. That is, the Party cell must support the absolute authority of the factory director by mobilizing the workers "for the fulfillment of production plans, for the strengthening of labor discipline, and for the development of socialist competition." At the same time, the Party cell is also called upon to "fight against mismanagement, control the administrative activity, and strengthen the masses in the struggle against bureaucratism and against conduct inimical to the state."[28]

The official interpretation denies the existence of any conflict between the absolute authority of the director and the apparently overlapping functions of the Party cell. The latter is said to support the director's authority and to assist in the implementation of managerial directives. The Party's struggle against bureaucratism and other deviations and failings is but another phase of its responsibility for aiding in the fulfillment of production goals and safeguarding the interests of the state. None of this, it is said, limits in any way the principle of "one-man management," for the director has ultimate responsibility for maximum production. He is enjoined to fight against "bureaucratism" and to rely on the support of the Party organization in meeting his responsibilities. The director and the Party cell are ultimately subject to the authority of the Party, whether the director is a member of the Party or not, and of course most of them are. Hence, the goals of both are the same: they are to collaborate in "fulfilling and overfulfilling" the plan. But despite this prescribed identity of goals and despite the common subordination to the same ultimate authority the division between management and "labor" is retained. The director represents management, while the Party cell represents the Party which in turn is said to represent and lead the workers. However, conflicts between management and "labor" which might result from common interests and patterns of thought within each group, are officially eliminated.

[28] *Ibid.*, pp. 134–135.

This is clearly revealed in the so-called collective agreements between management, the trade union, the Party cell, and individual "activists." With regard to the usual stipulations concerning wages and the conditions of employment, these "agreements" can only repeat what is already contained in the authoritative directives of the planning agencies. However, the agreements also have a substantive content which consists of pledges by all signatories concerning the detailed duties each obliges himself to fulfill during the coming year. A textbook on Soviet labor law defines this agreement between management and the trade-union representatives of the workers as "the *reciprocal obligations* of the participants . . . set down with regard to the fulfillment and overfulfillment of the production plan, the improvement of the organization of work and of labor safety, as well as the improvement of the material and cultural living conditions of workers and employees."[29] Thus, the collective agreements are in fact declarations of loyalty to the dictatorial Party, which pledge each group and individual to the utmost exertions and to eternal vigilance against the "enemies" of the regime. The complete centralization of control at the top of the two hierarchies is paralleled at the bottom by a joint pledge of "comradely cooperation and mutual help" on the part of all participants. Management and labor are not antagonistic classes and conflicts cannot exist, because "all have the common goal of increasing labor productivity, of improving the material well-being and the cultural level of the workers."[30]

In this formal description of the two interlocking hierarchies of authority, I have limited my illustrations to a hypothetical factory for the sake of simplicity. I must now add for the sake of accuracy that this principle of a double government applies throughout the society. Every factory, every government office, every unit of the army and the secret police, as well as every cultural or social organization is sub-

[29] N. G. Alexandrov, ed., *Lehrbuch des Sowjetischen Arbeitsrechts* (18. Beiheft zur Sowjetwissenschaft; Berlin: Verlag Kultur und Fortschritt, 1952), p. 161. My italics and translation.

[30] *Ibid.*, p. 157. These agreements are the product of a 30-year development, which is traced briefly in *ibid.*, pp. 156–161.

ject to two authorities rather than one. For the work of each unit is programed, coordinated, and supervised by some government agency. But it is also propagandized, expedited, criticized, organized, spied on, and incorporated in special-purpose campaigns by the Party cell within the organization, and that Party cell is of course subject to the higher Party authorities. Thus, the actual work done in any specific organizational unit *and* in its supervising agency (or agencies) is expedited, criticized, and spied on by Party cells which are responsible neither to the director of the unit nor to the head of its supervising agency, but to the independent hierarchy of the Party.[31]

At first glance, this whole arrangement bears out the common view that dictatorships inevitably develop a superbureaucracy with its inefficiency and confusion. But what appears irrational from one point of view may well be rational from another.[32] In view of the manifest success of Soviet in-

[31] For an attempt to depict this structure in the form of an organizational chart for East Germany, I refer to my *Work and Authority in Industry*, pp. 356, 359. I should add that my interpretation differs from that contained in C. J. Friedrich and Z. K. Brzezinski, *Totalitarian Dictatorship and Autocracy* (Cambridge: Harvard University Press, 1956). Though I agree with the authors' emphasis on the difference between autocracy and totalitarianism, I do not consider it useful to state that difference entirely in terms of Friedrich's descriptive syndrome of official ideology, a single mass party, a technologically based monopoly of arms and mass communications, and a system of police control. Apparently this doubt is shared by the coauthor who has pointed out that this syndrome leaves out the "institutionalized revolutionary zeal" of the Party. See Z. Brzezinski, "Totalitarianism and Rationality," *American Political Science Review*, L:3 (September 1956), 754. I attempt to include this essential element and point out its institutionalization in the double hierarchy of government.

[32] See Weber, *Protestant Ethic*, p. 26. For this reason it does not appear useful to me to conceptualize the inefficiency of totalitarian government by showing that in many respects it is the reverse of Weber's concept of bureaucracy. See Friedrich and Brzezinski, *op. cit.*, pp. 185–186, where the authors refer to the process of "debureaucratization," in which such characteristics of bureaucracy as centralization, separation of functions, recruitment on the basis of qualifications, objectivity and secrecy of official business have been abandoned under the influence of one-party rule. There is no

dustrialization an analysis of totalitarian rule has the task of seeing the organizational rationale which has achieved that success. This rationale can be stated in the framework of Weber's analysis. An ideally functioning bureaucracy in his sense is the most efficient method of solving large-scale organizational tasks, but only if these require the orderly administration of public affairs under the rule of law. However, a continuous and dependable operation which combines efficiency with a more or less stable norm orientation is usually obtained at the price of some inflexibility for the sake of maintaining the rule of law and achieving an equitable administration of affairs. Such a bureaucracy may not function properly where the task is the rapid industrialization of a nation. Under the simulated combat conditions of a totalitarian regime, the norms which govern conduct do not remain stable for any length of time. In the face of an unremitting drive for prodigies of achievement, officials will use their devices of concealment for a systematic, if tacit "withdrawal of efficiency" (Veblen). They will do so not only for reasons of convenience, but also because the demands made upon them by the regime are "irrational" from the viewpoint of expert knowledge and systematic procedure.[33] The Party, on the other hand, must prevent the types of concealment which make collective inaction possible, while putting all executive officials under maximum pressure to utilize their expertise to the fullest extent. This, I take it, is the rationale of a double hierarchy of government, which places a Party functionary

---

doubt, of course, concerning these effects of totalitarianism, but one would have to know about the degree of bureaucratization (in Weber's sense) under Tsarist rule, before one may properly speak of "debureaucratization."

[33] We have it on the authority of a thoroughly compliant Communist functionary in East Germany that "the word 'impossible' is banned once and for all from the vocabulary of the German language" and that the functionaries must learn that "what was correct yesterday is already outdated and incorrect today." See Walter Ulbricht, *Der Fünfjahrplan und die Perspektiven der Volkswirtschaft* (Berlin: Dietz-Verlag, 1951), p. 91, and in *Lehren des XIX. Parteitages der KPdSU für den Aufbau des Sozialismus in der DDR* (Berlin: Dietz-Verlag, 1952), p. 56.

at the side of every major official in order to prevent concealment and apply pressure. In a totalitarian regime these two
hierarchies would be required, even if all key positions in
government and industry were filled with Party functionaries.
For a functionary turned executive official would still be responsible for "fulfilling and overfulfilling" the plan, while the
new Party functionary would still be charged with keeping
that official under pressure and surveillance.[34]

This "double government" of a totalitarian regime has
certain consequences, which have been variously noted and
which are related to the tendency of the regime to centralize
authority at the top while shoving responsibility for results
downward.[35] At the level of policy this tendency has corollar-
ies which possess a rationale of their own, at least from the
viewpoint of the regime. The industrial situation may again
be used for illustration. I noted earlier that in the textbook
version of the Soviet regime the Party cell is given a regular
function in the operation of a factory, but that this function
is double-headed, so to speak. The Party must support the
director in mobilizing the workers for the overfulfillment of
the plan, but it must also control the administrative activity
and fight against mismanagement. This type of directive gives
rise to a familiar refrain of industrial relations under the
Soviet system. The Party organization in a factory will be
admonished not to interfere with the work of management,
because this violates the principle of "one-man management"
and constitutes a usurpation of economic functions by the
Party. However, the Party will also be reminded that it is
duty-bound to help management in overcoming the difficulties
facing the enterprise and that it must be vigilant in the detec-

[34] It should be added that the effort to prevent concealment and
exert pressure to procure greater performance is not confined to
executive officials. The techniques of mass agitation are surveyed
in Alex Inkeles, *Public Opinion in Soviet Russia* (Cambridge: Harvard University Press, 1950), esp. pp. 67–131. For a case study of
agitation in East German industry see my *Work and Authority in
Industry*, pp. 400–433.

[35] I assume that this is the tendency Barrington Moore has in
mind in his slightly different formulation in *Terror and Progress*
(Cambridge: Harvard University Press, 1954), p. 17.

tion of evasive and bureaucratic practices on the part of management. There are many examples of this kind, all of which indicate that the regime demands of its functionaries the simultaneous maximization of conflicting goals. Officially, it is denied that these goals conflict: the Party secretary and the director are leading members of the same Party organization and are admonished to discuss and resolve all decisive questions. But although this desired collaboration is endorsed as the principle of "collective leadership," that principle stands opposed not only to the principle of "one-man management" but it is also hedged in by the determined campaigns of the Party against collusive practices between executive officials and Party functionaries.[36]

This institutionalization of conflicting standards in the textbook version of the regime reflects the centralization of authority at the top and the allowance of controlled flexibility under pressure at the level of operations.[37] It may be stated

[36] From a Chinese source we have a formulation of the principle of "collective leadership" which reveals clearly that the collaboration envisaged is based on mutual distrust, or Bolshevik partisanship in the official terminology. "By collective leadership we understand a system, in which all principal questions must be decided by all leading personalities on the basis of careful examination and collective discussion. . . . No one should presume to decide principal questions by himself. . . . Collective leadership is the most important means to secure unity, improve criticism and self-criticism, and *facilitate the control of each functionary* regardless of his position." Quoted from a Chinese Communist newspaper in *Ostprobleme,* VI (May 1954), 731. My italics and translation. The party's opposition to collusive practices which underlies this formulation is spelled out in the comments on "cadre policy" by N. Khrushchev, *Report to the Nineteenth Party Congress on Amendments to the Rules of the CPSU* (Moscow: Foreign Languages Publishing House, 1952), pp. 23–25.

[37] Among the conflicting goals there exists a scale of priorities, but these priorities are frequently implicit, rather than explicit. My point is that this implicit character of the priorities together with abrupt changes in policy is aided by the institutionalization of conflicting goals in the textbook version of the regime, because this institutionalization increases the freedom of abrupt decision making at the center and intensifies the planned uncertainty below. Where officials are told to maximize both productivity and safety, failure to do either *can* be punished, while the authorities through their

as a principle of totalitarian rule that it implements an un-remitting drive for achieving the possible by continually de-manding the impossible. Conflicting demands are "on the books" and thus legitimate every demand the highest Party authorities decide to make. Under these conditions the hier-archy of Party functionaries may be said to serve the pur-pose of demanding the impossible, that is, the simultaneous maximization of conflicting goals (if they perform their tasks adequately from the viewpoint of the regime). When some success has been achieved, more success may be possible, and it is the responsibility of the Party in this system to test con-tinually whether this "more" can be achieved. The top agen-cies of the Party, therefore, treat every one of their own di-rectives as a minimum, because officially the "impossible" cannot be allowed to exist if the pressure is to be maintained below. Moreover, the Party authorities are well aware of evasions and collusive practices at the operational level. And although the pressure is presumably tempered and allocated in order to allow for the necessary maneuvering and to ob-tain the maximum of the possible, the official viewpoint of the regime is to consider all evasions or collusions as evi-dence of slack which may be taken up by additional pres-sure. The Party jargon reflects this orientation by speaking of "still further successes" which proper political agitation will make possible. Thus, the Party is eminently successful, but its functionaries can still do much more in tapping the underutilized resources of the country and the hallowed ini-tiative of the masses. There is a constant demand for "over-fulfillment," and it is standard practice to treat every suc-cessful performance as a *prima facie* indication that more could have been accomplished. At the agitational level there is in principle no reliable sign of success.

At the level of operations this drive of the Party meets

---

administration of incentives, controls, and penalties may in effect opt for productivity at the expense of safety. If this leads to pro-duction breakdowns, the officials will be called to account for their neglect of safety measures. In this way, an implicit scale of priori-ties is combined with the formal institutionalization of conflicting goals.

with considerable, tacit resistance. In his striking analysis of the "web of 'mutual involvement,'" Berliner has shown that Party officials and industrial managers support each other in their illegal practices, because their performance is judged by the same criteria.[38] A casual reading of this study might make it appear as if the relations between political functionaries and managers were free of tensions and conflicts of interest as long as the enterprise is successful, and that the drive of the Party for greater achievements was so much empty commotion. But this conclusion does not follow from the available evidence. Berliner himself emphasizes that illegal practices are condoned only where they lead to successful performance in terms of the official criteria, and that the collusion which makes such practices possible disintegrates quickly with the first signs of impending failure.[39] In addition, we have considerable evidence for the assertion that "the drive for industrial expansion comes almost wholly from the top."[40] My hunch is that both lines of analysis are right in their respective emphases on collusive alliances at the bottom *and* on organizational drive from the top through the agencies of the Party. Perhaps the experts would have to "give" a little on each side to become compatible with each other. This is already implicit in the fact that illegal practices thrive most where they lead to successful economic performance. Presumably this fact indicates a degree of that economic rationality which is feasible under totalitarian conditions. For to the extent that collusion leads to economic

[38] Berliner, *op. cit.*, Chaps. 13–16.

[39] *Ibid.*, pp. 295–300. One may wonder whether the portents of failure are easily discerned in this bureaucratic environment, and hence whether the collaboration between operating and control officials is as free of tension even in the successful enterprise, as the former Soviet managers make it appear.

[40] See Moore, *op. cit.*, pp. 71 and *passim*. See also Fainsod, *op. cit.*; David Granick, *Management of the Industrial Firm in the USSR* (New York: Columbia University Press, 1954); Leopold Haimson, "Decision Making and Communications in Russian Industry," *Studies in Soviet Communication* (Cambridge: Center for International Studies, Massachusetts Institute of Technology, 1952), Vol. 2; and other studies.

growth rather than to the "withdrawal of efficiency," it would seem to indicate that during the last generation the regime has in part produced a built-in ethic of work performance which does not possess a steady intensity, but which is nevertheless "rational" in the sense of being adapted to the bureaucratic fits and starts of forced industrialization.[41]

This speculation is related to the fact that the conflicting goals which are "on the books" cannot be enforced simultaneously. The result is a characteristic jerkiness of Party policy which tends to engage in campaigns for the achievement of one *or* the other goal, although officially the Party demands the simultaneous maximization of both.[42] There is a kind of organizational logic in this phenomenon. The executive officials and Party functionaries of the regime develop a "sixth sense" for the changes of the Party line, which may be detected in a daily press known to be an authoritative organ of the Party. Under the systematic pressure of the regime which pushes responsibility downward, implementation of the new Party line will eventually lead to exaggerations which make a "reversal" of that line mandatory, although officially this takes the form of emphasizing the "other" goal which is also "on the books." The history of industrial relations with its

[41] The energy and willingness with which such adaptations are made is perhaps evidence of a belief that the successful drive for industrialization legitimates the regime. But while this rationale for the drive is accepted, its bureaucratic manifestations and police-state methods are not. See R. A. Bauer, A. Inkeles, and C. Kluckhohn, *How the Soviet System Works* (Cambridge: Harvard University Press, 1956).

[42] This fact has been used as the basis for an organizational model by A. G. Frank, "The Organization of Economic Activity in the Soviet Union," *Weltwirtschaftliches Archiv*, LXXVIII (1957), 104–156. The author speaks of the selective enforcement of conflicting standards in order to maximize both authority at the center and flexibility in operation. As discussed in the text, I am inclined to emphasize the more or less "cyclical" character of policy enforcement. But this emphasis is compatible with Frank's interpretation, and my analysis of the underlying organizational structure may be regarded as a supplement to his economic analysis which relies in good part on the work of Berliner, Granick, Holzman, and others.

alternating emphasis on "one-man management" and "contact with the masses" is a case in point. A discussion of industrial reorganization makes the same point by examining the policy of decentralization in terms of the new problems created by that policy which may eventually lead to renewed centralization.[43] If this characterization is correct, it may not be too fanciful to suggest that at the apex of a totalitarian regime the authorities find themselves forced to "re-enact" a kind of organizational simulation of the business cycle with its cumulation of indices of performance in alternate directions.

THE PLEBISCITARIAN ENGINEERING OF CONSENT

In Western Europe, 200 years of moral and religious education occurred before technology and the administrative organization of economic enterprises began to make unprecedented demands on the discipline of the individual worker. The mass education of the people can be taken for granted by the time the scale of economic enterprises calls for a "scientific management" of their organizational problems. In Russia the mass education of workers coincided with the development of large-scale industry. Following the revolution of 1917, labor discipline and "scientific management" are developed at the same time under the leadership of a one-party dictatorship.

To fully utilize managerial expertise in the face of normative instability, the Soviet regime employs at least two hierarchies of authority: the planning agencies of government and the Party's organs of control and agitation. The functioning of these hierarchies has been analyzed by greatly simplifying the organizational complexities of the regime. In the model of an economic enterprise, to which I have referred, the decision-making authority of the managers is not only controlled by the planning agencies from above, but must be in

[43] See Alec Nove, "The Soviet Industrial Reorganization," *Problems of Communism*, VI (November–December 1957), 19–25.

line with the "experience of the masses," as this experience is represented and manipulated by the Party. Workers are not only subordinated to the managers, but are also called upon, under the guidance of the Party, to criticize and help correct the administrative and technical work of management. The social differences between managers and workers are thus disguised symbolically by the subordination of superiors and the superordination of subordinates.

According to Stalin, correct decisions, proper execution, and control are impossible without considering the experience and obtaining the support of the masses.[44] Work at all levels should be controlled, therefore, from below as well as from above.

> Verification by managers from above is combined with verification by the masses from below. This also assures the correct direction of production. Comrade Stalin says that the range of view of a manager is more or less limited: he sees people, things and events only from one side, from above and from the managerial summit. The masses, after all, see them from the other side—from below. Therefore, the field of vision of the masses is also limited to a certain extent. "In order to obtain a correct solution of a problem these two experiences must be united. Only in this case will management be correct."[45]

Accordingly, the differences between managers and workers are obliterated by the subordination of both ranks to the political controls of the Party. Differences of status and rewards may be as great under this system as in any "class society," but these differences are not allowed political expression. Instead, the work of each individual is turned into a test of his loyalty to the interests of all as represented by the Party.

Under Soviet rule the principle of plebiscitarianism is institutionalized. No representative body is permitted to intervene between the individual and the supreme authority of the Party, for the latter claims a monopoly on the representation of the

[44] Quoted in Kamenizer, *op. cit.,* p. 114.
[45] A. Arakelian, *Industrial Management in the USSR* (Washington: Public Affairs Press, 1950), p. 160.

interests of all the people. No doubt, the social differentiation of society gives rise to common understandings in Soviet Russia as it does everywhere else. But the Party either ignores the existence of these understandings, or denounces them as evidence of disloyalty and subversion. At the same time, the Party creates an authoritative interpretation not only of its own policies, but of all events in society and nature. The common understandings thus created are difficult to interpret at a distance, but it may be possible to characterize their general effect.

All policies of the highest Party authority are justified in terms of doctrinal orthodoxy as interpreted by that authority. The universal ideology justifies each successive Party line in absolute terms. Without these interpretations it would be impossible to test the continued commitment of Party members and hold them responsible for any failure to implement directives. Such tests are made to ensure the discipline and unity of the Party. Yet, the more disciplined and united the members of the Party are, the more problematic becomes their relation to the people at large. The more the Party seeks to develop among the people a consciousness and commitment which they do not possess, the greater will be the distance between Party and people. It is this ever open gap which each Party line is designed to "negotiate," but which the Party cannot permit to diminish very much or for too long unless it also accepts a diminution of its revolutionary momentum. As a result, declarations that the Party is the vanguard of the proletariat alternate with demands that the resulting distance must be overcome, that the Party must strengthen its contact with the masses. In this alternation we see the repercussions of the Party's claim to a monopoly of representation and its consequent suppression of all competing *pouvoirs intermédiaires*. This plebiscitarian position is the distinguishing characteristic of the Soviet system in its relation to the Western European tradition. It is also a token of the industrialization of an entire society by political means.

Consideration of the Japanese development in Chapter 6 will show a similar predominance of politics. Here a "modernizing autocracy" claimed to represent the people with a minimum of concessions to plebiscitarianism.[46] In Japan important features of the traditional social structure were employed in the effort to industrialize the country.

[46] For the term "modernizing autocracy," I am indebted to David Apter, *The Political Kingdom in Uganda* (Princeton: Princeton University Press, 1961), pp. 438 ff. and *passim*.

6

PRECONDITIONS OF DEVELOPMENT:
A COMPARISON
OF JAPAN AND GERMANY

The economic and political development of the modern world
was initiated in England and France during the eighteenth
century. Influences from abroad had played a role at an
earlier time, but with the emergence of modern industry in
these countries it became a convenient and useful abstraction
to consider changes as indigenous to the societies changing.
This model of an "indigenous development" is not very useful
for understanding the development of other countries. It is
as true of Russia as it is of Japan and Germany that many
ideas, technical innovations, and political institutions are
either taken over from abroad or developed in conscious
reference to changes that have taken place abroad. At times
such borrowing and adaptation are part of a concerted political effort to increase the economic and military viability of a
country. Military occupation and conquest are another major
source of change. The influence of the French Revolution and
of French culture on Russia and Germany during the eighteenth and nineteenth centuries; German borrowing of English
technology and the prominence of English thought and institutions as a "reference group" of German intellectuals; the
effect of the Napoleonic conquest in Germany; England and
Prussia as "reference groups" for the modernization of Japan
—these examples of cross-cultural influences from the nine-

teenth century have multiplied greatly in more recent times. As modern technology and various other aspects of modern Western societies have been "transplanted" by one means or another, Germany and Japan along with many other countries have had to cope with the problems arising from the symbiosis of tradition and modernity.

Germany and Japan are today highly industrialized countries. Consequently, the two countries share a large number of characteristics which follow from industrialization itself and are either the direct product of technical and economic change or variable by-products of that change. An incomplete list of the first would include the change from a traditional technology toward one based on the application of scientific knowledge, a change in agriculture from subsistence farming toward commercial production of agricultural goods, a change in industry from the use of human and animal power toward the use of power-driven machines, and a change in work place and residence from the farm and village toward urban centers. An incomplete list of the second would include the effects of a growing market economy upon the division of labor, the substitution of contractual and monetary ties for the earlier familial or quasi-familial relation between employer and worker, the diversification of the occupational structure, increased social mobility, the development of universal elementary education, and others. These and related changes have occurred in all countries that have industrialized successfully, though this is not to deny that quantitative and qualitative distinctions remain even with regard to these comparable products and by-products of industrialization.

Germany and Japan are comparable in a number of other respects. Both countries underwent rapid political changes at roughly the same time, Japan after the Restoration of 1868 and Germany after her political unification following the Franco-Prussian war of 1870–71. This accident of timing is less important than the political comparison. The two countries shared a preference for monarchical institutions and a tradition of bureaucratic government controlled by a ruling oligarchy—a similarity which accounts for the degree to which the Meiji oligarchs took the government of Imperial Germany as their model. In this setting most democratic tendencies were regarded with suspicion; autocratic or dictatorial forms of government were readily preferred to the development of parliamentary institutions. This common tradition of an autocratic and bureaucratic government also imparted a certain similarity to the aristocracies of the two countries, since aristocratic title was often directly associated with high office. Persons from aristocratic families enjoyed a social and political prominence which was a source of envy and resentment in the German and the Japanese "middle class." Economic similarities are not so pronounced, since Germany preceded Japan by several decades both in the development of science and technology and in the rapid industrialization of her economy. Still, both countries were industrial "latecomers" and as such dependent for a time on borrowing technical and economic know-how from abroad.

With reference to each of these similarities it is possible to point to striking differences as well, but the comparison between the Japanese and the German social structure is illuminating just because there is also some common ground between them. The dissimilarities are massive, nevertheless.

Japan is an island empire that was conquered only once in her recorded history—at the end of World War II. The tremendous internal divisions which mark Japanese medieval history had no adverse effect upon the cultural coherence of the country. Because of her insular position, Japan's political divisions and instability never exposed her to the cumulative effect of wars and alliances from the outside. On the other hand, Germany has experienced changes in her territorial composition throughout her history. Her exposure to outside forces at all times greatly intensified her cultural and political heterogeneity. This difference is associated with the dynastic and religious traditions of the two countries. In one case, there is an unbroken tradition of the Emperor as the single source of legitimacy (despite the political impotence of the Emperor for long periods of Japanese history). In the other, there is a succession of reigning houses during the medieval period and a history of conflicts over the principle of legitimacy as well as over questions of succession. Again, Japanese religious history is marked by a high degree of doctrinal syncretism, making for a considerable degree of toleration, whereas Germany reflects the doctrinal orthodoxies of Christianity generally and reveals to this day the legacies of past conflicts based on religious belief.[1]

Moreover, the basis from which the two countries began their most rapid industrialization is not the same despite the important similarities noted earlier. By the time of the Meiji Restoration, Japan had had 250 years of exclusion accompanied on the positive side by administrative consolidation, significant developments in agriculture, a population increasingly disciplined both by police supervision and education, and the pent-up preparedness for change on the part of the lower nobility analyzed below. On the negative side, there is the high cost of isolation. The exclusion of ideas from abroad retarded technical advance and contributed to a cultural provincialism which perhaps threatened even the native arts with stagnation. Above all, isolation entailed the danger, visible only in retrospect, that the precipitous industrialization following the opening of the country would subject its social structure to strains of a magnitude difficult to manage politically. By the time Germany became unified in 1870, she had undergone a very different experience. Instead of isolation she had been exposed to the impact of the French Revolution and its Napoleonic aftermath, thus setting the stage for her political bifurcation between revolution and reaction. During the eighteenth and nineteenth centuries, every idea propounded in England or France found a creative response or

[1] These religious and dynastic differences between Japan and Western Europe have important ramifications for the comparison of feudalism and the preconditions of representative institutions in the two settings. On feudalism, see F. Jonon de Longrais, *L'Est et L'Ouest* (Tokyo: Maison Franco-Japonais, 1958), and now John W. Hall's excellent essay, "Feudalism in Japan: A Reassessment," *Comparative Studies in Society and History*, V (October 1962), pp. 15–51. A comparative study of preconditions of representative institutions is contained in Otto Hintze, "Weltgeschichtliche Bedingungen der Repräsentativverfassung," *Staat und Verfassung* (Göttingen: Vandenhoeck & Ruprecht, 1962), pp. 140–185.

at least an echo in Germany. Her cultural cosmopolitanism was not matched for decades in the technical and industrial fields but from the late eighteenth century onward there was a steady advance here also, often based on borrowings from England. Her economy was stimulated also (and at an increasing rate) by indigenous developments, at first by bureaucratic initiative and scientific developments at academic institutions and supplemented eventually (roughly from the 1830's on) by entrepreneurial efforts.[2] Germany's liabilities were largely political. Instead of administrative consolidation of more or less equal component territories under the central government as in Japan, Germany was fragmented into very unequal units and hence lacked central authority. Moreover, one of the units (Prussia) was clearly ascendant over all others by virtue of military strength and efficient administration. Political unity, ensuing from the Franco-Prussian war, came under the aegis of Prussia, the Prussian army, and the Hohenzollern legacy of monarchical and bureaucratic rule. Economic development after 1870 was not nearly so precipitous in Germany as in Japan, but Germany's oligarchic rule was not nearly so undisputed as that of the Meiji bureaucrats who derived considerable strength from the cumulative legacies of Tokugawa rule, even though these did not include as much economic advance.

Against this background of similarities and differences the following analysis will compare three aspects of Japanese and German modernization. We saw earlier that in Western Europe the growth of the nation-state involved the concurrent development of a nationwide authority, the destruction of

[2] As a result of these early developments, Germany was at a markedly different economic level in the 1870's. In 1871, 36% of the German population was classified as urban whereas as late as 1890 only 10% of the Japanese population was so classified. Germany's railroads measured 37,650 kilometers in 1885, whereas Japanese railroads measured 1024 kilometers in 1887. Japan's distribution of her labor force in 1920 corresponds roughly to the German distribution of the 1880's. Perhaps most striking of all, Prussia had 86% of her children (7–14 years of age) attending school as early as 1820, as contrasted with Japan whose elementary school attendance developed from 28% in 1873 to 94% in 1903!

inherited privileges, and the gradual universalization of citizenship. In Germany as in other Western European countries this development was ridden with conflicts, since the established ruling groups resisted not only the extension of citizenship but all political reforms jeopardizing their own position. The striking feature of Japan is that her modernization began with the internal, social, and political reconstruction of the ruling groups themselves. Thus, resistance to internal reforms in Prussia as contrasted with the initiation of such reforms by the ruling groups in Japan is the first aspect to be considered. Specifically, why were the Japanese samurai willing to pioneer in this respect and the Prussian *Junkers* not? This first problem is considered in relation to the historical antecedents of the Prussian and Japanese social structure. It will be seen that these different antecedents also help to explain a second and third aspect of Prussian and Japanese modernization. Entering the modern era with an internally reconstituted ruling class, Japan possessed a greater ability of managing the country's political transition in the post-Meiji period than was the case in Germany after her unification under Prussian leadership in 1870–71. This difference in political modernization will be related to a comparison of the "consensus" achieved in Japan and in Germany. In the concluding section of this chapter an attempt is made to relate the comparative evidence examined under these headings to the theoretical problems in studies of social change discussed in Chapter 1.

TWO ARISTOCRACIES

All developed countries exemplify a more or less viable symbiosis between their traditional social structures and the consequences of industrialization. The task is, therefore, to distinguish between different types of "partial development." For Germany and Japan this may be attempted by comparisons between the samurai and the *Junkers,* two traditional ruling groups which exemplify how past formations of the social structure can facilitate or hinder the process of modernization.

A word is needed to explain this emphasis on ruling groups.

Most obviously, ruling groups are best documented in the history of any country. Since political initiative is important in countries that are "industrial latecomers," it is appropriate to give special attention to the social groups that were politically prominent in the traditional social structure. Whether or not such groups take a leading role in the modernization of the country, it is clear that their social and cultural influence is pervasive. If we are to understand types of "partial development," then we must give special attention to the "base line" of tradition with reference to which these changes are to be gauged. To do this, a knowledge of traditional ruling groups is indispensable, and a comparative analysis can help us to define their distinguishing characteristics. Professor Thomas Smith's interpretation of the "aristocratic revolution" in Japan represents and specifically calls for a comparative analysis of the kind attempted here.[3]

Smith points out that ordinarily one expects aristocracies to defend their established positions, not to take the lead in abolishing their own privileges and transforming the whole society. Why was Japan different? In his answer to this question, Smith examines the changes in the position of the samurai prior to the Restoration, how these changes are related to Japan's "aristocratic revolution," and what distinctive traits emerge in Japan because her revolution was aristocratic. On all three points Smith's treatment is a brilliant summation of research on the social history of Japan. Several specific points in his analysis invite comparison with the divergent history of the ruling strata in Prussia and Germany since the seventeenth century.

[3] See Thomas Smith, "Japan's Aristocratic Revolution," *Yale Review* (Spring 1961), pp. 370–383. Two other contributions of the same author, "The Discontented," *Journal of Asian Studies,* XXI (1962), 215–219 and " 'Merit' in Tokugawa Bureaucracy" (mimeographed; Second Conference on Modern Japan, Bermuda, January 1963), in addition to his earlier works, fit into the framework of this interpretation and will be noted in due course.

Ideological Articulation

Referring first to conditions under the Tokugawa Shogunate, Smith makes the hypothetical point that the Japanese aristocracy might not have initiated a wholesale transformation of their own position in society, if their privileges had ever been challenged by a rising "democratic" movement. They could be revolutionary only because there was no democratic revolution in Japan. Why did the Japanese townsmen fail to launch such a challenge? Neither numerical weakness, poverty, illiteracy, political innocence, nor a lack of resentment can well serve as an explanation.

> There was resentment aplenty and there were many instances of private revenge; but for some reason resentment never reached the pitch of ideology, never raised private hurts to a great principle of struggle between right and wrong.[4]

With this suggestion let us look at Prussia and Germany at the end of the eighteenth century. As in Japan, the aristocracy was *not* challenged in its privileged position. The quietism and pietism of the German burgher are proverbial, coming to consummate expression in Goethe's epic poem, *Hermann und Dorothea*, in which the upheavals of the French Revolution are recorded as from afar, while by contrast the modest well-being and contentment of the average citizen are praised in a quietly glowing panegyric.[5] It is true that liberal tendencies were present, but these were forced "underground" by the police. The Free Masons with their secret assemblies became the forum for mildly liberal, frequently mystical expressions of opinion.[6] However, if liberal views were hardly public enough

[4] Smith, "Japan's Aristocratic Revolution," p. 372.

[5] For a documentation of these quietistic tendencies in the middle-class society of the eighteenth century, see W. H. Bruford, *Germany in the 18th Century* (Cambridge: At the University Press, 1939), pp. 206–234. See also Koppel Pinson, *Pietism as a Factor in the Rise of German Nationalism* (New York: Columbia University Press, 1934).

[6] Two studies enable us to follow both trends in detail. For an analysis of the first very mild expressions of opinion and the rela-

to account for a strong aristocratic reaction, it was otherwise with their literary expression. The German classical drama of Lessing, Schiller, Goethe, and many lesser writers broadcast the message of the French enlightenment, of liberty and the inviolable claims of the individual personality. In this manner the widest possible audience was reached in a society in which public life, publicity, the expression of political views were virtually nonexistent.[7] Thus, in Germany, "private hurts [were raised] to a great principle of struggle between right and wrong," because the country's opinion-leaders were influenced directly by liberal ideas from abroad, even though there was very little internal stimulus in this direction. Conversely, the absence from Japan of a comparable ideological polarization may be attributed, at least proximately, to the effective seclusion of the country.[8] It is difficult to make a

tion of these expressions to public affairs see Fritz Valjavec, *Die Entstehung der politischen Strömungen in Deutschland, 1770–1815* (Munich: R. Oldenbourg, 1951). The Free Masons as a forum for the formation of "public" or politically relevant opinion are examined in Ernst Manheim, *Die Entstehung der öffentlichen Meinung* (Brünn: R. M. Rohrer, 1933).

[7] From the standpoint of the present we can only look back with nostalgia to a time when it was sufficient for a writer to place his action in the Middle Ages, in Spain, or the far-off Near East in order to disguise the contemporary political relevance of his theme. It should be mentioned, however, that most of the classical German literature originated outside Prussia and, although subject to some police controls, was probably more at liberty to reflect current ideas than would have been the case in Prussia. There are, of course, hundreds of studies of this matter, but one of the most comprehensive and judicious is probably Ernst Cassirer, *Freiheit und Form, Studien zur deutschen Geistesgeschichte* (Berlin: Bruno Cassirer, 1916).

[8] I am tempted by the intriguing byways which this contrast suggests. To understand the social-psychological correlates of modernization we require some basis for comparison between past and present. In the absence of interviews or questionnaires, we must rely on the indirect evidence of literature, the theater, diaries, and so forth. In this respect a comparison between Japan and Germany would seem to be especially rewarding. Perhaps the most striking contrast in the literature of the two countries is related also to the restrictionism of the Tokugawa regime. In Japan sumptuary laws and police controls sought to regulate the entertainment appropri-

convincing case for the absence of a phenomenon, such as the ideological articulation of middle-class resentments, even where a directly contrasting development can be found as in this instance. But these negative considerations do not stand alone.

Relation to Land and Its Implications

Smith points out that following the Restoration of 1868 the Japanese samurai were in no position to resist the transformation of their position in society, because some three centuries earlier they had been removed from the land. Until the late sixteenth century, warriors had been scattered over the land, where they were overlords of villages, levying taxes, administering justice, and keeping the peace. In the course of the protracted civil wars preceding the Tokugawa Shogunate the great lords restricted the power of these vassals over their fiefs, that is, forbade them to administer justice, eventually took the power of taxation into their own hands, and compensated their warriors directly by stipends in money or in kind. Thus, by 1560 fiefs had been consolidated into large

---

ate for each class and to exclude from the theater any politically suspect themes. As a result, Kabuki seems to have been channeled in the direction of situation comedy, taking its themes from the foibles of stock-characters derived from the social scene of the time. The fact that police controls proved very difficult to enforce and that political themes kept reappearing despite efforts to suppress them, only accentuates the political significance of cultural seclusion. Germany in the eighteenth century also witnessed considerable censorship, but she was the recipient of influences from abroad and her classical literature reflects this in the sense that here themes derived from the suppressed social and political controversies of the time were given a universal meaning. This classic literature then was joined to a romantic idealization of personality, this blend became the dominant "high culture" of Germany during the nineteenth century, and under the influence of a dominant militarism some unsavory syntheses resulted between this humanistic tradition and the power-orientation of *Realpolitik*. A glimpse of the contrast may be had by comparing Donald H. Shively, "Bakufu versus Kabuki," *Harvard Journal of Asiatic Studies*, XVIII (December 1955), 326–356, with Bruford, *op. cit.*, pp. 291 ff.

tracts of land and seignorial rights concentrated in the hands of some 200 daimyos, each governing on the average a population of some 100,000 people. These large realms were administered from the newly erected castle towns in which the expropriated samurai came to reside as retainers and officials of their lords. The chronology of these and related events is instructive. Hall states that most of the first-ranking castle towns were founded between 1580 and 1610 after a large number of lesser castles had been destroyed, a process which culminated in the Shogunal edict of 1615 ordering the destruction of all but one castle in each province.[9] This wholesale removal of warriors from the land was the action most likely to provoke their intense resistance, and there is evidence that it was accomplished by superior force.[10] It is significant in this respect that the first decree promulgating the expulsion of Christian missionaries was issued in 1587, in the midst of the struggles eventuating in the consolidation of daimyo-power. At the national level, the Battle of Sakigahara of 1600 established the supremacy of the Tokugawa family, which consolidated its power by requiring each daimyo family to maintain a residence in Edo. Mandatory attendance at Court by the daimyo or a member of his family (the so-called *sankin-kotai* system) provided the Tokugawa Shogunate with the personal guarantee of the daimyo's continued loyalty. In the 1620's prior to the introduction of this alternate-residence system, the Christian missions were suppressed with great ferocity and the policy of seclusion was introduced. These policies were prompted, in part at least, by the specific fear that continued contact with the West would provoke the warriors to organize a more concerted resistance against the con-

[9] See John W. Hall, "The Castle Town and Japan's Modern Urbanization," *Far Eastern Quarterly*, XV (November 1955), 42–44. He cites the case of Bizen which had some 20–30 castles during the fifteenth century, this number was reduced to four by 1615 at which time the edict led to the destruction of three more, leaving the castle town of Okayama.

[10] See the brief description of the principal methods used by Hideyoshi in C. R. Boxer, *The Christian Century in Japan, 1549–1650* (Berkeley: University of California Press, 1951), pp. 173–174.

solidation of daimyo and Tokugawa power.[11] Seclusion insulated the struggles of the Japanese warrior aristocracy sufficiently to enable them to fight it out among themselves, and continued insulation was used by the victors to stabilize the resulting power relationships.

The contrast with Prussia enables us to strengthen this interpretation, though in such complex matters one cannot expect confirmation. Here also the struggles among the ruling strata of the country culminated in the supremacy of one ruling family—the Hohenzollern Dynasty, but political unification was achieved to the accompaniment of a rapid decline of towns, the political and economic ascendance of the rural nobility, and an eventual victory of the ruler over the estates on the basis of military mobilization and foreign involvements. Toward the end of the sixteenth century the later state of Prussia consisted of a number of scattered territories in Northeastern Germany and elsewhere, only nominally held together by the Hohenzollern rulers whose center of power lay in the province of Brandenburg.[12] In these territories the towns had been relatively prosperous and the peasants free

[11] This is the interpretation of C. R. Boxer. See *ibid.*, especially pp. 338–339. Professor Boxer emphasizes that among Japanese Christian converts who remained true to their faith unto death during the persecution *heimin* (peasants, artisans, and merchants) constituted a much higher proportion than samurai. Out of two to five thousand martyrs who died for their faith in 1614–1643, less than 70 were Europeans (pp. 358, 448). Accordingly, it is probable that the persecution was motivated by the fear that conversion to Christianity would undermine obedience to temporal lords among the population at large as well as by the more specific fear of the disgruntled *ronin* and the possibility of an alliance between these elements and Catholic Spain (pp. 317, 373, and *passim*).

[12] The diversity of these territories is suggested by their divergent legal status. "The Prussian 'kingdom' was confined to the province of East Prussia only. The 'King of Prussia' (since 1701) was at the same time 'Elector' of Brandenburg, 'Duke' of Pomerania, Magdeburg, Cleves, and Silesia (since 1740), 'Prince' of Halberstandt and Minden, 'Count' of Mark and Ravensberg, etc." See Hans Rosenberg, *Bureaucracy, Autocracy, and Aristocracy* (Cambridge: Harvard University Press, 1958), p. 28. The territory of "East Prussia" was a Polish fief until 1657 when Poland recognized the sovereignty of Prussia.

under the stimulus of the Hanseatic towns on the Baltic Sea and the political stability provided by the Teutonic Order. By the sixteenth century, however, the Hanse was declining and the Order was dissolved in 1525. All resistance to the landed nobility crumbled. The result was a steady encroachment by the nobility on the commercial and political prerogatives of the towns and on the customary rights of the peasants, leading to an almost precipitous decline of the towns and the establishment of serfdom for the peasants by the middle of the seventeenth century. Still, the sixteenth century was a period of peace and prosperity. Feudal knights turned themselves into merchants and entrepreneurs who, once they had broken the urban monopoly on trade and industry, proceeded to make the most of the ample opportunities in foreign and domestic trade which were available to them.[13]

At first, the Hohenzollern rulers were entirely powerless against this landed but commercialized nobility. Although their territories were scattered, during the sixteenth century they succeeded in adding to them by a series of marriages. These marriages involved them in the power struggles of Europe—an important vantage point in their later struggles against the estates. But at the beginning of the seventeenth century the Hohenzollern were at the lowest point in their fortunes. The Thirty-Years' War (1618–48) engulfed all of their possessions. The Hohenzollern did not take part in these struggles; while the Elector chose to reside in far-away Prussia, his home province of Brandenburg was occupied by Imperial or Swedish troops from 1627 onward. Yet this occupation helped to change the internal balance of power. The foreign army leaders made short shrift of all existing privileges, so that prolonged occupation weakened the political power and economic strength of the landed aristocracy. This weakness played into the hands of the Hohenzollern who strengthened their military preparations especially in connection with the war between Sweden and Poland from 1655 to

[13] For documentation see F. L. Carsten, *The Origins of Prussia* (Oxford: At the Clarendon Press, 1954), Chap. XII. Note that the towns continued to pay two thirds of all taxes, even in this period of their decline, while the landed nobility was tax exempt.

1660, in which they took an active part. Frederick William, the Great Elector (1640–88),

> . . . considered it the obvious duty of the Estates not only of Prussia which was directly involved in the war, but equally of Brandenburg and of Cleves, to grant him the money for the conduct of the war. When they failed to do so, he raised it without their consent. At the end of the war he had gained great strength and a standing army, capable of breaking any resistance against the collection of taxes required for its maintenance.[14]

Frederick William and his successors compensated the aristocracy for its submission not only by a continuation of their privileges in all fiscal and local administrative affairs, but also by the transformation of an army of mercenaries into one in which especially the poorer nobility made up the overwhelming majority of the officer corps that was loyal to the Hohenzollern dynasty and indeed opposed to some extent the more parochial interests of the landed nobility.[15]

Japanese and Prussian social history in the sixteenth and seventeenth centuries provide a series of striking contrasts. In Japan, centralization of power occurred in the course of protracted civil wars under conditions of increasing isolation; in Prussia, it occurred as a result of (or in relation to) events outside the country which altered the internal balance of power (e.g., decline of the Hanse, dissolution of the Teutonic Order, Hohenzollern marriage alliances, Thirty-Years' War). The Hohenzollern used foreign involvements and the divisions within the aristocracy to subdue the recalcitrant nobility and

[14] *Ibid.*, p. 189. When the Great Elector came to power in 1640, the total revenue of his realm amounted to one million Taler; at the time of his death in 1688 the total came to over three million. During the same period the strength of the standing army increased from approximately 4500 men to some 30,000, although these numbers fluctuated greatly. The financial burden of this effort fell on a population of one million people, who had to pay nearly twice as much per head than their much more prosperous contemporaries in France. See *ibid.*, pp. 266–271.

[15] See Rosenberg, *op. cit.*, p. 70. Rosenberg's study contains an excellent comparative analysis of the "Prussian case" in its relation to the general European development. See *ibid.*, pp. 1–45.

weaken its opposition to specific policies. From the standpoint of the internal social structure the importance of external events for this build-up of the Prussian state may be considered "fortuitous." Yet in the present context these "fortuitous" events have significance, because their absence or deliberate exclusion from the course of the Japanese development helps to account for the successful removal of warriors from the land and hence for their greater receptivity to change in comparison with the Prussian landed nobility.

Japan experienced a rapid rise of urbanization, Prussia a rapid decline. In Japan the warrior aristocracy was separated from the land—which was tantamount to its urban concentration, its antirural bias, its relative demilitarization, or, conversely, its increasing bureaucratization. In Prussia the aristocracy strengthened its ties to the land by virtue of the widening of economic opportunities that resulted from the destruction of urban monopolies. This development led to a strong antiurban bias and a concerted resistance to the demands of the ruler and his officials; when this resistance was finally overcome in matters of taxation, military affairs, and foreign policy, it continued in all local affairs where the nobility remained paramount.[16]

This difference between an urbanized and a rural aristocracy is related in various ways to the different significance of military affairs for the political unification of the two countries. German unity was achieved through military victory over France. Prussia, the leading German state prior to uni-

[16] At the same time, we can speak of a "remilitarization" in so far as these Prussian aristocrats who now became army officers were descendants of feudal knights who had cultivated the military arts as a way of life at one time, but had become peaceful landowners and landed merchants during the peace and prosperity of the sixteenth century. However, we should remember that this was East European frontier territory, which had been settled not only by knights, but by "professional promoters of frontier settlements, and numerous noble *condottieri* immigrants." In addition, some of these noble families were descendants of "horse and cattle thieves, dealers in stolen goods, smugglers, usurers, forgers of legal documents, oppressors of the poor and helpless, and appropriators of gifts made over to the Church." See Rosenberg, *op. cit.*, p. 30.

fication, was itself largely the product of military preparedness and army organization. This accounts for the special position of the Hohenzollern kings and for the special virulence of the constitutional conflict of 1862–66. For the Prussian king was above all the personal leader of the army, the constitution of 1850 specifically noted this position and excluded military affairs from the purview of legislative oversight, so that the Prussian *Landtag's* refusal to endorse the proposed increase in military preparedness struck at the root of the king's prerogative. The subsequent military victory appeared to give a retrospective endorsement to the king's and Bismarck's position and brought about a genuine acceptance of "dynastic militarism" in the ranks of the liberal opposition. I note this development of ascendant militarism in Germany in order to emphasize the contrast with Japan. Seen in the large, we may characterize the Tokugawa Shogunate as a period of descendant or quiescent militarism. Hideyoshi's sword hunt of 1588, the consolidation of local daimyo rule through the establishment of castle towns (from 1580 to 1610), the consequent removal of samurai from the land, and the formalization of the *sankin-kotai* system for *tozama* daimyo in 1635 (and for *fudai* daimyo in 1642) were major steps in the thorough subjugation and control of the Japanese warrior aristocracy; and this control remained intact until the Meiji Restoration. In terms of their education, bearing, and ideas, the samurai remained attached to their tradition of physical prowess and chivalric honor, as Veblen might say, but this was a militarism without war and above all it was an individualized military stance. Thus, Japan entered the modern world in 1868 under the leadership of a demilitarized aristocracy that was turning its attention to the promotion of education and economic enterprise as a necessary precondition of the country's eventual political and military renaissance, whereas Germany did so under the leadership of the Prussian king, the Prussian army, and the Prussian bureaucracy whose *raison d'être* was a military posture and whose success in achieving national unity provided a framework of militancy for the resolution of most internal conflicts.

The foregoing comparative analysis has examined two

points. In the absence of a "democratic challenge" the Japanese aristocracy possessed a greater tolerance for change, even in its own privileged position, than would have been the case otherwise. Secondly, the Restoration movement under the leadership of the Meiji oligarchs could accomplish a wholesale transformation in the position of the samurai, because the latter had been removed from the land three centuries earlier and were in no position to resist. Both the lack of ideological articulation and the final failure of the warriors to resist removal from the land may be related to the policy of seclusion, an interpretation which is strengthened by the contrasting development of Prussia during the same period. But it is one thing to show why the Japanese aristocracy did not resist the development of their country; it is another to show why they took the lead in accomplishing this result and in so doing greatly altered the preconditions of their own privileged status. In his answer to this last question, Professor Smith points to a series of conditions which induced the samurai to take an active interest in development under the aegis of the Meiji government, even at the risk of actual or eventual deprivation. Conflicts of interest among the ranks of the aristocracy, the bureaucratization of *han*-government, the development of new aspirations, and changing interpersonal relations between lord and vassal are among these conditions.

Ruling-Class Traditions and Development

The Tokugawa settlement resulted in a genuine class division within the aristocracy. A few thousand families of superior lineage monopolized the important offices of government, while several hundred thousand families of samurai were cut off from all opportunities of appointment. Although some samurai became officials in their respective daimyo domains, most of them were modest retainers. Many samurai families lived in real poverty, resorted to by-employments they considered degrading, and greatly resented the impropriety of merchant wealth. Yet such differences in rank or condition did not affect samurai ideology. The tradition of loyalty to the lord, the cultivation of a militant stance of daring and prowess were not only retained by the samurai but encouraged by the Shogunate and the daimyo. We can suppose that the samurai sensed this discrepancy between their lives and their pretensions. Military men who live as retainers and have little chance to see action may strut about in language and gesture, but the most sensitive among them must have become restless and many more developed strong hostilities against the higher ranks of the aristocracy, especially at the Shogunal Court.

Other considerations support this speculation. The consolidation of daimyo power led to the bureaucratization of *han*-government and hence to increased career opportunities for some of the samurai who had been removed from the land and could now exercise a larger, albeit delegated authority. By the late eighteenth century writers on government were in strong and general agreement on merit as the criterion which should govern selection for office. It is uncertain at what levels and how widely this new principle was applied. But impressive public works were undertaken in some well-administered daimyo domains, and this suggests that merit was recognized occasionally.[17] Where such practices prevailed, upward mobility based on achievement became possible.

[17] Both the emphasis on "merit" and the uncertainty of applying this principle under the Tokugawa Shogunate are discussed in Smith, " 'Merit' in Tokugawa Bureaucracy." It would be instructive to know the social position of these writers and in particular whether they have reference primarily to the Tokugawa or the daimyo bureaucracy. The transformation of samurai from vassals into officials and the increasing use of impersonal, administrative considerations is described by John W. Hall, "Foundations of the Modern Japanese Daimyo," *Journal of Asian Studies*, XX (May 1961), 327–328. The same author discusses the construction of waterworks undertaken during and since the seventeenth century in Richard Beardsley, John W. Hall and Robert E. Ward, *Village Japan* (Chicago: University of Chicago Press, 1959), Chap. 3, especially pp. 51–55. However, the two studies cite evidence from the same area (Bizen and environs) and conditions varied among the *han*. One such variation is analyzed in Robert K. Sakai, "Feudal Society and Modern Leadership in Satsuma-han," *Journal of Asian Studies*, XVI (May 1957), 365–376. Note especially the decentralized administration of Satsuma and the quite high proportion of samurai in the population (26% in 1874 against 0.56% of the total population).

. . . men of lower rank were sometimes promoted to high office; merchants and occasionally even peasants with specialized qualifications were ennobled that they might hold office; and promotion in the bureaucracy became for warriors an important means of improving status.[18]

But however sporadic such instances may have been, the impoverished samurai families provided a ready audience for writers who made "merit" their watchword. Since the highest offices usually went to well-placed families, it was easy to exacerbate the invidious contrast between the incompetence of high officials and the lowly samurai whose sterling virtues went unrewarded. Accordingly, an ideology of "merit" was fashioned which satisfied the pride and aspirations of the samurai, while it also intensified the invidious contrast between the daimyo-domains and the corrupt and effete Shogunate in Edo.

Smith argues that the ideal of the warrior was gradually superseded by ideals of personal conduct more appropriate for a bureaucrat. After the samurai were removed from the land and the country had become pacified, relations between lord and vassal became more impersonal. The administration of the consolidated daimyo-domains became bureaucratic and a new ideology of aspiration developed among the lower samurai. For two centuries prior to the Restoration, the samurai had been schooled in envy and emulation by the example of *han* officials of samurai rank, whose successful careers presumably goaded on the pretensions and self-confidence of men who had to live on a modest rent or in penury.[19] Ac-

[18] Smith, "Japan's Aristocratic Revolution," p. 375.
[19] In this context, Smith refers in a review article to "able and rising men destined to form a new ruling class who felt unjustly cut off from positions of power and respect." See his "The Discontented," 218. Although this characterization applied to men from all social ranks, it applied with special force to the lower samurai. The curious combination of radicalism and conservatism among these petty and frustrated aristocrats may be explained by the fact that some of their number were successful; there was hope in principle, a condition highly conducive to revolution as Tocqueville already suggested; but no one in high office questioned that men of

cordingly, the very rapid expansion of opportunities after 1868 was tailor-made for men who suffered from the acute discrepancy between their high social rank and their lowly economic position, who were free of bias against change since they had long since been severed from the land, whose educational preferment under the Tokugawa regime provided them with an immediate advantage over all competitors, and whose traditional cult of action, habits of frugality, aristocratic aversion to money-making, and ideology of aspiration had prepared them psychologically for a bureaucratic career.[20] In a society which heavily underscored status distinctions, the samurai could now hope to rise to the highest positions. This hope, combined as it was with the collectivist ideal of national advance, outweighed the real deprivations to which they were at first exposed and this occurred the more easily because the Restoration leaders left no doubt that the new government's obligations toward the ex-samurai were taken seriously.[21]

---

samurai rank had first claim, certainly a reassuring note even in a dismal economic situation.

[20] Smith, "Japan's Aristocratic Revolution," pp. 378–379. Ronald Dore, "Mobility, Equality and Individuation in Modern Japan," *Second Conference on Modern Japan* (Bermuda, January 1963) states (p. 2) that the samurai class made up 6% of all families, and that two samples of samurai participation in the Meiji elite yield the proportions of 45 and 53% respectively. That the response of the samurai was instantaneous and disproportionately high is suggested by the fact that in the years 1863–1871 Fukuzawa's Western-oriented Keio school was attended by 40 commoners and 1289 samurai. See Johannes Hirschmeier, S.V.D., *Entrepreneurship in Meiji Japan* (Ph.D. Dissertation, Harvard University), p. 69.

[21] In 1867 payments in rice to the samurai amounted to 34.6 million yen, while in 1876 the value of yearly interest paid on a commutation basis had fallen to 11.5 million. But this decline should be compared with the fact that in 1871 the government spent 15.3 million yen or some 36% of its total budget on stipends for *han*-samurai who had become prefectural samurai. See Hirschmeier, *op. cit.*, p. 62. Note also Ito Hirobumi's telling comments that "most of the men of spirit and argument have come from among the former samurai," that these men have been deprived of their former high position in society and are, consequently, the source of unrest. Quoted in George Beckmann, *The Making of the Meiji Constitution* (Lawrence: University of Kansas Press, 1957), p. 131.

Once again, comparisons and contrasts with Prussia and Germany may be made. The consolidation of Tokugawa and Hohenzollern power was similar in one respect: the daimyos and the *Junkers* were left with considerable local powers in contrast to a country like France, where dynastic absolutism greatly disorganized or actually destroyed the old aristocracy. Yet, daimyos and *Junkers* or the samurai and the lower landed nobility of Prussia were not aristocrats of the same type, either in their relation to local government, in their military role, or in their manners and general culture.

In Prussia, the Hohenzollern rulers subjected a once-free peasantry to serfdom and thus vastly increased the local power of the landed aristocracy (even of its lesser ranks) in return for political submission. The Prussian nobles remained on the land and lorded it over a servile peasantry as landowners, administrators, judges, prosecutors, and police officers, thus combining personal dominance with governmental authority. In Japan, the samurai were removed from the land in the sixteenth century, while the social structure of the village community remained intact. The daimyos along with their samurai retainers became town residents and as such did not intervene in village affairs as long as they received their stipends and contributions from the villagers. This setting greatly encouraged local autonomy, albeit one combined with a strongly collectivist orientation. Under the Tokugawa Shogunate governmental controls were highly centralized, and responsibilities were imposed on the community as a whole. As a result the exercise of local authority by government officials tended to be relatively impersonal, in contrast to the Prussian estates with their highly personal exercise of authority. It is probable, therefore, that these two countries possess strikingly different traditions of interpersonal relations, despite their common and long-standing emphasis on status distinctions and hierarchy. For *in the sphere of local government* high social rank and governmental authority went hand in hand in Prussia, whereas in Tokugawa Japan the vast majority of samurai possessed rank but not authority.

In the military sphere the contrast is sharp also. The Tokugawa Shogunate pacified the country as a whole and sought to control their aristocratic vassals by elaborate police controls. At the same time the Shoguns protected the exclusive right of daimyos and samurai to carry a sword; this right was an index of high social rank. At first, Meiji military reforms retained this right in the new army, but eventually the right was abolished and a system of national conscription introduced a significant measure of equality through the army. In Prussia, the Hohenzollern kings also suppressed all independent military action on the part of the nobility while protecting its high social rank. But in this case supremacy was achieved by the organization of a standing army directly subordinate to the monarch. Both the high rank and the loyalty of the nobility were ensured by giving the sons of noble families exclusive access to the officer corps. High military rank in the standing army and high social rank were closely related. In the army, relations between officers and men were very harsh and tended to replicate and reinforce the harsh civilian relations between landlords and peasants, since the composition of the two groups largely overlapped. Accordingly, interpersonal relations between military ranks were a major buttress of inequality and invidious status distinctions in Germany. The individual militancy of the samurai in Tokugawa Japan contrasts sharply with this organized militarism of the Prussian nobility.

There are parallel distinctions in the field of culture and manners. The Tokugawa Shoguns required that all daimyos maintain a residence in Edo in which the daimyo or his relations by their presence at court vouchsafed for the loyalty of the absent. This *sankin-kotai* system imposed very heavy expenditures, increased still further by the conspicuous consumption through which the daimyo and his relations sought to hold their own in the competition for preferment at the Shogunal Court.[22] It would be of interest to compare the

[22] Incidentally, this put a premium on a more efficient organization of the *han*, which in many instances passed into the hands of samurai officials. May this not be an instance in which "wasteful expenditures" proved to be on occasion at least a positive incentive for a more efficient administration of the *han*-domains, Veblen to the contrary notwithstanding?

resulting refinement in etiquette with the development of polite manners at the French Court in Versailles, since both may be considered a by-product of absolutism following the decline of feudalism.[23] By contrast, the Prussian nobility was not subjected to comparable controls. The individual lord (*Gutsherr*) was complete master in his own domains, especially east of the Elbe River. As such he combined the arbitrary benevolence or punitiveness of the personal master with the authoritarianism of the government official and military commander. In the East these landlords became "experts in local tyranny" (Rosenberg) for several reasons. As colonizing territory East Germany attracted its complement of adventurers and outlaws. The serfdom of the peasantry brutalized masters and servants alike. And the masters, who stayed on the land and entertained themselves with the crude pleasures of provincial squires, lacked the polished manners and cultural refinements which in the seventeenth and eighteenth centuries were typical by-products of court life.[24] In the Prussian "garrison state" there was little room for the cultivation of manners, with the result that civilian life was "militarized" exacerbating the class and status distinctions of German society until well into the twentieth century.[25]

As a consequence of these and related differences the two aristocracies played quite different roles in the development of their countries. In Japan, the samurai took the initiative and at the beginning furnished the majority of the key figures in the economic as well as the political fields.[26] Among the samurai there was a strong antirural bias and much indignant

[23] Such an interpretation of the evidence from France is contained in Norbert Elias, *Über den Prozess der Zivilisation* (Basel: Haus zum Falken, 1942), two volumes.

[24] Until well into the eighteenth century many of these *Junkers* definitely preferred a military as against a bureaucratic career, because they lacked the educational background for the latter. See Rosenberg, *op. cit.,* p. 59.

[25] See Otto Büsch, *Militärsystem und Sozialleben im Alten Preussen, 1713–1807* (Vol. 7 of Veröffentlichungen der Berliner Historischen Kommission; Berlin: W. de Gruyter, 1962).

[26] See Dore, "Mobility, Equality and Individuation in Modern Japan," *passim.*

envy of wealthy merchants, but the prejudice against materialism and money-making disappeared quickly after 1868 when development of the country became a national cause. Among the *Junkers* an antiurban bias prevailed, which was combined with a strong prejudice against merchants and commercialism. These attitudes were buttressed by the real conflicts of interest between the agrarian East and the industrial West of Germany, and by the anticommercial sentiments typical among military officers. All this did not preclude an intense interest in money-making. Max Weber observes that these landlords from East of the Elbe had become rural capitalists with aristocratic pretensions, who use their privileged social position to exact economic concessions from the government and resist all attempts at constitutional reforms. Thus, in Germany initiative for reform came, not from the landed aristocracy but from the officials of an absolutist regime. These reforms met with determined opposition with the result that German nineteenth century history is marked by a basic cleavage between defenders of tradition and advocates of reform.

No comparable cleavage seems to have developed in Japan. As in other societies undergoing rapid change, there was considerable tension between tradition and modernity in Japan as well. But Professor Smith points out that in the absence of an aristocratic defense of the old regime there was no "radical cleavage of the two by ideology." When all parties are more or less reformist and more or less traditional, the past does not appear as a barrier to progress, but rather as an obstacle in some respects and an aid in others.[27] On the other hand, tradition and modernity appeared mutually exclusive where, as in Germany, the ideals of the French Revolution were brought into direct confrontation with "stiffly martial concepts of authority and of military virtues . . . as models for civil life in general."[28] Again, in Japan the absence of a revolutionary struggle against inequality meant that class consciousness remains relatively weak, even though status consciousness is strong. Professor Smith sees no con-

[27] Smith, "Japan's Aristocratic Revolution," p. 382.
[28] Rosenberg, *op. cit.*, p. 41.

tradiction in this, since the Japanese concern with status is relatively free of class feeling as long as higher-ups are looked on "as superior extensions of the self."[29] We have seen that this view is a typical feature of societies which take the existence of inequality for granted.[30] Professor Smith's assessment implies, therefore, that in Japanese society inequality remains unchallenged until well into the modern era and, perhaps, is rather widely accepted still. In Germany, on the other hand, inequality becomes controversial early in the nineteenth century, with the result that status differences are challenged and class consciousness increases. To this day, interpersonal relations tend to be marked by strong feelings of class in Germany, whereas in Japan such relations seem to be characterized by an acceptance of status differences, softened by kinship simulations and an elaborate ritual of collaboration among status equals, which have no analogue in Germany as far as I am aware.

THE ISSUE OF CONSENSUS

The preceding discussion emphasizes distinguishing characteristics of the Japanese development, exemplified by comparisons with Prussia and Germany. The century-long isolation of Japan is the most outstanding basis of these distinctions. In the modern world no other major society has been similarly isolated, certainly not England whose insularity invites comparisons with that of Japan. Yet the problems with which Japan has had to cope in the political management of her renewed contact with the outside world are recurrent problems that can be approached in general terms.

From a comparative perspective it is plausible to emphasize the nationalist consensus uniting the Japanese people and her leaders. To be sure, when contact was re-established after a virtual isolation of more than two centuries, Japan's intellectual response showed a bifurcation between nativism

[29] Smith, "Japan's Aristocratic Revolution," p. 382.
[30] See the earlier discussion of "traditional authority relationships" above, pp. 48–57.

and westernism that is superficially similar to what occurred elsewhere, notably in nineteenth-century Russia. Nor should one minimize the personal violence accompanying this difference of opinion. But Japanese opinion leaders and intellectuals were principally recruited from the samurai. As such they were oriented toward action and united in their common goal to ensure Japan's greatness as a nation, however divided they were on the best way of achieving that goal. Socially and culturally homogeneous, Japan's educated elite was *not* alienated from the establishment of autocratic government with the Emperor as its symbolic apex. In this respect the elite was at one with the people at large. To the outsider it remains something of a puzzle that the Emperor, who for many centuries of Japanese history remained a shadowy figure even in the cultural sense, could become within a year or two the focus of national loyalty for the entire population—a development clearly manipulated by the leaders of the Restoration but just as clearly meeting with a genuine popular response. If we compare this development with the symbolism of personal rule in Tsarist Russia, we are struck with the complete absence of populist themes from Japanese culture, in contrast to the apotheosis of "Holy Russia" and her people which goes back to medieval times and is radically transformed only in the course of the nineteenth century.[31] We can speculate that in Japan loyalty to the Emperor was of a kind with loyalty to the immediate overlord which had been fostered assiduously for many centuries prior to the Restoration. Even kinship loyalties were subordinated to personal loyalty of this kind, which was defended at the inception of the Tokugawa regime by the destruction of Christianity as a competing focus of personal loyalty. When kinship relations are stressed as strongly as they are in Japan, it is again puzzling to find that loyalty to the overlord is emphasized more strongly still—so much so in fact that we can speak of an absolute supremacy of hierarchy and authority over all competing values and loyalties.

[31] Michael Cherniavsky, *Tsar and People* (New Haven: Yale University Press, 1961), Chap. 4.

There are many other types of hierarchy in Japan, which affect different individuals—business, religious, social, intellectual and artistic hierarchies—but the one which takes precedence over all others is the political hierarchy. In late feudal times the supreme loyalty, the supreme obligation, was due one's feudal lord and through him the Shogun. The family as a unit was definitely inferior to the feudal realm. The real moral of the story of the "Forty-Seven *Ronin*," when viewed in the context of the Far Eastern milieu, is that these forty-seven men ruthlessly sacrificed their families, in some cases sending wives and daughters into prostitution, in order to fulfil their obligations to their lord.[32]

The puzzle is less the supremacy of the Emperor in the Japanese rank-order of values than this supremacy of hierarchical authority at all levels of the social structure. Whatever the reasons of this phenomenon may be, its effects are manifest. Respect for established authority strongly buttressed the solidarity of the Meiji oligarchy, once the basic compromise of the Restoration movement had been achieved. There is evidence that very tortuous negotiations and elaborate ritual were needed to achieve this compromise among equals but that the compromise was retained with extreme tenacity once it had been achieved.[33] This particular kind of consensus within the ranks of the governing elite is surely one reason for the success of a "modernizing autocracy," just as the absence of a comparable degree of cohesion helps to explain the failure of the Tsarist autocracy.

[32] Edwin O. Reischauer, *The United States and Japan* (New York: The Viking Press, 1957), pp. 165–166. The lord of these retainers had wounded another lord on the premises of the Shogunal court, thus violating his own duty of absolute obedience to the Shogun. In punishment of this violation the Shogun demanded that he commit suicide and the "Forty-Seven *Ronin*" avenged their lord's death by killing the man who had provoked the initial aggression.

[33] In this respect the study by Marius Jansen, *Sakamoto Ryoma and the Meiji Restoration* (Princeton: Princeton University Press, 1961), may be compared with R. J. C. Butow, *Japan's Decision to Surrender* (Stanford: Stanford University Press, 1959). Different as the setting of the two studies is, it is instructive to consider both as case studies of the "art of compromise" among status equals.

But undeviating respect for hierarchical authority is also a pervasive aspect of Japanese society as a whole. At the lower levels of the social structure it takes the form of respect for elders and a highly developed capacity for collective action as long as the elders achieve agreement among themselves. Both aspects of local solidarity were greatly strengthened under the Tokugawa regime by the collective legal responsibility for tax payments on the part of each village community. In medieval Europe such collective responsibility was associated with the development of urban autonomy, while a landed aristocracy exercised personal authority over a dependent peasantry. Tokugawa Japan experienced a reversal of this pattern in so far as collective responsibility was imposed on the village (thus leading to considerable, albeit highly paternalistic autonomy), while an urbanized aristocracy exercised personal authority in the castle towns. From the standpoint of political management by the Meiji oligarchs the effect was that governmental instructions concerning agricultural improvements were followed with alacrity by the village communities—in marked contrast to the tendency of peasants elsewhere to resist the exercise of governmental authority.[34]

The relative solidarity of the governing elite and the readiness with which governmental leadership was accepted by the population are outstanding attributes of state and society in Japan during the initial period of rapid development following the opening of the country. The significance of these attributes is accentuated further if we consider the management of political modernization in comparative perspective.

DEVELOPMENT AS A POLITICAL PROBLEM

The leaders of the Meiji Restoration simultaneously sought to advance their country economically and contain the consequences of that advance politically. In this they resemble the elites of other countries attempting to cope with the eco-

[34] For evidence concerning this response of Japanese peasants see R. P. Dore, "Agricultural Improvements in Japan: 1870–1900," *Economic Development and Cultural Change*, IX, Part 2 (October 1960), pp. 69–91.

nomic and political momentum emanating from Western Europe and America, though because of Japan's long isolation her confrontation with that momentum was especially precipitous. The attempt of the Meiji government to promote industry but contain or suppress democratization has notable parallels in nineteenth-century Europe. In Russia the Tsarist autocracy under Count Witte and in Germany the Wilhelmian autocracy under Bismarck attempted much the same thing. But in these cases autocratic rule not only aided the rapid economic development of the country, it also provoked political disaffection of segments of the population and especially its intellectual elite. By comparison, the Japanese case is remarkable because here a "modernizing autocracy" succeeded for a significant period of time in advancing the country economically while containing her political conflicts within manageable limits.

Compared with England, France, or the United States, both Japan and Germany are latecomers to industrialization and industrialization of the latecomers typically involves a rela- curred in the late eighteenth and early nineteenth centuries with considerable emphasis upon private initiative and a curtailment of political controls over the economy, whereas the industrialization of the late comers typically involves a relatively high degree of political initiative.[36] Japan and Germany are, therefore, early examples of this spread of "development," not only because they borrowed a ready-made technology from the industrially more advanced countries but

[35] Veblen was perhaps the first to emphasize this distinction. Since the renewal of interest in this problem after World War II, a number of scholars like Alexander Gerschenkron, Bert F. Hoselitz, Marion Levy, Henry Rosovsky, E. A. Shils, and others have developed the distinction in several directions.

[36] See Talcott Parsons, "Some Reflections on the Institutional Framework of Economic Development," in *Structure and Process in Modern Societies* (Glencoe: The Free Press, 1960), pp. 99, 102, and *passim* for an elaboration of these points. The importance of political initiative in industrialization is, of course, a matter of degree. It was never absent even in England at the height of *laissez-faire* policies and it varies greatly among countries like Germany, Japan, and Russia which are notable for their emphasis upon political measures.

also because both countries witnessed the importance of political initiative in attempts to promote economic change and to cope with the intensified divisions of the population.[37] In Japan as well as in Germany, government and political ideas were considered major factors in the development of these countries. This emphasis together with the political considerations animating it are another basis on which the two countries may be compared and contrasted.

To do this, it will be useful to cite a forceful statement made in 1880 by Ito Hirobumi, one of the architects of the Meiji Restoration. After referring to the major transformations brought about in Japanese society by the destruction of the relatively autonomous daimyo-domains (*han*), the system of conscription, and the decline of the samurai, Ito continues as follows:

> It is easy to control the popular sentiments of a single village, but it is difficult to control the public opinion of an entire nation. Moreover, it is easy to change the conditions of a country, but it is difficult to alter world-wide trends. Today, conditions in Japan are closely related to the world situation. They are not merely the affairs of a nation or province. The European concepts of revolution, which were carried out for the first time in France about one hundred years ago, have gradually spread to the various nations. By combining and complementing each other, they have become a general trend. Sooner or later, every nation will undergo changes as a result.
>
> In this period of changes from old to new, revolution often broke out. In fact, revolution continues at present. It has not

[37] I note in passing that in the absence of abundant resources and a widespread "achievement motivation" many countries borrow selected aspects of modernity, and some of these like education or medicine are more easily borrowed than modern technology. Under these conditions politics and administration can become a panacea for all the ills besetting an economically backward country. For an interesting discussion of this perspective in the context of the contemporary African experience see the analysis by David Apter, "Political Religion in the New Nations," in Clifford Geertz, ed., *Old Societies and New States* (New York: The Free Press of Glencoe, 1963), pp. 57–104. However, we are dealing here with Germany and Japan, countries which possessed the requisite resources and motivation.

yet stopped. Elsewhere enlightened rulers, with the help of wise ministers, led and controlled these changes, thus solidifying their nations. In brief, all have had to discard absolutist ways and share political power with the people.

Now, European ideas and things are coming into our country like a tidal flow; moreover, new opinions concerning the form of government have become popular among the ex-samurai. Within a few years' time, these ideas have spread into the towns and countryside, and this trend cannot be halted immediately. Thus, there are persons who surprise the public by voicing misleading views. Their thoughtless, disorderly acts pay no attention to the considerations of the Emperor. They groan although they are not sick, and their violent acts have evil effects upon others. However, if we take a general view of causes, it appears that this experience is common to the whole world. Like the rain falling and the grass growing, it is no wonder that we, too, have been affected.

. . . At present it is the responsibility of the government to follow a conciliatory policy and accommodate itself to these tendencies so that we may control but not intensify the situation, and relax our hold over government but not yield it. . . .[38]

There is a whole literature dealing with the comparable orientation of ruling strata in Imperial Germany. Among the many sources that could be cited, I call attention to an analysis by the German historian Otto Hintze, who points out in 1911 that owing to the rifts characterizing German society English parliamentary methods are inapplicable. Then, turning to the factors which make a monarchical constitution mandatory for Germany, Hintze states that first Prussia and then Germany are specifically military states by virtue of their location in Central Europe.

In his relations to the army the monarch is not bound by any constitutional considerations (*Rücksichten*). The constitution is in fact only related to the people in its capacity as a bourgeois society. But the military structure is after all the backbone of the organization of the state, so that the represen-

[38] Quoted in George M. Beckmann, *The Making of the Meiji Constitution*, pp. 131–132.

tation of bourgeois society, i.e., the Landtag, can never acquire a dominant influence in the state. Moreover, this representative body thoroughly lacks the necessary inner unity which would be the indispensable precondition of a dominant political role (*politische Machtrolle*). Unity and cooperation are prevented by the great social and economic cleavage which has always divided East from West in Prussia, a division which has its origin in the diversity of the agricultural economy in the two regions and the different distribution of agrarian and industrial interests between them. Likewise, unity is prevented by the conflict of religious faiths, whose virulence and repercussions in Prussia and the German Reich are greater than in any other state in the world. There is further the radical opposition to the state (*radikale Staatsfeindlichkeit*) on the part of the Social Democratic Party.

In England, the development of a parliamentary regime was conditioned by the unity of the polity (*Einheit und Geschlossenheit der politischen Gesellschaft*), which was reflected in the party-system of the old Whigs and Tories. Both of these were aristocratic parties of the same political, social and religious basis, and the distinctions between them involved relatively subordinate nuances. A system of party-government can be constructed only on such a homogeneous basis. . . . [However] among us parties are not so much political as economic and social or religious group-formations. This is related to the fact that our representative bodies only reflect the life of bourgeois society in contrast to the specifically political structure. From the standpoint of monarchical government Bismarck wishes to have the parties appear as clearly articulated, socioeconomic interest-groups, with which one can bargain and do politics on the du-ut-*des* principle.[39]

These statements present some interesting similarities and differences. Foremost in both is the conviction that the monarchical or imperial government is the guarantor of order and to this end the inviolable authority of the Emperor (or Kaiser) must be assured. In both cases the government is conceived as the indispensable "balance wheel" among the antagonistic forces which threaten the stability of the coun-

[39] Otto Hintze, "Das monarchische Prinzip und die konstitutionelle Verfassung," in *Staat und Verfassung*, pp. 377–378.

try.[40] Yet beyond these well-known similarities, many contrasts stand out.

First, there is the difference between Japan coming into contact with Western ideas after 250 years of seclusion, and Germany being a seedbed as well as a recipient of these ideas throughout her history. Hence it is quite appropriate for Ito to refer to the intrusion of ideas which have disturbed Japan's domestic tranquility, while Hintze speaks of the religious and political divisions of the German population as an established fact. Ito's implication is that the upheavals and divisions resulting from the Western intrusion are controllable in principle, Hintze's that the divisions are so pervasive as to make national unity precarious. Both, of course, consider the Emperor or Kaiser as the mainstay of the nation.

Second, Ito's principal concern is the internal unity and development of the country. Japan's military weakness at the time of the Restoration is so manifest that any attempt at an immediate and rapid military build-up was foreclosed as unrealistic. Eventually, a gradual build-up was undertaken, but in the years immediately following the Restoration, Japan benefits from the fact that her situation makes the promotion

[40] No doubt these two considerations prompted the statesmen of the Meiji Restoration to look to Imperial Germany as the constitutional model most appropriate to their own needs. George M. Beckmann has described the visit of the leading Meiji oligarchs to Europe and especially their attendance at lectures delivered by Rudolf Gneist and Lorenz von Stein. While the general affinity between the German and the Japanese outlook is clear enough, the actual differences between the two countries were considerable. I have the impression, which I cannot document, that men like Gneist, von Stein, and others made a system out of the uneasy truce between Wilhelm II and the Landtag, or that they extrapolated the claims of the Kaiser in the light of what they thought their Japanese visitors wanted to hear. In the process they may have greatly enlarged the prerogatives of the Kaiser, large as these were, while underemphasizing their limitations and the considerable development of quasi-parliamentary methods, of political parties, freedom of the press, etc. Or, perhaps, this extrapolation was the work of the Japanese since in Germany at the time knowledge of Japan was rudimentary. See George M. Beckmann, *The Making of the Meiji Constitution*, Chap. VI. No other monographic study of this "borrowing" process has come to my attention.

of industry the precondition of a later military preparedness.[41] The German situation is quite the reverse. Some of
the earliest governmental efforts to promote industrial production (in the eighteenth century) are directly related to
military considerations.[42] Moreover, the predominance of the
army and of the monarch as its personal leader is related by
the fact that many scattered territories are first united into
the state of Prussia through these means. It is on the same
foundation that Prussia eventually becomes the predominant
political and military power within Germany and the fountainhead of her political unity. Accordingly, "militarism" is
a building-block of the German social structure which cannot
be explained as a response to the strains arising from the
precipitous confrontation between tradition and modernity,
whereas in Japan that explanation appears to be more nearly
correct.[43]

[41] See Thomas Smith, *Political Change and Industrial Development in Japan: Government Enterprise 1868–1880* (Stanford:
Stanford University Press, 1955), p. 35.

[42] The contrast is perhaps lop-sided, since in the interval between the reign of Frederick the Great and the years following the
Meiji Restoration military technology underwent a complete transformation. In the eighteenth century production of simple arms and
the promotion of industrial enterprises could go hand in hand,
while in the later nineteenth century it was necessary to create an
industrial base before the production of military equipment could
be undertaken. See Henry Rosovsky, *Capital Formation in Japan
1868–1940* (Glencoe: The Free Press, 1961), p. 27 for related comments. These considerations do not, however, nullify the major
contrast made in the text.

[43] Otto Hintze's major work, *Die Hohenzollern und Ihr Werk*
(Berlin: Paul Parey, 1915), especially pp. 202–221, 280–306 and
passim is the classic analysis of the early development of Prussian
militarism. Note also Hintze's comparative treatment of this problem in his essay "Staatsverfassung und Heeresverfassung," *Staat
und Verfassung*, pp. 53–83. In the latter essay, Hintze shows that
the militarism of the German Reich is a continuation on a larger
scale of the militarism which was the foundation of the Prussian
state. It is impossible to ignore this background of militarism when
an attempt is made to interpret the rise of National Socialism. However much this movement may have been a "fundamentalist reaction" against "the rationalization of the Western world," the fact
remains that this reaction took a paramilitary form and thus fol-

Third, there is the matter-of-fact manner in which Ito refers to the vast changes which the Restoration government has brought about: the abolition of the *han*-system, the establishment of universal conscription which is tantamount to the final "demilitarization" of the samurai, and the fact that several hundred thousand samurai are deprived of their property and their stipends. Manifestly, the Meiji government possessed a great reservoir of power and unity to have accomplished such results—a fact which stands out in bold relief against the confusion and disunity and powerlessness of the immediately preceding period.[44] In a comparison with the contemporaneous German experience this unity of the Restoration government is impressive. The Meiji oligarchs constitute a relatively cohesive group of political leaders, largely from the Satsuma and Choshu clans, who have acquired considerable political experience in achieving a compromise prior to the Restoration.[45]

---

lowed as well as bastardized models derived from the Prussian military tradition. The great social and political strain between the Reichswehr and the Nazi Party and its paramilitary formations reveal, among other things, the great social distinction between the failures and outlaws who rose to leadership in the Party and the aristocratic officers who commanded the army. In this respect it is indeed striking, as Masao Maruyama has observed, that the Nazi elite consists of "rejects" from bourgeois society, while the top-leaders of the Japanese military establishment certainly belong to the highest strata of Japanese society. See Masao Maruyama, "Japan's Wartime Leaders," *Orient/West*, VII (May 1962), 37–45.

[44] See the characterization of successive constellations of leadership and compromise from the 1830's on in Yoshio Sakata and John W. Hall, "The Motivation of Political Leadership in the Meiji Restoration," *Journal of Asian Studies*, XVI (1956), 31–50. The authors conclude with the observation that the leaders of the restoration movement had no aim other than the elimination of Tokugawa despotism, and in particular that social and economic reorganization was not part of their objective.

[45] More than opposition to the Tokugawa united these men, as Beasley has shown in his analysis of the latent unity underneath the conflict between the *joi* and the *kaikoku* advocates. See W. G. Beasley's introduction to *Select Documents in Japanese Foreign Policy, 1853–1868* (London: Oxford University Press, 1955), pp. 8–10, and *passim*. This unity could emerge once the Bakufu had turned to the Imperial Court for an endorsement of the treaty with

There is nothing really to equal this record in the German case. Hintze maintains correctly that the ascendance of Prussian military might is the foundation of the German Reich and hence of her monarchical constitution. Here political unity is achieved by the ascendance of one territory and its leading strata over all other territories and strata. We could say that this ascendance of Prussia is not unlike the rise of the Tokugawa Shogunate, but this comparison is vitiated by the fact that the ascendance of Prussia was *not* accompanied by any significant transformation of her ruling groups. These ruling groups simply expanded the range of their social and political predominance, culminating in the unification of the German Reich in 1870 as a result of the successful war against France. In the process the social and economic divisions of the population are intensified, accentuating the militarism of the Prussian ruling strata and the drive for unification. These facts are reflected in a striking speech by Max Weber, given in 1893:

> Tremendous illusions were necessary to create the German empire, but now that the honeymoon of unification is over these illusions are gone and we cannot recreate them artificially. . . . No doubt, the nation would rally to the colors to defend the frontiers of the country. But when we undertake the peaceful defense of German nationality on the eastern border, we encounter several mutually conflicting interest groups. . . .[46]

Townsend Harris. The steps by which this opening wedge was eventually used to effect a compromise between the Satsuma and Choshu leaders which took the form of "returning" the *han*-lands to the Emperor are traced from a worms'-eye perspective in Marius B. Jansen's study of *Sakamoto Ryoma* cited earlier (see footnote 33). These superb studies appear to give evidence both for the difficulty of interpersonal contacts leading to eventual compromise, but also for the tenacity with which a compromise once achieved is maintained. The balanced discussion of the positive aspects of this cultural characteristic, such as that contained in Reischauer, *op. cit.,* pp. 133–140, may have to be put alongside an analysis of the same traits in their negative potentialities as revealed by Masao Maruyama, "Japan's Wartime Leaders," pp. 37–53.

[46] Quoted in Reinhard Bendix, *Max Weber, An Intellectual Por-*

Accordingly, the German slogan of the *Primat der Aussen-politik* (primacy of foreign policy) over all internal political issues reflects the military and political vulnerability of Germany. The country's internal divisions reinforced the need for diplomatic and military successes as a means to unity —certainly a major theme in the political role of Bismarck. It is not surprising that in this use of foreign policy-issues for the purpose of maintaining an internal balance less could be done about the internal transformation of the country than in Japan, quite aside from the question whether or not there was any intention of pointing in this direction. Moreover, comparison with Japan during this critical period makes one thing quite clear: the unity of leadership in Japan was collective, while in Germany it depended on one man—Bismarck.

Both government and political ideas play a major role in the development of Germany and Japan, and more particularly in the attempts to cope with the divisions of the population. It is not clear, however, that these divisions are primarily a result of that confrontation between modern technology and "archaic institutions," which Veblen emphasized in his earlier analysis. When Hintze cites the religious divisions of the German population as one major reason for the need for a strong monarchical constitution, it is apparent that these divisions antedate the impact of modern technology, even if it is true that they were also compounded by that impact. This consideration supports Schumpeter's view that once they are formed social structures and attitudes persist, sometimes for centuries. Many tensions observed today are,

---

trait (Garden City: Anchor Books, Doubleday and Co., 1962), pp. 30–31. Hintze appears to confirm this view when he stresses the endemic disunity of Germany and this confirmation has additional weight in view of his profound political disagreement with Weber. To my knowledge, the works of the two men have not been analyzed in relation to each other. Since I have quoted from Hintze's essay "Das monarchische Prinzip . . . ," it is worth adding a reference to Max Weber's "Parlament und Regierung im neugeordneten Deutschland," *Gesammelte Politische Schriften* (Tübingen: J. C. B. Mohr, 1958), pp. 294–431, which is the liberal counterargument to Hintze's conservative position.

therefore, influences persisting from the past which have little to do with the development process. Nor is it clear that these influences are inimical to development. When the Meiji oligarchs "engineered" major changes of the Japanese social structure, they relied upon certain aspects of Japanese tradition in order to facilitate their effort to meet the Western threat. A comparison of development in Japan and Germany clearly underscores the consideration that traditions can facilitate as well as hamper rapid development. But to what extent "tradition" will do the one or the other depends not only on given characteristics of a country, but also on the manner in which these "givens" enter into the "political management" of development.

THEORETICAL IMPLICATIONS

Emphasis on decision-making as an aspect of social change recalls the "fallacy of retrospective determinism" against which I warned in the introduction to these studies. It is easy to see all past changes as inevitable. The conspicuous success of managed social change in Japan can be attributed to long isolation, cultural homogeneity, and the widespread acceptance of political hierarchy and national advance. Similarly, the manifest failure of "political management" in Imperial Germany can be attributed to the constant exposure of the country to radical ideas from abroad, long-standing divisions on religious and economic lines, and the absence of a consensus on political guidelines and national goals. But all this is deceiving. It makes the contingencies with which men must reckon into a system, the parameters of which are merely reflected in the actions of men. In the present case it would consider the rather sudden introduction of modern technology as creating "strains" or "malintegration" in the established institutions of a society. This assertion implies an earlier time when tensions were absent, which is false, or when society functioned "more smoothly," which is vague, as long as scholars cannot agree on a rank-order of tensions or integration. The whole approach overlooks the precarious balance of decision-making and substitutes for it some concept of "equilibrium" attributed to society as a "system."[47]

To this day sociologists (like Marxists before them) consider political ideas and solutions matters of negligible interest compared with the imperatives of the social structure. Yet comparative studies which consider social structures as enduring, but timebound phenomena, suggest a different perspective. If "partial development" is the rule, and if men are active in reconciling tradition and modernity (though they often fail), then the further development of a country depends in some degree on the political management of the problems besetting every developing society. In Japan there is evidence that this management was remarkably effective, aided though it was by a high degree of consensus, traditions favorable to effective, oligarchic rule, and (last but not least) a good bit of luck. In their assessment of economic fluctuations, Professors Ohkawa and Rosovsky state that Japanese economic history looks like a success story. The country's need to grow rapidly was recognized clearly in view of the real or imagined threats to her national sovereignty. But a closer look reveals "weak spots," the omnipresence of dangers and the fortunate turn of random events. Among the most important of these fortuitous factors were,

> the decline in the growth rate of agricultural output beginning in 1905–10, the permanent built-in international payments problems, and beginning in the 1920's, the rapidly developing productivity disparities between the modern and traditional sectors [of the economy]. The best example of a random event which proved fortunate for Japan was World War I, which created an unprecedented opportunity for export expansion.

[47] This is one of the basic assumptions made by Talcott Parsons, *The Social System* (Glencoe: The Free Press, 1951), pp. vii, 3, and *passim*. Use of the equilibrium-model in social theory requires some criterion by which one can judge when and at what level a social structure has attained equilibrium, a point originally and perhaps more simply discussed by Emile Durkheim under the term "social health." According to Robert K. Merton, *Social Theory and Social Structure* (Glencoe: The Free Press, 1957), p. 52 "this remains one of the cloudiest and empirically most debatable concepts in functional theory."

In addition, Japan was never a rich country, and her reserves
—social and material—for sitting-out a period of stagnation
were very small. If growth did not continue speedily, there
was the real danger of slipping once more into backwardness,
and at certain early stages the danger of disappearance as a
nation. It seems to us highly probable that these issues were
understood by economic and governmental leaders. And this
could explain the expansionist atmosphere and the recurrence
of credit creation when price levels began to decline and a
prolonged recession was in view.[48]

Such considerations are not confined to economic history.
A similar case has been made concerning possible historical
alternatives with regard to the exacerbation of class-relations
in Imperial Germany prior to World War I.[49] More generally,
such cases weaken structural explanations of development
which, in the manner of nineteenth-century evolutionary
theory, impute to the attributes of tradition or modernity "a
strain of consistency with each other, because they all answer
their several purposes with less friction and antagonism when
they cooperate and support each other."[50] Once we recognize
that a given admixture of tradition and modernity may be
both enduring and affected by "political management," we
will give less weight to the "malintegration" which impedes
that "strain of consistency." Also, we will rely less exclusively
on structural explanations of development, once we recognize
that societies that come late to the process of development
are influenced profoundly by ideas and institutions which
originate beyond their geographic frontiers and the "bound-
aries" of their social structure. The cases of Germany and
Japan have a special interest in this respect. Both countries
industrialized successfully. Both were characterized by a symbiosis between tradition and modernity that was tension-ridden

[48] Kazushi Ohkawa and Henry Rosovsky, "Economic Fluctuations in Prewar Japan: A Preliminary Analysis of Cycles and Long
Swings," Hitotsubashi Journal of Economics, III (October 1962),
p. 19.
[49] Guenther Roth, The Social Democrats in Imperial Germany
(Totowa: The Bedminster Press, 1963), pp. 311–325, and passim.
[50] William G. Sumner, Folkways (Boston: Ginn & Co., 1940),
pp. 5–6.

but enduring. In both cases this symbiosis was subjected for a considerable time to the cumulative impact of the "industrial arts" and the "process of rationalization," which Thorstein Veblen and Talcott Parsons consider to be the source of instability and strain. Veblen believed that such instability would eventually result in "full modernization," and Parsons' interpretation tends in the same direction.[51] Yet the most drastic social and political change of both countries has *not* occurred as a result of that slow adaptation to the matter-of-fact outlook of modern technology which Veblen extrapolated from the English experience. In both countries, the mainstays of social and political tradition in the midst of modernity have been destroyed by conquest, military occupation, and partition.

In a field in which few things are certain, it will probably be agreed that the expropriation and physical decimation of the *Junkers* in East Germany in 1945 did more to subdue, if not destroy, the "archaic" features of German culture and politics than did the preceding 75 years of industrialization —especially if the result is compared with the unsuccessful or very incomplete subordination of this group following World War I.[52] Here would seem to be that rare thing, the approximation of a test case, for there is no doubt that the *Junkers* were more effectively eliminated from public life after World

[51] See above pp. 7–9 for a discussion of Veblen's views. Similar issues are analyzed in Talcott Parsons, "Democracy and Social Structure in Pre-Nazi Germany," and "Population and Social Structure in Japan," in *Essays in Sociological Theory* (rev. ed.; Glencoe: The Free Press, 1954), pp. 104–123, 275–297. Parsons states that both countries have failed to "continue in what many have thought to be the main line of the evolution of Western Society." (*Ibid.,* pp. 116, 287.) That failure is evidenced in German Naziism and Japanese militarism, which are not consequences of industrialization (since nothing comparable has occurred in other industrial societies) but of "malintegration, tension and strain in the social structure" (*ibid.,* pp. 117, 277).

[52] See *ibid.,* pp. 118–119, 286, and *passim.* For an interpretation of this new bourgeois, social structure in the Federal Republic of Germany, see Ralf Dahrendorf, "Demokratie und Sozialstruktur in Deutschland," *Archives Européennes de Sociologie,* I (1960), pp. 86–120.

War II than after World War I. The different repercussions of these two situations can be studied empirically. At a guess, I would suggest that the crucial difference was expropriation, since without their land the *Junkers* have not been in a position to continue their political dominance, though their decline after the war was certainly prepared by Hitler.[53]

In the different setting of Japan, the impact of American occupation probably has been more diffuse, though perhaps equally thorough-going. There is, of course, the notable difference that the sources of Japanese tradition and ultra-nationalism are not nearly as group-specific as in Germany. Professor Maruyama suggests that, with the exception of some radical groups, everyone in prewar Japan was a nationalist; thus, nationalist sentiments cannot account for the specific development of militarism. He attributes the rise of Japanese militarism after World War I to the cumulative resentments arising from the startlingly precipitous contrasts between farming villages and cities created by a rapid development. Extreme militarism provided an alternative career pattern for the local boys who lost out in the stiff competition for bureaucratic or military positions, and for the young officers who saw their career chances frustrated politically and shared the resentments of the provincial against modernity and metropolis.[54] Japanese surrender brought a complete breakdown

[53] A recent study enables us to follow the declining position of the aristocracy. In an analysis of Senior Foreign Service Personnel, Lewis Edinger has shown that German diplomats were recruited from the aristocracy in the following proportions: 1906—89%; 1926—42%; 1936—61%; and 1956—17%. Thus, while the proportion of aristocrats in the German Foreign Service was cut in half by the November Revolution of 1918, their participation increased once more under the Nazis and then plummeted to a new low after World War II. See Lewis J. Edinger, "Continuity and Change in the Background of German Decision-Makers," *The Western Political Quarterly*, XIV (1961), 28. See also the comparative study of purges in the two countries by John D. Montgomery, *Forced to be Free: The Artificial Revolution in Germany and Japan* (Chicago: University of Chicago Press, 1957).

[54] See Masao Maruyama, "Introduction," to Ivan Morris, *Nationalism and the Right Wing in Japan* (London: Oxford University Press, 1960), pp. xxiv–xxv.

of the military imperialism which had been fostered by these recruits, and Japanese nationalism was dispersed to its traditional foci of family, village, and small local group. As Professor Morris states:

> Discredited, chauvinist symbols [were replaced] by older, non-political but traditional symbols. At the same time loyalty to the Emperor made way for loyalty to bosses of local groups, sports and racing were substituted for militant nationalism, an atomized desire for better material life took over from below what had previously been pre-empted by nationalist aggrandizement from above.[55]

In addition, the considerable success of land reform has presumably diminished the hiatus between village tradition and modern technology and city life, so that the basis for a recrudescent nationalism from the same sources as before has probably shrunk. These considerations strongly suggest that in Japan also major steps in the decline of her "feudal legacies" resulted from conquest and foreign occupation as well as from the gradual, cultural impact of modern technology.

This emphasis is likely to provoke at least two reactions: that it is obvious or that it is extraneous. The point is obvious to those who accept Schumpeter's theory of "partial development." From this vantage point, it is easy to concede that military conquest and occupation can be, and in these cases have been, more important than industrialization in destroying the legacies of the past.[56] Yet this does not dispose of the second objection which considers foreign policy or more broadly the international power position of a country extraneous from the viewpoint of the social sciences and hence regards military defeat and occupation as factors that fall under the "all other things being equal" clause of scientific analysis. The reason for this position is the endeavor to consider the social or economic structure of a country as a functioning system possessing regularities that can be discovered by sys-

[55] *Ibid.*, p. 39.

[56] This approach fits in with Schumpeter's theory of imperialism. See Joseph Schumpeter, *Imperialism and Social Classes* (New York: Augustus M. Kelley Inc., 1951), *passim*.

tematic inquiry. This position is supported by the judgment that even in the absence of conquest and foreign occupation, German and Japanese industrialization *would have* dispelled the "feudal legacies" of these countries eventually.[57] However, for present purposes, it is sufficient that drastic changes *were* brought about by the German and Japanese military defeat. In the absence of these events each country's symbiosis of tradition and industrialization would have been *more* enduring than it has been in fact, an inference which is quite compatible with the possibility of a further decline of tradition in the still longer run. The point is that countries which come late to the process of development possess social structures which must be understood in their own terms rather than merely as "transitional stages" to the type of industrialized society exemplified by the English or, better still, the American case.

[57] As Otto Hintze pointed out two generations ago, these considerations do not justify the elimination of state-power as a major factor in the comparative study of social structures. See Otto Hintze, "Staatenbildung und Verfassungsentwicklung," in *Staat und Verfessung*, pp. 34–51. The essay was published originally in 1902.

7

PUBLIC AUTHORITY IN A DEVELOPING POLITICAL COMMUNITY: THE CASE OF INDIA

The following case study examines "community development" as an effort to organize mass support for the program of modernizing India. Attention will be focused on the lowest rungs in a hierarchy of authority which tries to reach from the center down to the local community. The quality of public response, compliance with laws or administrative directives, and the willingness of the people to collaborate in undertakings that will help them and aid the national effort—these are most apparent at the local level.

We know from the history of the Soviet Union that after more than 40 years her leaders continue to encounter resistance at this local level, especially in agriculture. Even when it is not a question of resistance, it has remained necessary to supplement directives from above by intermittent campaigns of mass agitation from below. These are organized by the totalitarian party and synchronized with regular directives and tests of performance in order to remove bureaucratic bottlenecks and reduce to a minimum all attempts to maximize personal advantage at the expense of official plan-goals. The degree to which mass support or participation is forthcoming depends partly on the prior existence of a political community and partly on the consensus or dissension which emerges along with the efforts to develop the country.

The sacrifice of large numbers of human lives in Russia since 1917 and the effective isolation of the country have been steps taken toward ensuring mass compliance in the industrialization of the country. Although the combat conditions of this drive were simulated in part because the tradition of a political community was lacking, it is possible that material success has gradually established more consensus than existed before.

In India, a concerted effort has been made since 1947 to utilize the heritage of British political institutions in order to achieve comparable results by democratic means. This effort involves a policy of rapid industrialization and of community development which aims to advance the social and economic level of the bulk of the Indian population in the rural areas. Examination of the latter policy furnishes clues to the development of a political community in India. To understand these clues, it is necessary to take a broad inventory of the historical-structural context in which that community is taking shape in the second decade of its independence. With this long-run view, comparisons and contrasts with the Western European experience provide a vantage point for the following analysis of Indian policies of development, particularly at the local community level.

GOVERNMENT AND LOCAL COMMUNITY: THE HISTORICAL BACKGROUND

In India, historical and institutional legacies militate against the economic and political mobilization of people in the countryside. For centuries prior to the modern period, if not indeed throughout her history, Indian society has been divided between centers of secular political rule and more or less autonomous, rural settlements inhabited by the vast mass of the population. In his survey of political life and thought in ancient India, A. L. Basham gives a picture of kingship which accords well with the ideas and practices of patrimonial rule, or government conceived as an extension of the royal household. Like a patriarch ruling over his private domain, the king rules over his country with the aid of personal servants, retainers, and dependent rulers. Patrimonial ideology typically vacillates; it asserts the august status and omnipotence of the king but also his great duties as the protector and benefactor of his people. The king is admonished to adhere to sacred tradition, yet custom supports the image of a ruler whose will is supreme. Under conditions of primitive transport patrimonial rule entails frequent moves of the royal household, partly to ensure the king's control over his realm and partly to maintain his large retinue from the revenue in kind which is collected and consumed on the spot. Territorial extension of such rule increases the resources of the king and supports the myth of his power, but also jeopardizes his control over vassal kings, provincial governors, and other subordinate local rulers. Tendencies toward independence from the king and territorial aggrandizements at his expense increase with distance, rivalries at court, disputes over succession, encroachment of rival kingdoms, and so forth. Basham points out that in India the relations between overlord and vassal were not regularly based on contract, and that after the end of the Mauryan Dynasty (183 B.C.) "it became usual for kings to pay their officers and favourites not with cash, but with the right to collect revenue from a village or a group of villages."[1] These relations of the king and his dependent rulers gave rise to personal struggles for power that did not involve conceptions of time-honored rights—a feature of major significance as we shall see later.

Contact between the king's officials (or officials of dependent rulers) and the villages was characterized by a more or less explicit recognition of "separate jurisdictions." No doubt, this term is too legalistic; nor is the general injunction that

[1] See A. L. Basham, *The Wonder That Was India* (New York: Grove Press, 1954), pp. 94–96. See also pp. 81–93 for Basham's discussion of kingship and the royal function. The same problems are surveyed in Charles Drekmeier, *Kingship and Community in Early India* (Stanford: Stanford University Press, 1962), Chaps. 14–15. At the ideological level, the parallels between kingship in India and Western Europe are emphasized in Louis Dumont, "The Conception of Kingship in Ancient India," *Contributions to Indian Sociology,* VI (December, 1962), pp. 48–77. See the earlier discussion of patrimonialism on pp. 39–44.

the king must respect and protect the age-old, divinely ordained customs of the people different from patrimonial ideology elsewhere. But the ancient sources suggest, according to Basham, that the village headman, the last link in the chain of governmental control, could be the champion of the villagers as much as he was the king's agent. To be sure, the headman was formally charged with the duty of tax collection and in many areas he occupied a hereditary position according him special privileges. When such privilege went together with wealth, the village headman easily became a local tyrant. But for all his official status, the headman was also a permanent resident of the village, probably belonged to one of the most prominent families, and was thus dependent in his social position as well as for the collection of taxes upon establishing some effective relation with the villagers. Moreover, he was under immediate and constant pressure from prominent fellow villagers if a village council existed. Such councils on which the other prosperous landowners were represented, were "independent of the government and continued to function, whatever dynasty was ruling the district." Given the fact that the control by royal officials was often intermittent, depending as it did on periodic visitations, it is not surprising that the headman could be seen "as the mother and father of the village, protecting it from robbers, from the king's enemies and from oppressions of the king's officers."[2]

[2] Basham, *op. cit.*, pp. 105–106. Note also the critical comments in Hugh Tinker, "The Village in the Framework of Development," in Ralph Braibanti and Joseph Spengler, eds., *Administration and Economic Development in India* (Durham: Duke University Press, 1963), pp. 95–100. Conditions, no doubt, varied considerably in space and time and the scarcity and vagueness of most records on local government must be kept in mind. Village councils seem to have been more prominent in the South than in the North, but the accident of a detailed record for one community in the Cola kingdom may also be misleading. A quite elaborate secret service was an important feature of the Maurya Dynasty and other empires, but it seems more probable that these agents supervised the people in the towns rather than controlled village headmen directly. On balance, the evidence would seem to point to a considerable identification of the headman with his village. A modern instance of such

Ancient Indian theories of kingship seem to have accepted the communal allegiance of the headman. In practice, the king's authority did not extend to the internal affairs of the village or its constituent units—the caste communities—unless taxes were in arrears, civil order was jeopardized, or the villagers appealed to the king directly. It is difficult not to apply the term "separate jurisdictions" where Indian villages enjoyed *de facto* autonomy in the conduct of their affairs.[3] From a

identification and a telling characterization of the "ambassadorial role" of the headman is described in John T. Hitchcock, "Leadership in a North Indian Village," in Richard Park and Irene Tinker, eds., *Leadership and Political Institutions in India* (Princeton: Princeton University Press, 1959), pp. 395–414. Note also the similar analysis of the village-headman as the "personality in whom the domestic kinship and the political systems intersect," in Max Gluckman, *Order and Rebellion in Tribal Africa* (London: Cohen & West, 1963), p. 151, and *passim*.

[3] The ancient sources are so allusive that no firm statement is warranted. For example, a standard text refers to the fact that villages had to be self-reliant in defense in view of unsettled conditions and that the organization of defense was the foremost duty of the headman. On another page of the same chapter it is stated that the jurisdiction of the village council in civil cases was complete. Yet the same writer strongly rejects the theory of some early writers (Henry Maine among others) that the village councils owed their judicial powers to the prevailing anarchy. Smriti texts refer to the enforcement of local decisions by the State which has "duly invested them [the councils] with judicial powers." And the author cites several instances in which kings refuse to entertain a legal suit brought before them, referring them to the proper village council instead. With this "evidence" the character of village-jurisdiction is surely an open question, while circumstantial considerations favor the view that in many instances the villages were autonomous in fact with the delegation of jurisdiction to them a legal "gloss" reflecting royal pretensions more often than actual surveillance of local jurisdiction. The distinction may have made little difference, since the theory of kingship unequivocally endorsed the view that the king was duty-bound to maintain local custom, i.e., prevailing caste practices. My wording in the text should be read as a short-hand expression of these considerations. The statements referred to are found in A. S. Altekar, *State and Government in Ancient India* (Delhi: Motilal Banarsidass Publications, 1958), pp. 226–227, 237. From the viewpoint of the legal historian, the "separate jurisdiction" of the village panchayat is emphasized clearly. See U. S. Sarkar, *Epochs in Hindu Legal His-*

comparative viewpoint it is significant that on the lowest rung of the hierarchy of authority the village headman was prompted by circumstances and prevailing ideology to mediate between the village to which he belonged and the authorities whom he had to obey.

The theory which admonished secular rulers not to intervene in the internal affairs of the village also reflects countervailing forces and circumstances which require comment. One of these forces arose from the repeated invasions of the Indian subcontinent. The resulting decimation of the warrior class probably contributed to the long-run weakness of secular rule in India.[4] If villages had to rely on the organization of self-defense under their headmen, they did so presumably because secular rulers were not strong enough to provide protection. These circumstances had other ramifications. Invaders were aliens who preferred to reside in the towns rather than the countryside, at least as long as they remained unassimilated by Hindu society, and sometimes even thereafter. This meant farming out the task of government and a distrust of those to whom central authority had been delegated, which in turn curtailed the growth of a hereditary, land-holding aristocracy.

The same factors which weakened the native warriors (Kshatriya) strengthened the Brahmin caste of house priests.[5]

---

tory (Hoshiapur: Vishveshbaranand Vedic Research Institute, 1958), Chap. 11.

[4] See Marc Bloch, *Feudal Society* (Chicago: University of Chicago Press, 1961), p. 56, for his emphasis upon the eventual immunity from invasion in both Western Europe and Japan. Internal strife was presumably as intense in Japan and Europe as in India. But outside India such strife appears to have been compatible with an effective domination at the local level, perhaps because the invasions had ceased.

[5] In his *The Religion of India* (Glencoe: The Free Press, 1958), esp. pp. 125, 138, Max Weber makes the point that the Moslem conquest of Northern India greatly strengthened the position of the Brahmins, and hence the rigidities of the caste system, because the invaders defeated the princes and warriors who were capable of opposing or curbing the claims of the Brahmins. At the same time, it is necessary to discount the impression of Brahmin dominance on the basis of their priestly position alone. As elsewhere, domi-

Brahmins were the house priests of all royal and noble families, the teachers of all Brahmin boys, the priests at the ceremonies of all twice-born castes, and hence influential at the apex of Indian society as well as in every village. This dispersion through the social structure could be a source of strength under unsettled conditions. Defeats at the hands of self-assertive, secular rulers could be neutralized by the Brahmins' continued control over ritual observances at other (especially the "lower") levels of society. Hence the Brahmin priests helped to buttress the capacity of local castes to regulate their own affairs and arbitrate disputes. Effective self-regulation at the local level enabled village leaders to forestall or circumvent the exercise of secular authority over village affairs.

Having said this much, it is necessary to guard against the idealization of these self-regulating "village republics" which is a standby of the literature on India. Some writers convey the impression that through many centuries of Indian history there was a clear-cut separation between the government and its officials on one hand, and the vast majority of the village population on the other. The following passage illustrates this point of view:

> India presents the rare and remarkable phenomenon of the State and society coexisting apart from, and in some degree of independence of each other, as distinct and separate units or entities, as independent centers of national, popular and collective life and activity. Both of them were independent organisms with distinct and well-defined structures and functions of their own and laws of growth and evolution. The limits of State interference were accordingly so defined and fixed as not to encroach upon the sphere of the activities of the social organization. A policy of non-interference was recognized as the ideal policy of the State, the functions of which were ordinarily restricted to the "irreducible minimum," viz. the protection of life and property and realization of the revenue for the proper exercise of duty. There was a well-understood delimitation of the respective boundaries of the political and

---

nance to be effective requires a material basis of wealth; "domination" by words alone must be discounted.

social organizations, both of which were cooperating agencies for the promotion of the common weal.[6]

This, I would submit, is not a plausible interpretation, even if one recognizes the general tendency of peasant populations to withdraw from contact with government officials and, perhaps, the superior ability of India's villagers to do so effectively.

Since all authority relations are bilateral, strategies of withdrawal are typically met by appropriate counterstrategies. Among these are surveys of land and resources, periodic assessment of the revenue to be paid by the cultivators, central appointment of local tax collectors, periodic checks on their conduct, as well as systematic espionage to prevent concealment.[7] The extent and intensity of such controls will depend presumably on the stability and the resources of royal government, and in pre-British India these attributes were often wanting. Where kings are too weak to collect revenue through their own officials, or too much in need of supplies and cash to rely on their own centralized, cumbersome, and expensive methods, they typically resort to tax-farming. In exchange for services rendered or payments in cash or kind, they delegate the authority of tax collection to local rulers and these, as often as not, redelegate that authority to powerful local families. For the Banaras region in eighteenth-century India, Bernard Cohn has described the resulting system as follows:

> The Raja's [local ruler's] main concern with his dominion was the assessment and collection of revenue. The āmils (tax farmers) obligated themselves to pay a stipulated amount into the Raja's treasury every month which they were to collect from a parganā. The āmil did not collect the revenue directly from the actual cultivator but rather from representatives of lineages or from one or two persons in a village who claimed

[6] R. K. Mookerji, *Local Government in Ancient India* (Oxford: Clarendon Press, 1919), pp. 3–4.

[7] For a description of these and other methods see W. H. Moreland, *The Revenue Administration of the United Provinces* (Allahabad: The Pioneer Press, 1911), *passim*.

to be superior through wealth, caste or family to others in the village.[8]

In this system intervening and overlapping authorities multiplied readily, each presumably intent upon increasing its receipts from the next lower "level" and escaping controls from above as much as possible. Professor Cohn observes that it was easier for the king to destroy an intransigent Raja than it was for the king or the Raja to "completely destroy the web of allegiances of cultivators to the dominant lineage."[9] By the same token it is plausible to assume that the village people's capacity to conceal produce and reduce tax payments depended on the degree to which such a dominant lineage of tax farmers had developed its personalized domination of the local castes and their internal divisions.

For in India, the "separate jurisdiction" of the village and its relative autonomy vis-à-vis the claims of authorities outside the village are related to caste. Castes may be defined as endogamous communities of persons whose social status is indicated by their birth. Castes maintain or enhance their position by observing ritual practices, based on religious beliefs and involving ideas of pollution that serve to regulate each community's relations with castes of inferior and superior status. Such mutually exclusive communities exist in a context of ritually based status distinctions. Although common beliefs and interests may support the internal cohesion of a caste, that cohesion is based above all upon neighborhood relations in which the high social visibility of ritual practices daily reinforces the affiliation of the individual with the community of his birth.[10] Accordingly, castes can dispense with formal organization without thereby losing their capacity for collective action. Since the status of each mem-

[8] Bernard S. Cohn, "Political Systems in Eighteenth Century India: The Banaras Region," *Journal of the American Oriental Society*, Vol. 82 (July–September 1962), p. 319.

[9] *Ibid.*, pp. 317–318.

[10] The term "community" is often used to mean "caste community," a usage which seems to be common among English-speaking Indians, who refer to "my community" when they mean my caste."

ber of such a community affects and is affected by the status of all other members, castes are the guardians of their own rules, discipline the individual transgressor, expel him if need be, readmit individuals after penalties have been imposed and satisfactions exacted, and negotiate with other castes where questions of relative status can be resolved by discussion rather than force.[11]

In this context we can see the insulation of villages from governmental authority as a by-product of caste dominance. When leaders of a caste combine preponderant economic power with control over a large following due to kinship ties, educational advantages, and a sufficiently high ritual status, they need not confine themselves to a regulation of their own affairs.[12] Local dominance of this kind can become a very important means of self-regulation at the village level. Patrons of the dominant caste use their bonds with clients, kinsmen, and friends for the settlement of disputes between individuals outside their own caste, though the dominant caste may be divided into factions and hence into competing "jurisdictions." Srinivas reports that in rampura, except for untouchables, persons from all castes in the village and in the environs of the village bring their disputes for settlement to elders of the dominant caste. Many factors are responsible: local elders have intimate personal knowledge of the disputants, decisions at the local level can be cheap and swift, they will adhere to the caste customs of the disputants. Above all the local elders can combine in their decisions whatever judiciousness they are capable of with the full range of positive and negative sanctions which their preponderant position in the village automatically puts at their disposal.[13]

[11] This is a paraphrase and expansion of J. H. Hutton's characterization in his *Caste in India* (London: Oxford University Press, 1951), p. 92.

[12] For the following I am indebted to M. N. Srinivas, "The Dominant Caste in Rampura," *American Anthropologist*, LXI (February 1959), pp. 1–16 and Bernard S. Cohn, "Some Notes on Law and Change in North India," *Economic Development and Cultural Change*, VIII (October 1959), pp. 79–93.

[13] Srinivas, *op. cit.*, pp. 8–10. See Cohn, "Some Notes . . . ," pp. 85–88, for a characterization of dispute settlement in a North

Even today this pattern of village life reflects customary practices of which we have evidence from inscriptions going back to the tenth century:

> The population looked to their natural leaders to apply pressure to delinquents. Only when pressures were nearly equal would what approaches litigation in the modern sense arise, and then the representatives of the government would take part only in the last stages. The ancient principle was that unanimity was more important than "abstract" justice. Those that have and merit prestige should retain it, and the perquisites that go with it. Compromise was better than the disappointment of one party, who was equally the "child" of the authority who lent his support to the decision. The prevalent methods of adjustment, bargaining, waiting for pressures to emerge or evaporate, frequent adjournments, appeal to higher authority to evade the responsibility for recommending an unpopular course, and the other essentials of decision-taking amongst closely-knit societies consisting of interdependent castes, gave the impression to foreign observers that no law existed.[14]

Modern India's imagery of the ancient village community resembles the idealization of traditional societies that has accompanied the modernization of Western Europe. Yet the decisive dominance of a caste may mean oppression of a whole village. In that case effective autonomy in relation to controls that are external to the village may be the result of ruthless exploitation. Ordinarily, villagers will not be in a position to resist such caste dominance. Typically, they are

---

Indian village. One may see in such a local, customary jurisdiction directly dependent upon community consent some parallel to earlier European types of adjudication, especially the *Thing* of the ancient Germanic tribes in which elders would decide a dispute before an assembly that had to voice its consent before the decision was considered valid. See Max Weber, *Law in Economy and Society* (Cambridge: Harvard University Press, 1954), pp. 86 ff.

[14] J. Duncan M. Derrett, "The Administration of Hindu Law by the British," *Comparative Studies in Society and History*, IV (November 1961), pp. 15–16. See also Bernard S. Cohn, "From Indian *Status* to British *Contract*," *Journal of Economic History* (December 1961), pp. 613–628.

personally dependent on members of the dominant caste, and the latter exploit this dependence for private gain and on occasion for the enforced performance of "public works" such as road repair, maintenance of tanks and wells, relief work in case of famine, and so forth. Standard texts frequently refer to such public works as if they were decided on and implemented more or less spontaneously by all the villagers,[15] but such an idyllic community is a romantic illusion. Only the leaders of the principal caste or castes have an effective voice in these matters, and like dominant groups the world over they identify their own interests with those of the "public." Even so, exploitation may result in the construction of *public* works. They will benefit the village leaders first of all, and only incidentally the villagers at large. Nevertheless, such works will help to legitimate the very exploitation and dominance which went into their construction. In India as in Europe, coercion within was an important factor in achieving local autonomy against the encroachment of royal officials, though this same constellation had very different consequences in the two areas.

However, *decisive* dominance of the leaders of one caste over the whole village is not the only, and perhaps not the most general, condition. The possible dimensions of dominance such as ritual status, education, numerical preponderance, economic power, and others may be distributed among several castes in a village.[16] When this is true, factionalism becomes exacerbated, often within a dominant caste as much as between castes. Together with his followers and dependents each leader represents an "enclave" of solidarity which he seeks to protect and enhance *vis-à-vis* other leaders and their factions.[17] If disputes occur between persons belonging to the same faction, they may be settled internally. When disputes arise between persons belonging to different factions, the leaders may attempt a negotiated settlement. If negotiation

[15] See, for example, Altekar, *op. cit.*, pp. 239–244.
[16] Srinivas, *op. cit.*, p. 2.
[17] See K. N. Sharma, "Panchayat Leadership and Resource Groups," *Sociological Bulletin*, XII (March 1963), pp. 47–52.

and arbitration fails, protracted feuds ensue which occasionally erupt in violence. Stereotyped as this description is, it calls attention to the fact that entire caste communities within the village or individual leaders with their followers and dependents may be "self-regulating" at the expense of the village "as a whole."[18] But however divided a village may be, the groups forming within it are islands of dominance and solidarity. Even the strife between them does not necessarily create a power vacuum in which an outside authority can intervene readily. The settlement of disputes and the construction of public works will be less effective presumably than in villages where one caste is dominant, relatively united, and utilizes its powers to the full. But one should not simply equate factionalism with the cessation of dispute settlements and "public works." The gains of factional groups in these activities are distinct from mere personal aggrandizement and may have to be considered quasi-public functions in the absence of an authoritative organization of such functions for the village as a whole.[19]

Indeed, even where they belong to different factions, villagers may unite to resist intervention from the outside. For although local autonomy is strife-ridden and involves all the abuses of personalized exploitation, the alternative is to resort to higher juridical authority outside the village. To do so exposes what concerns the villagers most directly, to the formalities and vagaries of an outside power—in addition to exposing the individual villager to possible retaliation at the local level. Since from a local point of view these are mani-

[18] This phenomenon has led some scholars to question the appropriateness of the term "village" with reference to Indian conditions. But there is no reason to assume that elsewhere villages are always cohesive communities. It is not really the term "village" but the nature of the groups within the village which is in question. See the comments of Louis Dumont and D. Pocock in *Contributions to Indian Sociology*, I (April 1957), pp. 26–27.

[19] Even in strife-ridden villages people are preoccupied with their daily tasks, much as this is the case in any society if the time and energy devoted to disputes and daily tasks were to be compared with one another. The relevance of the "faction phenomenon" to issues of government awaits further clarification.

fest hazards, it is striking that for centuries past villagers have appealed time and again to the king for the adjudication of local disputes.[20] When disputes cannot be settled locally, this is evidence for the existence of factions, since by themselves individual "litigants" would not resist community pressure and appeal to outside authority. In this picture the village appears as a community capable of independent action where it possesses internal unity and effective leadership, and still capable of resistance to outside authority even where factionalism prevails and leadership is at a discount. It is pious fiction to contrast the unity of the ancient or medieval with the strife of the modern Indian village, though this does not rule out significant differences between then and now.

Some elements of this disjunction between the village and centers of secular rule are found wherever local communities come in contact with metropolitan government. This is an archetypical reaction, variously called provincialism, localism, traditionalism, etc., and often associated with "backwardness." Natives of a community or a region defend their way of life against all intrusions and especially against the twin dangers of taxation and conscription emanating from government. From Italy we have striking examples of this reaction, involving an ethic of brotherhood within and enmity against the world.[21] But such cases are on the fringes of the political experience characteristic of Western civilization. The reluctant, hostile, and exploitative but still willing acceptance of ties between the small community and centers of

[20] Ancient and medieval texts contain many specific injunctions which remind secular rulers to uphold the proper duties (dharma) and customary practices of each caste when they act as arbiters in caste-disputes. For a survey of such secular jurisdiction in questions of caste see Hutton, *op. cit.*, pp. 93–97. Further discussion and documentation concerning this question may be found in Sarkar, *op. cit.*, pp. 50–53 and P. V. Kane, *Hindu Customs and Modern Law* (Bombay: University of Bombay Press, 1950), pp. 38–39.

[21] See the reference to the Sicilian experience, pp. 44–45. See also Carlo Levi, *Christ Stopped at Eboli*, for a vivid eyewitness account of this anti-governmental mentality. See the related points in George A. Floris, "A Note on Dacoits in India," *Comparative Studies in Society and History*, IV (July 1962), pp. 467–472.

secular rule is the more familiar and general phenomenon.[22]

Although the hiatus between local community and government is in this sense a general occurrence, India was and is a case apart. Almost a century ago Sir Henry Maine pointed out that this difference was due to the absence in India of the rule of law in the sense in which this rule is understood in the Western tradition. Laws for us are *commands* which political *sovereigns* address to the subjects of a country. As citizens we have an *obligation* to abide by the laws of our country and are threatened by *sanctions* if we do not. Particular members of the community possess *rights* in so far as they are invested with the power to draw down sanctions on neglect or breaches of duty. Maine observed that it was impossible to apply the italicized terms to the customary law under which Indian villages had lived for centuries,[23] and his interpretation is confirmed by the more recent analyses of the British legal system and its effect in India.

The early British courts received a flood of Indian cases and this "success" was due to the immediacy and violence of the remedies the courts offered. The risks of appealing a dispute to the British courts were great, but the prizes to be gained if the case was won were also great, and many times greater than those to be obtained under the system of customary law. In introducing a system of formal jurisprudence of the Western type, the British supposed

> . . . that Indian litigants would elsewhere suffer from corruption or prejudice. It did not strike them at once that the Hindu could take advantage within the British jurisdiction of rules of law which did not exist outside it. He could not only get his decrees executed, without delay or appeal, to the great discomfiture of the opposite party, but he would be able to gain legal advantages of which the native legal system knew nothing.[24]

[22] Modern examples are furnished by Granville Hicks, *Small Town* (New York: Macmillan, 1946), and Arthur Vidich and Joseph Bensman, *Small Town in Mass Society* (Garden City: Anchor Books, Doubleday & Co., 1958), Chap. 8 and *passim*.

[23] Henry Maine, *Village Communities East and West* (London: John Nurray, 1887), pp. 67–68.

[24] Derrett, *op. cit.,* p. 18. For a telling descriptive statement con-

The differences between Western jurisprudence and customary law are made abundantly clear by this exploitation of the British courts for the "extraneous" ends of native society. The "exploitation" of court procedure for the extralegal ends of caste disputes certainly points to one of the mechanisms by which Indian caste practice could become increasingly rigid under the impact of the British rule of law.[25] Similarly, the decline of village panchayats is often considered an unintended consequence of British rule. Such repercussions would have to be balanced, however, against other consequences, such as the decline of certain caste practices. Concerning this whole subject sentiments run high, the evidence is equivocal, and no early resolution of the issues is in sight. But whatever the conclusion of this debate may be eventually, it will have to take into account that the conflict between British rule and customary law was not a by-product of British rule alone, but also reflected ancient Indian antecedents. For the customs and religious ideas sanctioning the caste-order probably militated at an early time against the development of a secular system of rights and of representation.

We may compare the headman of the Indian village, for instance, with the bailiff on a medieval manor in Europe. The latter was the direct and personally dependent agent of his lord who controlled the villagers in his lord's behalf, but who together with them was subject to the lord's jurisdiction.

---

cerning the problems of criminal procedure under these conditions see Philip Woodruff, *The Guardians* (New York: St. Martin's Press, 1954), pp. 52–53.

[25] See the extended discussion in G. S. Ghurye, *Caste, Class and Occupation* (Bombay: Popular Book Depot, 1961), Chap. VIII on "Caste and British Rule." See also the discussion by M. N. Srinivas, *Caste in Modern India and Other Essays* (Bombay: Asia Publishing House, 1962), esp. Chap. I. Since the emphasis in these writings is upon the decisive impact of British rule it is worth noting that some features of village India which have been attributed to British rule in all probability existed long before the British came to India. See D. Kumar, "Caste and Landlessness in South India," *Comparative Studies in Society and History,* IV (April 1962), pp. 337–363.

Note that the medieval village is in this case part of a larger jurisdiction; the villagers are personal subjects, they enjoy immunity from outside intervention only as a part of their lord's own immunity. They enjoy his protection at the price of being subjected to his will. Personal subservience to their protector is an important part of the local custom which the lord upholds and protects against competing jurisdictions of other lords as well as of the king. For each local lord enjoys a recognized immunity which he upholds by military action if need be, so that feuds on behalf of well-established rights are an essential part of the medieval legal order. He has obtained the privilege of the immunity he is defending in exchange for his pledge of loyalty that obliges him to render certain services to his lord in turn. In this manner the village is part of a larger jurisdiction which is often in turn part of a still larger legal order under a sovereign ruler.

We can examine the Indian situation in a similar, ideal-typical fashion, starting with the lowest rung in the hierarchy of government. We saw that the headman in India is a part of his village community and that Indian social theories tend to endorse this affiliation through their stress on the inviolability of the caste-order. (Western feudal theories with their stress on personal loyalty could hardly endorse a similar communal allegiance of the bailiff, who is the servant of his lord just like the villagers, though as the lord's agent the bailiff occupied a higher position than they.) Accordingly, the Indian villagers are subject first to the customary rules of their respective castes, which constitute a body of law that was recognized as overruling or supplementing the written law of the Smritis.[26] Secular rulers who were admonished to uphold caste custom were thus maintaining rules and practices over which they had no jurisdiction, and which did not originate, however remotely, in a contractual undertaking as did the oath of fealty and grant of immunity. Conversely, villagers are subject not to a personal lord but to the practices of their communities, sanctioned by ancient custom and belief. In this

[26] N. C. Aiyar, ed., *Mayne's Treatise on Hindu Law and Usage* (Madras: Higgenbothams, 1950), 11th ed., p. 8.

setting they enjoy immunity from outside intervention as part of a religiously sanctioned, inviolable order which in theory is upheld by all secular rulers. In practice, the villagers engage in strategies of withdrawal and evasion in order to achieve such immunity, whereas the medieval villagers had no choice but to share the vicissitudes of their lord's fortune. Dependency relationships in India are, thus, part of a rank-order sanctioned by religious belief, ritual practice, Brahmin interpretations, and the control of caste leaders. Social theory and practice reserve their worst castigations and penalties for the individual who has been "outcast," for by his transgression he threatens the status of all his caste fellows as well as the order of society. Secular rulers become involved in these questions upon appeal; and their own arbitrary elevation or downgrading of individuals contrary to the local rank-order of castes cannot by itself alter that order though over the generations it may contribute toward the increased or decreased status of a whole caste. Unlike India, dependency relationships in Europe were incorporated in a legal system in which rights and duties originated in agreements that were defended against arbitrary alteration; local lords had the right to order internal village affairs and this privileged jurisdiction was conceived as part of a "just order" which ultimately had divine sanction.

The contrast between these two structures is especially clear in the ideological sphere. For the Indian social structure the key concept is "dharma." Each caste has its appropriate duty. That man is righteous who unhesitatingly acts in accord with the duties of his caste. Warriors have the duty to excel in the manly virtues of strength and courage; fulfillment of this caste duty is their supreme obligation. In the classic Bhagavad-Gita, the warrior Arjuna is admonished to give no further thought to the fact that the ranks of his enemies are manned by relatives and friends. True to his caste, he must fight them. His life and theirs are mere way stations, while dutiful action free from the things of desire brings true happiness. In this view each way of life is justified, if properly adhered to, and each individual's caste duties in this life are a phase in an eternal recurrence. No effort is made to subordinate action to a higher, unified principle. Indeed such efforts are seen as futile or worse, conducive to man's vanity and productive of those attachments or desires from which the truly wise seek escape. The same military virtues are praised in ancient and medieval India as in medieval Europe. But in India they do not call for any further justification, since as an attribute of caste rank they are justified already, while in Europe they are subordinated to the ideas of feudal loyalty and the Christian faith.

This subordination of action to a higher principle pervades all medieval thought in Europe and bears directly upon the relation between local community and secular government. We saw that even the military feuds so characteristic of early European feudalism were fought in defense of well-established rights, and it is significant that in Europe the intellectual break with this tradition, Machiavelli's *Prince*, originated in Italy where feudal institutions developed only feebly. When, subsequently, the secular authority of rulers gained ascendancy over these competing jurisdictions of early feudalism, the idea of a rule of law was retained. The sovereign ruler was obliged to maintain peace and justice in the land, while assemblies developed in which representatives of the several estates saw to the protection of established rights and thus upheld "justice." This development helped to incorporate the local community in a countrywide political order. For the village which had hitherto enjoyed the protection of its lord and had been subject to his jurisdiction, now was bound to follow this lord when he sought to defend his rights (and thus protect "his" villagers) in the estate assembly and through it in negotiation with the king's officials. Although much idealization occurred, it is probably true that the tradition of reciprocal loyalties was strong enough to color the relations between aristocratic landowners and their dependents in this period of an emerging sovereign state. At any rate, the idea of a "representative assembly" in which all the estates of the realm were represented had caught the popular imagination. For when the absolutist regimes of Western Europe were overthrown in turn, the ensuing popular agitation took the form of demanding representation for the "fourth estate."

In Indian history there is no comparable legacy of an abstract principle of justice or of a sovereign political order in which the several estates and local communities could be integrated through a system of representation. In the absence of such legacies modern India faces difficult problems of integration, that is, of establishing orderly relationships between the constituent units of her society and the centers of governmental authority. These problems were foreshadowed in the relations between the leaders of the movement for independence and the masses of the Indian people. Here the contrast with nation-building in Western European societies is not as noteworthy as the similarity with countries which, like India, have come under the sway of Western ideas and institutions.

RESPONSES TO BACKWARDNESS AND EMERGING PROBLEMS OF REPRESENTATION

The economic and political transformations of Western Europe since the eighteenth century have affected entire social structures. Technical changes and economic growth gradually modify the traditional way of life under the leadership of innovators and entrepreneurs who are largely unconcerned with social and cultural matters. In the political sphere protracted struggles occur over the extension of citizenship, and eventually those persons formerly excluded acquire the right to participate in the public life of their country. In their double role as citizens and private individuals, people express their views on public issues and join political parties and a large variety of other associations. Middle-class leadership in the development of the economy and a gradual but pervasive economic and political mobilization of the people are accompanied, however, by a sense of alienation among certain intellectuals. Although professionals and government officials participate actively in the development of their country, special groups of writers and artists find themselves at odds with the middle-class materialism of industrial society and are repelled by the popular tastes of an expanding mass public. The trends suggested here have been characteristic in varying degrees of England, France, Germany, Italy, the Scandinavian countries, and to a lesser extent of other countries in Western Europe.

The discordant relationship between economic growth and intellectual activity is of special interest as we turn toward the countries of Eastern Europe as well as toward "new nations" such as India. There, less economic growth and less mobilization of the people than occurred in Western Europe are accompanied by very intense intellectual activity, which may be one response to a country's relative lack of economic growth. This is not a new insight. Writing on the basis of his experience during the revolution of 1848, the German folklorist and social philosopher, Wilhelm Riehl, put the matter succinctly:

> If one examines the legions of this intellectual proletariat in Germany, one can only conclude that this group . . . is in no country of Europe as numerous as it is with us. This goes to prove that the turnover of the economic capital of the nation is disproportionately small compared with this whole sale and retail trade, this haggling and speculation in spiritual goods. Germany produces more intellectual products than it can use or pay for. . . .
>
> We are confronted with a paradox. Intellectual work grows like the weeds, because economic enterprise does not provide sufficient opportunities, and these opportunities cannot, on the other hand, develop fully, because every surplus of energy is wasted in this endless foliage of books. . . . It is only during the most recent period that industry has begun to weigh the scales in favor of the middle class. The lush growth of the intellectual proletariat occurs only as long as there is no spirited development of the middle class.[27]

[27] This citation is taken from a chapter entitled "Die Proletarier der Geistesarbeit." See Wilhelm Riehl, *Die Bürgerliche Gesellschaft* (Stuttgart: J. G. Cotta'sche Buchhandlung, 1930), pp. 312–313. My translation. The book was written (together with several companion volumes) in 1847–51.

Although Riehl notes this inverse relationship between economic growth and esoteric intellectual activity, he has no use at all for the latter. Yet the intellectual agitation he decries, may mean that sensitive men seek to find a way out for their country, albeit in a disorganized, critical, and sometimes exasperating fashion.

We saw that Japan's long cultural isolation had the effect of creating a consensus on national goals so that men were divided only in their opinions on the best way of achieving these goals. On the other hand, nineteenth-century Russia exemplifies a country long exposed to ideas from abroad and this cultural contact had a divisive and alienating effect upon her intelligentsia. In a setting of great economic and political backwardness as compared with the "advanced" countries, Russian intellectuals "planned" the future development of their country and sought intimate contact with "the people" as the prospective mainspring of a national renaissance.[28] Both tendencies have recurred in countries engaged in a concerted drive to overcome their comparative backwardness. Planning the future *and* a renaissance of the country's spirit through contact with the people are seen as imperatives of national development. Yet, under these circumstances the social structure typically reveals a major cultural hiatus between the educated elite with its modern ideas and a people whose view of life is largely bound by tradition—a hiatus which hinders rather than furthers the desired development. In India, as elsewhere, a tiny, upper segment of the native population changed its outlook and way of life during the nine-

[28] See, for example, the study by Arthur P. Mandel, *Dilemmas of Progress in Tsarist Russia* (Cambridge: Harvard University Press, 1961), Chap. II, who points out (see especially pp. 66–76) that current writings on the economic problems of industrialization and particularly the thinking behind the Indian Five-Year Plans reiterate the themes of Russian "legal populism" of the late nineteenth century. Similarly, there is a parallel between the "go-to-the-people" movement in Russia and the community development movement in India and elsewhere. A comprehensive study of the first movement is contained in Franco Venturi, *Roots of Revolution* (New York: A. A. Knopf, 1960), Chap. 18.

teenth century as a result of ideas originating in the industrial and democratic revolutions of Western Europe.

> If the prime mover of the 19th century social revolution in England and some other Western countries was technology, in India, as in some other underdeveloped countries, it was education.[29]

The masses of the people remain unaffected by these ideas and adjust to, or subvert, whatever influences from abroad they cannot escape. Although the elites are separated from the masses in every complex society, the gulf between them is increased greatly when the educated few move far ahead —if only in the realm of ideas—while the masses of the people remain tied to traditional ways.[30] It is probable that in Western Europe the social distance between the elites and the masses narrowed, as both were affected by rapid industrialization and democratization, whereas that distance has increased in most of the countries that are latecomers to these processes of development.

In India, Brahmins had always been the interpreters of society, as house priests and advisors of her secular rulers. According to the ancient legal texts, Brahmins attained extraordinary legal privileges, presumably by exploiting their expert knowledge of religious ritual and by representing their own position in the caste-order in as favorable a light as possible. Emphasis on the exclusive importance of ritual status tended to overstate the unity of Indian culture as well as the Brahmin's dominance at all levels of Indian society.[31]

[29] Shanti S. Tangri, "Intellectuals and Society in 19th Century India," *Comparative Studies in Society and History*, III (July 1961), p. 368.

[30] The ramifications of this "gulf" between modernity and tradition are analyzed in E. A. Shils, "Political Developments in the New States," *Comparative Studies in Society and History*, II (1960), pp. 265–292, 379–411.

[31] Examples of the Brahmin's legal position are given in Sarkar, *op. cit.*, esp. pp. 78–79 and the references listed under "Criminal Law" in the index. The significance of the literary upgrading of Brahmin dominance in contrast to the actual diversity of criteria of dominance has been emphasized by André Beteille, *The Domi-*

Under British rule this interpretive or ideological activity of Brahmin literati probably acquired greater currency than had been possible before. No previous Indian rule had possessed a sovereignty over the whole of India or a legal and administrative system comparable to that of the British. Moreover, the British introduced a Western system of higher education and provided educated Indians with occupational opportunities in several branches of their government, albeit in subordinate positions. As the caste traditionally preoccupied with learning, Brahmins were the first to take advantage of these opportunities.

Brahmins acted as informants for British administrators and judges who sought to obtain systematic evidence on native customs and ancient Hindu law. The British wished to preserve customary practices where these did not interfere with their political and commercial interests or their own sense of morality. Whereas the ancient legal texts as well as the pandits who interpreted them were often in conflict, the exigencies of colonial administration made it necessary to resolve these conflicts. The resulting legal and administrative decisions militated against the flexibility inherent in customary law. As one British writer on Hindu law put it, the essential policy was that law should be certain, no matter which rule was chosen. And although the legal texts themselves left room for the discretion of the judge even with regard to the rule he chose to apply, the European judges were not equipped to exercise such discretion.[32] Thus, it is probable that Brahmin interpretations of Hindu society, through the medium of British rule, had a greater impact than had been the case earlier. In addition, Brahmin leaders with a Western education were concentrated in urban areas, where they could interpret Hindu society and propose reforms at a considerable distance from the very diverse local practices in the country as a whole.

---

nant *Caste in Indian Society* (unpublished manuscript, Department of Sociology, University of Delhi). I am indebted to Professor M. N. Srinivas for the opportunity to examine this valuable study.

[32] See Derrett, *op. cit.*, p. 32 n. 83 and p. 33 n. 89 for the source of these statements as well as Derrett's incisive characterization on pp. 32–34 of the over-all rigidities which resulted.

Something resembling a representative principle was introduced inadvertently when the Brahmin elite was given privileged access to educational and occupational opportunities
and allowed participation, however indirectly, in legal and
administrative decision-making. Thoughtful observers were
aware, even in the early nineteenth century, that this policy
would have far-reaching consequences. In a letter written in
September 1823 to a friend in England, Mountstuart Elphinstone commented:

> We are educating the natives from the same feeling but not
> with the same enthusiasm as you describe at home. Here it
> is even a more important and more hazardous experiment than
> in Europe, but it is I think our very first duty and it will be
> better for us to lose the country by the effects of our liberality
> than to keep it like Dutchmen or Spaniards, not that I think
> the immediate danger of our losing the country increased by
> education, on the contrary, the immediate danger is much
> diminished. But there can be no doubt that when the natives
> get more extended notions they will expect first a share of their
> own Government and then the whole.[33]

Elphinstone's analogy with the situation in Europe is revealing, if inept. In Europe the extension of educational facilities
to the "lower classes" involved the disenfranchised masses who
would aspire "above their station" and demand a voice
in government once they were educated, though education
might also prepare them for active citizenship. But although
in Europe elementary education was being made available to
the illiterate and uncultured, in India elementary and higher
Western education became available to the educated elite.[34]
Since British administrators and judges had to rely upon native informants and assistants, this native, Western-educated
elite acquired preponderant (if tacit or indirect) influence
upon the ideas and practices of British rule long before Indians were accepted in significant numbers in legal, administrative, advisory, or quasi-legislative positions. We have to

[33] Quoted in Kenneth Ballhatchet, *Social Policy and Social
Change in Western India* (London, Oriental Series Vol. 5; London: Oxford University Press, 1957), p. 250.
[34] See Tangri, *op. cit.*, p. 369, and *passim*.

keep firmly in mind that the leaders of modern India who formulated her constitution and have been at the helm of affairs since independence are Western-educated Indians who "represent" the masses of Indians today in ways that were foreshadowed by their nineteenth-century forebears of the Indian Renaissance who "represented" these masses at that earlier time.

The term "representation" has many connotations, as we have seen. In nineteenth-century European societies it referred to identifiable notables who were distinguished among the people by their wealth and social standing and also by their considered opinions on public affairs, or so it was supposed. These notables naturally reflected the groups and associations with which they were personally affiliated. But they also "represented" the public at large, as they saw it. However partial, their opinions were attempts to identify and articulate the "public interest." The degree to which political leaders fell short of this ideal is less important than the assumption that they sought to approximate it. As Walter Bagehot pointed out, the electors were deferential enough to believe that those who were superior to them in rank and wealth were "superior also in the more intangible qualities of sense and knowledge."[35]

Subsequent reflections turned primarily on the question of what would happen when under an extended franchise the vote of every ordinary, uneducated man would be solicited by well-appointed spokesmen of the opposing parties. Those who feared this prospect often failed to recognize that the people who were now enfranchised, shared a good many opinions with their "betters." In nineteenth-century Europe the consensus of an earlier day sometimes helped to make the few and the many parts of the same nation, however divided they were by rank, wealth, and education.[36] It is true that

[35] See Walter Bagehot, *The English Constitution* (World's Classics; London: Oxford University Press, 1958), pp. 263–264.

[36] Contrast in this respect Bagehot's argument, *op. cit.*, p. 271 and *passim* where the fear of the ordinary man is expressed unequivocally, with Max Weber's astringent observations on the incorrigible probity of German social democrats despite their radical

consensus varied from country to country and that in some instances it was greatly weakened. But as the earlier discussion suggested, lower-class agitation in Western Europe emerged from a mobilization of people previously excluded from participation in public life in a setting basically favorable to the development of representative institutions. Hence, it is plausible to assume that such agitation was directed at obtaining representation in the "going establishment," equal rights before its tribunals, and equal access to its facilities, until such efforts failed too often and agitation became more radical.

The problem of "representation" in India was fundamentally different. During the nineteenth century Western education became more directly important than rank or wealth in determining entry to the Indian elite wherever the latter was defined in relation to British law and administration. Even the leaders of radical opposition to British rule, spokesmen for a militant Hinduism who stood for a revival of Indian traditions, were Western-educated Indians. Hence the educated elite rather than India's men of affairs or her traditional community leaders was in the forefront of the movement for independence.[37] The ability of this socially distinct

---

language. See Max Weber, *Gesammelte Politische Schriften* (Tübingen: J. C. B. Mohr, 1958), page references under "Sozialdemokratie" in the index.

[37] This contrasts with Western Europe where an intelligentsia that emerged with industry and democracy commented critically on both while being only equivocally involved with either. See Schumpeter's comment in *Capitalism, Socialism, and Democracy* (New York: Harper and Brothers, 1950), p. 147 who emphasizes "the absence of direct responsibility for practical affairs" as the distinguishing characteristic of intellectuals, but without noting also that this characteristic is itself a by-product of the industrial order in Europe. Western European intellectuals have been preoccupied ever since the eighteenth century with the cultural repercussions of industrialization and democracy, and in this sense they have shown a considerable sense of responsibility. See the analysis of this preoccupation in Leo Lowenthal and Marjorie Fiske, "The Debate over Art and Popular Culture in 18th Century England," in Mirra Komarovsky, ed., *Common Frontiers of the Social Sciences* (Glencoe: The Free Press, 1957), pp. 33–112. But this concern involves the values of "high culture" and is in part responsible for

elite to speak for an inchoate public opinion or to represent the long-run interests of the Indian people is speculative. However, for an understanding of the relation between the governmental elite and the people since independence, it is important to arrive at tentative judgments concerning the "representative" role of the leaders of the movement for independence.

Articulate opposition to the oppressive regime of the foreigner made educated Indians representative in the literal sense of reflecting popular sentiment. The British regime disrupted Indian society (more probably than earlier types of secular rule), because the legal and administrative devices of the British introduced unfamiliar and impersonal rigidities even in the effort to uphold native customs. We can assume that most Indians resented this intrusion, perhaps especially because unlike earlier foreign rulers the British could not be assimilated into Hindu society.

All Indian leaders of the opposition to British rule were Western-educated themselves, most of them recruited from the highest Brahmin castes. These facts probably imparted an element of ambiguity to the leadership of the movement. Traditionally, education is a mark of high status in Indian society, and some of the respect for education probably remained even when the Brahmins' traditional learning was replaced by Western education. However, Western-educated Indians also aspired to positions under British tutelage and considered Indian problems from the vantage point of Western thought, especially the liberalism of mid-nineteenth-century England. Moreover, adaptation to Western speech, dress, and manners presumably placed them at a greater distance from their own society than their preoccupation with Western ideas as such.[38] We can assume that these "Western-

---

the fact that European intellectuals are ill-suited to "represent" interest groups or the "public interest" in the more ordinary sense of these words.

[38] For a general review of this social distance in its several dimensions see B. T. McCully, *English Education and the Origins of Indian Nationalism* (New York: Columbia University Press, 1940), Chap. IV.

izing" tendencies of the leaders tended to alienate them from the people at large. On the other hand, there was widespread respect (mixed with apprehension) with regard to the prestige, overwhelming power, and frequent efficiency of the British Raj. The Indians who were in close contact with the agents of that power may have risen in the eyes of their countrymen despite the fact that they were also held in some suspicion.[39]

But the ambiguities of their position were a source of great ambivalence to the Western-educated Indians themselves. These men experienced a lack of ease in their exposure to two civilizations in a manner similar to other intellectuals in countries that have come late to the industrial and democratic revolutions of the nineteenth century. Debates concerned the merits or disadvantages of traditional learning and Western education, of service to the colonial government in subordinate capacities, or of remaining aloof from all contact but also from all influe nce upon affairs, of the need for reform of Indian customs and institutions or the need to preserve them against the corrupting influences emanating from the West. Justice M. G. Ranade, the great Maharashtrian reformer (1842–1901), saw this issue perhaps more clearly than others when he points out that protest against the oppressor is straightforward and superficial compared with the much more difficult social reforms that are needed to prepare Indians for citizenship in a political community of their own.

[39] In commenting on India at the time of the mutiny, de Tocqueville speculated that it had been the aloofness of English officers and administrators which had triggered that revolt. But he observed also, with an eye as much to Algeria as to India, that native feeling was likely to be aroused by foreign settlers rather than by a foreign government, especially if it manages well. "Government by foreigners is opposed," he said, "only to national feelings, which are weak. The foreign settler injures, or appears to injure, in a thousand ways, private interests which are strong." One wonders whether this observation is not indeed a clue to the manifest differences between English and French colonial rule. See Alexis de Tocqueville, *Memoirs, Letters and Remains* (Boston: Ticknor & Fields, 1862), II, pp. 398–399, 401–402 for the text of these letters to Henry Reeve and Lord Hatherton.

We resent the insult given by the oppressor. We protest against the unjust judge. Here, however [in the field of social reform] we are judge and jury and prosecutor and accused ourselves, and we are sometimes consciously and more often unconsciously committed to a course of conduct, which makes tyrants and slaves of us all and, sapping the strength of our resolution, drag us down to our fall—to be the laughing stock of the whole world. Till we set these matters right, it is almost hopeless to expect that we can have that manliness of character, that sense of our rights and responsibilities without which political and municipal freedom is hard to achieve and impossible to preserve.[40]

But Ranade emphasizes that the social reformer is forced to live a "twofold life" in the midst of two civilizations, two forms of faith, and two ideals of life conduct. This conflict does not exist for those who live entirely in the past or entirely in their dreams for the future. The task is to maintain a balance between these conflicting imperatives.

If to resolve were the same thing as to act, life would have no difficulties and no discipline. You are not strictly correct when you think that men like Telang paused and halted for want of earnestness or from fear of offending people. Those who live in the past secure popularity. Those who bury their past obtain neither ease nor popularity by the very fact that they can neither hold by the past nor forget it altogether.[41]

Inevitably, this ambivalence gave rise to sharp ideological disagreements.[42] But this agitation consisted of newspaper

[40] M. G. Ranade, *Miscellaneous Writings* (Bombay: Manoranjan Press, 1915), p. 124. I owe this and the following reference to Mr. D. K. Bedekar who cites them in his instructive essay "Must Social Reform Precede Political Reform?", in Poona University Teachers' Social Sciences Seminar, *Thought Currents in Maharashtra, 1850–1920* (mimeographed, Poona, 1962), pp. 103–114.

[41] G. A. Mankar, *The Late Mr. Justice Ranade* (Bombay: 1902), pp. 109–110 cited in Bedekar, *op. cit.*, pp. 108–109. K. T. Telang (1850–1893) was another Maharashtrian reformer.

[42] A highly informative study of these disagreements is contained in Stanley A. Wolpert, *Tilak and Gokhale: Revolution and Reform in the Making of Modern India* (Berkeley: University of California Press, 1962). These two leaders stood for the "nativist" and the "assimilationist" program of political action. The parallel

editorials, discussion meetings, public speeches in the big urban areas, petitions, and other activities which primarily concerned executive officials of the government and a small number of oppositionists recruited from the Western-educated Indian elite. It was agitation of this kind, rather than the later, popular opposition to British rule, which would eventually have to provide the basis for the political community of an independent India. The heated arguments within the movement for independence were in effect a rehearsal of the grounds upon which future governments of an independent India would claim to rest their legitimacy. It is for this reason that I touch on these debates in so far as they concern the relationship between the educated minority of Indian leaders and the masses of the Indian people whom they sought to "represent."

As elsewhere during the nineteenth century social reform and political emancipation were debated by an urban intelligentsia at some remove from the people and their everyday experience. In India the Western-educated elite was heir to a tradition which had created an idealized theory of Indian society. Such cultural dominance by one social group for so long a period of time had probably led to a widespread acceptance of the codes and ideals of behavior which marked the ranks at the top of the caste hierarchy. For example, such practices as child marriage, suttee, and the enforced celibacy of widows were prevalent in the main among the high castes, while in the villages and among the castes below the highest rank just these practices were either absent or more or less infrequent.[43] As long as these practices were part of a cultural ideal, they were valid for all. Even those castes which in practice accepted widow remarriage and the marriage of chil-

---

with the controversies in nineteenth-century Russia between Slavophiles and Westernizers is obvious and striking. For a broader interpretation of Congress leadership over time see the analysis by Robert I. Crane, "The Leadership of the Congress Party," in Park and Tinker, *Leadership and Political Institutions in India*, pp. 169–187.

[43] I am indebted for this information to the unpublished study of André Beteille, *The Dominant Caste in Indian Society*, cited previously.

dren after puberty or later, would endorse the contrary practices as ideal. By so doing they would accept their own lower status into the bargain or seek to raise that status by emulating the practices of the higher castes; and such emulation would confirm the validity of the rank-order itself. But once spokesmen of the highest castes began to excoriate what their predecessors had idealized, a cultural rift appeared between the elite of Western-educated Indians and the castes below them who continued to achieve mobility in terms of the old practices. Inadvertently, during the nineteenth century, a cultural differentiation between town and village was being added to the physical and political insulation between government and village, discussed previously.[44] This differentiation also intensified the division between modernity and tradition within the Western-educated elite itself.

This background helps to explain the dramatic and revitalizing influence of Mahatma Gandhi. Through his way of

[44] The emulation of higher-caste practices by lower castes has been called "sanskritization" by M. N. Srinivas. For the original exposition of this much discussed process see Srinivas, *Caste in Modern India*, Chap. II. See also Harold A. Gould, "Sanskritization and Westernization," *Economic Weekly* (June 1961), pp. 945–950 who suggests that Westernization is as much a means of mobility for Brahmins as Sanskritization is for non-Brahmins. It should be remembered, however, that in the course of time social mobility changes in its terms of reference. If it be true that during the nineteenth century (and earlier) non-Brahmin castes strove to raise their status through Sanskritization, this resulted in part from the fact that they could not aspire to Westernization since they had no chance to be considered for positions under the control of the British. It may be, however, that since Independence the terms of reference have changed once more. If an untouchable succeeds in escaping from his low position in his village by appointment to an administrative position reserved for members of his caste, he is likely to have acquired at least a modicum of "Westernization." On the other hand, Brahmins who turn (or return?) to local politics are likely to adhere to traditional practices, in part because they have remained traditionalists and in part because at the local level traditionalism has political appeal. Under the circumstances it would not be surprising to find instances of "Re-Sanskritization" and "Re-Westernization" as the mobility of individuals increases while the contrast between Indian tradition and modernity remains great.

life and the specific reforms he advocated, Gandhi could mitigate the ideological cross-currents of the urbanized elite. Indeed, he reflected every current of Indian sentiment and thought, but by not yielding to any he possessed a vantage point from which to appeal to all. Western-educated Indian reformers were attracted by his determined advocacy of social reforms such as his attack on untouchability, his advocacy of women's education, his opposition to child marriage, his use of conciliatory measures as far as possible in the opposition to British rule—even his arguments for cleanliness and energy in personal conduct. Yet in important respects Gandhi was a convinced conservative who could appeal to the upholders of Indian traditionalism just to the extent that he would disappoint his "Westernizing" followers. His program for solving India's poverty was inspired by opposition to modern technology and Western civilization. Personally reluctant even to use the railroad or modern medicine, he advised his countrymen to adopt foreign ways only after the most searching scrutiny. He advocated the cultivation of handloom weaving as a means of boycotting foreign goods and of revitalizing the village economy. He was a determined advocate of Hindustani as the national medium to be taught as a required second language in all schools together with the respective regional languages; English would remain only as the language of diplomacy and foreign trade. Gandhi opposed intermarriage and commensality between the castes. He favored cow protection, though not without advocating model dairies. If in these respects he pleased the traditionalists, it was not presumably without disquieting them. For Gandhi's traditionalism was never merely that: he insisted upon examining the classic traditions from a moral standpoint, yet felt free to reject customary practices he considered morally repugnant, such as untouchability. It could hardly have appealed to Indian conservatives when Gandhi personally rejected the sacred thread, the emblem of the twice-born castes, on the ground that it constituted an unwarranted symbol of superiority and hence should be discarded.[45] By

[45] Mahatma Gandhi, *An Autobiography, The Story of My Experiments with Truth* (Boston: Beacon Press, 1957), p. 393.

thus endorsing and opposing some tenets from each of the camps Gandhi appealed to the Indian elite despite the controversies dividing it.

But the secret of his ability to bridge the gulf between an urbanized elite of reformers and the mass of the people in village India lies elsewhere. Gandhi was an "exemplary leader" who inspired his disciples with a sense of his mission while the masses of the people attributed to him the possession of charismatic powers.[46] In his *Autobiography* he states that his "life is based on disciplinary resolutions."[47] By means of self-discipline Gandhi set examples, symbolizing a line of action which others could follow. The masses, however, looked upon Gandhi in the tradition of the self-denying holy man to whom they attributed extraordinary powers, and whose appearances they greeted as if these were epiphanies of a deity. He opposed such idolatry, deplored the cruelty of the love which the people manifested toward him, and suffered from the great responsibility and power which the peoples' belief in him engendered. But he utilized that power to advance his causes. Gandhi never escaped the dilemma that his power was derived from mass beliefs which he considered false, a mindless adulation which made him feel ill in the literal sense of the word.[48] He would seek to meet his responsibility, especially for the violence and abuses which he could not prevent, by further acts of self-denial. But objectively considered these acts only enhanced his power, since the people considered them evidence of holiness, de-

[46] This formulation seeks to take account of Gandhi's distinguishing characteristics, rather than merely apply the term "charismatic leadership" which would not do justice to the complexities of Gandhi's political role. The phrase "exemplary leader" is modeled after Max Weber's "exemplary prophecy" since the appeal through exemplary conduct is the same in both; but Gandhi steadfastly denied that he was a prophet, even though the people treated him as if he was. So far as I know the conceptually most differentiated study of Gandhi is that of W. E. Mühlmann, *Mahatma Gandhi, Eine Untersuchung zur Religionssoziologie und Politischen Ethik* (Tübingen: J. C. B. Mohr, 1950).

[47] Gandhi, *op. cit.*, p. 390.

[48] See Mühlmann, *op. cit.*, pp. 267–268.

spite Gandhi's denials. Conceived in humility and following the ascetic traditions of Indian culture, fasting and the possibility of self-immolation were transformed by the mass-media and the political context into a form of blackmail to bludgeon opponents and keep followers in line.

It is necessary to say this in order to understand the uniquely personal way in which Gandhi appealed to the elite *and* the masses. His combination of reforms which could enlist modernists and traditionalists under his banner, was too esoteric a creation to provide an enduring basis for compromise among these warring factions of the independence movement. But Gandhi's personal humility and sweet reasonableness had their effect even on those who disagreed and his unrivaled ability to stir the imagination of the people side-tracked controversies, if it did not terminate them. He left no doubt that he considered the indifference of the educated few responsible for the bad habits and ignorance of the people, that through Western education these few had isolated themselves from the masses, and that he was better equipped than any other educated Indian to understand the motives of the people and rally them to the cause of reform and independence.[49] Although his success in this respect is unquestioned, Gandhi tended to confine himself in the political realm to the paramount task of achieving India's independence. He did not or would not bring his great gift of leadership to bear upon the task of constructing a political framework and thus provide an enduring basis for the link between the centers of rule and the countryside which he had built by the force of his personality in the fields of social action and reform. Perhaps his talent in the latter fields was so great precisely because he could not bring himself to think in institutional rather than personal terms; in all probability he would have argued with Justice Ranade that in India social reform was the *sine qua non* of a viable political structure.[50] Perhaps

[49] Gandhi, *op. cit.*, p. 379 and Mühlmann, *op. cit.*, p. 241.

[50] These remarks are not contradicted, in my judgment, by Gandhi's reorganization of the Congress Party at the Nagpur session of 1920. While the constitution adopted at that session established a viable mass organization which reached into the villages,

those Indian leaders who emphasize political at the expense of social reforms have done so in part because they lacked Gandhi's great power as a personal leader. But whatever the reason, Gandhi's legacy to an independent India has been in the fields of social reform and rural uplift. The difficulties of transferring that legacy into the political realm are nowhere more evident than in the debates concerning village panchayats during the meetings of the Constituent Assembly.

ATTEMPTS TO DEFINE THE ROLE OF THE VILLAGE

India became independent on August 15, 1947. The Constituent Assembly first met on December 9, 1946, adopted a resolution on objectives on January 22, 1947, and appointed a number of committees to report on various aspects of the proposed constitution. The Draft Constitution, prepared by this committee, was published in February 1948, following the establishment of independence, and the Assembly began its debate of the Draft in November 1948. Following this debate further revisions were prepared, and the final version of the Constitution was debated and adopted in November 1949.

The Constitution was formulated and debated under extraordinary circumstances. Independence was won while the Constitution was under consideration, the Muslim League boycotted the Constituent Assembly, the representatives of the Princely States had still to join the nation-building effort, and Mahatma Gandhi absented himself from the Assembly and had proposed the abolition of the Congress Party. Despite the social and political turmoil the deliberations went forward in an orderly fashion and despite Gandhi's aloofness his spirit swayed the minds of those who had met to discuss the Con-

its objective was solely to win independence for India. Though the earlier organization of the Congress Party has been carried over into the postindependence period, a party-organization is not a sufficient basis or an appropriate model for the administrative structure of government.

stitution.[51] The discussion of village panchayats by the Constituent Assembly is crucial in the present context, because in it the place of the village in India's emerging political community was under consideration. Nothing reveals this more clearly than the striking contrast between two statements which set the theme of the ensuing debate.

One of these statements came from Mahatma Gandhi. In December 1947, a little more than a month before his assassination, Gandhi was told by a reporter that the Draft Constitution contained no directives about village panchayats and decentralization and he responded by declaring that this "is certainly an omission calling for immediate attention if our independence is to reflect the peoples' voice. The greater the power of the panchayats, the better for the people. . . ."[52] His own ideas concerning the role of the village in an independent India were clearly expressed in an earlier discussion with Louis Fischer, and these words were quoted at the very outset of the meetings in which the aims of the future Indian Constitution were debated.

> The Center of power now is in New Delhi, or in Calcutta and Bombay, in the big cities. I would have it distributed among the seven hundred thousand villages of India . . .
> There will then be voluntary cooperation between these seven hundred thousand units, voluntary cooperation—not cooperation induced by Nazi methods. Voluntary cooperation will produce real freedom and a new order vastly superior to the new order in Soviet Russia. . . .[53]

This double front against the coercive methods of the Nazi and the Soviet regime strongly influenced the debate that

[51] In an interview in December 1947 (published in *Harijan*), Gandhi stated that he had "not been able to follow the proceedings of the Constituent Assembly," but he expressed strong opinions, nevertheless, with regard to what the Assembly should consider.

[52] Quoted from *Harijan*, December 21, 1947.

[53] Quoted in Louis Fischer, *A Week with Gandhi* (New York: Duell, Sloan, & Pearce, 1942), p. 80. This interview took place in 1942, several years before the debates of the Constituent Assembly, but the importance of Gandhi's ideas for the members of the Assembly did not diminish during the intervening years.

followed. In addition there was Gandhi's elaboration of his meaning which was familiar to the men who had followed his leadership for decades and were now assembled to construct a political framework for the independence which the masses of the people had won under his guidance.

> There are seven hundred thousand villages in India each of which would be organized according to the will of the citizens, all of them voting. Then there would be seven hundred thousand votes and not four hundred million votes. Each village, in other words, would have one vote. The villages would elect the district administration; the district administration would elect the provincial administration and these in turn would elect the President who is the head of the executive. . . .[54]

The Constituent Assembly never considered this proposal as a viable alternative, and we can wonder how seriously it was put forward by Gandhi himself.[55] Still, the proposal reflected Gandhi's profound conviction that fundamentally India is village India and that his principles of social action and reform are of paramount importance in the task of political reconstruction.

The second statement was made by Dr. B. R. Ambedkar, the impressive leader of the untouchables, who for many decades had opposed Gandhi and many policies of the Congress Party but who had won for himself a position of national eminence nonetheless. Indeed, in August 1947 Ambedkar had been chosen as a member of the Committee charged with the responsibility of scrutinizing the Draft Constitution, and, as it turned out, a major part of this responsibility devolved upon him personally. In introducing the Committee's recom-

[54] Ibid., pp. 55–56.
[55] See Fischer's discussion in ibid., pp. 118–119 of the element of playfulness and sentiment in Gandhi's thinking on this topic. However, Gandhi's own awareness of the impracticality and anachronism of some of his ideas did little to diminish their effect upon his followers. It may even have reconciled those of his immediate disciples who themselves were more "modern" in outlook, while strongly attracting masses of the Indian people who only "heard" the traditional sentiment but missed Gandhi's own, ironic undertone.

mendations dealing with village panchayats Ambedkar refers
to criticisms of the Draft Constitution:

> . . . It is said that the new Constitution should have been
> drafted on the entire ancient Hindu model of a state and that
> instead of incorporating Western theories the new Constitu-
> tion should have been raised and built upon village panchayats
> and District panchayats.

Such criticism, according to Ambedkar, is based on the tendency of intellectual Indians to idealize the village community.
In fact, the villages have played no significant part in the
affairs of the country.

> . . . Knowing this, what pride can one feel in them? That the
> village-communities have survived through all vicissitudes may
> be a fact. But mere survival has no value. The question is on
> what plane they have survived. Surely on a low, on a selfish
> level. I am therefore surprised that those who condemn pro-
> vincialism and communalism should come forward as cham-
> pions of the village. What is the village but a sink of localism,
> a den of ignorance, narrow-mindedness and communalism? I
> am glad that the Draft Constitution has discarded the village
> and adopted the individual as its unit.[56]

In this provocative statement, Dr. Ambedkar expressed not
only his personal views but the strong feelings of the untouchables who seek emancipation from their oppressed position in the village by recourse to an external political authority. Although it did not reflect the views of the other
members of the Committee, the Ambedkar statement served
to focus the debate upon an issue of paramount importance
for the future of India. Gandhi's idealization and Ambedkar's
condemnation of the village community highlight the ancient
dilemma of India's political community—the separation be-

[56] This and the following quotations are taken from *Avard News
Letter*, IV (January–February 1962), pp. 1–27, a publication of
the Association of Voluntary Agencies for Rural Development
which has devoted this special issue to extensive reprints from the
discussion of village panchayats in the Constituent Assembly.
Comparison with the original sources indicates that the essential
materials have been faithfully reproduced.

tween central authority and the relatively autonomous village community.

The discussion following these major statements may be summarized briefly. The complaint is voiced that the Draft Constitution gives no place to the importance of local government, that "instead of being evolved from our life and reared from the bottom upwards [it] is being imported from outside and built from above downwards." The need for centralization is admitted, but only decentralization is a safeguard against totalitarianism. This initial statement by Damodar Swarup Seth was adumbrated in many ways. The ancient tradition of local government is praised and it is argued that it had been destroyed by British rule. The drafters are condemned for having followed foreign constitutional models and hence for having produced something "un-Indian" that would have no meaning for the people. It is pointed out that the Constitution is worth nothing unless it declares the peoples' basic right to food, clothing, and employment. Throughout the discussion the theme is reiterated that the village republics must be reconstituted and that the emerging Indian polity must be made meaningful to the people by ensuring their participation in the deliberative process at the local and national levels.

There were, of course, other voices. It is pointed out that the Constitution could be revised subsequently, but that even in its present formulation it allows the Provincial Assemblies to enact legislation establishing panchayats. In its recognition of fundamental rights and the other welfare provisions the Constitution in fact incorporates major Gandhian ideas. Occasionally, even Dr. Ambedkar's statement is defended in view of the poverty and ignorance, the factionalism and oppression characteristic of village life; panchayats can be introduced more safely at a later time when some of these primary evils have been removed.

From the beginning, however, most speakers seem to agree on the desirability of village panchayats. Perhaps the basic mood and issue of the discussion are reflected most accurately in this simple emotional statement:

. . . with the spread of western education in our schools and colleges we had lost contact with the villages, and it was our leader, Mahatma Gandhi, who advised the intelligentsia to go back to the villages, and that was some thirty years ago. For the last thirty years we have been going into the villages and making ourselves one with the villagers. . . .

. . . this love of ours for the villages has grown, our faith in the village republics and our rural communities has grown and we have cherished it with all our heart. It is due to Mahatma Gandhi . . . that we have come to love our village folk . . . If we do not cultivate sympathy and love and affection for our villages and rural folk I do not see how we can uplift our country.[57]

This sentiment may have been an important emotional and practical link between the urban elite and the countryside in the years preceding Indian independence. But now the men and women who had participated in the struggle for freedom, were called upon as leaders of the new nation to transform the solidarity of that struggle into an enduring institutional framework.

The very success of the earlier European development has a magnetic attraction for the elites of countries like India. As a result, some leaders of the Indian movement for independence and the governing elite of India today have a high level of aspiration for themselves, their country, and the masses of her people. As they see it, it is necessary to mobilize the people. The political community is envisaged in terms of a new consensus which demands positive action on the part of the average citizen, not mere compliance. But the hiatus between leaders and the people tends to widen at exactly the time when the people are called upon to participate actively in the building of the new nation. For the mobilization of the masses, which was powerful enough to win independence, is not enduring enough to alter the peoples' way of life. Hence, after

[57] *Ibid.* At the end of the debate Dr. Ambedkar accepted for the Committee and the Assembly adopted as one of the Directive Principles of State Policy the following resolution: "The State shall take steps to organize village panchayats and endow them with such powers and authority as may be necessary to enable them to function as units of self-government."

independence the government elite sets out to implement those massive social changes which it considers necessary for development—a task which greatly exceeds the more conventional functions of government. Yet this greater task is itself a product of the fact that so far the social and economic life of the people at large has not been transformed sufficiently from the viewpoint of Indian development policies.

INDIAN POLICIES OF DEVELOPMENT

The Constitution of India contains a most comprehensive declaration of "fundamental rights." Fully implemented, these rights would revamp Indian society. It is acknowledged, however, that legal enforcement can play only a small part in achieving that objective. Hence, the "Directive Principles of State Policy," though stating these aspirations explicitly, are not enforceable in the courts. They are guidelines which enjoin the state by solemn Constitutional mandate to proceed towards the implementation of such rights as are within reach, given the present resources of the Indian nation. In addition, the government declares its purpose to be the establishment of a socialist society and accordingly the Planning Commission plays a central role in the allocation of governmental resources from year to year.

Many-sided as the responsibilities of the Indian government are, its policies emphasize economic development.[58] The over-all setting of these policies is best revealed by comparing the distribution of the work force, the national income, and the outlays under the First and Second Five-Year Plans among the three major sectors of the economy (see Table 7.1). Some three quarters of the work force contribute about 48% of the national income, working in agriculture and allied activities. A little over one fourth of the expenditures under the first two Five-Year Plans was devoted to this sector of the economy, a proportion which is being increased under the Third Five-Year Plan to provide more food for a

[58] See I. S. Gulati, "Central Government's Capital Expenditure, 1950/51–1961/62," *Economic Weekly*, XIII (July 1961), pp. 1195–1198.

TABLE 7.1

Percentage distribution of work force, national income, and plan outlays by sectors (all India for indicated years).

Sector of the Economy	Working Force 1961	National Income 1955–1960 (Average for Period)	Plan Outlays (First and Second Five-Year Plans)
Primary			
Agriculture, animal husbandry, forestry, fishing, hunting, plantations, orchards, and allied activities	72.28	47.6	26.6
Secondary			
Manufacturing, small enterprises (incl. household industry), mining, construction, power	11.70	17.9	26.9
Tertiary			
Commerce, transportation, communication, warehousing, marketing, and other services (incl. professions, government administration, social services, etc.)	16.02	34.4	46.5

Sources: Data for working force and plan outlays are taken from Census of India, *1961 Census, Final Population Totals* (Paper No. 1 of 1962), pp. xxii, 397. National Income Data are based on S. K. Bose, *Some Aspects of Indian Economic Development* (Delhi: Ranjit Printers and Publications, 1962), I, pp. 161–162.

Note: The proportion of the work force in primary industries is a little too high since it includes workers in mining. For plan outlays I have added, those for community development and housing under *Primary* which overstates the outlays under this heading slightly, since outlays for housing are made in the nonagricultural sectors as well. On the other hand, outlays for "power" also benefit agriculture, but are here included in the *Secondary* sector; note, however, that outlays for multipurpose projects, irrigation, and flood control are included in the *Primary* sector.

rapidly increasing population. About 12% of the work force contribute about 18% of the national income, working in manufacturing, mining, construction, and power; and a little over one fourth of the Plan outlays are devoted to this sector. Again, 16% of the work force produce some 34% of the national income in the tertiary sector, but Plan outlays here come to 46.5% of the total.

These are very gross figures. To some extent they understate the proportion of public expenditures going to the primary sector, because outlays for power, transportation, and social services benefit agriculture as well. Still, public investment policy puts its heaviest emphasis on the capital-intensive sectors of the economy, since more than half of all outlays under the First and Second Five-Year Plans were made in industry, mining, power, transport, and communications.[59]

However, expenditures from public funds are only one aspect of the development program. The government necessarily counts upon private investments to aid the national effort. In this respect it is instructive to compare the fields in which public outlays greatly outweigh private investments with those in which this pattern of expenditures is reversed (see Table 7.2). The public sector has overwhelming importance in the fields considered crucial for rapid industrialization. With the total population remaining 82.2% rural even in 1961 (though not all these people are engaged in agriculture), while in 1959–60 preliminary figures put the national income derived from agriculture at 61.8 billion rupees (out of a total of 128.4 billion), it is certainly noteworthy that *public* investment in agriculture, irrigation, and village and small industries represents less than one half of total investment in these fields—amounting to about one fourth of all public investments made during the First and Second Five-Year Plans.[60]

[59] See Census of India, *1961 Census, Final Population Totals,* p. xxii. Under the Third Plan agriculture and community development are to receive 14% of the proposed outlay, while irrigation and power are to receive 22% of a greatly increased total budget of 75 billion rupees (compared with 46 billion under the Second Plan).

[60] For purposes of orientation some reference to the distribution of burdens should be added here. In 1958–59 agriculture contributed 48.6% to the national income, but only 21.8% to total tax revenue. Over the years per capita income in agriculture has fluctuated at between one third and two fifths of per capita income in the rest of the economy, while per capita tax in agriculture has been between 10 to 15% of the per capita tax level in nonagricul-

TABLE 7.2

*Public and private investment in the second plan**

Investment Area	Public	Private	Total	Per Cent
Major and medium irrigation	420	—	420	6
Power	445	40	485	7
Organized industry and minerals	870	675	1545	23
Transport and communication	1275	135	1410	21
Subtotal	3010	850	3860	57
Agriculture and community development	210	625	835	12
Village and small industries	90	175	265	4
Social services and miscellaneous	340	950	1290	19
Inventories	—	500	500	8
Subtotal	640	2250	2890	43

Source: Third Five-Year Plan, op. cit., p. 59.
* In units of 10,000,000 rupees.

Major policy decisions are reflected in these figures. The attempt is made to stimulate the industrial sector of the economy through public investments in the most capital-intensive branches of production such as railroads, steel plants, hydroelectric power projects, and others. In a poor country private capital is unable to attempt such large undertakings, which are considered indispensable to rapid industrialization. To maximize the national resources available for this over-all purpose, public policy decisions on the most desirable pattern of growth are given top priority, though in a democracy such decisions are inevitably subject to cross-pressures from many quarters. However, even a full implementation of the Plan can do no more for the time being than maintain the present level of employment. The investment policies envisaged in the Third Five-Year Plan mean that, given the antici-

---

ture. Given this low level of taxation, it has been estimated that governmental disbursements to agriculture in 1951–56 were perhaps 60% higher than the revenue flow from agriculture. For the source of these figures and a comprehensive analysis of trends in the 1950's see Ashok Mitra, "Tax Burden for Indian Agriculture," in Ralph Braibanti and Joseph J. Spengler, eds., *Administration and Economic Development in India*, pp. 289–291, 295, and *passim*.

pated increase in population, the number of people to be absorbed through increasing employment may just about equal the number of new entrants to the labor force. There is no expectation of a decrease in the 9 million unemployed and the 15–18 million underemployed which were estimated at the end of the Second Five-Year Plan.[61] Thus stark poverty will continue as the country seeks to establish and develop its basic industrial potential.

Although these policy decisions have engendered controversy, in India as well as abroad,[62] I shall concentrate in this discussion on problems of implementation. Governmental policies must be administered. Even where the government's role in the economy is to be minimal, private enterprise requires for its success the maintenance of internal peace and of the essential utilities; both are major tasks in economically underdeveloped countries. India possesses a great administrative apparatus left as a legacy of British rule. In this respect she is uniquely favored among the "developing nations" of the world. But she faces the task of maintaining and extend-

[61] See *Third Five Year Plan* (Delhi: Government of India, n.d.), p. 156 where it is estimated (on pp. 159–161) that the Plan will provide 10.5 million additional opportunities in nonagricultural employment and 3.5 million such opportunities in agriculture. Leaving aside present unemployment, this target falls short by 3 million of the total number of new entrants into the labor force during the Plan period, and special efforts are planned to create job opportunities for this additional number.

[62] Among Western economists the policies of the Second and Third Five-Year Plans have been criticized in a manner that more often than not recapitulates the old arguments over free enterprise vs. centralized planning. See in particular, P. T. Bauer, *Indian Economic Policy and Development* (London: Allen & Unwin, 1961), *passim* for a vigorous presentation of the *laissez-faire* argument. Inside India some of the same arguments are presented in the programmatic statements of the Swatantra Party. See the resolutions of the party at its Bombay and Patna sessions, reprinted in S. L. Poplai, ed., *1962 General Elections in India* (Bombay: Allied Publishers Private Ltd., 1962), pp. 374–401. On the basis of more equalitarian values they also reappear in modified form in the writings of Professor D. R. Gadgil as, for example, in his essay "An Approach to Indian Planning," *Economic Weekly*, XIII (July 1961), pp. 1127–1138.

ing that apparatus with its supposed principle of impersonal operation in a society in which the vast majority of the people retain a primary allegiance to their family and caste community. Hence, the policy of rapid industrialization through governmentally controlled, capital-intensive enterprises may reflect not only a belief in socialism, but also the reasoned conviction that the government must concentrate its major effort in fields it can control directly. The hope is that changes in the industrial sector will be massive enough to raise the peoples' standard of living and modify their way of life. Such an outcome partly depends on conditions that favor efficient administration and a willing public response. A knowledge of the conditions under which the directives of public authority are implemented will contribute to an understanding of the Indian political community.

Such knowledge is called for, it seems to me, by the paradox of the Indian planning effort. India is a country in which 72% of the work force produces 48% of the national income. The remaining 28% represents the nonagricultural work force which produces the other 52% of the national income, with the industrial sector producing 35%. The growth potential of the industrial sector appears to the government so much greater than the rural-agricultural sector that it proposes to invest under the Third Plan more than twice as much of its development expenditures in the first than the second.[63] It is true that this overemphasis is counterbalanced to a degree by the expectation of a reverse emphasis in the private sector.

[63] Disregarding expenditures for social services, the government proposes under the Third Plan to spend 41.5 billion Rs. for power, industry and mining, transport and communications, and small industry and 18.5 billion for agriculture, community development, major and medium irrigation, and village industries. In these very approximate figures, I have ignored investment in social services and have included half of the expenditures for "Village and Small Industries" in each of the sectors. It may be added that the above estimate of income derived from agriculture (expressed as an average for the years 1955–60) may be somewhat on the low side, since different estimates have placed agriculture's contribution since the 1920's between 44 and 57%. See J. P. Bhattacharjee, ed., *Studies in Indian Agricultural Economics* (Bombay: Indian Society of Agricultural Economics, 1958), p. 4.

But this does not alter the fact that in terms of the larger objectives this is a policy of delayed gratification for the vast mass of the Indian population.

This approach is analogous to the priorities of Soviet planning, albeit in the absence of the totalitarian methods used by the Russians to implement these priorities.[64] But this is not all. The constitution clearly establishes the welfare of all the people as a cardinal principle of state policy. Given its priorities, the Indian government devotes what efforts it can spare to the task of increasing agricultural productivity and of alleviating the myriad problems of poverty and ill-health which beset the country. Moreover, the government is limited by the concentration of land ownership which persists despite land reforms.

According to a study conducted by the National Sample Survey in 1953–54,

> . . . of the 66 million rural households in the country, nearly 15 million, or 22 per cent, do not own any land at all, another 25 per cent hold less than one acre each, while, at the other end, 13 per cent of the total households exercise permanent ownership rights over almost 65 per cent of the total area.[65]

Increases in agricultural productivity and most other additional facilities which are provided locally, tend to accrue to the advantage of those groups within the village which possess most of the advantages already. To this must be added that, true to its democratic principles, the government makes a very conscientious effort to reach the countryside through the universal franchise, so that gradually the rural people as a whole are mobilized politically. Yet for the time being the efforts to increase agricultural productivity remain a palliative in view of the priority of the industrial sector, the sheer magnitude of rural problems, and the fact that the gains made do not benefit the nonlanded segments of the rural popula-

[64] See Gadgil, *op. cit.*, p. 1132.

[65] See Mitra, *op. cit.*, p. 298. Since the elimination of intermediaries was largely completed by 1953–54, the author believes that this pattern of land ownership has not been altered substantially since then.

tion. The latter seek to compensate for these disadvantages by recourse to preferments and services under the control of the central government.

It is a race against time. The speed and magnitude of success in the industrial sector together with the lesser efforts in agricultural productivity and social welfare are pitted against the mounting problems of destitution, aggravated by rapid population growth. These problems are made hazardous politically by the simultaneous extension of communication facilities and democratic procedures to the vast rural population of the country, whether political controls remain in the hands of the rural elites or become available to some extent also to the nonlanded castes. For in either case it is difficult to see how economic growth can be rapid enough to satisfy the rising expectations of the rural population. Friends of India hope that the race will be won. If it is not won soon, there still remains the possibility that, despite all general declarations in favor of modernity and democracy, the political mobilization of the countryside will in fact be sufficiently slow so that the villagers despite their grinding poverty and the rural elite despite its drive for personal gain will moderate their demands until the country is in a better position to satisfy them.[66] The physical context of government in India gives ample indication, at any rate, that the mobilization of the countryside in terms of economic growth for a majority of the population is a slow and arduous process.

GOVERNMENT AND LOCAL COMMUNITY: THE ADMINISTRATIVE TASK

The Indian subcontinent covers an area of 1,261,597 square miles. In 1961, the total population numbered some 439 million people. The Census classifies all settlements of 5000 and above as towns or cities and all those containing less

[66] The point has not escaped attention, though it is not discussed prominently, since emphasis on it would conflict with the drive for rapid economic growth. See Sisiu Gupta, "Indian Democracy, What Gives it Stability," *Economic Weekly*, XII (June 1959), pp. 843–845.

than 5000 as villages.[67] In all there were 2690 cities and towns with a total population of 78.8 millions (17.3%) and 564,718 villages with a total population of 359 millions (82.7%). In 1951, the urban population had been 62 millions and the rural 295 millions, so that by 1961 the rural population alone was about as large as the total population had been a decade earlier.

In its program of development the Indian government faces the task of eliciting public cooperation. For the purpose of describing the magnitude of this task, the census of villages is insufficient, since its enumeration is based on units of revenue administration rather than inhabited settlements. If the latter are made the basis of enumeration, rural communities are found to number 840,033. Of this number 681,036 or 81% are hamlets inhabited by less than 500 people, comprising a little more than 116 millions or 41.5% of the rural (almost one third of the total) population. Another 105,495 villages (12.5%) are inhabited by between 500 and 999 people and some 72.9 millions or 26% of the rural population live in communities of that size. In other words, half of India's total and 67.5% of her rural population live in communities of 999 inhabitants or less.[68]

The All-India Educational Survey refers to "central tendencies" of urban and rural areas based on calculated averages such as dividing the total area of a state by the number of

[67] In the 1951 Census a judgment of borderline cases was made so that some habitations with less than 5000 people but definite urban characteristics were included among cities and towns while some definitely rural communities with more than 5000 people were classified as villages. These criteria have been altered somewhat in the 1961 Census, but this need not concern us.

[68] Figures refer to 1957. See Report of the *All-India Educational Survey* (Delhi: Ministry of Education, Government of India, 1960), pp. 160, 163–165. Aside from some outlying areas this survey does not cover the state of West Bengal (see *ibid.*, pp. 15–16), so that figures based on this survey always understate the case. However, the survey is a very scholarly inventory of educational facilities, and since it was undertaken with a view to assess India's position with reference to the goal of universal elementary education, it also provides a comprehensive inventory of rural and urban settlements.

towns or cities located in it or establishing the ratio between
the number of rural communities in every 100 square miles
of its territory. The density of settlement, on the fictitious
assumption of an even spread over each of the states, provides
us with an estimate of the diversity of the country which all-
India figures necessarily hide (see Table 7.3). Thus, Andhra
Pradesh has on the average one town of 5000 inhabitants or
above for every 371 square miles of its territory. All such
towns together influence the surrounding countryside to a
distance of a five-mile radius, thus encompassing 22,560
square miles or 22% of the total rural area of Andhra Pradesh. The state possesses an average of 49 rural communities
for every 100 square miles of its territory. Roughly 45% of
all its settlements have a school located in them, another 29%
are within a distance of from $\frac{1}{2}$ to $1\frac{1}{2}$ miles, and 26% of its
settlements were without access to primary schools, assuming
that small children cannot or will not walk more than 3 miles
a day. Broadly speaking, the table shows the varied degree of
urbanization in the different states, the corresponding variation of the rural areas affected by urbanization, the density
of rural settlement, and the spread of primary school facilities.

It must be borne in mind, however, that availability of
facilities is not enough. Enrollment even of primary school
children depends upon their economic dispensability and the
positive interest of parents in education. When such factors
militate against enrollment, the location of the school in another community may well discourage it. Although 71% of
all settlements in India had schools in them or near them (in
1957), only 61% of the total population aged 6 to 11 was
enrolled in 1960–61, with the averages ranging among the
states from a low of 42% to a high of 100%.[69] Under the
circumstances it is realistic to assume that in, say, half the

[69] Enrollment of boys varied between a low of 66% and a high
of 100% (with the average at 81.5%), while that of girls varied
from a low of 15% to a high of 100%, with the average at 40%.
The State of Kerala has 100% primary school enrollment for both
boys and girls, but this is an exception which tends to distort the
picture. See *First Year Book of Education* (New Delhi: National
Council of Educational Research, 1961), p. 930 for a detailed
tabulation of these figures.

TABLE 7.3

Settlements in urban and rural areas, extent of urban influence, and the distribution of educational facilities
(March 31, 1957)

State	Urban Areas			Rural Areas			
	One Town per Total Area (sq. miles)	Rural Area under Urban Influence (5-mile radius about towns)		Communities per 100 sq. miles	Per Cent of Settlements		
		in sq. miles	% of total rural area		With School	School Near	Without School
Andhra Pradesh	371	22,560	22	49	44.77	29.09	26.14
Assam	1578	2,320	2	54	43.07	29.39	27.54
Bihar	651	8,240	12	165	23.99	55.50	20.51
Bombay*	280	50,560	29	44	53.22	26.54	20.24
Jammu and Kashmir	6138	720	1.3	20	17.38	46.20	36.42
Kerala	555	2,160	15	72	53.95	31.32	14.73
Madhya Pradesh	847	16,160	9	48	25.34	30.40	44.27
Madras	169	23,600	49	107	34.65	53.64	11.71
Mysore	271	21,680	30	56	44.61	37.51	18.18
Orissa	1542	3,120	5	86	29.22	47.25	23.53
Punjab	236	15,520	34	61	40.28	43.95	15.77
Rajasthan	581	18,160	14	36	19.08	32.28	48.64
Uttar Pradesh	238	38,160	34	210	11.11	54.89	34.00
Delhi	53	880	100	59	65.74	22.15	12.11
Himachal Pradesh	960	960	8	111	7.86	54.71	37.43
Manipur	8622	80	1	22	34.82	25.12	40.06
Tripura	4116	80	2	126	17.25	52.82	29.93

Source: All-India Educational Survey, pp. 176, 177, 266.
* The 1951 Census gave figures for the state of Bombay which was separated in 1960 into the two states of Maharashtra and Gujarat.

communities with a school nearby, the children of primary school age are either not enrolled or do not attend.

These data on the isolation of India's villages can be supplemented by a nationwide survey which gives a more differentiated picture. A representative sample of villages was ranked by their relative distance from various modern facilities and centers of communication (see Table 7.4). The results from two surveys agree closely. Figures for villages up to 200 and 500 inhabitants have been added from the eleventh sample survey, in order to facilitate comparison between the over-all results and those for the smallest and presumably most isolated communities. According to the 1951 Census more than a third of India's total (and 41.5% of her rural) population lived in these smallest settlements, and figures from the 1961 Census are not likely to alter this picture significantly. Clearly, all centers other than primary schools are located at a considerable distance from the villages and many of these distances are no doubt prohibitive except under the most compelling circumstances.

TABLE 7.4

Average distance in miles from villages to nearest important center

	Average Distance in Miles			
	All Villages		Villages up to	
Center	(Tenth Round)	(Eleventh Round)	200	500
Primary school	1.29	1.35	2.12	1.16
Post office	4.00	3.81	5.13	3.65
Police station	7.58	8.15	—	—
Hospital	8.99	8.83	9.83	9.09
High school	10.54	10.24	12.25	10.59
Telegraph office	11.49	11.52	13.40	11.90
Railway station	20.45	20.23	—	—

Source: Cabinet Secretariat, *The National Sample Survey, No. 45, Report on Indian Villages* (Tenth to Twelfth Round, December 1955–August 1957; Delhi: Government of India, 1961), p. 9.

Yet, it is easy to misinterpret this physical isolation of the countryside. Difficulties of access to *modern* facilities have not been a bar to the spread of Hindu religious and cultural ideas throughout the Indian subcontinent. To this day the vast majority of the villages have significant social and cultural contacts through the traditional village fairs (see Table 7.5), and village fairs are only one of the traditional channels of communication. (Pilgrimages are another, for example.) As we examine the great physical isolation of the Indian countryside, we must be aware, then, of these traditional means of communication which through governmental initiative are also used today for the diffusion of modern ideas and practices.[70]

TABLE 7.5

*Percentage distribution of villages by source of
social and educational services*

	Percentage of Villages	
Source	Eleventh Round	Twelfth Round
Village fairs		
Religious	64.7	65.6
Nonreligious	6.2	7.4
Mixed	7.9	10.6
Weekly or daily newspapers	19.4	19.2
Radio	11.6	14.2
Library	7.1	6.9

Source: Cabinet Secretariat, National Sample Survey, *loc. cit.*, p. 16. Percentages add up to more than 100, since some villages have more than one of these services.

[70] For evidence that at the cultural level a network of communications existed through the Indian countryside, see Bernard S. Cohn and McKim Marriott, "Networks and Centres in the Integration of Indian Civilization," *Journal of Social Research*, I (Ranchi, Bihar: 1958), pp. 1–9, and McKim Marriott, "Changing Channels of Cultural Transmission in Indian Civilization," in L. P. Vidyarthi, ed., *Aspects of Religion in Indian Society* (Merrut: Kedar Nath Ram Nath, 1961), pp. 13–25, and the references cited there. The implications of this cultural communications network for the distribution of power still need to be explored.

To this background may now be added more summary figures on communications facilities, community development agencies, and the implementation of the franchise. Since half of the total and two thirds of the rural population live in communities of 999 inhabitants or less, possessing little or no contact with the "outside world," this large segment is yet hardly a part of India's developing political community. But since her constitution establishes the principle of a universal franchise, India faces the prospect that this large but inarticulate and isolated segment of the nation will be mobilized politically with every extension of modernizing facilities. The scarcity of such facilities surely impedes mobilization, even though their availability is only a necessary, not a sufficient condition of increased political involvement.

In 1959 India had an estimated total of 393,051 miles of extramunicipal roads, surfaced and unsurfaced. That worked out on an average to about 31 miles of roads and 75 settlements for every 100 square miles of territory. It is hoped that during the next 20 years the average length of extramunicipal roads can be built up to 52 miles per 100 square miles, which would still mean that for every 100 square miles there is less than 1 mile of extramunicipal road for every settlement in that area.[71] In 1962 India had 46,195 permanent and 28,401 temporary rural post offices, which meant that 8 or 9% of India's villages have direct access to written communication. With 71% of all settlements having a school in or near them in 1957 and average male literacy having increased from 25% in 1951 to 34% in 1961, it is reasonable to assume that by now some written or printed communications are trickling down to the villages. By 1961 electrification had reached only 25,470 towns and villages below 10,000 population, but it is probable that battery-powered radio communication has spread rather widely through community institutions in the larger villages.[72]

[71] See *India, A Reference Annual, 1961* (Delhi: Publication Division, Ministry of Information and Broadcasting, 1961), pp. 359–360; for the average number of settlements per 100 square miles see *All-India Educational Survey*, p. 177.

[72] For the figures on post offices and literacy see *India, 1963,*

The great physical isolation of Indians in the rural areas has been of much concern to the government of India and efforts to overcome its effects have been under way since independence. In community development and agricultural extension, the country has been divided into blocks, comprising on the average 100 villages with an area of 150–200 square miles and a population ranging between 60,000 and 70,000. As of January 1963, 4187 out of a total of 5223 blocks had been covered by the program, comprising about 80% of India's villages and about 74% of her rural population.[73] This quantitatively impressive achievement has been questioned, however, and the efficacy of this centrally organized contact with the villagers is in some doubt.

No such question has been raised with reference to the equally widespread organization of national elections. In the 1962 elections to the state assemblies and the national legislature, registration and returning officers prepared a roll comprising 210 million persons entitled to vote. At the rate of some 1000 voters to each station and at a maximum distance of 3 miles between each voter's place of residence and the polling station, the election required the establishment of 240,000 polling stations throughout the country. At these stations supervisory polling personnel on the days of the 1957 election consisted of 926,328 governmental personnel, 273,-762 policemen, and 168,281 village watchmen (chowkidars). In all, 1,166,459 government servants and 363,008 persons who were not government servants participated in the organization of that election in various capacities. In the 1962 election the total personnel employed had increased to 1,680,-000.[74] For thorough coverage of the entire country and for

---

pp. 332, 369. Figures on past electrification are given on p. 243. In this edition of the Reference Annual, the number of broadcast receiver licenses is given as 2,598,608 (p. 129), but it is not known what proportion of this total refers to the use of radios in villages.

[73] See *ibid.*, p. 170. Percentages calculated on 1961 census figures.

[74] Figures are taken from *Report on the Second General Elections in India, 1957* (Delhi: Election Commission, 1959), I, pp. 33, 35, 142, 156, and 211. Figures for the 1962 election are based on press-releases of the Press Information Bureau, Government of India.

administrative skill under conditions of staggering difficulty the Indian organization of elections can have few equals. Polling booths at a distance of no more than 3 miles from every Indian settlement are, thus, second only to primary schools among the modern facilities which have reached the people in the countryside. We can speculate that with reference to elementary education and the holding of national elections the Indian people have achieved a national consensus.[75]

The administrative tasks of the Indian development program cannot be assessed in terms of such external indexes alone. We tend to take for granted that more roads, post offices, radios, and so forth will facilitate the breakup of traditional ideas and practices. But such an effect, even when it occurs in the long run, is by no means automatic; traditional and modern elements will blend in the process in ever new ways. Not only is the physical availability of modern facilities at issue, but there is also the concern of how a given, tradition-bound people will avail themselves of their new access to these facilities. When external indexes indicate the increasing availability of modern facilities, and in India this is true only to a limited extent, they pose the urgent political problem of inducing the people to put these facilities to use. The twentieth century witnesses a unique spectacle. Governments seek to modernize countries in which they are supported (to the extent that one can speak of popular support) by a vast number of people who spend (or only recently

[75] To achieve a 57% (in 1962) voting participation in a population that has a literacy rate of 23.7% is remarkable enough. It is also noteworthy that in the 1957 elections voting participation in the rural areas exceeded participation in the urban areas in 7 out of 17 states and territories. See *ibid.*, p. 95. Western experience with parliamentary elections would lead one to expect an excess of urban over rural voting-participation. Two reasonable explanations for the reverse pattern in India are that in the rural areas elections are welcome, almost festive interruptions of routine and that the ability of local leaders to enforce participation is great in view of their considerable personal control over the villagers. The two explanations are not necessarily incompatible.

have spent) their lives in physical and social isolation from modern ideas and means of communication.

It is necessary to distinguish this great distance between government and society in India from parallels that are more familiar to a Western observer. Even in the most modern and developed country a large bulk of the population takes no interest in public affairs and has no knowledge of them; indeed the percentage of voter participation in the United States, while somewhat larger than in India (64% in 1960 compared with 57% in the Indian elections of 1962), is very low both in comparison with European countries and in view of the educational level of the American people. But even the most passive segments of the American public have ready access to all aspects of modern culture. In the most isolated rural settlements many people are a part of the national community in the sense that their activities involve them with and make them conscious of their country and the modern world. This kind of involvement even of the "isolated and backward" is conspicuously absent from the Indian scene, and the proportion of such people is, of course, very large.

IN QUEST OF PUBLIC COOPERATION

An Official Perspective

The following discussion analyzes the community development movement as a clue to the emerging structure of the Indian nation-state, beginning with the perspective of the Five-Year Plans. This approach is subject to major limitations. It takes as its starting point the official perspective on the problem of rural development, a position that is ideologically congenial to many Indians but endorsed wholeheartedly only by certain public officials and others who are concerned directly. The facts are that community development is not a major or principal part of the government's development effort. Public expenditures under this head during the First and Second Five-Year Plans amounted to Rs. 298 million out of a total of Rs. 6.56 billion, or about 4.5%, constituting about one fifth of the public funds directly devoted to agricultural improvements.[76]

Nor should the rhetoric of community development be allowed to disguise the massive inequalities of the Indian rural economy. In 1953–54, 11.9% of the agricultural population (or 30.8 out of 259.3 million people) owned 50.84% of the land in holdings of 15 acres or more, earning an average per capita income of 858 Rupees annually, while the other 228.5 millions earned an average per capita income of 112 Rupees. There are indications, moreover, that in recent years these disparities have increased, with the proportion of income going to cultivators declining and the proportion of income paid out in interest increasing.[77]

In view of these facts the plebiscitarian statement may seem disingenuous that "public cooperation has been recognized as an essential condition for the success of our Plans." However, there is no reason to question the sincere dedication of those concerned and it is candidly admitted that "of the many assumptions on which a Five-Year Plan is based, this [public cooperation] is not only the most important but also the most difficult."[78] It may be that efforts to promote community development are insufficient and/or misguided. Yet these efforts are part of India's emerging political community. If the quest for public cooperation with development plans fails to meet with the response hoped for, then this gap between aspiration and reality provides clues for an understanding of that community.

One other caveat is needed. The rhetoric of community development will be used below as symptomatic evidence of the problems encountered in the exercise of public authority at the local level. This rhetoric dwells on the apathy of the rural masses, appeals for their cooperation, speaks in positive terms of the peoples' productive potential, and depicts a better

[76] *Census of India, Final Population Totals, op. cit.,* p. xxii.

[77] See Ashok Mitra, "Tax Burden in Indian Agriculture," in Braibanti and Spengler, eds., *op. cit.,* pp. 299, 302; and S. A. Shah and M. Rajagopal, "Distribution of Agricultural Income in India," *The Economic Weekly,* XV (Oct. 12, 1963), pp. 1735–1738.

[78] *Third Five Year Plan,* pp. 291, 276.

future. For all its encomiums to the Indian peasant, this imagery is full of innuendos concerning the traditionalism and narrow-mindedness of these rural people. Such views are characteristic features of India's political life. But in analyzing them we do well to remember Max Weber's shrewd comment that

> Peasants become "dumb" only where they . . . face a presumably strange, bureaucratic machine . . . of a great state, or where they are abandoned as serfs to landlords, as happened in Egypt, Mesopotamia, and in the Hellenist and late Roman states.[79]

India's Five-Year Plans rest on the assumption that "at each level in the national life . . . an attempt will be made to implement [the Plan] with the utmost efficiency."[80] The statement is hortatory. It is recognized that much remains to be done to improve the implementation of the Plan and elicit public cooperation. The authors of the Third Five-Year Plan address themselves to both problems. They note

> . . . the slow pace of execution in many fields, problems involved in the planning, construction and operation of large projects, especially increase in costs and non-adherence to time-schedules, difficulties in training men on a large enough scale and securing personnel with the requisite calibre and experience, achieving coordination in detail in related sectors of the economy.[81]

But although reforms are needed in the administration of the Plan, administration alone is not sufficient. Declaring that public cooperation is essential, the Planning Commission states that

[79] Max Weber, *Ancient Judaism* (Glencoe: The Free Press, 1952), p. 206. Elsewhere Weber states that the idea of the peasant as the pious man who is pleasing to God, is a distinctively modern phenomenon. See his *Sociology of Religion* (Boston: Beacon Press, 1963), p. 83. In the nineteenth century this belief is frequently associated with the invidious contrast between town and country. The idea about the peasant's "purity of heart" is related in turn to the populist notions about his strength and productive capacity.

[80] *Third Five Year Plan,* p. 276.

[81] *Ibid.,* p. 277.

The concept of public cooperation is related, in its wider aspect, to the much larger sphere of voluntary action in which the initiative and organizational responsibility rest completely with the people and their leaders, and does not rely on legal sanctions or the power of the State for achieving its aims. . . . Properly organized voluntary effort may go far towards augmenting the facilities available to the community for helping the weakest and the most needy to a somewhat better life. . . . Material gains to the nation from this source can be widespread and large. What has been achieved so far on this account is, however, of small proportions. There should, therefore, be an early appraisal of the activity in this field to remove hindrances in the way of a much more massive advance.[82]

These statements suggest that India's planners hope for much more than the rather passive compliance or confidence which helps to sustain a policeman's authority or a bank's credit. They assume or hope that the efforts of the Central and State governments can be met halfway or more than halfway by the willingness of the Indian people to do for themselves what the government cannot do for them. In a setting of comparative backwardness national aspirations by the few easily give rise to idealized conceptions of the productive potential of the people which only needs to be harnessed to accomplish the desired development.

The Indian Constitution contains a whole array of political and social rights. The foremost task of the government is to implement these rights through modern technology and administration. A highly centralized government appears as the *sine qua non* of national development. But the society which this government confronts is characterized by tribes and castes whose hold on peoples' beliefs and loyalties is not weakening as rapidly as was the respect of inherited privilege in eighteenth-century Europe. Moreover, castes and their organizations are no longer confined to a local base but have spread out horizontally with urbanization and the franchise, so that the sentiments of caste affiliation are used in an ever-increasing range of social, civic, and political activities.[83]

[82] *Ibid.*, pp. 291–292.
[83] Systematic surveys of social and civic activities of caste or-

These activities are constantly condemned as "casteism" by the leaders of the country. They do *not* represent the public cooperation which the authors of the Five-Year Plans consider indispensable for the success of the national effort. Accordingly, there is a hiatus between what the government considers vital for the industrialization of the country and the activities in which Indians engage spontaneously. Divisions between capital and countryside, between planning at the center and social activity in the over 800,000 settlements of India, between the long-run rationale of the plan and the immediate rationale of family and neighborhood mark and mar the political consciousness of India today. We saw that distinctions like these have existed for a long time, but that they acquired a new intensity under the British as the social distance increased between the educated elite and the masses of the people.

Public Authority and the People in Community Development

The Community Development Movement of the Indian Government is an attempt to bridge the gap between the ruling elite and the masses of the Indian people, although the resources devoted to the development of the industrial sector have absolute priority. This governing decision is reflected in the relatively small number of officials who are charged with the responsibility for agriculture and community development at the local level. According to a tabulation of January 1961,

---

ganizations are lacking so far. However, a good beginning is contained in D. R. Gadgil, *Poona, A Socio-Economic Survey* (Poona: Gokhale Institute of Politics and Economics, 1952), II, pp. 172–222. The most comprehensive survey of caste politics is contained in Selig Harrison, *India, The Most Dangerous Decades* (Princeton: Princeton University Press, 1960), *passim*, but many graphic details are also discussed in M. N. Srinivas, *Caste in Modern India*, esp. Chaps. I, VI, and VII. See also the discussion in Myron Weiner, *The Politics of Scarcity* (Chicago: University of Chicago Press, 1962), Chaps. II and III; and F. G. Bailey, *Politics and Social Change, Orissa in 1959* (Berkeley: University of California Press, 1963), Chap. V, and *passim*.

a total of 61,449 persons had been employed in over 3000 blocks, covering 66% of India's villages. On a rough average this comes to one village level worker for every 6000 and one specialist extension officer for every 15,000 villagers.[84] If current plans are implemented fully, there will be one village level worker for every 5000 and one extension officer for every 10,000 villagers.[85]

In a country as large and diverse as India national averages cover up tremendous contrasts. One sample study of development blocks revealed hill-blocks in Uttar Pradesh with a density of 148 persons per square mile in contrast to a density of 1628 per square mile in the rice bowl area in Kerala. Again, if accessibility is defined in terms of the percentage of villages within 1 mile of a surfaced road, then blocks varied as much as 3.7% of the villages being accessible in one block, and 100% in another. Although some of the other contrasts among the blocks studied are not as great, they are frequently substantial enough to seriously affect the ability of officials to contact the villages for which they are responsible.[86] It is

[84] See Administrative Intelligence Unit, *Important Figures at a Glance* (mimeographed release, Ministry of Community Development and Cooperation, March 31, 1961), p. 4.

[85] Under the Third Five-Year Plan emphasis is being shifted between agricultural production and community development. To some extent this shift is reflected in the personnel requirements envisaged during the Plan period, namely 29,558 additional village level workers and 18,527 additional extension officers. Compared with the number currently employed under these two categories, village level workers are reduced by one seventh, while extension officers are increased by one half. See *Third Five Year Plan*, p. 177. The averages given in the text result when the totals of currently employed and planned VLW's and extension officers are divided by the 5223 blocks into which the country has been divided. There are some other categories of officials employed under this program (like block development officers at the top of the local hierarchy or social education organizers) which have not been considered in these rough calculations.

[86] For further details see Committee on Plan Projects, *Report of the Team for the Study of Community Projects and National Extension Service* (New Delhi: 1957), II, pp. 37–40. Cited below as *Mehta Report*, after Balvantray G. Mehta, the chairman of the study committee charged with the task of evaluating community development and national extension.

difficult, however, to take such contrasts into account, when
the endeavor is to cover the entire countryside in the shortest
possible time. Great progress has been achieved in the administrative coverage of the blocks, with plans calling for a
completion of that coverage ten years after the program was
initiated. This speed has come in for considerable criticism,
and there is evidence that administrative coverage has been
achieved at the expense of actual rural development.[87]

The problem is not only one of resources and administrative
organization, however. At the level of the village, development
officials have the difficult task of enlisting cooperation with
projects of whose soundness and desirability the villagers must
first be convinced. To do this officials must strike a balance
between making suggestions and listening to demands, taking
advantage of modern knowledge but also adapting it to the
local situation. In addition, villagers must exert themselves
with considerable determination if the change in production
methods and village amenities is to be an enduring attribute
of village life. The intricacies of this assignment are reflected
in a statement by the former Union Minister of Home Affairs,
Govind Ballabh Pant, entitled "The Right Approach to the
People." A pointed contrast is made with British rule, which
for all its admitted achievements was an alien and authoritarian system. Now, in independent India, an entirely different
spirit should prevail. Pant calls upon the officials to understand
their mission in a new sense. No longer are they to work in
the old manner, with an attitude of condescension towards the

[87] See the criticism by Prime Minister Nehru in *Kurukshetra,
A Symposium* (Delhi: Ministry of Community Development and
Cooperation, 1961), p. 318. (The title of this volume is also the
title of a periodical, edited and published by the Ministry; the
articles contained in this volume are taken from this periodical.
New editions of the symposium are published from time to time.)
A review of the whole program in 1958 came to the conclusion that
the extension of coverage was still proceeding faster than was com-
patible with an intensive development of the rural economy. See
U.N. Commissioner for Technical Assistance, *Report of a Community Development Evaluation Mission in India, 1958–59* (Delhi:
Government of India, Ministry of Community Development and
Cooperation, n.d.), pp. 7–9. Cited below as *U.N. Report.*

villagers as "superstitious men who deserve contempt."[88] Yet, the people have to be taught how to adopt modern methods of agriculture, develop amenities and keep the surroundings clean. Above all, they have to be inspired so that "they may put in their best for their own advancement."[89] Thus the officials must be authoritative but not authoritarian, knowledgeable but not overbearing.

> To serve the villagers, you have to identify yourself with rural life; to find joy in the air you breathe in and the consciousness of the fact that you are engaged in the act of building a new society. You have to train people in the art of life and the art of living. You have to see that they move, they move onward and they are not pushed onward artificially. Let them learn the art which will enable them to secure for themselves what we want them to possess. Unless you try to influence them without imposing something from above, your success will be shortlived.[90]

The whole thing is not a "mercenary undertaking." It depends upon winning the peoples' confidence so that they accept the new ways of working and living.

These appeals clearly call for excellence in a combination of virtues that requires consummate skill in the person who would possess them all. Yet they are addressed to officials who are ordinary men even where they are talented and who work under conditions which militate in some measure against the fulfillment of their many exacting duties. Time and again local officials are told that they must identify with rural life, rather than place before the villagers the "high-sounding theories" they have learned in the agricultural college. "You have to work in the filth and the cowdung and out of it create a clean and wholesome atmosphere."[91] Such a task is difficult for officials who have acquired an "urban orientation" by virtue of the very education which technically qualifies them for the task of promoting rural development. The following statement characterizes the resulting dilemma:

[88] *Kurukshetra*, pp. 61–62.
[89] *Ibid.*, p. 60.
[90] *Ibid.*, p. 59.
[91] *Ibid.*, p. 60.

... I have a feeling that public services in our country are manned primarily by the urban sections of the population, while the Plan that we are trying to put through and the series of Plans which will follow, are directed primarily to making an impact on the rural life of the community. I do not know whether the kind of faith that we would like to see in the public services would be generated among the people who are really not so much at one with the interests of the bulk of the population. It is true, of course, that as education advances there will be greater and greater degree of urbanization and since in the public services you get educated sections, they have to be perhaps more urban in their ideal and outlook than the rest of the countrymen. But I always feel that there is this sort of an initial hiatus between the public services and the major section of the population. I do not know how this gap could be reduced, whether the methods of recruitment could be suitably altered in order to see that there is not much emphasis on urbanization, so that there is greater realization of the needs of the rural population among the Services.[92]

In addition, development officials have to overcome the legacies of the freedom movement which discredited not only British rule but inadvertently administration as such, and hence intensifies the personal and social distance between villagers and official representatives of government. Moreover, after independence, rapid expansion of staff militated against the maintenance of standards, and the missionary spirit of development work was difficult to sustain wherever public cooperation was not forthcoming.[93] The number and diversity of duties assigned to village workers often exceed what even the most devoted person can accomplish.[94] Pressure for speedy expansion together with the very genuine

[92] *Morale in the Public Services* (Report of a Conference, January 3–4, 1959, C. D. Deshmukh, Chairman; New Delhi: Indian Institute of Public Administration), p. 17.

[93] See *ibid.*, pp. 75, 127 for comments along these lines by Indians directly associated with rural development work.

[94] *U.N. Report*, pp. 41–42, 48; *Kurukshetra*, pp. 126, 198, 389. A vivid description of the task of development work at the local level is contained in S. C. Dube, *India's Changing Villages* (London: Routledge & Kegan Paul, 1958), pp. 192 ff. See also *Mehta Report*, II, pp. 126–145.

national need for increased agricultural production have had the unintended consequence of accentuating central control of community development. For all these reasons, the achievement of "visible targets" (like the construction of block headquarters) has been emphasized at the expense of the more time-consuming and intangible task of drawing out the initiative and wholehearted cooperation of the villagers.[95]

There is acute awareness of these problems. G. Ramachandran, the secretary of the Gandhi National Memorial Fund, points out that "80% of the people is almost the whole of the people, what affects them will affect the whole nation, . . . what does not touch them is of little consequence." Yet programs of national improvement tend to concentrate "in some vivid patches in our towns and cities," and for the present it is no answer to assert that only the massive changes now occurring in, or planned for, the industrial sector will be capable of affecting the rural masses eventually. Mr. Ramachandran points to the magnitude of the task in the villages when he states that:

> . . . the caste system with its menace of untouchability must go root and branch. Many of the feudal characteristics of the old order must also be swept away. But we must destroy nothing which will weaken the basic vitality of the village tradi-

[95] See *Mehta Report,* I, p. 4 which states that welfare activities have been emphasized more than economic development. For specific examples of this emphasis and also of excessive expenditures for the more easily achieved objectives like construction of block headquarters, etc., see *Mehta Report,* I, *passim,* and *U.N. Report,* pp. 14, 21–23, 48–50. These emphases are clearly reflected in the frequently repeated admonition that "the people must be allowed to make mistakes." (E.g., *Kurukshetra,* p. 173.) Presumably this means that frequently they have not been permitted to make the costly and time-consuming mistakes that would have to be tolerated, if local officials are to encourage but also await the articulation of local wants and desires. In a national emergency it is difficult to allow public cooperation to emerge at its own pace, especially if development officials depend for their own careers upon their demonstrated ability to get things done. The fact seems to be that the construction of facilities and amenities is more easily accomplished than extension services to increase agricultural production, since it requires less public cooperation.

tion. We must not destroy anything we cannot replace with something better and in time . . . It is in these villages we will make or mar the history of India.[96]

Thus, the tremendous problem of reaching more than 800,-000 settlements by administrative means rather than in the exemplary, Gandhian fashion as before, is complicated further by the task of actively transforming the caste-practices of the villagers and without detriment to the values of their traditional way of life. To these complexities is added the further task of greatly increasing agricultural production and of providing public amenities to the village people—in conformity with the objectives of the Five-Year Plans. Officials are eagerly seeking the public cooperation which will facilitate the achievement of these objectives, *but not at the price of accepting the present outlook of the village people or tolerating the factions which divide them.*[97] Thus, economic development *and* the transformation of village society are clearly formulated as the two major aims of the Constitution, which abolishes untouchability and directs the State to promote the interests of the weaker sections of the people and to secure for all citizens an adequate means of livelihood.[98]

The drive to revolutionize village India while devoting the

[96] See G. Ramachandran, "Gandhian Approach to Rural Welfare," in Planning Commission, *Social Welfare in India* (New Delhi: Government of India, 1960), pp. 87–88. New editions of this work appear from time to time.

[97] In its report of 1959 the U.N. Mission refers to the caste system as one of the major causes of stagnation in the rural sector. The traditional land tenure system has favored a class of land owners, who spend little or none of their rents on land improvements, while the lower castes are generally not in a position to purchase land and grow commercial crops. Other factors cited are the erosion of the land due to uncontrolled cultivation, extension of cultivation to marginal or submarginal lands due to population pressure, the persistence of money lending, share-cropping, and the fragmentation of land holdings. In one way or another, many of these factors are also related to caste. See *U.N. Report*, p. 20.

[98] See V. T. Krishnamachari, "The National Extension Movement," *Kurukshetra, op. cit.*, p. 35, for an expression of these objectives by the former Deputy Chairman of the Planning Commission.

bulk of development expenditure to rapid industrialization has resulted in a characteristically urgent and ambivalent rhetoric. Public statements alternate repeatedly between praise and blame of India's villagers. One writer states, for example, that "the rural people have almost limitless capacity to fashion a better life for themselves if properly aided by State action."[99] Similarly, the Minister for Community Development, S. K. Dey, states:

> We have in this country villages full of vital people. All that they desire is a scope for expression such as we have not given them in our anxiety to avoid possible errors and mistakes by local institutions.

Or, on another occasion:

> People are ready to do what we ask them, but we do not yet know how to ask them.[100]

But the Minister also states that:

> In a planned developmental economy for an underdeveloped people such as the vast masses in India represent, it is but natural that the initiative for development, at least in the early stages, will have to rest preponderantly on the government apparatus.[101]

And another writer, while acknowledging the "tremendous awakening" in the country, observes that:

> . . . the main difficulty which is likely to face the administrator and the social welfare worker is this resistance and apathy towards measures to improve the conditions of the village. There is a strong tendency for people therefore to expect Government or someone else to do everything for them while they continue in the same groove in which they are accustomed to move.[102]

Thus, the untapped potential of the masses is praised in phrases of soaring panegyric, followed by declarations which

[99] *Ibid.*, p. 27.
[100] *Ibid.*, pp. 173, 240.
[101] *Ibid.*, p. 176.
[102] *Ibid.*, p. 204.

decry the apathy and traditionalism that beset village life. That is, the potential of the rural masses for greater productivity can be realized only when the obstacles of apathy and tradition are removed, when the people themselves actively desire and achieve the better life which the government seeks to establish. But it is not put that way, because India's leaders tend to have an ambivalent outlook on the rural problem. With its mixture of wishful thinking and fearful apprehension the prevailing rhetoric envisages a tremendous outburst of constructive effort, denounces the obstacles which seem to prevent its release, and time and again admonishes development officials to deal sympathetically and imaginatively with the realities of village life. The higher echelons of government tend to transmit these unresolved issues downward and charge those directly responsible for rural development with the task of reconciling conflicting policies and the imperatives of India's rural development problem. Accordingly, it is up to the locally responsible officials to obtain the public cooperation upon which rural development and the success of the Plans depend.

At the level of policy it is now acknowledged that this approach has not been successful. The development effort is to

TABLE 7.6

*Government expenditure and people's contribution under the first and second five-year plans**

Period	Government Expenditure	People's Contribution
First Five-Year Plan (annual average)	9.24	5.26
Second Five-Year Plan		
1956–57	23.93	16.32
1957–58	31.53	16.30
1958–59	40.45	16.84
1959–60	42.93	14.15
1960–61 (provisional)	51.40	12.13
Total	190.24	75.74

Source: Administrative Intelligence Unit, *op. cit.*, p. 11.
* Rs. Crores or units of Rs. 10,000,000.

be decentralized. Under the Panchayati Raj scheme to be mentioned presently, the officials concerned with rural development are subordinate to locally elected bodies. This capacity to critically assess and reorient a policy that has been found to fail is a great credit to the Indian government. But it is still necessary to understand the reasons for that failure, for under the new policy the task of enlisting public cooperation with centrally devised plans remains the fundamental problem.

In a "new nation" such as India, the government sees itself faced with the task of mass mobilization. It is thus important to examine the amount and nature of public cooperation which has been elicited even though the evidence is incomplete and difficult to interpret. The *Mehta Report* which subjected the Community Development Program to a searching critique, explicitly criticized the inadequate methods of assessing the value of such cooperation, especially the tendency to inflate the figures to show a good record on paper.[103] Still, the available figures (see Table 7.6) on public contribution seem to tell us that despite a considerable rise in government expenditure public contributions have declined during the Second Five-Year Plan, rather than increased.

But figures in the aggregate do not reveal the nature of public involvement. In what manner have India's villagers shown initiative in supporting and advancing governmental projects designed to improve their own living conditions and agricultural productivity? Some measure of the villager's involvement in the development effort can be found in the extent to which they acknowledge that upkeep of the facilities constructed under the community development program is a responsibility of the village and its people. In a sample of 467 respondents, the following over-all results (Table 7.7) were obtained.

Some tentative interpretations of these results seem possible. The people who did not reply either have no knowledge of these matters or no concern with them. By this token public concern with roads, schools, and wells is clearly greater than

[103] *Mehta Report*, I, pp. 43–44 and II, pp. 57–58.

with drains and community centers. Taking these "no replies" together with the response that either the government or only direct beneficiaries should be responsible for continuous maintenance, it appears that some two thirds of the respondents show no concern or express the belief that responsibility does not rest with the village as a community, while one third acknowledges such village responsibility. However in another study (of 573 respondents from 13 blocks in six states) 54% assigned responsibility for continuous maintenance to the panchayat, 20% to the local cooperative society, and only 22% to the government.[104] Since 59% of the respondents in this latter sample were literate (in contrast with a national average of 17%), it may well be that increased education helps to develop a sense of involvement and local civic responsibility.

Considering the formidable difficulties of mobilizing an illiterate, tradition-bound population by democratic means, this record of public cooperation may well be quite impressive.

TABLE 7.7

*Per cent of respondents allocating responsibility
for the maintenance of facilities**

Type of Facility	Continuous Maintenance Should Be Responsibility Of			
	Government	Beneficiaries	Panchayat	No Reply
Roads	13	25	30	32
Schools	21	23	22	36
Wells	5	23	37	35
Drains	—	50	7	43
Community Centers	2	11	33	57

Source: Mehta Report, II, pp. 66–67.
* *N* = 467.

[104] Another 24% assigned that responsibility to "other institutions" and the meaning of this response is unclear, except that no one in this study seems to have considered "beneficiaries" responsible as individuals. The percentages add up to more than 100 since more than one response was possible. See *Mehta Report,* II, pp. 96–98, 114.

If it has fallen short of the goals set, then perhaps these goals have been excessive.[105] There is logic in rhetoric of the peoples' creative potential in a nation that makes a major effort to advance her economy by an image of unity and purposeful exertion. But this language of agitation hides the divisions of a caste society.[106] These divisions inevitably influence the peoples' contribution to the development of their village and to increased agricultural productivity.

In a study prepared for the *Mehta Report* two surveys were made, dealing respectively with the degree to which various occupational groups in the villages contributed to different community projects or benefited from agricultural extension programs. In a sample of 467 villagers in ten blocks (selected from six states) it was found that 79% or 368 had contributed their labor to at least one community project since 1952. Table 7.8 compares the degree of voluntary participation in the different projects. Clearly, villagers in different occupations and castes have greatly divergent interests in the several projects. Most conspicuous is the lack of interest in drains and community centers among the lower groups and among businessmen. Equally conspicuous is the paramount interest which small and medium cultivators show in schools, drains, community centers, bridges, and wells. Given such differential participation, it is not surprising to learn from another study that "considering the village popu-

[105] That excess is especially noteworthy in populist phrases which attribute a "giant potential" or "limitless capacity" to the people. See *Kurukshetra,* pp. 27, 399, and *passim.* For a listing of the physical achievements of the community development program see *India, 1963,* pp. 187–188.

[106] Lest I be misunderstood, I should add that the rhetoric of unity is often associated with denunciation of the caste system. But when the public's creative potential is declared to be great if only the state will lend a hand, then the people are urged to avail themselves of the great benefits which are theirs for the taking, and the obstructions arising from the caste system, factionalism, or disparities in landownership are significantly omitted. By such omissions relevant facts of rural India are not brought into direct confrontation with the peoples' creative potential, which is also treated as a fact. See below for further discussion especially with reference to the rule of unanimity in local elections or deliberations.

TABLE 7.8

Number and per cent of respondents who have given free labor for different projects (by occupational category)

Occupational Category	Number of Respondents	Participants		Per Cent of Respondents Who Have Given Free Labor For					
		No.	%	Roads	Wells	Schools	Drains	Centers	Bridges
Large cultivator	23	25	7	8	4.5	3	24	9	9
Medium cultivator	107	99	27	29	3.5	29	24	36	9
Small cultivator	126	104	29	20	33	26	48	45	36
Tenant	23	15	4	3	—	5*	—	—	9
Cultivator and laborer	9	10	3	2	3.5	6	—	—	18
Agricultural laborer	63	40	11	10	23	13	—	—	9
Service	28	29	8	8	14	5	4	9	5.5
Artisans	18	22	6	12	14	11	—	—	—
Business	47	22	6	6	5	2	—	—	4.5
Others	18	—	—	—	—	—	—	—	—
Total*	462	367	101	98	99	100	100	99	99

Source: Mehta Report, II, p. 63 and passim. Where the number of participants exceeds the number of respondents in the sample the same participant contributed labor to more than one project.
* The numerical totals differ slightly from those contained in the report because numbers had to be recomputed from percentages. In the case of schools, participants contributed labor repeatedly. Also one percentage printed as "49" has been corrected, since it is an obvious misprint for 4.9 or 5.

lation as a whole the owner-cultivators—large, medium and
small—altogether represent the largest single group of beneficiaries of the facilities made available by community
projects."[107]

The quest for public cooperation has not had the results
for which the Indian planners had hoped. The official assessment of the record of community development and agricultural extension draws the conclusion that the "attempt to
evoke popular initiative" was clearly the least successful aspect of these programs.[108] Although there is certainly evidence of change in the outlook of India's villagers, it is gradual and probably affects the areas involving their economic
interests more readily than those involving the beliefs and
customs of the caste structure, at least where these two spheres
are distinguishable.[109] From the standpoint of India's development plans rural change has been too slow, while the effort
to enlist public cooperation has given rise to basic issues of
public policy.

Some Unresolved Issues of Public Cooperation in Rural Development

More often than not, the faulty design or execution of
community development and national extension is held responsible for the failure of India's villagers to respond "adequately" to the emergencies facing rural India. One such
diagnosis puts the blame on the speed with which these programs have been extended to all parts of the country and
upon the rapid growth of staff that resulted. The program
has moved away "from the original impetus and clarity of

[107] *Mehta Report,* ii, p. 103.

[108] *Ibid.,* I, p. 5.

[109] For a survey of some of these changes see the essay "The
Industrialization and Urbanization of Rural Areas," by M. N. Srinivas, *Caste in Modern India,* Chap. V. However, evidence for this
"urban impact" on the rural areas must be considered together
with evidence showing that in many instances such impact is tenuous and superficial. See Richard Lambert, "The Impact of Urban
Society upon Village Life," in Roy Turner, ed., *India's Urban Future* (Berkeley: University of California Press, 1962), pp. 117–140.

vision," while the "philosophy of community development" which was to have preserved that impetus has come to be "remote from village realities."[110] Another and related critique attributes the overemphasis on construction at the expense of extension activities to the fact that program leaders do not believe in the willingness of the villagers to solve their own problems. Too many resources are devoted to the misguided attempt to motivate the people.[111] There is some merit and illusion in both comments, but they do not deal with the political ideologies and strategies which first led to the quest for public cooperation and has now led to the policy of "democratic decentralization."

The public cooperation sought by the Indian planners is not cooperation at any price. Although it is acknowledged that so far community development has benefited the upper sections of village society, it is constantly stressed that in this way the objective of community solidarity is defeated. National and local leaders should be troubled in their conscience by this failure to achieve social justice.[112] Nor does the objective of promoting rural economic development have exclusive priority. Rather,

> Our Community Development approach stands for . . . the dual purpose of building democracy from the base and harnessing it to the cause of development. . . . It is not so much a question of protecting the individual and the community from the evil effects of too much State action as of revitalizing the community and building up democracy from the roots upwards. The people have to be made conscious of their rights and responsibilities as citizens of a free country. They must be ready to bear the main burden of re-building the communities in which they live, which have been disintegrating over a period of centuries. To re-integrate the life of these village communities must be an important objective of Community Development.[113]

[110] *U.N. Report*, pp. 49–50.

[111] Carl Taylor, "Two Major Evils," in *Kurukshetra*, p. 396. For several years Dr. Taylor has been advisor on community development to the Ford Foundation and the Indian Government.

[112] *Kurukshetra*, pp. 28–29.

[113] *Ibid.*, p. 26. This statement may stand for many of its kind; I

This explicit duality of purpose is related to the special meaning of "democracy" as used in this context. The rhetoric of the community development movement refers to "democracy" in the two senses of "equality" and "solidarity," and both meanings are linked with economic development.

It is said that development cannot succeed unless it has nearly universal and entirely voluntary support from the villagers. Officials are admonished to promote the solidarity of the village as well as "effective" leadership, since development will inevitably suffer where factions divide the village and local leaders fail to promote village development.[114] "Democracy" in the ordinary sense of a free competition for public office is not considered applicable or suitable at the local level. Rather, at the "lower levels of democracy" responsible political parties have an important "constructive" role to play, and only at the "higher levels" should they play a "political role."[115] Again, political parties are characterized as "essentially undemocratic," because they foster ideological differences and "foment divisions at the village and Panchayat levels on every issue in order to form a rural political base for themselves."[116] To prevent both the natural and these "fomented" divisions, an organization representing the village as a whole is demanded. In its discussion of the new policy of "democratic decentralization" the Third Five-Year Plan urges the village panchayat to encourage unanimity or near unanimity "so that various activities are undertaken with the general consent and good will of the community."

---

choose it because of its clarity. From a policy standpoint the same points are made in a statement by Tarlok Singh (Additional Secretary, Planning Commission), "Planning at the Village Level," *ibid.*, pp. 134–135.

[114] *Ibid.*, pp. 17, 19, 20, 23, 32, 70–71, and *passim*.

[115] *Ibid.*, p. 32. Note in this connection the statement by S. K. Dey, Union Minister for Community Development, Panchayati Raj and Cooperation, according to which village democracy should be safeguarded from the pressures of power politics. Although admitting that it would be difficult to isolate panchayat work from the activities of political parties, Mr. Dey said: "What we want to avoid is power politics," adding that there could be no objection to "good politics." See *Economic Weekly*, XIV (July 1962), p. 1106.

[116] *Kurukshetra*, p. 332.

In the absence of such unanimity and of an effective village organization "the approach to rural problems is [said to be] better organized from the side of the administration."

This drift toward centralized administration is a response of equalitarian officials to the stark inequalities of village life.[117] But the results of this "drift" have not always been salutary. Emphasis on centrally directed actions runs counter to the explicit demands for public initiative and cooperation at the local level. Plans for agricultural development are prepared at the state and central levels "independently of local plans" and hence lack responsiveness to local demands.[118] Local development officials are admonished to elicit cooperation, but they also have to prove their worth, which as we saw leads to concentration on physical construction and welfare activities in the absence of the desired cooperation in increasing agricultural production. Moreover, achievements in both fields tend to accrue to the benefit of the better-situated segments of village society, so that the drift toward centralization which partly arises from the government's unwillingness to tolerate the inequalities of village society nevertheless intensifies these inequalities in many instances. This inadvertent effect has been severely condemned, and equalitarian reforms have been instituted. In practice planners and administrators proceed as if the public cooperation for which they ask and the caste divisions and inequalities which they denounce exist in two separate, watertight compartments. Yet the villagers are asked to cooperate today, not tomorrow, and today they are deeply divided by great economic inequalities and intense communal affiliations. The fact is that the "public" does not possess that capacity for a villagewide solidarity and organization which may arise in some distant future if and when the conditions of village society have been transformed.

[117] The plea for an organization representing the whole village and the statement concerning the administrative approach are contained in Tarlok Singh's statement of 1954 (ibid., p. 134). The statement concerning unanimity and supporting arguments appear on p. 339 and *passim* of the *Third Five Year Plan*.

[118] *Third Five Year Plan*, p. 334.

In themselves these facts are clearly acknowledged. Solidarity is commended, factions are denounced, and it is frankly stated that "there is considerable weakness in the organization available in the village."[119] But the weakness referred to is the incapacity or unwillingness of villagers to organize themselves along equalitarian lines. Government leaders reject the capacity of villagers to organize along caste lines or in factions as an evil legacy of the past. Accordingly, the Indian political community is envisaged as consisting of organized government on one hand, and the masses of the Indian people on the other. Nowhere is this attitude more forcefully put than in this statement by Kaka Kalelkar, the Chairman of the "Backward Classes Commission":

> National solidarity demands that in a democratic set-up Government recognize only two ends—the individual at one end and the nation as a whole at the other—and that nothing should be encouraged to organize itself in between these two ends to the detriment of the freedom of the individual and the solidarity of the nation. All communal and denominational organizations and groupings of lesser and narrower units have to be watched carefully so that they do not jeopardize the national solidarity and do not weaken the efforts of the nation to serve all the various elements in the body politic with equity.[120]

This plebiscitarian framework is identical with the approach formulated at the end of the eighteenth century by such men as La Chalotais and Le Chapelier. It rules out any positive attention to the communal organizations which have sprung up with the advance of urbanization and the spread

[119] Tarlok Singh in *Kurukshetra*, p. 134. See also the statement by Raghubir Sahai in 1959 which declares that "we are woefully lacking in this kind of non-official element at each and every level" (*ibid.*, p. 354).

[120] *Report of the Backward Classes Commission* (Delhi: Government of India Press, 1956), I, p. iv. This commission was appointed pursuant to Article 340 of the Constitution authorizing the president to initiate an investigation of the conditions of socially and educationally backward classes. These classes are distinct from the scheduled castes (untouchables) and tribes which are provided for separately in the Constitution and the government.

of communication facilities. In India, it has given rise to the quixotic effort of assisting *voluntary* organizations.

The government's purpose is to stimulate cooperation and initiative along noncommunal lines.[121] Inevitably, this new scheme has raised major problems: the difficulty of making an officially sponsored "nonofficial" organization appear as a "voluntary effort" is only too apparent. At a meeting of the National Advisory Committee on Public Cooperation a galaxy of public figures examined the government's role in sponsoring "voluntary" organizations. Since the need for public cooperation is all-pervasive, why should there be a separate allocation for this purpose? If the government sponsors voluntary organizations, they will mushroom and the resulting rivalries will get out of hand. Voluntary agencies and their workers should strengthen existing institutions with their assistance rather than become another agency. One speaker states that the central government has publicized full particulars about the program under which voluntary organizations could secure grants-in-aid; now, the states should do likewise, and some criteria should be laid down so that the voluntary organizations applying for grants-in-aid can be properly assessed. From here it is only a short step to the suggestion that all voluntary organizations should evolve a uniform program on the national scale and that the government should encourage their activities since otherwise

[121] The Planning Commission set up a "Public Cooperation Division" which was authorized to give grants to the Bharat Sevak Samaj (Indian Service Society), a nonpolitical and nonofficial organization that seeks to secure public participation in the work of the Five-Year Plans. In 1958 the Bharat Sevak Samaj was invited to set up on an experimental basis Lok Karya Kshetras (areas especially designated for the purpose of enlisting cooperation). Through these special organizations voluntary labor and local resources were to be used to assist in local programs of development, to create popular enthusiasm for the plan programs, to draw out promising young workers from the masses and to strengthen local institutions like panchayats and cooperatives. For a period of three years each of these Kshetras would receive Rs. 5000 per annum. See Programme Evaluation Organization, Planning Commission, *A Study of the Lok Karya Kshetras of the Bharat Sevak Samaj* (New Delhi: Government of India, 1960), p. 1.

vested interests might oust them from their field of endeavor. There were, of course, warnings. Voluntary organizations maintained or run by the government would cease to be voluntary; that efforts to raise donations from the public are terminated when financial assistance by the government becomes available; the government comes to duplicate activities carried out by voluntary organizations already. But the tone is set by statements which refer to uniform training for all workers in voluntary organizations, to the periodic official assessment of these organizations to make sure they have the desired results, to the required degree of planning and continuity in nonofficial voluntary action, to the need to entrust voluntary organizations with certain specific responsibilities. The discussion reveals little awareness of its self-defeating character; it seems to take for granted that public cooperation can and should be organized from the side of the administration.[122]

But such plebiscitarian doctrines cannot disguise the failure of the Indian government to "evoke popular initiative" in its program of community development and agricultural extension. In their exhaustive study of this program, published in 1957, the authors of the *Mehta Report* state:

> So long as we do not discover or create a representative and democratic institution which will supply the "local interest, supervision and care necessary to ensure that expenditure of money upon local objects conforms with the needs and wishes of the locality," invest it with adequate power and assign to it appropriate finances, we will never be able to evoke local interest and excite local initiative in the field of development.[123]

Such institutions have not been developed so far, because "decentralization of responsibility and power has not taken place below the state level in recent years." Accordingly,

[122] But it is not surprising under these circumstances that of the Rs. 50 million set aside for "public cooperation" in the Second Five-Year Plan only Rs. 150,000 were actually spent. The preceding summary is based on Planning Commission (Public Cooperation Division), *Summary Record of the Meeting of the National Advisory Committee on Public Cooperation* (August 1960), *passim.*

[123] *Mehta Report*, I, p. 5.

it is recommended that in agriculture, animal husbandry, cooperation, minor irrigation works, village industries, primary education, local communications, health and medical relief, local amenities, and similar subjects the government would devolve all of its functions in these fields upon the local bodies, reserving to itself the functions of guidance, supervision, and higher planning.[124] Since this recommendation was made, implementing legislation has been passed or is under consideration in the several States. Although the details vary, the over-all objective is to replace administrative institutions below the state legislature with a three-tier structure of directly or indirectly elected bodies. At the bottom are the panchayats, elected from one or several villages depending on their size. Secondly, a new statutory body—the Block Panchayat Samiti—will be established, composed of elected heads of panchayats and coopted members representing women and scheduled castes. All administrative personnel at the block level and all government resources at this level will be at the disposal of this body, which will have responsibility for all community development and other governmental programs within its jurisdiction. The presidents of all Panchayat Samitis together with members of the state legislature, the collector, and the technical personnel at the former district level will constitute the Zila Parishad, which will advise and assist the Panchayat Samitis, especially in articulating local with state and national plans, but without exercising control over them.

This drastic reorganization of local institutions has been in operation since 1959 in the two states of Rajasthan and Andhra Pradesh, it is being implemented rapidly in a number of other states, and there is little doubt that it will soon cover the country. At the time of writing data for a comprehensive evaluation are not available, though a few surveys of the new system have been made already. However, the new administrative structure can be analyzed in terms of the problems of "authority and public cooperation" discussed previously. To do this, it is necessary to characterize the basic

[124] *Ibid.*, p. 7.

institution upon which the new system rests—the village panchayat—which is seen as representing the entire village community and which is now to be given added powers and resources to exercise leadership in the implementation of the development program. From this vantage point it will also be possible to obtain some perspective concerning the conflicting claims of planners and administrators on one hand, and of local and state politicians on the other, whereby the future relations between centers of government and village India can be studied.

RURAL SOCIAL STRUCTURE AND INDIA'S POLITICAL COMMUNITY

India's planners approach her villagers with high hopes for their contribution to the economic development of the nation. Now that Community Development has been found wanting, attention is focused on the village-panchayat as the central institution of the local community. The panchayat is to mobilize and, if necessary, redirect the cooperative capacity of the village. There is evidence to show that these hopes are largely unrealistic.

Panchayats Then and Now

B. B. Misra has formulated three models of the Indian village panchayat for the pre-British period, the period under British rule, and the present as conceived under the Panchayati Raj legislation of several Indian states.[125]

Under Type I the authority of a village panchayat was the by-product of custom and caste dominance. Custom governed

[125] See B. B. Misra, *The Indian Middle Classes* (London: Oxford University Press, 1961), pp. 310–312. In lieu of quoting this passage at the required length, I attempt here to formulate the threefold typology which it implies. Necessarily, this is a simplified developmental model. For a more differentiated, but still typological discussion of panchayats see Ralph H. Retzlaff, *Village Government in India* (New York: Asia Publishing House, 1962), Chaps. 1–3.

all procedures and decisions in accordance with considerations of caste, which legitimated the authority exercised by the village elders. Typically, these elders were the chief proprietors of the village many of whom held respected positions in the caste hierarchy as well. As *primus inter pares* among the village elders, the village headman combined the functions of leader, judge, and local administrator, who was responsible to government for the payment of revenue on behalf of the village. This condition was stabilized wherever the economic dominance of the elders was intact. Dominance based on land ownership reinforced established caste practices, precluded the uncontrolled transfer of land especially outside the community, and saw to the completion of "public works" through forced labor.[126]

Under Type II British revenue and rent laws defined different kinds of landed interest, the resulting proprietary rights were recorded, and individuals were consequently able to transfer their interest in land independently of the chief proprietors. By making every villager in principle an independent proprietor and thus destroying the collective responsibility of the headman and the immobile nature of the land, British rule deprived the village of its earlier corporate structure. Through legal and administrative rules the British also introduced considerations in village affairs with which the traditionally consensual and adjudicatory deliberations of the old panchayat were not equipped to deal.[127]

[126] Misra emphasizes the isolation of village lands from marketing relations with the outside, but the point concerning "public works" should not be attributed to him. In the literature on Indian villages much is made of economic dependence, as in the jajmani relationship, but I can find little reference to "public works." This may be due to the fact that a large part of what might be so called consisted of irrigation works which primarily benefited the economically dominant land owners and hence were constructed by socially and economically dependent villagers. But even then somebody must have dug the community wells or built the road which incidentally benefited all villagers however privileged the access of the dominant few, and I infer that this "community service" was exacted by the dominant and from the most dependent castes.

[127] The contrast with Type I is real enough, but it is uncertain how common village panchayats were. Moreover, British rule did

Under Type III, as envisaged under Panchayati Raj, village panchayats are required to administer laws and regulations in accordance with legislative enactments. Typically, this involves the principle of legal equality which is repugnant to caste privileges, and procedural technicalities which are alien to the customary practices of village life. From the deliberative tribunal regulating village affairs within and serving, through the headman, an "ambassadorial function" toward the world outside, the village panchayat is to be transformed into an executive agency—the lowest rung in the hierarchy of government—which is elected by the people and charged with the responsibility of enlisting their cooperation in the national endeavor. These multifarious functions are exceedingly difficult to reconcile, so that there are calls not only for an educational program commensurate with the tasks assigned to the panchayat but also for an extension of state machinery to supervise and control the administrative functions which are to be performed by the panchayat.

Panchayati Raj is still in its beginning. In Rajasthan, the state in which it has been in operation for the longest time, the program was initiated in 1959. But the Indian government has put special emphasis on village panchayats since independence, and a certain amount of information concerning this institution is available. In 1957 the Planning Commission sponsored a study of 60 panchayats in 15 evaluation blocks (in 14 different states); of the 175 villages covered by these panchayats, 102 were selected for detailed examination. The following table (Table 7.9) gives the personal characteristics of the 547 members (panches) and 47 presidents (sarpanches) of these panchayats. The overwhelming majority of village representatives are from the older, better educated, propertied, wealthy, high-caste groups of village society. Moreover, a comparison between

---

not introduce inequality and exploitation, which were an integral part even of the corporate village structure. The point is worth reiterating in view of the persistent idealization of the traditional village in contrast with the strife-torn community under British rule and since.

members and presidents reveals that on the average the top leaders of the village are older, more educated, better off economically, and of a higher caste than the elected members, and the latter are favorably distinguished in these respects from the general village population.

TABLE 7.9

Personal characteristics of members and presidents in sixty panchayats

Personal Characteristics	Per Cent of Members (N = 547)	Per Cent of Presidents (N = 47)
Age group		
Below 25 years	1.1	—
25 to 40 years	38.9	46.8
40 years and above	59.6	53.2
Educational qualifications		
Illiterate	42.2	17.0
Primary school	36.4	44.7
Middle school	17.0	27.7
Matriculation	2.9	8.5
Above matriculation	1.5	2.1
Ownership of land		
Land holders	88.1	95.7
Nonland holders	11.9	4.3
Financial status		
Rich	32.5	89.4
Others	67.5	10.6
Caste group		
High	69.8	97.9
Low	30.2	2.1

Source: Programme Evaluation Organization, Planning Commission, *A Study of Panchayats* (Separate reprint of Chapter IV of Fifth Evaluation Report; May, 1958), p. 10.

These results pertain to village panchayats charged with responsibilities under the earlier community development program. It is of interest, therefore, to learn whether significant changes in the personal composition of the panchayats have occurred under Panchayati Raj.[128] There is clear evidence of change in only one respect. Of the sarpanches (panchayat presidents) in Rajasthan, 57.4% are below 40 years of age compared with 46.8% in the Planning Commission's study cited above. The Rajasthan report goes on to say that the age distribution of the panches (panchayat members) is not significantly different. We may infer, therefore, that on the whole a younger group of men are coming to the fore than was true only a few years ago, and that this change is due to the greater interest aroused in local elections under Panchayati Raj.[129]

With regard to financial status the Rajasthan study provides us with quite specific information. The earlier study of the Planning Commission only revealed the greater economic prosperity of panchayat presidents compared with panchayat members. The Rajasthan study gives a more differentiated picture. (See Table 7.10.) To assess its findings it is important to note that 80% of rural households have an income of less than Rs. 1000 per annum, and 50% of

[128] The following remarks are based on Evaluation Organization, Government of Rajasthan, *The Working of Panchayati Raj in Rajasthan* (Jaipur: June 1962), Appendix II, which is identical with the same organization's Report on the Panchayat Elections in Rajasthan, 1960 (Jaipur: 1961), pp. 26–32, although the two reports differ in other respects. These reports are very poorly put together and in view of the uncertainties of the original my interpretation can only be tentative. However, so far as I know, this is the most up-to-date information available.

[129] Other comparisons between the PEO study of the Planning Commission and the study from Rajasthan do not show marked differences to the extent that the data are comparable. For example, 78% of the sarpanches in Rajasthan have completed less than middle school education, which compares roughly with the 72% with primary or middle-school education in the PEO study. There may be a somewhat greater proportion of sarpanches from scheduled tribes and castes in Rajasthan than from "low" castes in the PEO study, but inadequate reporting makes a reliable judgment impossible. For two preliminary assessments of the administrative experience in Rajasthan see Ralph Retzlaff, "Panchayati Raj in Rajasthan," *Indian Journal of Public Administration*, VI (1960), pp. 141–158; B. Maheshwari, "Two Years of Panchayati Raj in Rajasthan," *Economic Weekly*, XIV (May 1962), pp. 845–848.

TABLE 7.10

*Percentage distribution by annual income of reelected and
newly elected sarpanches and panches in Rajasthan
1961–1962*

Average Annual Income	Panches*		Sarpanches	
	Re-elected	Newly elected	Reelected ($N = 2779$)	Newly elected ($N = 2801$)
Rs. 1000 or less	24	29	16	16
Rs. 1000–3000	57	62	45	41
Rs. 3001 or above	19	9	39	43
(Rs. 5001 or above)†	—	—	(23)	(21)

Source: Evaluation Organization, Government of Rajasthan, *The Working of Panchayati Raj,* Appendix II, pp. ix–x.
* The sample size for panches is not given in this report; for sarpanches this number will be found in Appendix C to the *Report on Panchayat Elections, 1960.*
† Figures in parentheses are contained in those immediately above.

the households have less than Rs. 500 per annum.[130] Accordingly, the great majority of representatives belong to the middle- and upper-income groups, with more panches than sarpanches in the low- and middle-income groups, and sarpanches clearly representing the local economic elite. The most notable difference between "old" and "new" panchayat representatives is the fact that the proportion of well-to-do panches has declined, while that of well-to-do sarpanches has increased—certainly not an indication that the new institution of Panchayati Raj has helped to increase the representation of the lower strata on these local bodies. For the rest there is a remarkable continuity between the personnel of panchayats before and after the introduction of Panchayati Raj: the middle and upper strata of the village virtually monopolize these elected positions. And since

[130] Data cited from the report of a Study Group on the Welfare of the Weaker Sections of the Village Community by R. Jagannathan, "Weaker Sections of the Village Community and Panchayati Raj," *Indian Journal of Public Administration,* VIII (October/December 1962), pp. 590–591.

for the first time the new panchayats and especially the Panchayat Samitis are authorized to spend considerable financial resources, it may be that service on these bodies has become more attractive to a younger generation of well-to-do peasants than was the case earlier.

These local elections have elicited very great interest at any rate. Out of 5835 elections for sarpanch in the 1960 panchayat elections for Rajasthan, 2271 or 39% were unopposed; of the remaining 3564 elections, 2131 were straight contests between two candidates, and 1433 involved contests among three or more candidates. More than one third of the elections was uncontested, but the total number of contestants was about twice the number of available positions. Voting participation in selected villages ranged from 58 to 78%, well above the rate of participation in national elections.[131] Another survey of panchayat elections in Uttar Pradesh indicates that 400,000 nominations were filed for a total of 72,000 positions (as sarpanch), while 1,500,000 nominations were filed for 1,100,000 positions as panchayat members.[132] Elsewhere interest in local elections is likely to be equally intense.

Such developments have been accompanied by admonitions that political parties should not enter and exacerbate local contests. Time and again, unanimous local elections are demanded to combat factionalism. Where unanimity occurs, it is cited as evidence of solidarity. In Rajasthan this position was institutionalized when prior to the elections the government offered a special grant of Rs. 25 per head to villages in which the sarpanch and at least 80% of the panches were elected unopposed.[133] At the same time the

[131] See *Panchayat Elections in Rajasthan*, Appendix C, Table 1.

[132] See Programme Evaluation Organization, Planning Commission, *A Note on Panchayat Elections in Punjab, Rajasthan and U.P.* (mimeographed), p. 9. In U. P. voting participation went as high as 80%.

[133] The Punjab government has a similar scheme of "grants-in-aid" to unanimity. See Tinker, *op. cit.*, pp. 126–127. According to Maheshwari, *op. cit.*, p. 847, 27.2% of the panchayats in Rajasthan qualified for this grant. The Rajasthan study shows that the percentage of unanimous panchayat elections ranged from a high

new role of the panchayats is praised in the name of enlisting the people's unity and enthusiasm in their efforts to advance themselves and their country.

The intensification of local politics can also be considered an inevitable and even salutary aspect of democracy. In the Indian context this view does not commend itself on ideological grounds, but in the years to come it is likely to grow to the extent that administrative controls and financial decisions are decentralized. As a member of the Lok Sabha put it in a recent symposium:

> We cannot possibly divide Rural India between persons who are interested in Panchayati Raj institutions in one camp and those who are interested in politics at the State and Central level in another. Anybody who is aware of realities is fully aware that Pradhans and Pramukhs are involved in politics and they need support at the State level. The government at the State level, official machinery at the district and block levels and the non-officials are so interlinked that each has an impact on the other.[134]

---

of 76% in one district to a low of 6% in another and that the proportion of unanimous elections correlated inversely with the size of the population covered by each panchayat. That is, unanimity increases as the constituency declines in size. See *Panchayat Elections in Rajasthan*, pp. 7, 19–20. The greater social homogeneity of the smaller communities explains this phenomenon only in part, since unanimous elections also reflect apathy or the use of pressure tactics, as the PEO study has pointed out. See *A Study of Panchayats*, p. 9. The most elaborate ideological defense of this antipolitical position and of the pre-eminent importance of decentralized self-government is contained in the writings of Jayaprakash Narayan. For the present context see his essay "The Role of Political Parties in Panchayati Raj," *Indian Journal of Public Administration*, VIII (October/December 1962), pp. 602–608. See also the discussion of the contrast between "consensual" and "adversary" politics in India by Susanne Rudolph, "Consensus and Conflict in Indian Politics," *World Politics*, XIII (April 1961), pp. 385–399.

[134] Harish Chandra Mathur, "Panchayati Raj and Political Parties," *Indian Journal of Public Administration*, VIII (October/December 1962), p. 615. Note also the subsequent statement in the same article: "Panchayati Raj will essentially mean relieving the State Government of a considerable amount of power and pa-

Accordingly, political parties will enter increasingly into local contests and the factionalism of village life will be intensified. The power to be gained at the local level has increased, and the extension of the franchise, involving as it does local as well as state and national issues, will lead to greater political mobilization than before.

Prospects of Change

At first glance the two positions just outlined merely represent the "old" and the "new" in Indian politics, the Gandhian vision of self-contained village republics on the one hand, and the acceptance of power politics as an inescapable aspect of Indian life on the other. Yet this conventional picture is too simple. Among the spokesmen for decentralization, democracy, and unity at the grass-roots level there are strong advocates of rapid economic change and centralized planning. Among those who accept the prospect of intensified political life at the village level are Indian traditionalists who defend the caste system, federalists who oppose excessive centralization, and "modernists" who endorse a "pluralist" structure as "democratic." Evidently, the familiar ideological positions have divergent political implications. To discern the prospects of change, bound up with these implications, this concluding discussion will focus attention on the relation between inequality and administrative authority.

The finding that panchayat members and panchayat presidents primarily come from the upper strata of village society comes as no surprise to students of village India. Ten years ago it was pointed out that panchayats are an inappropriate agency for community development on an equalitarian ba-

tronage. Resistance from the State level and the bureaucracy is natural. Officers through whom the State rules and administers will lose position and power. What we have today is a tug-of-war between these two forces." *Ibid.*, pp. 616–617. Pradhans are presiding officers of the Panchayat Samiti, pramukhs are presiding officers of the Zilla Parishad, and "nonofficials" is Indian jargon for elected local representatives.

sis, since local bodies inevitably reflect the great economic disparities of Indian villages.[135] These facts are well known, but the ideology of community development has tended to put a gloss over them, as, for example, when panchayats are called upon to spark development programs of benefit to the village as a whole. Still, there is full realization of the effects of social and economic inequalities at the village level.

A case in point is the discussion of land reform in the Third Five-Year Plan. In one respect this reform has been successful: some 40% of the area of the country had been covered by intermediary tenures, and the abolition of these tenures has brought more than 20 million tenants into direct relationship with the State.[136] Yet it has proved difficult to go beyond this initial step, so that the total impact of land reform has been less than had been hoped for.

> Where there is pressure on the land and the social and economic position of tenants in the village is weak, it becomes difficult for them to seek the protection of the law. Moreover, resort to the legal process is costly and generally beyond the means of tenants. Thus, in many ways, despite the legislation, the scales are weighed in favour of the continuance of existing terms and conditions.[137]

Consequently, the government has frequently been frustrated in its efforts to reduce rents, ensure security of land tenure, strengthen the enforcement of the rights of ownership, and redistribute land by prescribing a ceiling on agricultural holdings. The Third Five-Year Plan states that the aims of the law have been defeated, because the land-

[135] See Daniel Thorner, "The Village Panchayat as a Vehicle of Change," *Economic Development and Cultural Change*, II (1953), pp. 209–215. See also the confrontation of Thorner's position with the equalitarian assumptions of the "project approach" to community development, as represented in the work of Albert Mayer, in John T. Hitchcock, "Centrally Planned Rural Development in India," *Economic Weekly*, XIII (March 1961), pp. 435–441.

[136] *Third Five Year Plan*, pp. 221–222.

[137] *Ibid.*, p. 223.

transactions which have occurred have tended to evade the legal requirements. To prevent such evasions (or counteract their effects) reference is made time and again to the need for vigorous governmental action which would make it obligatory for owners to furnish receipts, find land for a tenant left without land to cultivate, have tenants pay for the acquisition of land directly to the government rather than the owner, and which in general would *"bring tenants into a direct relationship with the State."*[138] In this view the central government is the guardian of equality in India.

The preceding analysis has shown that the efforts to achieve more equality are based on: (1) the decision to achieve rapid economic growth through central planning and administration of capital-intensive enterprises; (2) the decision to reduce or combat existing inequalities arising from economic conditions (like concentration of land-ownership) and social practices (especially the caste-system), to do so simultaneously and—if need be—in the absence of an economic growth rapid enough to facilitate these efforts; and (3) the belief that in the face of little economic growth and great inequalities the initiative to increase the first and decrease the second must remain with the administration as long as the villagers will not do so of their own accord.[139]

[138] *Ibid.,* pp. 223, 226, 228, and *passim.* My italics. Note the similarity of this "plebiscitarian" approach with the statement by the Chairman of the "Backward Classes Commission," who would recognize only the individual and the nation as a whole as compatible with democracy. See above p. 334.

[139] This belief lends support to an "even spread" of the rural development effort which is an "administrative bias" in any case and which is supported in India by the government's reluctance to be anything other than "even-handed" for that would be "discriminatory" and allow for the intrusion of "communalism." Pressures for the satisfaction of regional demands have a comparable effect. For a critique of this approach see Kusum Nair, *Blossoms in the Dust* (London: Gerald Duckworth & Co., 1961), *passim.* Mrs. Nair strongly emphasizes the differential levels of aspiration and aptitudes for genuinely productive endeavor among different "communities" of agriculturalists, even in the same or adjacent localities, and accordingly she criticizes the "official" assumption that given

These decisions and beliefs support a centralization of administrative controls, a tendency which is enhanced by several other forces as well. The Constitution provides that special consideration and aid be given to the "weaker sections" of the Indian population; accordingly, there is continuous pressure upon the central government for assistance and preferment. Such pressure also arises from the dependence of the states and, through them, of districts and local bodies on the continued ability of the center to provide them with financial resources and other aids—a dependence which is increased further by the widespread and persistent reluctance of elected representatives to tax their own constituencies. These tendencies toward a centralization of administrative controls are strengthened in turn by conditions peculiar to public administration in India.

Among these conditions perhaps the most important is one that is implicit in the preceding discussion. In India, public administrators are called upon to implement egalitarian policies in a social structure marked by great inequalities. Typically, two things happen. Subordinates tend to look to their superiors for further instructions or review and authorization to proceed; they shun responsibility and seek reassurance. This tendency arises from the low pay and prestige of many positions, the insecurity bound up with the excess of applicants over available government positions, the consequent efforts of officials to "play it safe," and the resistance encountered in dealing with the public.[140] Superiors

---

similar financial incentives and physical resources all communities will respond similarly in their productive efforts.

[140] Since resistance frequently involves demands for favors, the most obvious consequence is corruption. For documentation of such a corrupt "web of mutual involvement"—a phrase coined by Joseph Berliner in his study of Soviet factory management—see *Report of the Railway Corruption Enquiry Committee, 1953–55* (Delhi: Government of India, Ministry of Railways, 1961), *passim.* It is worth emphasizing that the opposite of corruption is not just honesty, but the willingness of honest officials to assume responsibility for the decisions needed to implement policies even in the face of resistance. That considerable discretion is needed even at the lower echelons of the hierarchy, if planning is to succeed, has

frequently encourage the evasion of responsibility. In a poor and inequalitarian society subordinates are subject to great pressures. Their superiors may wish to guard against the resulting danger of corruption and policy sabotage, when they do not connive in promoting that danger. Accordingly, superiors request reports and initiate reviews which by their number interfere with or even jeopardize the work of subordinates, though the purpose is only to check and control. These practices suggest a lack of trust within the administration which appears to characterize not only superior-subordinate relations but also the spirit of administrative procedure.[141]

Thus, the great inequalities of Indian society, the plebiscitarian insistence on a direct relation between the "weaker sections" and the state, the desire to maximize economic growth and equality at the same time, the demand for state assistance by weak and strong alike, and the excessive centralization of administrative controls in response to political and administrative pressures—these are interrelated tendencies of the political community which make for much government and much inefficiency. Above all, centralized controls and an excess of consultation and referral interfere with the effective delegation and exercise of authority. As Paul Appleby has put it:

---

been emphasized by D. R. Gadgil, "Public Enterprise Administration," *Journal of the National Academy of Administration* (Mussourie), VI (July 1961), pp. 1–10.

[141] My reference here is to the abuse of advisory and reviewing functions. According to Paul Appleby, subordinate officials in various ministries tend to transform these "checking" functions into policy-decisions through excessively narrow construction of their responsibility. For an over-all analysis of the failure to delegate authority within and among ministries and other governmental agencies, and for documentation also of the tendency to substitute administrative procedures for decisions on policy, see Paul Appleby, *Re-Examination of India's Administrative System* (Delhi: Government of India, Cabinet Secretariat, 1956), *passim*. Mr. Appleby emphasizes that the tendencies he analyzes critically are not only intrinsic to the executive branch, but arise in part from the "negative influence" of Parliament. See *ibid.*, pp. 39–48.

One of the most important single facts about the Indian governmental system in general is that the drive to expand and to fulfill Plan objectives is extraordinarily confined to [the programmatic] agencies, while the long-established practices of review in Finance, in Home Affairs, in the activities of the Comptroller and Auditor General, in Parliamentary committees and in too frequent references to ministers and cabinets, are definitely hostile to governmental expansion and programme achievement. . . .

[Yet] growth requires a widening and deepening of hierarchies. . . . Room must be made for the insertion into hierarchy of new levels to take care of new functions and to receive more and more delegations of responsibility.[142]

The decentralization under Panchayati Raj may be seen as a partial response of the Indian government to the contingencies here analyzed.

With regard to rural development official spokesmen have denounced the excessive centralization of earlier efforts and demanded that villagers be given a voice in their own affairs. Rapid economic development cannot be achieved unless the villagers display greater initiative than they have hitherto. In the words of Prime Minister Nehru:

. . . the only way to get a response is to trust the peasant and give him power and authority to go ahead. The argument is used that he does not know enough. But this is fundamentally a wrong argument. . . . You should give them authority, technical help and, of course, such other help as you can give. But, essentially, authority and power must be given to the people in the villages. Let them function and let them make a million mistakes. Do not be afraid about it. [That risk should be cheerfully faced.] We are restricted in our thinking, and in our movement because of the way of our thinking. Let us give power to the Panchayats.[143]

[142] *Ibid.*, p. 14.

[143] See *Kurukshetra*, p. 269. The interpolated sentence is taken from another statement of Mr. Nehru's, *ibid.*, p. 318, but fits into this context as well. The last phrase recalls a slogan of the Russian revolution ("All power to the Soviets!"), but this allusion is primarily rhetorical.

Yet, from the standpoint of the egalitarianism embodied in the Constitution, the fear against which Nehru inveighs is very real. To give power and authority to the panchayats means in the foreseeable future to give it to the upper strata of village society. This runs counter to the aims of land reform, which have been evaded by the rural elites that are now given added powers under Panchayati Raj. It contravenes the aims of community development in so far as the same elites have exploited this program primarily for their own advantage. And it is an open question whether decentralization will result in a more rapid economic development of the rural areas.

It is not surprising, therefore, that the program of "democratic decentralization" has been greeted not only by the usual rhetoric praising the "dynamism of the people," but also by the demand that in practice the panchayats must "carry out the policies embodied in the Plan."[144] Yet this insistence upon the continued centralization of administrative controls even under Panchayati Raj poses a very large question. For the policy of decentralization is not only an administrative device for the distribution of funds by local bodies; it also entails a political mobilization of the rural electorate with regard to issues that really concern it. And while the predominance of the rural elite among the elected representatives is overwhelming at present, it must be re-

[144] Both are statements of V. T. Krishnamachari, former Deputy-Chairman of the Planning Commission. See his inaugural address in D. G. Karve, ed., *The Pattern of Rural Government* (New Delhi: Indian Institute of Public Administration, 1958), p. 21 and the quotation from his address to the 1961 Conference on Community Development, in Association of Voluntary Agencies for Rural Development (AVARD), *Report of a Study Team on Panchayati Raj in Andhra Pradesh* (New Delhi: 1961), p. 43. It should also be noted that State Governments are reserving the right to cancel or suspend particular resolutions of Panchayats and indeed to dissolve local bodies altogether. Evidence that currently the panchayati bodies have at best an advisory function in the formulation of the Plan and that "planning from below is more or less an illusion" is discussed in Yoginder K. Alagh, "Formulation of a State Plan, Rajasthan: A Case Study," *Economic Weekly*, XIV (July 1962), pp. 1051–1055.

membered that many of these upper-caste representatives already have solicited votes among the poor and low-caste majority of the village population. This is certainly a new fact in the Indian political community. Although it is not possible to anticipate its long-run repercussions, we can attempt to formulate schematically the terms of reference within which the prospects of political change in India may be examined.

For the vast majority of the Indian people in the rural areas these terms of reference are perhaps clearest. A large, if undefined segment of this majority at the bottom of the social and economic scale is passive, remote from contact with modern ideas and facilities, entirely dependent on the rural elite, its energies taken up with the task of staying alive. According to one estimate, this segment includes some 30% of the Indian people whose dire poverty will not be alleviated even if the most optimistic forecasts of Indian economic growth materialize.[145] Another, equally undefined segment of this bottom stratum has come in contact with one or another aspect of the government and modern facilities, and a minority of the most active have transcended the limitations of their low status. Some join an active religious organization, such as neo-Buddhism; others migrate to the city. Under special provisions of the Constitution some members of the scheduled castes obtain positions in institutions of higher education or in the government. And in the course of an increased political mobilization under Panchayati Raj a number will run for public office or at least become active politically. The major problem is posed by the relation between careers based on Constitutional privileges in favor of the disadvantaged and those associated with political mobilization. For education and government position (as well as migration to the city) remove the most active persons from the lower strata of the village and thus deprive these strata of the potential for leadership that

[145] This estimate was made in a lecture on Indian economic planning, by Dr. Morton C. Grossman (Consultant, Ford Foundation, New Delhi) at the University of California, December 17, 1962.

could find expression in political activities encouraged by Panchayati Raj.[146]

It is more difficult to outline the prospects of change from the standpoint of the rural elites, however schematic the attempt. The reason is simply that by definition the upper strata of the villages have more alternatives than do the scheduled castes and tribes. We can assume, of course, that these upper strata will defend their privileged position to the best of their ability, as they have done in the past. They can be counted on to attempt three things: (1) minimize the demands made locally by the lower strata; (2) maximize the resources made available locally by the government; and (3) minimize central controls over their local utilization. We have seen that under Panchayati Raj they can pursue these goals under conditions which allow for greater participation of local leaders in the distribution of available funds. At present, the declared goal is to introduce this degree of decentralization in all the states and territories. Eventually, the upper strata of India's villages may obtain more local power than they have acquired so far under Panchayati Raj; when some power is delegated, more delegation of power will be demanded. And to the extent

---

[146] Constitutional discrimination in favor of scheduled castes and tribes presumably has the purpose of becoming superfluous, once these lower strata have acquired a sufficient degree of social and economic equality with the higher strata. The political mobilization under Panchayati Raj is important because it could eventually provide career opportunities that are alternatives to those based on constitutional privileges. In that eventuality low-caste leaders could remain in the village or at least in local affairs, rather than leave these for the large cities. That is a potential gain of increased village factionalism which is rarely mentioned. For some of the paradoxes of "positive discrimination" see the discussion by Lelah Dushkin, "Special Treatment Policy," *Economic Weekly,* XIII (October 1961), pp. 1665–1668; "Removal of Disabilities," *loc. cit.* (November 1961), pp. 1695–1705; and "Future of Special Treatment," *loc. cit.* (November 1961), pp. 1729–1738. Note also the analysis by Marc Galanter, "The Problem of Group Membership: Some Reflections on the Judicial View of Indian Society," *Journal of the Indian Law Institute,* IV (July–September 1962), pp. 331–358.

that this drive for local authority is successful, it is likely to bring into the open the great conservatism of these village leaders. In this context conservatism means a preference for some or all of these eventualities:

1. Since under modern conditions it would be difficult to withdraw universal franchise once it has been granted, local leaders may prefer to see the most active individuals from the lower strata go to the cities and to government positions rather than remain in the village and make the political control of these lower strata more difficult than it would be in their absence.

2. One disadvantageous consequence of this line of action would be that through the recruitment of low-caste men to government positions it would tend to reinforce the equalitarian policies of the government. Still, the possibilities of evasion are numerous and the upper strata are interested in the minimization of central controls over local affairs in any case.

3. Given their reluctance to tax locally, the upper strata are interested in maximum benefits of all kinds from the government and in local control over their distribution, but not necessarily in the modernizing aims of the Five-Year Plans.

Perhaps the last point is of special importance. Communication and the franchise can spread to the countryside more rapidly than upper strata of the villages will transform their way of life which yields them the substantial advantages of a privileged position. In mobilizing the countryside politically and allowing for a measure of decentralization, the government may, therefore, succeed in mobilizing social forces that are inimical to policies which curtail the privileges of the local elites. From the standpoint of the upper strata the balance of advantage may lie in an increased drive for locally available resources, even if this results in less economic growth and still greater economic inequalities.[147]

[147] See the statement that "the modern idiom is moving out of its base in the elite just as surely as the traditional idiom is emerging from its hidden habitat" and the related discussion in W. H. Morris-Jones, "India's Political Idioms," in C. H. Philips, ed., *Poli-*

The question may become to what extent the planners of the central government—in conjunction with such grass-root support as they can obtain—can resist demands to this effect.

---

tics and Society in India (London: George Allen & Unwin, 1963), p. 146, and *passim*. An assessment of community development and Panchayati Raj which parallels the preceding analysis at several points is contained in Hugh Tinker, "The Village in the Framework of Development," in Braibanti and Spengler, eds., *op. cit.*, pp. 94–133. Professor Tinker's essay appeared after the completion of my study.

Concluding Considerations

India's Prime Minister Nehru died in 1964. Since then, the leaders of the independence movement have been replaced gradually by a new generation of political figures. For them the development *since* independence, the threat of China and the emerging rearrangements among the super-powers—rather than opposition to British rule and English ideas and institutions—will be the formative experience of their lives. Time will tell whether the foundations of a nation-state have been laid firmly. Although uniquely favored by relatively viable political institutions, India yet shares this uncertainty with a large number of countries for which independence is but a first step on the road to nation-building.

Governments possessing nationwide authority and a national citizenry are gradual and proximate achievements, even when these achievements are unquestioned. The foregoing studies have emphasized these "success stories," but without subscribing to the comfortable view that past patterns of nation-building will be followed elsewhere. We have seen rather that the Western, the Russian, and the Japanese experiences already encompass several meanings of the phrase "political modernization" and even in these cases successful nation-building is a difficult achievement. The case of India serves to remind us that the expansion of European ideas and institutions has placed the task of nation-building on the agenda of most countries, whether or not they are ready to tackle the job. In a broad sense, the problems faced by India are duplicated in the many countries attempting to build viable political communities in the middle of the twentieth century. The outcome of such attempts is uncertain and instances of "failure" at nation-building may be more numerous in the end than those of success. We may well face a period in history in which fragments of nation-building—like the quest for a national culture, the unification of language, the detribalization of a population, the assimilation of ethnic communities, the formalization of laws, the elimination of corruption, the maintenance of order, the demilitarization of quasi-autonomous groups, and a thousand other issues—are tackled piecemeal and without immediate prospect of a definitive outcome. In that perspective the dominant experience of our generation appears to be that the unanticipated repercussions of European expansion were effective enough to undermine or destroy existing social frameworks, but often not nearly effective enough to provide viable structural alternatives.

To future historians it may appear as a touching if minor irony that an organic conception of society based on the idea of equilibrium is one of the major intellectual perspectives of our time. In their eagerness to develop systematic social theory some scholars would have us look principally at the universal social processes which can be found in all countries, those which have built nation-states as well as those which may not succeed in this respect. But the life-chances of millions are affected by this difference between success and failure. An evolutionary perspective either ignores that difference or espouses the view that it will be obliterated eventually as sooner or later societies around the world will follow the development of the industrialized countries. I cannot accept these neo-evolutionist assumptions and propose to subject them to a critical examination in the concluding Part III of this volume.

PART THREE

8

TRADITION AND MODERNITY
RECONSIDERED

Modernization is a term which became fashionable after World War II. It is useful despite its vagueness because it tends to evoke similar associations in contemporary readers. Their first impulse may be to think of "the modern" in terms of present-day technology with its jet-travel, space exploration, and nuclear power. But the common sense of the word "modern" encompasses the whole era since the eighteenth century when inventions like the steam engine and the spinning jenny provided the initial, technical basis for the industrialization of societies. The economic transformation of England coincided with the movement of independence in the American colonies and the creation of the nation-state in the French revolution. Accordingly, the word "modern" also evokes associations with the democratization of societies, especially the destruction of inherited privilege and the declaration of equal rights of citizenship.

These changes of the eighteenth century initiated a transformation of human societies which is comparable in magnitude only to the transformation of nomadic peoples into settled agriculturalists some 10,000 years earlier. Until 1750 the proportion of the world's active population engaged in agriculture was probably

An earlier version of this essay was published in *Comparative Studies in Society and History*, IX (April 1967), pp. 292–346. Published by Cambridge University Press.

above 80 per cent. Two centuries later it was about 60 per cent, and in the industrialized countries of the world it had fallen below 50 per cent, reaching low figures like 10 to 20 per cent in countries that have a relatively long history of industrialization. In Great Britain, the country which pioneered in this respect, the proportion of the labor force engaged in agriculture reached a low of 5 per cent in 1950.[1]

Wherever it has occurred, the modernization of societies originated in social structures marked by inequalities based on kinship ties, hereditary privilege and established (frequently monarchical) authority. By virtue of their common emphasis on a hierarchy of inherited positions, pre-modern or traditional societies have certain elements in common. The destruction of these features of the old order and the consequent rise of equality are one hallmark of modernization; hence the latter process shows certain uniformities. These changes in the social and political order were apparent before the full consequences of the industrial revolution were understood. As a result, most (if not all) thinkers of the nineteenth century

> ... exhibit the same burning sense of society's sudden, convulsive turn from a path it had followed for millennia. All manifest the same profound intuition of the disappearance of historic values—and, with them, age-old securities, as well as age-old tyrannies and inequalities—and the coming of new powers, new insecurities, and new tyrannies . . . .[2]

And, as Professor Nisbet adds, "sociology in Europe was developed almost wholly around the themes and antitheses cast up

[1] See Carlo M. Cipolla, *The Economic History of World Population* (Baltimore: Penguin Books, 1964), pp. 24–28. By focusing attention on the technical and economic effects of the process, Cipolla provides a comprehensive formulation of what is meant by industrialization. Nothing like that clarity can be achieved with regard to "modernization," which is more inclusive and refers, albeit vaguely, to the manifold social and political processes that have accompanied industrialization in most countries of Western civilization. The following discussion contains contributions towards a definition of "modernization."

[2] See Robert A. Nisbet, *Emile Durkheim* (Englewood Cliffs: Prentice-Hall, 1965), p. 20.

by the two revolutions and their impact upon the old order."[3] We owe many insights to this intellectual tradition. Yet today there are indications that this perspective gave an oversimplified view of traditional societies, of modern societies, and of the transition from the one to the other. Oversimplification resulted from ideological interpretations of the contrast between tradition and modernity, and from undue generalizations of the European experience. Today, a more differentiated and balanced analysis of modernization should be possible; the following discussion is presented as a contribution to that end.

Its first part deals with an aspect of the history of ideas. The rise of industrial civilization in Europe engendered a new conception of society, invidious contrasts between tradition and modernity, and a theory of social change culminating in the work of Karl Marx and most recently in a revival of theories of social evolution. My effort will be to show how our conceptual vocabulary in studies of modernization developed. The second part offers a methodological critique of this intellectual tradition and proposes an alternative conceptualization of the contrast between tradition and modernity. In the third part I shall attempt to develop a comparative approach to the study of modernization and illustrate it by application to the field of social stratification.

PERSISTENCE AND CHANGE OF IDEAS ABOUT MODERN SOCIETY

A New Perspective

The sense that the late eighteenth century represents a hiatus in intellectual perspective as well as a new departure in the history of Western civilization is as common among scholars as is the related connotation of the term "modern" among people at large. Before the 17th and 18th centuries, the world of nature and of man was conceived as an emanation of Divine providence. Since then our thinking has been restructured in all fields of learning. As the idea

[3]*Ibid.*, p. 21 n.

of God became fused with that of Nature, the concept of the universe created at the beginning of time was gradually replaced by the idea of an infinitely various and endlessly active process of evolution. The idea was applied in parallel fashion to our understanding of the growth of knowledge, to a new conception of God as in Schelling's *Natur philosophie*, and to an ethical interpretation of world history as in Kant's view that "all the excellent natural faculties of mankind would forever remain undeveloped" if it were not for man's nature with its quarrelsomeness, its enviously competitive vanity, and its insatiable desire to possess or to rule.[4] Here was one of many schemes by which thinkers of the late eighteenth and early nineteenth centuries linked the fractious qualities of individual men with the concept of a self-contained regularity or lawfulness attributed to the social world. While Kant used a teleological construction in this respect, classical economists like Adam Smith asserted that man's propensity to truck, barter, and exchange one thing for another gave rise to actions obeying an impersonal law of supply and demand. By their actions in society individuals conform to a regularity or higher principle without intending to do so. Phrases like the "end of nature" or the "invisible hand" by which Kant and Smith referred to such a higher principle may be considered a survival of an earlier belief in Divine providence or a harbinger of later concepts of "society" and "economy." In any case, they helped to usher in a new view of the social world as an impersonal structure possessing attributes or principles of its own.

The following discussion presents an historical sketch of ideas about the new, industrial society in the making—with special emphasis upon the effects of that society on different social classes. My purpose is to show that the invidious contrast between tradition and modernity is the master-theme which underlies a great diversity of topics and influences our understanding of modern society to this day.

[4]Immanuel Kant, "Idea for a Universal History with Cosmopolitan Intent," in Carl J. Friedrich, ed., *The Philosophy of Kant* (New York: Random House, 1949), p. 121. Note the relation of this view to the intellectual tradition traced in Arthur Lovejoy, *The Great Chain of Being* (New York: Harper and Bros., 1961), passim.

In his *Essay on the History of Civil Society*, first published in 1767, Adam Ferguson attributed the progress of a people to the subdivision of tasks (Adam Smith's division of labor) which at the same time improves the skills of the artisan, the profits of the manufacturer, and the enjoyment of consumers.

> Every craft may engross the whole of a man's attention, and has a mystery which must be studied ... Nations of tradesmen come to consist of members, who beyond their one particular trade, are ignorant of all human affairs, and who may contribute to the preservation and enlargement of their commonwealth, without making its interest an object of their regard or attention.[5]

Ferguson's discussion formulates ways of looking at modern society which have become commonplace. The division of labor necessarily restricts the understanding of those who specialize. In so doing it also increases their productivity and the wealth of the country. Hence, private ends, a lack of conscious concern for public welfare, and public benefits go together. This laissez-faire doctrine is joined, as Marx already noted, with a theory of social action, at least in rudimentary form. By only attending to his business, each man is distinguished by his calling and has a place to which he is fitted. In Ferguson's view the differences among men are a direct outcome of the habits they acquire in practicing different arts: "Some employments are liberal, others mechanic. They require different talents, and inspire different sentiments."[6] In his assessment of these corrolaries of specialization, Ferguson combines the older conventional wisdom with insight into the emerging problems of modern society. The old division of society into a leisured, ruling minority and the bulk of a working population is reflected in his view that social rank depends on the work men do. Those who must eke out a mere subsistence are degraded by the "objects they pursue, and by the means they employ to attain it." Those who belong to the superior class are bound to no task and are free to follow the disposition of their mind and heart.

At the same time, Ferguson is well aware that increasing di-

[5]Adam Ferguson, *An Essay on the History of Civil Society*, 5th ed. (London: T. Codell, 1782), pp. 302-3.
[6]*Ibid.*, pp. 308-9.

vision of labor exacts a price. The ends of society are best promoted by mechanical arts requiring little capacity and thriving best "under a total suppression of sentiment and reason."[7] Another Scotch philosopher, John Millar, points out that art and science improve with the division of labor, but produce in the worker, who is employed in a single manual operation, a "habitual vacancy of thought, unenlivened by many prospects, but such as are derived from future wages of their labor, or from the grateful returns of bodily repose and sleep."[8] The human cost of manual labor under modern conditions of production is thus a theme from the very beginning of industrial society.

It was argued that this human cost is inevitable. The burdens of the laboring classes under the new conditions are simply a new form of the ancient division of society into masters and servants. Attempts to relieve these burdens only decrease the wealth of a country and hence ultimately aggravate the lot of the workers themselves.[9] Yet this advocacy of the traditional rank-order under new conditions did not in the long run match the significance of another, much more critical body of opinion.

Conservative and Radical Critiques of Industry.

In many parts of Europe men of letters viewed the discrepancies between rich and poor with alarm and with a feeling that the destitution of the people represented a new phenomenon and an

[7] *Ibid.*, p. 305.

[8] See John Millar, "Social Consequences of the Division of Labor," reprinted in William C. Lehmann, *John Millar of Glasgow, 1735–1801* (Cambridge University Press, 1960), pp. 380–82. This volume contains a reprint of Millar's *Origin of the Distinction of Ranks*, first published in 1771.

[9] Edmund Burke, "Thoughts and Details on Scarcity (1795)," in *Works* (Boston: Little, Brown and Co., 1869), V, pp. 134–35. Burke himself used the laissez-faire doctrine to support his argument. The law of supply and demand governed the wages paid to labor and interference with that law would merely aggravate the condition of the poor. The traditional argument against the injustice of this system is exemplified by William Godwin, *Enquiry Concerning Political Justice and its Influence on Morals and Happiness* (Toronto: University of Toronto Press, 1946), I, pp. 15–20.

increasing threat to the social order. The ideas of a growing bi-furcation of society into two opposed classes, as well as the doc-trine of pauperization, which are familiar to modern readers from the writings of Karl Marx, were in fact beliefs spelled out by many European writers during the seventeenth and eighteenth centuries.[10] Their sense of crisis is reflected in ideas about social rank which sought to take account of the changes occurring in industrializing societies. To exemplify these ideas, indicate some-thing of their ubiquity, and show how strongly they have influ-enced modern social thought, I shall take examples from Ger-many, France, and the United States. These judgments about social ranks in a period of transition reflect both the experience and moral sense of men of different social ranks and the moral sense with which the writer himself regards the role of different groups in that transition.

The first example contrasts a conservative and a humanist cri-tique of commercialization in late eighteenth-century Germany. In 1778 the publicist Justus Möser complained in an article on "genuine property" that in his day the German language had lost its capacity to designate an owner's inalienable relationship to his property.[11] At one time ownership of land included associated rights in addition to those of proprietorship, such as the right to hunt, to vote in the National Assembly, and others. These rights had been known by distinctive terms which gave a clue to the specific rights an owner enjoyed in perpetuity. He could sell or otherwise dispose of the land itself, but he could not divest himself of these rights any more than a purchaser of the land could acquire them. Möser's critique of the change of language is thus at the same time an indictment of moral decay resulting from an easy transfer of property. The relationship between an owner and his property is in his view a source of personal identification and social stability. These are ensured as long as ownership of land confers on the proprietor rights and privileges which give him status in the

---

[10]Cf. the survey of these opinions by Robert Michels, *Die Verelen-dungs theorie* (Leipzig: Alfred Kroener, 1928), passim.

[11]Justus Möser, *Sämtliche Werke* (Berlin: Nicolaische Buchhandlung, 1842), IV, pp. 158–62. I owe this reference to the article by Karl Mannheim, cited below.

community and can be obtained by inheritance only, not by purchase.

The humanist critique of commercialization looks at first glance very similar to that of Möser. Trading as well as the ownership and care of property undermine an individual's integrity, because his every act and thought turns on considerations of money and economic expediency. Man is ruled by that which should be at his service. In his novel, *Wilhelm Meisters Lehrjahre*, originally published in 1796, Goethe expresses this view when he writes:

> What can it avail me to manufacture good iron whilst my own breast is full of dross? Or to what purpose were it to understand the art of reducing landed estates to order, when my own thoughts are not in harmony?[12]

But Goethe's hero goes on to relate this anticommercial view to the conflicting personal values of the *Bürger* and the aristocrat. The latter, he claims, has polished manners in keeping with his lofty social position, but he does not cultivate his heart. The *Bürger* cannot make such pretensions. For him the decisive question is not "who he is," but what "discernment, knowledge, talents, or riches" he possesses.

> He must cultivate some individual talent, in order to be useful, and it is well understood that in his existence there can be no harmony, because in order to render one talent useful, he must abandon the exercise of every other.[13]

Thus, to Goethe's hero, the aristocrat has high social standing but a cold heart, the *Bürger* may gain distinction by his attainments, but only the artist is in a position to pursue the "harmonious cultivation of his nature."[14]

[12]Johann W. Goethe, *Wilhelm Meister's Apprenticeship*, trans. By R. Dillon Boylan (London: Bell and Doldy, 1867), p. 268. See also Baron Knigge, *Practical Philosophy of Social Life* (Lansingburgh: Perriman and Bliss, 1805), pp. 307-8.

[13]Goethe, *op. cit.*

[14]See Werner Wittich, "Der soziale Gehalt von Goethes Roman 'Wilhelm Meisters Lehrjahre'," in Melchior Palyi, ed., *Hauptprobleme der Soziologie, Erinnerungsgabe für Max Weber* (Berlin: Duncker and Humblot, 1923), II, pp. 278-306.

The resemblance between these views does not go beyond their common rejection of commerce. Möser looks backwards towards a society characterized by a rank-order of privilege and subordination based on land and the rights associated with landownership. He attributes to that society not merely stability, but ideal qualities of mind and feeling such that man's relations to his fellows are in harmony and his work an adequate outlet for his capabilities. Against this mythical image of the past, the commercialization of property appears as a decay of civilization. During the century and a half which followed, Möser's praise of inalienable, prescriptive rights was associated again and again not only with the benevolence of paternalistic rule but also with the warmth of personal relations and the sense of personal belonging, made possible by a closely knit, hierarchic community. Against this benign view of tradition Goethe's hero defines his own position by referring to the empty, cruel heart which goes together with the polished manners of the aristocrat. Bourgeois man stands forth by virtue of his *individual achievements*, which represent greater personal worth than the ease and poise which are an unearned, and hence unmerited, byproduct of inherited privilege. The *Bürger* may lack manners, but at least his individual attainments establish his personal worth. Yet like Ferguson and Millar, Goethe's hero decries the stultifying effects of specialization. The merit of achievement is only relative, for in the ordinary man it is the result of a one-sided development; all his other capacities are sacrificed so that he may be useful. This praise of man's protean capacities—here put as the artist's many-sided cultivation of his personality—has been associated ever since with the radical critique of bourgeois civilization. An emphasis on achievement as an attribute of that civilization entirely misses this inherent ambiguity of the value of individual striving and creativity.

The two opinions from late eighteenth century Germany reflect a provincial setting in which economic change was slow, but in which imaginative men witnessed more rapid changes taking place in England and France. The classic document portraying this response is Goethe's epic poem *Hermann und Dorothea* in which the upheavals of the French revolution are commented on from afar and in eloquent contrast to the well-being and contentment of an average, small-town *Bürger* family.[15] Under these circumstances reflections about the effects of commerce on the ranks of society tended to be abstract, whether they consisted of nostalgic references to the past or humanistic celebrations of personal values.

With the advance of commerce and industry during the first decades of the nineteenth century, critical reflections on the impact of these changes continued. Invidious contrasts between tradition and modernity, and between one-sided utility and individual creativity, were elaborated and reiterated, but with more direct attention to the nature of work. Across an interval of more than two generations one may compare the contrast between Möser and Goethe's hero in Germany with the contrast between de Bonald and Proudhon in France. According to Bonald, industry has increased the material wealth of the country, but it has also produced civic unrest and moral decay. Members of families employed in industry

> ... work in isolation and frequently in different industries. They have no more acquaintance with their master than what he commands and what little he pays. Industry does not nourish all ages nor all sexes. True, it employs the child, but frequently at the expense of his education or before he is sufficiently strong for such work. On the other hand, when a man has reached old age and can no longer work, he is abandoned and has no other bread than that which his children may provide or public charity bestow . . . .
>
> The [industrial laborer] works in crowded and sedentary conditions, turns a crank, runs the shuttle, gathers the threads. He spends his life in cellars and garrets. He becomes a machine himself. He exercises his fingers but never his mind . . . . Everything debases the intelligence of the industrial worker . . . .[16]

[15]For documentation of the social and literary life of the period cf. W. H. Bruford, *Germany in the 18th Century* (Cambridge University Press, 1939), passim. The literary and philosophical response to the French revolution is analyzed in Alfred Stern, *Der Einfluss der französichen Revolution auf das deutsche Geistesleben* (Stuttgart: Cotta, 1928), but I know of no comparable summary treatment of the German response to English industrialization. Cf., however, Hans Freyer, *Die Bewertung der Wirtschaft im philosophischen Denken des 19. Jahrhunderts* (Leipzig: W. Engelmann, 1921), for some relevant materials.

[16]M. de Bonald, *Oevres Complètes* (Paris: J. P. Migne, 1864), II, pp. 238–39.

In this critique of industry emphasis on the incapacities resulting from specialization are related to the industrial worker and his family. To eke out a subsistence, members of the family are dispersed, they work in isolation, and have no human relationship with their employer. In addition, industry as a whole abuses the child and gives no care to the aged.

In all these respects agricultural work is superior. On the land the different classes work alongside each other and at the same tasks; hence there is no social isolation between them. Children and old people are cared for and productively employed at tasks commensurate with their capacities. Agricultural work is not only healthy in contrast with industrial, it also furthers the intelligence of the peasant or farm laborer. Cultivation of the land demands attention to varied tasks, furthers neighborly cooperation, and through contact with natural processes lifts thought "to that which endows the earth with fertility, gives us the seasons, makes the fruit ripen."[17] Where Möser emphasizes the social stability and moral worth achieved by inalienable property rights, Bonald emphasizes that similar values are inherent in the nature of agricultural work. For Bonald as for Möser, the material benefits of commerce and industry are not worth the price in human values they exact. For both, the traditional social order represents sociability, meaningful human relations, proper security, care for young and old, and man's opportunity to develop his capacities to the full. In all these respects industry is said to fail; its sole accomplishment is the increase of wealth.

This critique of industry is not very different at points from Proudhon's radical attack upon the new industrial order (1846). Proudhon also believes that specialization has a destructive effect upon the individual. Like Bonald he deplores the helplessness of industrial workers and feels that the advance of technology turns

[17] *Ibid.* Note in passing that this contrast between agricultural and industrial work is made in almost identical terms by John Millar, years earlier. The difference between Millar's liberalism and Bonald's conservatism seems to be reflected only in Millar's emphasis on the knowledge of the peasant and Bonald's greater stress on his religion. Cf. Lehmann, *op. cit.*, pp. 380–82. As Max Weber has pointed out, this emphasis on the piety of the peasant is a distinctly modern phenomenon, related to invidious contrasts between town and country. See Max Weber, *Economy and Society, op. cit.*, II, p. 470.

men into machines.[18] But their common critique of industry and praise of agriculture shows that Proudhon and Bonald see the same facts in entirely different terms. For example, both agree that agricultural work is many-sided, not one-sided and stultifying like industrial work. Yet Proudhon finds this praiseworthy as the foundation of individualism, not like Bonald as the foundation of neighborliness and cooperation. Proudhon sees the agricultural proprietor as the solitary man who tills the soil for his family and does not depend upon the assistance of others; "never have peasants been seen to form a society for the cultivation of their fields; never will they be seen do do so." This ability to maintain his family by his own efforts makes the peasant into the ideal anarchist. By contrast Proudhon emphasizes that certain industries "require the combined employment of a large number of workers" involving subordination and mutual dependence. "The producer is no longer, as in the fields, a sovereign and free father of a family; it is a collectivity."[19] Thus, for Proudhon, industry is the locus of an enforced collectivism, mutual dependence, and subordination, whereas agriculture enhances freedom and individualism. He favors agriculture, because he rejects the "hierarchy of capacities" as a "principle and law" of social organization.[20] By contrast, Bonald accepts inequalities among men as a fact of nature which is merely recognized by society. For him the distinction between industry and agriculture turns on the question of which activity furthers the community, not the individual; and in this respect industry enhances human isolation, while agriculture promotes human solidarity.

Clearly, both writers structure the evidence to suit their purpose. For Proudhon neighborly assistance disappears from the agricultural community, because he searches for a personification of the individualism which is his ideal; for Bonald the harshness of the peasant's struggle with nature, and the human abuse which is endemic in close neighborly relations, disappear in the roseate

---

[18]P. J. Proudhon, *A System of Economic Contradictions or The Philosophy of Misery* (Boston: Benjamin R. Tucker, 1888), I, p. 138.

[19]P. J. Proudhon, *General Idea of the Revolution in the 19th Century* (London: Freedom Press, 1923), p. 215. This work was written in 1851.

[20]Proudhon, *Philosophy of Misery*, p. 132.

image of the community modelled on the familial pattern. Much the same is true of the two views of industry. For Proudhon the *relative* freedom of the industrial worker does not exist, and he ignores the fundamental subordination of the farm laborer in agriculture. Bonald, on the other hand, sees the worker's freedom only in its negative side, as human isolation in contrast to a benign solidarity in agriculture. One man idealizes agriculture as the bulwark of traditional society; the other, however, mistakenly, as the principal means of leveling social differences, decreasing mutual dependence, and enhancing individual freedom. Transparent as they are, such ideological constructions have had a profound influence upon the contrast of tradition and modernity down to the present.

To these examples I wish to add a brief reference to similar arguments on this side of the Atlantic. They will show something of the persistence of the intellectual tradition I am characterizing, even under quite divergent conditions. In the United States conservative views like those of Bonald had been openly expressed during the first decades following the Declaration of Independence. During the 1830's the public disclosure of these views became politically inexpedient, even among New England conservatives.[21] At the same time, the belief in inequality became a matter of deep conviction in the Southern states. In this regional context, conservative views became linked with an attack on Northern industrialism, on the one hand, and a defense of slavery, on the other. In his *Sociology for the South*, George Fitzhugh denounced men of property who are masters without the feelings and sympathies of masters, engaged in the selfish struggle to better their pecuniary condition and hence without time or inclination to cultivate the heart or the head.[22] Fitzhugh reiterates the theme which is already familiar to us: that the division of labor may make men more efficient, but also confines the worker to some monotonous employment and makes him an easy prey of the capitalist,

[21]Cf. Norman Jacobson, *The Concept of Equality in the Assumptions of the Propaganda of Massachusetts Conservatives*, 1790–1840, Ph.D. Dissertation (University of Wisconsin, 1951).

[22]George Fitzhugh, *Sociology for the South* (Richmond: A. Morris, 1854), pp. 233, 235.

who considers him solely in monetary terms.[23] In this setting the standard argument against the division of labor, which Marx emphasized so much, is used in a defense of slavery! For Fitzhugh contrasts the moral destitution of the free laborer, hated by his employer for the demands he makes and by his fellow workers because he competes for employment, with the moral attainments and domestic tranquillity of the South, which is founded upon the parental affection of the masters and child-like obedience of the slaves.[24]

This view is strangely echoed by Orestes A. Brownson, a New England cleric and radical Christian who had identified himself with the workers in the 1830's, and later became converted to Catholicism. Brownson contrasts the moral degradation imposed on both employers and workers with the benign features of paternalism:

> Between the master and the slave, between the lord and the serf, there often grow up pleasant personal relations and attachments; there is personal intercourse, kindness, affability, protection on the one side, respect and gratitude on the other, which partially compensates for the superiority of the one and the inferiority of the other; but the modern system of wages allows very little of all this: the capitalist and the workman belong to different species, and have little personal intercourse. The agent or man of business pays the workman his wages, and there ends the responsibility of the employer. The laborer has no further claim on him and he may want and starve, or sicken and die, it is his own affair, with which the employer has nothing to do. Hence the relation between the two classes becomes mercenary, hard and a matter of arithmetic.[25]

This language is not essentially different from that of the *Communist Manifesto*; it culminates in the contrasting images of exploiters and exploited, of haughty indifference, on the one hand, and injured hostility, on the other. Brownson even uses Marx's

[23]*Ibid.*, pp. 161.

[24]*Ibid.*, pp. 106-7, 253-54. A major analysis of this Southern ideology in historical perspective is contained in W. J. Cash, *The Mind of the South* (Garden City: Doubleday & Co., 1954), passim.

[25]Orestes A. Brownson, *Works* (Detroit: T. Nourse, 1884), V, pp. 116-17. This passage was written in 1857, after the author's conversion to Catholicism.

symbol of the worker as an appendage to the machine, though the phrase may have been common among social critics of the mid-nineteenth century.

The examples I have cited suggest that from the late eighteenth century on men of letters were made deeply anxious by what they considered the moral crisis in human relations, brought on by the coming of industry. Karl Mannheim has pointed out that critics like Möser and Goethe or Bonald and Proudhon were deeply divided in their political views but nonetheless based their opposition to industrial society on grounds that are similar to quite a striking extent.[26] Industry depends upon the division of labor and as that division progresses men cease to be masters of the machines they use and instead become their victims. As labor becomes more monotonous, workers are increasingly deprived of the opportunity to develop and apply their human faculties. More generally, the specialized development of one capacity in the interest of productivity and commercial success entails the atrophy of many or most other capacities. Industrial man appears as the counterimage of Renaissance man, and that at all levels of the social structure. At the same time, commercialization loosens the ties which bind men to each other. Freedom from paternal rule and the hierarchy of rank is obtained for the individual, but only at the price of fraternity. The ties among men lose their basis in sentiment and the sense of moral obligation and come to depend on economic interest alone. As equals men compete with one another rather than cooperate and as employers and workers they strike bargains solely in terms of material advantage.

These themes have been standbys of social thought for almost two centuries.[27] They owe their profound emotional appeal to the

[26]Karl Mannheim, "Conservative Thought," in *Essays in Sociology and Social Psychology* (London: Routledge and Kegan Paul, 1953), pp. 74–164.

[27]Different meanings of "alienation" as the common theme of anti-industrial sentiment are examined in Lewis Feuer's essay on this concept in Maurice Stein and Arthur Vidich, eds., *Sociology on Trial* (Englewood Cliffs: Prentice-Hall, 1963), pp. 127–47. That men of opposite political persuasion have come to employ this concept is analyzed sociologically by René König, "Zur Soziologie der Zwanziger Jahre," in Leonhard Reinisch, ed., *Die Zeit ohne Eigenschaften* (Stuttgart: W. Kohlhammer, 1961), pp. 82–118.

invidious linkage between the transition to an industrial society and the decline of the two ideas of individual creativity and human fraternity. Obviously, conservatives attribute both of these values to a largely symbolic, hierarchic order of the past, but implicitly (and sometimes explicitly also) radical critics of industrial society use the same clichés. By their incorporation in the work of Karl Marx these clichés have become a dominant influence on modern thought because of the unique way in which Marx combined the sense of moral crisis described above with his claim that his approach represented a scientific study of society. Reflections on Marx's theories are legion; here they will be pursued only to the extent that the reader can form an independent judgment of the differences between the presentation which follows and the most influential treatment of social classes in the process of modernization.

The Marxian Perspective

"The history of all hitherto existing societies is the history of class struggles." The *Communist Manifesto* begins with this sentence, yet Marx's work as a whole does not contain a sustained analysis of social classes. The third volume of his lifework, *Das Kapital*, breaks off after four paragraphs of a chapter which was to be devoted to this topic. The paradox has often been commented on, but it is more apparent than real. Probably Marx had said what he had to say about social classes, since it is not difficult to summarize his views.[28]

For Marx classes are but the agents of social change, their ultimate determinant is the organization of production. His reasons for this assumption go back to early philosophical considerations. Today these would be considered existentialist in the sense of inferences derived from basic exigencies of human experience. Men cannot live without work; they also propagate their kind and

[28]The following account is based in part on Reinhard Bendix and Seymour M. Lipset, "Karl Marx's Theory of Social Classes," in *Class, Status and Power* (New York: The Free Press, 1966), pp. 6–11.

hence enter into the social relations of the family. Men use tools to satisfy their needs; as needs are satisfied, new needs arise and techniques of production are improved. The proliferation of needs and improved techniques put a premium on cooperation based on some division of labor, for divided labor increases productivity. How labor is divided depends on the organization of production, specifically on the distribution of property in the means of production. It is, therefore, the position the individual occupies in the organization of production, which indicates to which social class he belongs.

In the unfinished chapter on class, Marx distinguishes between wage-laborers, capitalists, and landlords which form the three great classes of capitalist society, and he emphasizes the "infinite distinctions of interest and position which the social division of labor creates *among* workers as *among* capitalists and landowners."[29] In a complex society, individuals are distinguished from one another in a great many ways, even when they belong to the same class. Thus, individuals who depend entirely upon wage-labor may still differ greatly in terms of income, consumption patterns, educational attainment, or occupation. Efforts to ascertain class membership by grouping people in terms of their similar share in the distribution of material goods, skills, and prestige symbols, only produces statistical artifacts in Marx's view. For him "class" refers to a process of group formation in which people are united despite the "infinite distinctions of interest and position" which divide them.[30] To be sure, a shared position in the organization of production is the necessary condition of a social class. But only the experienced gained in making a living, and particularly the experience of economic and political conflict, would prompt workers, capitalists, or landowners to develop a consciousness of class and become united in action. Marx specified

[29]See Thomas B. Bottomore and Maximilien Rubel, eds., *Karl Marx, Selected Writings in Sociology and Social Philosophy* (London: Watts and Co., 1956), p. 179. My italics.

[30]Cf. T. H. Marshall's definition of class as "a force that unites into groups people who differ from one another, by overriding the differences between them." See his *Class, Citizenship and Social Development* (Garden City: Doubleday & Co., 1964), p. 164.

a number of conditions that would facilitate the process. Where communication of ideas among individuals in the same class position is easy, repeated economic conflicts will lead to a growth of solidarity and a sense of historic opportunities. Profound dissatisfactions arise from an inability to control the economic structure in which the ruling class curtails the economic advance of the group and subjects it to exploitation. In Marx's view a social class becomes an agent of historical change when these dissatisfactions lead to the formation of political organizations. A fully developed class is a politically organized group, capable of overcoming in action the distinctions of interest and rank that divide it.

This interpretation of social class was based in the first instance on Marx's detailed observations of the English labor movement which he himself systematized in the following words:

> Large-scale industry assembles in one place a crowd of people who are unknown to each other. Competition divides their interests. But the maintenance of their wages, this common interest which they have against their employer, brings them together again in the same idea of resistance—*combination*. Thus combination has always a double aim, that of putting an end to competition among themselves, to enable them to compete as a whole with the capitalist. If the original aim of resistance was that of maintaining wages, to the extent that the capitalists, in their turn, unite with the aim of repressive measures, the combinations, at first isolated, became organized into groups, and in face of the unity of the capitalists, the maintenance of the combination becomes more important than upholding the level of wages. This is so true that English economists have been astonished to observe the workers sacrificing a substantial part of their wages in favour of the associations, which in the eyes of the economists were only established to defend wages. In this struggle—a veritable civil war—all the elements for a future battle are brought together and developed. Once arrived at this point the association takes on a political character.[31]

This conception of class as a group gradually emerging to self-consciousness and political organization was at once analysis and projection. Analysis in so far as Marx systematized his observations of emerging working-class movements in England from the

[31]Bottomore and Rubel, *op. cit.*, pp. 186–87.

late eighteenth to the middle of the nineteenth century.[32] Projection in so far as Marx generalized from this analysis, both with regard to the formation of classes in the past (for example, that of the bourgeoisie under feudalism) and with regard to the development of a revolutionary working class in the future. The latter views applied not only in England but in all countries undergoing a capitalist development such as England had experienced since the eighteenth century. We should understand what gave Marx confidence in predicting that the struggle he analyzed would eventuate in a revolutionary overthrow and reconstitution of society.

The first point to be mentioned is Marx's acceptance and dramatic elaboration of the ideas briefly described above. Like Ferguson, Millar, Möser, Goethe, Bonald, Proudhon, Fitzhugh, Brownson, and a host of others, Marx was deeply impressed by the moral crisis which capitalism had wrought in man's relation with his fellows and his work. To cite Marx's views on alienation at this point would be to repeat many of the moral reflections cited earlier (albeit in more Hegelian language) and what has been elaborated in a thousand ways by critics of modern society since his day.[33] But Marx's elaboration of widely shared beliefs assumed special significance. The reason is, I believe, that for him the mounting alienation of men was part of an economic process in which repeated and severe depressions together with the capitalists' restrictive practices would create an ever-increasing discrepancy between the forces and the organization of production, or, in

[32]A recent massive study by E. K. Thompson, *The Making of the English Working Class* (New York: Pantheon Books, 1964), passim, enables us to appreciate this Marxian perspective in that it describes the movements Marx observed with the benefit of another hundred years of scholarship. However, the author faithfully reproduces Marx's own blindness to the strongly conservative elements that were an enduring part of working-class agitation (by treating these elements as a passing phase) as well as to the mounting gradualism of the labor movement (by terminating his study in the 1830s).

[33]A convenient compilation of relevant quotations from Marx is contained in Bottomore and Rubel, *op. cit.*, Part III, Chap. 4. To my knowledge the most comprehensive analysis of this complex of ideas is that of Karl Löwith, *From Hegel to Nietzsche* (New York: Holt, Rinehart and Winston, 1964).

simpler language, between the economy's capacity to satisfy human needs and the satisfaction of needs which is actually achieved. Marx's economic analysis seeks to support this interpretation, and in view of the importance he attached to it he had no reason to feel that he had neglected the analysis of social class. His analysis is distinguished from the many other writers who developed similar themes by the belief that he had proved man's alienation to be a symptom of the *final* phase of "pre-history."

Secondly, Marx welcomed the technical and economic changes which were revolutionizing the old order but, he saw the difference between then and now in a very special way. Earlier epochs were marked by "manifold gradations of social rank," but the modern era tends towards a simplified antagonism between bourgeoisie and proletariat. While this prediction has not stood the test of time, it is of a piece with his view that all previous history is pre-history. Never before had the social world been stripped of all its traditional practices and religious beliefs; only now had it been revealed as it really is, capable of a rational ordering by men who have come within reach of satisfying all their desires. Eventually, the classless, communist society of the future would establish both a true fraternity among men and on that basis an opportunity for each to develop and apply his capacities. Though he refused to speculate about this new order, Marx was emphatic that world history was nearing its decisive turning point. In his view man's productive potential had become so great that the deprivations of inequality and hence the substitute gratifications of religious beliefs had become obsolete. For the same reasons human relations have become transparent so that the social order is now capable of being "consciously regulated by freely associated men in accordance with a settled plan."[34] Marx believed that this equalitarian society of the future would bring about a complete break with the

---

[34] Karl Marx, *Capital* (New York: The Modern Library, 1936), p. 92. Marx attributed religious beliefs and ideologies which disguise the "actual" relations of men in society to the conflicts of interest engendered by its class structure. It was therefore logical for him to anticipate that the advent of a classless society would coincide with the "end of ideology," since then the "need" for ideology would disappear. Cf. the earlier discussion in Chapter 2, pp. 35–40.

past, leading to a cessation of class struggles and freeing men from being at the mercy of circumstances not of their own choosing. For the first time in history men had the opportunity to establish a rationally planned society. To cope with this world historical turning point, Marx devoted his life work to an analysis of those cumulative conditions, endemic in the capitalist organization of production, which would bring about the final revolutionary struggle.

The third point to be noted is the famous paradox of Marx's determinism. On the one hand, he predicted that the contradictions inherent in capitalism would inevitably produce a class-conscious proletariat and a proletarian revolution. On the other, he assigned to class-consciousness, to political action, and to his own scientific theory a major role in bringing the inevitable about. The paradox is "resolved" once it is remembered that for Marx the eventual revolution as well as the subjective actions and ideas which help bring it about, are consequences of the mounting contradictions between the potential for productivity and the actuality of exploitation. Marx "explains" the eventual political maturity of the proletariat, the constructive role of "bourgeois ideologists" as well as his own scientific theory as creative responses to contradictions which are the product of capitalism.

For Marx "all hitherto existing societies" encompass the "prehistory" of class struggles as contrasted with the classless society of the future. All his attention is focused on analyzing the last phase of that pre-history. Accurate, scientific understanding of this phase is indispensable for guiding political action, but capitalism also jeopardizes all constructive and undistorted use of intelligence. Between these two positions there is a fundamental ambivalence. Marx wants to know, accurately and dispassionately, but since his own theory of the socio-historical foundation of knowledge casts doubt upon the possibility of a science of society, he also wants to make sure that the knowledge gained will play a constructive role in human affairs. Science "shows" that alienation must get worse, and the worse alienation gets, the more it will function as the historical precipitant of the truth which will make men free. Accordingly, his lifelong work on economic theory, cast in a scientific mold, and his moral vision of an ultimate revolt against alienation, support each other. In his view a moral and world-historical crisis is upon us because we face the prospect of immiseration—relative deprivation and the loss of fraternity and creativity—just when an era of plenty has become possible. Marx's confidence in the contribution of his own theory was greatly reinforced by this coincidence—as he saw it—of a moral and an historical crisis. But at the same time we should note that this combination of a moral concern, a world-historical perspective, and a scientific stance greatly reinforced the invidious contrast between tradition and modernity as the foundation of a scholarly understanding of modernization.

Critique of an Intellectual Tradition

The interpretations of modernization which I have reviewed, established an intellectual tradition which has remained predominant down to the present. By their frequent reformulations of the contrast between tradition and modernity, such writers as Ferdinand Toennies, Emile Durkheim, and, among American sociologists, Charles Cooley, Robert Park, Robert Redfield, and Talcott Parsons have strongly reinforced that tradition. For all their diversity, these and related writers have the idea in common that "traditional society" and "modern society" constitute two systems of interrelated variables. The tendency is (1) to treat societies as "natural systems," (2) to search for the "independent variables" which—if altered initially—will cause changes in the related, but dependent variables in the process of transition from one type to the other, (3) to conceive of the transition as one of declining tradition and rising modernity, and, finally, (4) to assume that social change consists of a process that is internal to the society changing.

Marx was probably the most prominent expositor of this approach. England was the first country to industrialize. In Marx's view she exemplified the "laws of capitalist development" which he had analyzed in *Capital*. Writing in 1867, in his preface to the first edition of that work, Marx declared England to be the classic ground of the capitalist mode of production. He explained his analytic procedure in the following terms:

The physicist either observes physical phenomena where they occur in their most typical form and most free from disturbing influence, or, wherever possible, he makes experiments under conditions that assure the occurrence of the phenomenon in its normality. In this work I have to examine the capitalist mode of production, and the conditions of production and exchange corresponding to that mode. Up to the present time, their classic ground is England. That is the reason why England is used as the chief illustration in the development of my theoretical ideas. If, however, the German reader shrugs his shoulders at the conditions of the English industrial and agricultural laborers, or in optimist fashion comforts himself with the thought that in Germany things are not nearly so bad, I must plainly tell him, *"De te fabula narratur!"*

Intrinsically, it is not a question of the higher or lower degree of development of the social antagonisms that result from the natural laws of capitalist production. It is a question of these laws themselves, of these tendencies working with iron necessity towards inevitable results. The country that is more developed industrially only shows, to the less developed, the image of its own future.[35]

Marx made these predictions on the assumption that the same organization of production generates everywhere the same or similar transformations of social classes and the political structure. As an empirical proposition, this assumption is misleading because it treats societies as if they were entirely self-contained structures, each evolving in terms of given, internal tendencies. Actually, once industrialization had been initiated in England, the technical innovations and the institutions of the economically advanced country could be used as a model to move ahead more rapidly than England had while mitigating or even avoiding the problems encountered by the pioneering country. I shall consider this possibility in more detail below; Marx himself also noted it but did not think it significant. Instead, he declared that his analysis of the advanced country could help to "shorten the birth-pangs" of similar developments in other countries. By making social change in the long run entirely dependent upon the economic structure, Marx precluded recognition of the importance which international emulation and governmental initiative, na-

[35] *Ibid.*, pp. 12–13 (from the preface to the first edition).

tionalism and the diffusion of ideas could have in countries that followed in the wake of English industrialization. It is a measure of the surpassing influence of the intellectual and ideological tradition culminating in Marx that basically similar assumptions still inform many recent and empirical studies of "development." Some of these studies will here be considered in brief review in order to substantiate this statement.

Studies of social change typically operate with a "before-and-after" model of the society under consideration. The earlier and the later social structure are distinguished by two sets of dichotomous attributes, and one has great difficulty in resisting the view that each set constitutes a generalizable system of interrelated variables. On that assumption societies can be classified according to the degree to which they exhibit one set of attributes rather than another, resulting in a rank-ordering of countries in terms of their relative modernization. An example of this procedure appears in Daniel Lerner's well-known study *The Passing of Traditional Society*.

The great merit of Lerner's study consists in its candid use of Western modernization as a model of global applicability. For Marx, England, as the country that is "more developed industrially," exemplified universal "laws of capitalist development"; for Lerner, Western modernization exhibits "certain components and sequences whose relevance is global."[36] He recognizes that the "North Atlantic area" developed first and rather gradually, while other countries came later and sought to develop more rapidly, but like Marx before him he dismisses this as a secondary consideration. As Lerner sees it, the central proposition is that in the process of modernization, then as now, four sectors or dimensions are systematically related to one another, namely urbanization, liter-

---

[36]Daniel Lerner, *The Passing of Traditional Society* (New York: The Free Press, 1964), p. 46. The reasoning in this work (originally published in 1958) is paralleled at many points by that contained in Walt W. Rostow, *The Stages of Economic Growth* (Cambridge University Press, 1961). For a critical evaluation of the latter cf. Walt W. Rostow, ed., *The Economics of Take-Off into Sustained Growth* (*Proceedings of a Conference by the International Economic Association*) (New York: St. Martin's Press, 1963).

acy, media participation, and political participation.[37] The author appears to regard the following statement as central to his purpose:

> The book seeks to explain *why* and show *how* individuals and their institutions modernize together. It denies a unique role to "human nature" or to "social determinism." Having no taste for beating dead horses, we do not even acknowledge these as issues, but go directly to a "behavioral" perspective. To wit: social change operates through persons and places. Either individuals or their environments modernize together or modernization leads elsewhere than intended. *If new institutions of political, economic, cultural behavior are to change in compatible ways, then inner coherence must be provided* by the *personality matrix* which governs individual behavior. We conceive modernity as a participant style of life; we identify its distinctive personality mechanism as empathy. Modernizing individuals and institutions, like chicken and egg, reproduce these traits in each other.[38]

This vigorous assertion of a behavioral perspective rejects a psychological as well as a social determinism, but is still beholden to the conventional contrast between tradition and modernity.[39]

Professor Lerner puts the case in a conditional form which is hard to reconcile with his emphasis on behaviorism. He says in effect that either new institutions change in compatible ways (meaning, presumably, ways similar to the Western model), or modernization leads elsewhere than intended (meaning, presumably, in directions differing from the Western model). He believes that the high association between urbanization, literacy, media participation, and political participation in modern societies points to an underlying, systemic coherence (which Lerner calls "the participant style of life") such that societies can be ranked in accordance with their degree of tradition, transition, or modernity. Yet I do not believe there is any assurance that once

[37]Lerner, *op. cit.*, pp. 65–68. Cf. also the 1964 preface to the paperback edition.

[38]*Ibid.*, p. 78. My italics.

[39]Cf. the discussion of the "system" of modernity in *ibid.*, pp. 54–65. See also David Riesman's comment on p. 13 of his introduction.

initiated economic growth will be self-sustaining or that new institutions will change in "compatible ways." Professor Lerner himself asserts that "traditional societies exhibit extremely variant "growth" patterns; some are more urban than literate, others more media participant than urban."[40] Such "deviations from the regression line" are due to the fact that "people don't do what, on any rational course of behavior, they should do"[41]—hardly a consistent, behaviorist position. And although Professor Lerner recognizes that in the emerging nations people have not done what according to his model they should have done, he still considers his model validated by events.[42]

In recent years Lerner's work has been followed by a whole series of studies which compile attribute-checklists on which the countries of the world are ranked by the degree to which they approximate the characteristics of Western industrial societies.[43]

[40]*Ibid.*, p. 65.

[41]*Ibid.*, p. vii (1964 preface).

[42]*Ibid.*, pp. vii–x. The fact that Lerner chooses to ignore what he so clearly recognizes was explained by David Riesman in his introduction to the original edition by "the general belief that there must be a way—a way out of poverty and the psychic constriction of the "Traditionals'—which links the author of this volume with his own national tradition.—But this very American belief that there is a way is a dream. And Professor Lerner, as a student of communications, understands that it is dreams that inspire not only new wants but new solutions—as well as violent gestures toward modernity. What seems required from his perspective is an allopathic rationing of dreams, enough to spark the religion of progress, of advance without inciting to riot." To which Riesman adds the observation that "the emotional and political fluency of newly-liberated illiterates can be quite terrifying," and that "a movie image of life in America . . . is a radical 'theory' when it appears on the screens of Cairo, Ankara or Teheran." *Ibid.*, p. 10.

[43]See Seymour M. Lipset, *Political Man* (Garden City: Doubleday & Co., 1950), Chap. II and the references cited there. Cf. also Phillips Cutright, "National Political Development," *American Sociological Review*, XXVIII (1963), pp. 253–64; by the same author, "Political Structure, Economic Development and National Security Programs," *American Journal of Sociology*, LXX (1965), pp. 537–50; but also the critical contribution by Stanley H. Udy, Jr., "Dynamic Inferences from Static Data," *ibid.*, pp. 625–27. Meanwhile massive studies along similar lines are underway. See A. S. Banks and R. B. Textor, *A Cross-Polity Survey* (Cambridge: Massachusetts Institute of Technology Press, 1963); and Bruce M. Russett,

Such an approach rests on an application of evolutionary theory to very short time-periods despite earlier warnings that this is highly questionable even from the standpoint of evolutionism.[44] If the earlier and the later social structure constitute two generalizable systems of interrelated variables, it may be logical to infer that the transition from one to the other is characterized by admixtures of attributes from both, and over time by a decline of attributes from the first and a rise of attributes from the second. Yet attribute-checklists of the relative modernization of countries do not easily avoid the implication that change once initiated must run its course along the lines indicated by the "Western model," and that in the transition to modernity all aspects of the social structure change in some more or less integrated and simultaneous fashion. Only on these assumptions is it reasonable to ignore the timing and sequence of modernization of countries in their several and distinct aspects.

Just this timing and sequence can make a crucial difference for the success or failure of the effort to modernize.[45] In his introduction to Lerner's book, David Riesman notes that the transitional individual is defined as one who attends to the mass media, but cannot read, to which he appends the disturbing question: "What will a society look like which is dominated by such 'post-literate' types?"[46] This question points to the possibility of a "transition" of long duration, a contradiction in terms which arises from evolutionist assumptions and leads to a questionable nomenclature about "developing" or "transitional" societies which may never

Hayward R. Alker, et al., *World Handbook of Political and Social Indicators* (New Haven: Yale University Press, 1964).

[44]See Margaret Mead, *Continuities in Cultural Evolution* (New Haven: Yale University Press, 1964), p. 7. The author cites Boas's acceptance of evolution on a planetary scale, but also his rejection of the application of evolutionary concepts to a few centuries since short-run changes can go in any direction—a position accepted by most modern evolutionists.

[45]Despite cautionary comments, the tendency is to substitute a "horizontal" compilation for the "vertical" dimension of history. Cf. Raymond Grew and Sylvia L. Thrupp, "Horizontal History in Search of Vertical Dimensions," *Comparative Studies in Society and History*, VIII (January 1966), pp. 258–64.

[46]David Riesman in Lerner, *op. cit.*, p. 14.

become developed enough to be called modern. Related questions are raised as efforts at modernization in these so-called developing countries have led, or are leading, to changes of sequence and timing as compared with the Western model. For example, in many European countries the franchise was extended rather slowly, while in many newly independent countries universal suffrage has been adopted all at once.[47] Such a difference is ignored where countries are merely ranked at one point in time in terms of the degree to which the franchise has been extended to the adult members of their populations. The matter is not necessarily improved by the addition of another index, say that of literacy, because such data—even if they were reliable—would not reveal the level of education attained by the population. More generally, checklists of attributes of modernization are not likely to yield reliable inference, if—without regard to sequence and timing— their several items are interpreted as indices of approximation to the Western model.[48]

Nevertheless, comparative studies of modernization necessarily rely on the Western experience when they *construct* developmental sequences. This practice becomes hazardous only when past experience is used to extrapolate to the future of "industrializing"

[47]In the countries of Western Europe that extension was relatively gradual during the nineteenth century; the establishment of universal suffrage dates only from the first World War or the early 1920s. See Stein Rokkan, "Mass Suffrage, Secret Voting, and Political Participation," *Archives Européennes de Sociologie*, II (1961), pp. 132–52. By contrast, a compilation shows that of thirty-nine nations that have become independent and joined the United Nations between 1946 and 1962 only seven do not have universal suffrage. The restrictions usually refer to members of Buddhist religious orders, whose rules do not permit them to vote, and to members of the armed forces.

[48]Sometimes, as in statistics on economic growth and democratic trends, data of current trends from one country are superimposed onto the past trend data of another, more advanced country, but the similarity of current with past trends does not resolve the question of sequence and timing. Note the critical analysis of this approach by Simon Kuznets, "Underdeveloped Countries and the Pre-industrial Phase in the Advanced Countries," in Otto Feinstein, ed., *Two Worlds of Change* (Garden City: Doubleday & Co., 1964), pp. 1–21.

societies. In their book, *Industrialism and Industrial Man*, Clark Kerr and his associates explicitly emphasize that the "logic of industrialism" they have constructed involves abstractions on the assumption that the "transition stage of industrialization" has passed. Indeed, they emphasize that tendencies *deductively* arrived at (albeit by illustrative reference to the experience of "developed" societies) are not likely to be fully realized in the *actual* course of history. Yet, throughout the volume phrases recur which betray a confusion between these two levels of analysis. On the same page tendencies are alternately called logically constructed and inherent (33–34), emphasis on the contrast between abstraction and history is followed by the assertion that "the empire of industrialism will embrace the whole world" (46), industrialization is called an "invincible process," while the uncertainties of the future are relegated to variations of length and difficulty in the transition or to the several types of past industrializations (19–20, 47 ff.). Perhaps the most arresting feature of this deterministic view of the future is that the "industrialism" of the whole world is predicated, not on the organization of production as in Marx, but on the initiating or manipulating actions of five different elites whose capacity to "industrialize" whole societies is simply assumed. Exceptions, delays, and what not are seen as deviations which "cannot prevent the transformation in the long run,"[49] while neither the possibility of failure nor that of unprecedented types of industrialization is given serious consideration. Seldom has social change been interpreted in so managerial a fashion, while all contingencies of action are treated as mere historical variations which cannot alter the "logic of industrialism." Though the recognition of alternate routes to industrialization is a distinct improvement over the unilinear evolutionism of the study by Lerner, the authors abandon the gain they have made when they predict one system of industrialism for all societies in much the same way as Marx predicted the end of class struggles and of history for the socialist society of the future.

[49]Clark Kerr, John T. Dunlop, Frederick Harbison, and Charles A. Myers, *Industrialism and Industrial Man* (Cambridge: Harvard University Press, 1960), p. 49, and passim.

AN ALTERNATIVE APPROACH
TO TRADITION AND MODERNITY

The studies cited above may suffice as examples of the persistent influence of an intellectual tradition which originated with the emergence of industrial society in Western Europe. Necessarily, studies of social change rely on historical experience. But Western modernization has been accompanied throughout by a particular intellectual construction of that experience, prompted by moral or reforming impulses often presented in the guise of scientific generalizations. Theories of social evolution have had a particularly important influence in this respect in that they tend to use historical experience to construct contrasting ideal types of tradition and modernity and then use that contrast to make contingent generalizations about the transition from one to the other. In this section, I turn to a critical assessment of evolutionism and to the proposal of an alternative.

Ideal Types Are Not Generalizations

At a minimum, considerations of change involve two terminal conditions so that the word "change" refers to the differences observed before and after a given interval of time. Without knowing in what respects a later social structure differs from an earlier one, we would not know what changes to look for and explain. Accordingly, we are obliged to characterize the earlier (pre-modern) and later (modern) social structure by two lists of mutually disjunctive attributes.

The abstract formulation of such contrasts can be as seriously misleading, however, as the moral evaluations reviewed earlier. The point may be illustrated by using Talcott Parsons' contrast between universalism and particularism as attributes of modernity and tradition, respectively. In Europe traditional society, though particularistic in many respects, involved a major element of universalism through the Christian faith and the institutions of the Catholic church; in China traditional society involved other universalist elements through Confucianism and the examination system; even in India, where Hindu religion and the caste system fostered an extreme particularism, the basic cultural themes of that particularism spread throughout the sub-continent. Evidently, "particularism" characterizes traditional societies only in some respects, while in others it is combined with a "universalism" which may be as different as Catholicism, Confucianism, or the ideas of reincarnation. Hence, the disjunctive characterization of "tradition" and "modernity" by such abstract terms as "particularism" and "universalism" exaggerates and simplifies the evidence, as Max Weber pointed out in his discussion of the ideal type. Such characterization says nothing about the strength or generality with which any one attribute is present. Also, the use of one or several abstract terms to characterize either tradition or modernity tends to mistake labelling for analysis, since apparently societies vary not only in the degree but also in the kind of their universalism or particularism. At this abstract level it is quite probable that no society is without some elements from both ends of the continuum, leading some writers to use phrases such as "the modernity of tradition" or "the tradition of the new."[50]

These problems are compounded when we turn from the contrast between social structures "before and after" to a consideration of change from the one to the other. In this respect we can be guided by Max Weber's own discussion of this problem:

> *Developmental* sequences too can be constructed into ideal types and these constructs can have quite considerable heuristic value. But this quite particularly gives rise to the danger that the ideal type and reality will be confused with one another.[51]

Accordingly, ideal-typical constructs of development must be sharply distinguished from the actual sequence of change, but this distinction is "uncommonly difficult" to maintain. For in *constructing* a developmental sequence we will use illustrative ma-

---

[50]The first phrase occurs several times in Lucian W. Pye and Sidney Verba, eds., *Political Culture and Political Development* (Princeton: Princeton University Press, 1965), passim. The second is the title of a book by Harold Rosenberg.

[51]Max Weber, *The Methodology of the Social Sciences* (Glencoe: The Free Press, 1949), p. 101.

terials in order to make clear what we mean and hence may confuse the sequence of types with a course of events.

> The series of types which results from the selected conceptual criteria appears then as an historical sequence unrolling with the necessity of a law. The logical classification of analytical consepts on the one hand and the empirical arrangements of the events thus conceptualized in space, time, and causal relationship, an the other, appear to be so bound up together that there is an almost irresistible temptation to do violence to reality in order to prove the real validity of the construct.[52]

The hazards referred to by Weber have not gone unnoticed. Following the tradition of Maine, Durkheim, and Toennies, Robert Redfield compared four contemporary communities in Yucatan. He emphasized that his method was not to be recommended to those wishing to raise questions

> as to whether changes in any of the characters are related to or conditioned by changes in any of the others, and as to how they are interrelated . . . .

But while Redfield clearly stated that he had not answered such questions, he nevertheless supposed that

> there is some natural or interdependent relation among some or all of the characters in that change with regard to certain of them tends to bring about or carry with it change with respect to others of them . . . .[53]

In thus seeing his problem as one of causal "relations among variables" Redfield unwittingly disregards his own warning concerning the disjunction between ideal types and historical sequences. We should try to understand why this confusion is as widespread as Weber already suggested.

In operating with a "before-and-after" model of the society under consideration, one has difficulty in resisting the view that the two sets of attributes characterizing the earlier and the later social structure constitute generalizable systems of empirically interrelated variables. But in adopting this view, we entirely ignore

[52]*Ibid.*, pp. 102–3.

[53]Robert Redfield, *The Folkculture of Yucatan* (Chicago: University of Chicago Press, 1941), pp. 343–44.

that the specification of a list of attributes is ideal-typical and hence simplifies and exaggerates the evidence. If we are to avoid mistaking ideal types for accurate descriptions, we must take care to treat the clusters of attributes as *hypothetically*, not as actually, correlated. We need these clusters to distinguish between social structures, we illustrate them by historical examples, but these are still abstractions, constructs that should be used as tools of analysis. Redfield, for example, suggested that the relative isolation and the occupational homogeneity of communities coexisted in many instances and was perhaps causally related. No doubt there are many isolated communities with relatively little division of labor, but degree of isolation and occupational differentiation are correlated very imperfectly, and over time communities have varied independently in both dimensions. If one wishes to get away from the artificiality of ideal types one can visualize two overlapping frequency distributions in which either isolation or occupational heterogeneity are treated as the dependent variable. Such distributions would approximate historical reality more closely. whereas the ideal type of an isolated and homogeneous community is best employed as a *suggestion* for the investigation of isolated communities with considerable division of labor, or non-isolated communities that are relatively homogeneous.[54]

That these cautions are often ignored may be illustrated by reference to two related and quite common lines of reasoning. One of these has to do with the notion of "prerequisites." Beginning with the contrast between tradition and modernity (in one of its many versions) the analyst takes all the basic traits of modernity to be prerequisites of modernity, a procedure which implies that regardless of time and place all countries must somehow create all the conditions characteristic of modernity before they can hope to be successful in their drive for modernization. But

> Obviously, some of the factors listed are not prerequisites at all, but rather something that developed in the course of industrial development. Moreover, what can be reasonably regarded as a prerequisite in some historical cases can be much more naturally seen as a product of industrialization in others. The line between what is a precondition

[54]Cf. the related discussion above in Chapter 5.

of, and what is a response to industrial development seems to be a rather flexible one.[55]

Such a distinction could be made only if the specific processes of industrialization are analyzed. However, causes and consequences tend to become confused, if instead a uniform process is assumed such that countries entering upon industrialization at a later time will repeat in all essentials the previous industrialization of some other country.[56]

Another line of reasoning involves an undue generalization of a limited historical experience (rather than working back from present characteristics to necessary prerequisites). For example, the decline of kinship ties and the concomitant rise of individualism were aspects of Western modernization. Today we are learning how many meanings and exceptions were in fact compatible with this overall tendency, though these are quite properly ignored when we construct an ideal typical sequence. But, rather than using that sequence as an analytical tool to show how and why actual historical developments deviate from it, we use it to make contingent predictions about the future of "developing" societies. To be sure, no one is likely to say simply that these societies will develop; he states instead that they will not develop unless kinship ties decline. There are at least three things wrong with this procedure: (a) it ignores the exaggerations and simplifications which went into the ideal type in the first place, and hence blinds us to the role which kinship ties and collectivism played in the modernization of Western Europe; (b) it also blinds us to the possible ways in which kinship ties and collectivism might be, or might be made, compatible with the modernization of other areas (tacitly we have misused the ideal type as a generalization); (c) it diverts attention

[55]Alexander Gerschenkron, *Economic Backwardness in Historical Perspective* (New York: Frederick A. Praeger, 1965), p. 33. My indebtedness to Gerschenkron will be evident throughout; in several respects my analysis represents a sociological extension of points first suggested by him in the context of economic history.

[56]*Ibid.*, p. 40 Cf. also Gerschenkron's critical discussion of Rostow along similar lines in Rostow, ed., *The Economics of Take-Off, op. cit.*, pp. 166-67. See also for a related discussion Albert O Hirschman, "Obstacles to Development." *Economic Development and Cultural Change*, XIII (1965), pp. 385-93.

from the very real possibility that modernization may never arrive at modernity, so that terms like "development" or "transition" are misnomers when applied to societies whose future condition may not be markedly different from the present.

These critical consideration do not stand alone. Several writers have examined the assumptions of the intellectual tradition which I have characterized and have also found it wanting. Elkan and Fallers have examined specific local developments, like the mobility of wage labor in Uganda, and shown in what respects this experience differs from the mobilization of a work-force in early industrial England.[57] In his discussion of the changing craft traditions in India, Milton Singer has questioned the assumption of a uniform recapitulation of the process of industrialization, and the tendency to employ the concept of "tradition" as a generalization rather than an ideal type.[58] Similar questions have been raised and systematized by Neil Smelser, who distinguishes clearly between ideal-typical constructs of, and generalizations about, social change, and who emphasizes that the latter are difficult to achieve. Even if the "vicious circle of poverty" is broken, subsequent changes of the social structure will vary with the pre-industrial conditions of the country, the particular impetus to develop, the path which modernization takes, the significant differences that persist in developed economies, and finally with the impact and timing of dramatic events.[59] As Wilbert Moore has pointed out in a similar context:

> The manner in which history prevents its own replication creates difficulties in generalizations that will unite historical and contemporary experience and deal with the diversity that optional paths of change introduce . . . . In addition to minimum, required sequences and results, what is needed, and is mostly not at hand, is the construc-

[57]Walter Elkan and Lloyd A. Fallers, "The Mobility of Labor," in Wilbert E. Moore and Arnold S. Feldman, eds., *Labor Commitment and Social Change in Developing Areas* (New York: Social Science Research Council, 1960), pp. 238-57.

[58]Milton Singer, "Changing Craft Traditions in India," in Moore and Feldman, eds., *op. cit.*, pp. 268-76.

[59]Neil J. Smelser, *The Sociology of Economic Life* (Englewood Cliffs: Prentice-Hall, 1963), pp. 105-6.

tion of limited-alternative or typological sequences where total generalization is improper.[60]

Strictures of this kind are of rather recent date, though Gerschenkron had already expressed them in 1952. They have not replaced the dominant, evolutionary approach to the comparative study of modernization.

The impetus to generalize even where generalization is improper, derives not only from the intellectual tradition I have traced. It derives also from the desire to put policy directives on a "scientific" basis, and from the indispensability of ideal types in studies of social change. The fact that time and again the distinction between tradition and modernity has been oversimplified does *not* mean that we can dispense with that contrast entirely. Studies of social change are not possible without a "before-and-after" model of the social structure in question.

The Contrast Restated

The contrasts between pre-modern and modern social structures may be formulated along the several dimensions that are conventionally distinguished in the analysis of social structures. The problem of the causal interrelation among these dimensions is one of empirical research which cannot be replaced by logical deductions, as long as the evidence argues against the assumption of one uniform process of modernization. Nor is it proper to turn the two attribute-checklists by which we may distinguish tradition from modernity into two systems to which certain properties are imputed. For in this way a set of separate or separable attributes is transformed into the structural propensities of a collective entity. Such reification is closely related to the moralism and scientism

[60]Wilbert Moore, *The Impact of Industry* (Englewood Cliffs: Prentice-Hall, 1965), p..19. Cf. also the same writer's earlier monograph on *Social Change* (Englewood Cliffs: Prentice-Hall, 1963), Chap. V. Similar critiques of evolutionism are contained in the writings of S. N. Eisenstadt, esp. in two recent essays "Social Change, Differentiation and Evolution," *American Sociological Review*, XXIX (1964), pp. 375–86; and "Social Transformation in Modernization," *ibid.*, XXX (1965), pp. 659–73.

that has characterized many reactions to industrialization, as we have seen.

Smelser has suggested the concept of "structural differentiation" as a basic analytical tool for the study of modernization. He sees the transition between tradition and modernity as involving changes in several spheres of life. In technology there is a change from simple techniques to the application of scientific knowledge, and in agriculture from subsistence farming to the commercial production of agricultural goods. In industry human and animal power are replaced by power-driven machinery. And with industrilization the population shifts increasingly from the farm and the village to the city and the economic enterprises located in it. These processes of change consist of, or are accompanied by, structural differentiation in he sense that in each case an earlier structure that combines sveral economic functions is eventually replaced by a later one characterized by greater specialization, or by a greater division of labor as the older writers called it.[61] Smelser is careful to point out that, while these processes may occur jointly, it is also true that each has occurred independently of the others. He emphasizes that structural differentiation in such other realms as the family, religion, and stratification is not simply a consequence of "industrialization" alone; it has occurred in "pre-industrial" areas, for example as a result of colonialism.[62] In this way, "structural differentiation" provides us with a summary designation of the contrast between "tradition" and "modernity" without prejudging the systemic character of either term. The designation allows us to investigate the causal relation between different processes of structural differentiation.

Such investigations are needed, if we are to employ the indispensable, ideal-typical contrasts between "before" and "after" without imparting a spurious, deductive simplicity to the transition from one to the other.[63] A case in point is the cultural ramifications of changes in economic institutions which are properly

[61]See Smelser, *op. cit.*, pp. 101-2, 106.

[62]*Ibid.*, p. 112.

[63]Cf., for example, the analysis of changes in industrial organization by H. Freudenberger and F. Redlich, "The Industrial Development of Europe: Reality, Symbols, Images," *Kyklos*, XVII (1964), pp. 372-401.

conceived as instances of structural differentiation. The German historian Otto Brunner has shown that in the pre-modern societies of Europe the facts of economic life were typically incorporated in treatises on estate or household management, in which instructions concerning agriculture and the keeping of accounts occurred side by side with advice on the rearing of children, marital relations, the proper treatment of servants, and related matters. Technical and economic considerations were very much a part of the moral approach to human relations. This juxtaposition belongs to a world in which the household or estate typically constituted a unit of production, consumption, and social life, whereas the separation of morals from economics belongs to a society in which the family household is typically separated from the place of work.[64] In this case, the change in economic institutions and in intellectual outlook may be considered related instances of "structural differentiation," but it should be clear that this relationship is complex and requires detailed investigation.

Such investigations can help us avoid the ambiguities which remain at the abstract level, because terms like differentiation are not as neutral and unequivocal as one would wish. Following Durkheim, Smelser notes that modernization involves a "contrapuntal interplay" between differentiation "which is divisive of established society, and integration which unites differentiated structures on a new basis."[65] Here certain cautions are needed to avoid the value-implications of the evolutionary model. A traditional economy is characterized by little differentiation between economic and familial activities *within* more or less self-sufficient households or estates. *Within* the family and the community a high degree of integration exists in the sense, say, that the authority of social rank and religious norms are accepted without question. But we must take care not to commit the romantic fallacy so prominent in the intellectual tradition I have surveyed.

---

[64]The characterization of pre-modern treatises on economics is contained in Otto Brunner, *Neue Wege der Sozialgeschichte* (Göttingen: Vandenhoeck and Ruprecht, 1956), pp. 33–61. Cf. also the analysis by Peter Laslett, *The World We have Lost* (London: Methuen and Co., 1965), passim.

[65]Smelser, *op. cit.*, p. 110.

First, high integration and lack of differentiation *within* the family and community go together with much fragmentation *among* them. Second, within families and communities everyday life is one of "proud and cruel publicity," as Huizinga puts it. Since all activities occur within the household or estate personal interdependence is not only benign but also extremely coercive; it fosters sentimental attachments but also the most intense personal hatreds; it encourages fraternity but also mutual surveillance and suspicion. When structural differentiation is divisive of the established family households, not only their group solidarity and stable norms (integration of established society) are disrupted, but also their lack of privacy, their personalized cruelties and oppressions from which no member of the household could previously escape. This disruption of the household as one form of integration goes hand in hand with integration between households through increased interdependence. It is also accompanied by increased differentiation *within* these structures—increased privacy and freedom from personal coercion. A modern economy is characterized, therefore, by the separation of family household and workplace (structural differentiation) and by increased interdependence of the family with the market or of workers in the factory (integration on a new basis). Only assiduous attention to the liabilities and assets of each structure can avoid the ideological implications of the ideal-typical contrast between tradition and modernity. Otherwise, we merely nurse the discontents of industrial society by contrasting the liabilities of the present with the assets of the past.

To avoid this pitfall, it is useful to summarize the preceding discussion in explicit contrast to the received conventions of sociology. Social structures may be distinguished by the solidarities they achieve. Typically, traditional societies achieve intense solidarity in relatively small groups isolated from one another by poor communication and a backward technology. These groups create for their individual participants an intensity of emotional attachment and rejection which modern men find hard to appreciate and which they would probably find personally intolerable. Typically, modern societies achieve little solidarity in relatively small groups and by virtue of advanced communication and technology these groups tend to be highly interdependent at an impersonal level. In this setting individual participants experience an intensity of emotional attachment and rejection at two levels which hardly exist in the traditional society, namely in the nuclear family at its best and its worst, and at the national level where personal loyalties alternate between being taken for granted in ordinary times and moving up to fever pitch during national crises or other direct confrontations with alien ways of life.

Analogous considerations apply to the invidious personification of modernity and tradition. We saw that the stultifying effects of the division of labor became a major theme of social philosophers from the beginning of industrialization. Generations of writers have reiterated the theme with different contrasting images of man ranging from "the aristocrat" and "the medieval craftsman" to the several versions of "the Renaissance man" of protean capacities who has been the daydream of intellectuals from Goethe's Wilhelm Meister and Baudelaire's Dandy to Herbert Marcuse's "Multi-dimensional Man."[66] This romantic utopia of intellectuals in an era of industrialization must be taken seriously indeed, since the ideal images of a culture affect the changing social structure. But the idea of unlimited creativity by "the individual" or "the people" is as much a chimera as is that of a womb-like security and warmth in human relations attributed to a bygone age. These are projections of the discontents of intellectuals with a civilization that induces in them an intense ambivalence between elitism and populism—a point to which I return in the following discussion.

The contrast between tradition and modernity may be recast accordingly. It is probably true that traditional societies are characterized by universally accepted cultural norms. But this goes together with the subservience of men of letters to the church and to private patrons, and with the prevalence of illiteracy in the general population. It is, therefore, not accidental that terms like

[66]See Cesar Grana, *Bohemian Versus Bourgeois* (New York: Basic Books, 1964), passim, for a sympathetic analysis of this imagery. Herbert Marcuse's *One-Dimensional Man* (Boston: The Beacon Press, 1964) appeared too late to be included in Grana's concluding analysis.

"ideology," and "intellectuals" originated in Europe during the eighteenth century, when traditional beliefs were challenged, men of letters were emancipated from their previous subservience and literacy increased along with printed materials and a market for literary products. The universal cultural norms of traditional society also go together with a low level of productivity and communication and with a consequent fragmentation of the social structure in economic, legal, and political terms. One implication of this fragmentation is the prevalence of force and fraud and of jurisdictional disputes among a large number of solidary groups which depend for their cohesion not only on common norms but also on the imperatives of self-help and defense.[67] In each of these solidary groups and in the polity as a whole, society tends to be divided sharply between rulers and ruled. Those of gentle birth have a disproportionate share of the wealth, privileged access to positions of formal authority, enjoy sociability, leisure, and culture, whereas the bulk of the population lives in the drudgery of physical labor and in poverty, without access to literacy, culture, or positions of influence, and without recognized means of airing their grievances. In this setting the term "society" is applied only with difficulty, since the people themselves live in fragmented subordination, while their rulers constitute "the society" because they are the persons worthy of note in the country. These attributes

[67]It may well be the present-day absence of a need for self-help and defense which makes the closely knit solidarity of such groups appear oppressive to a modern observer, especially if he discounts the romanticism of past interpretations. By the same token, it may be the absence of that need for self-help and defense which weakens the solidarity of groups in modern societies and allows for the development of individualism. The older pattern often arose from the imposition of taxes in return for privileges, which necessitated the organization of communities for self-help and defense; Max Weber discussed this device under the concept of "liturgy." Cf. Max Weber, *The Theory of Social and Economic Organization* (New York: Oxford University Press, 1947), pp. 312–13. A society like the Russian in which this older pattern was preserved up to the present may well engender customs and attitudes markedly different from those that are familiar to us today. For an insightful discussion of these customs and attitudes see Wright W. Miller, *Russians as People* (New York: E. P. Dutton, 1961), Chap. 5.

may suffice as a contrast-conception for a reformulation of modernity.

It is probably true that modern societies are characterized by relatively few cultural norms that are universally accepted, and this goes together with a relative emancipation of men of letters and a nearly universal literacy in the general population. Structural differentiation in technology and communications has led to high levels of productivity and a high degree of impersonal interdependence. Associated with this interdependence are the attributes of the nation state which were noted earlier. The adjudication of legal disputes, the collection of revenue, the control of currency, military recruitment, the postal system, the construction of public facilities, and others have been removed from the political struggle among competing jurisdictions and have become the functions of a national government. Another and related characteristic of modern society is the process of fundamental democratization by which "those classes which formerly only played a passive part in political life," have been stirred into action.[68] The old division between rulers and ruled is no longer clear-cut, since the ruled have the vote, and the rulers are subject to formal controls at many points. Status distinctions no longer coincide with hereditary privileges. In this setting the term "society" is appropriately applied to all people in a country who constitute that society by virtue of their interdependence and equality as citizens.

The foregoing discussion has attempted to "de-ideologize" the conventional contrast of tradition and modernity. At this general level the contrast holds good for many societies that have undergone a process of modernization. Most "traditional societies" lack means of rapid communication so that the bulk of the population lives in relatively small enclaves isolated from one another. However, if one goes beyond such generalities, one is obliged also to go beyond the simple contrast discussed here. What is true of *all* traditional societies is by the same token not very illuminating about any one of them. For example, a key-feature of the European experience was the tie-in of universal cultural norms

[68]See Karl Mannheim, *Man and Society in an Age of Reconstruction* (New York: Harcourt, Brace & World, 1941), p. 44.

[69]See above pp. 230–34.

with the organization of the Church and hence with the enduring, if rather unstable balancing of centralizing and decentralizing tendencies of government which culminated in the development of representative institutions.[69] In countries like Russia and Japan universal cultural norms came to prevail in a manner that is quite different from this Western-European pattern. The study of social change in these societies would, therefore, require a more specific conceptualization of the contrast between tradition and modernity, in order to be analytically useful. The general contrast here discussed should be only the beginning of analysis, though often it has been mistaken for analysis itself.

Another limitation becomes apparent when one applies these concepts to colonial and post-colonial societies. Can any colonial society be said to have the characteristics of "tradition"? Does it have universally accepted norms? And since the prevailing norms surely do not apply to the subject population, in what sense can one in fact speak of one society? To contrast the past and present social structure one should take account of at least two traditions: the native tradition and the tradition of a dual society created by the colonizing country. Analogous questions apply to the European frontier settlements abroad, as in the United States, Canada, Australia, and New Zealand, but here the native populations were not strong enough to create the problem of a dual society, while the imported culture of the European settlers already represented a major break with the medieval tradition. The point of these comments is to suggest that several models of change are needed and are preferable to any attempt of forcing all types of change into the Procrustes bed of the European experience.

That ideal types of social change are of limited applicability, makes them more, not less useful. Once the weakness of the most general formulation as well as the limitations of the Western-European model are observed, it is then appropriate also to recognize the utility of focussing attention on the area in which the breakthrough to modernity was achieved first. The following analysis attempts to spell out the implications of this breakthrough and to interpret the process of modernization in the light of the foregoing discussion.

MODERNIZATION IN COMPARATIVE PERSPECTIVE

Theoretical Orientation

As European societies approached the "modern era," men of letters came to think about differences of social rank with an awareness of a new society in the making. Although political and ideological rather than scholarly, these ideas about modern society have strongly influenced the concepts with which social scientists have approached the study of modernization. At this point it is useful to state the common denominator of this intellectual tradition in terms of three related tenets.

A. The industrial revolution in England and the contemporary political revolution in France had a profound cultural impact, frequently leading men of letters to formulate pervasive and invidious contrasts between the old and the new social order. As a result "tradition" and "modernity" came to be conceived in mutually exclusive terms, not only as a conceptual aid but also as a generalized, descriptive statement about the two, contrasting types of society. Related to this approach is a conception of each type of society as a social system, characterized by the functional interdependence of its component parts and a balance of forces among them. Hence, "traditional" and "modern" societies appear as two types of societies, each with its own, built-in tendency towards self-maintenance or equilibrium.

B. From the vantage-point of Europe in the late eighteenth and early nineteenth centuries, both revolutions and much of the social change that followed appeared as phenomena that were internal to the societies changing. This mode of explanation goes back to influences emanating from Plato and characteristic of Western philosophy down to the present.[70] In the late eighteenth century

---

[70]For the link between the theological conception of emanation with theories of social evolution and functionalism cf. Arthur Lovejoy, *The Great Chain of Being, op. cit.*; Karl Loewith, *Meaning in History* (Chicago: University of Chicago Press, 1949); and the comprehensive historical treatment in Robert A. Nisbet, *Social Change and History* (New York: Oxford University Press, 1969), passim. The intellectual tradition discussed in these works has been criticized very effectively by Ernest Gellner, *Thought and Change* (Chicago: University of Chicago Press, 1964), passim. Gellner's analysis corroborates the present discussion at several points.

this intellectual tradition was reflected in interpretations of the growth of commerce and industry. Specifically, many writers of the period considered the division of labor a major factor in promoting social change. To a man like Ferguson that growth depended ultimately on the subdivision of tasks, which determines the ideas and actions of men, provides the basis for the difference between social classes, and gives rise to political actions.

The view that social change is the product of internal social forces has a certain basis in historical fact, difficult as it is to separate facts from reflections upon them. Most observers of early industrialization thought economic change the primary factor, whether they believed that governmental measures reflect that change, as the radicals did, or that these measures were needed to avert its worst consequences, as the conservatives did. In England, the work of the classical economists enhanced this consensus, because opposition to mercantilist policies argued for less regulation of economic affairs and hence for a secondary role of government. As governmental controls over the economy were reduced, as guild regulations were abandoned, as labor mobility increased along with population, trade, and manufacture, it became very plausible to consider that society and economy possess a "momentum" of their own, while government merely responds to the impact of social forces. At this time, office holding was still a form of property ownership so that the idea of authority as an adjunct of ownership partly described the society. In addition, the industrial revolution first occurred in England; among the continental countries England (along with Holland) lacked an absolutist tradition with its basis in a standing army, and she was also characterized by a more permeable upper class than the countries of the Continent. It was indeed a unique constellation of circumstances which gave new emphasis to the old view that social change is internal to the society changing, that social change originates in the division of labor, and that, consequently, government or the state are products of the social structure. It may be suggested that this intellectual perspective unduly generalizes from a very limited phase of the English experience.

Accordingly, both the intellectual tradition of Europe and the specific historical constellation at the end of the eighteenth century encouraged explanations of social change which emphasize the continuity and interconnectedness of changes *within* society, a tendency which was reinforced when modern nationalism came into its own. As a result a certain lawfulness was attributed to the social structure, while the relative autonomy of government and the impact of external factors upon every society were ignored or minimized. Paradoxically, this perspective also prevailed during a period of absolutist regimes, of European overseas expansion and of worldwide industrialization, when societies were increasingly subject to influences from abroad in contrast to the relative integrity of national societies in Western Europe. This cultural and historical background may help to account for the prominence of explanations which attribute change to a society's internal functional differentiation, such as the increasing division of labor, an observation that can alert us to the limitations of this intellectual perspective without questioning its analytic utility in the proper context.

C. The third tenet asserts that ultimately industrialization will have the same effects wherever it occurs. This follows, or appears to follow, from a combination of assumptions rather loosely linked with the preceding points. Where the causes of social change are conceived as intrinsic to a society, industrialization (and, more vaguely, modernization) is considered to have certain necessary and sufficient prerequisites without which it cannot occur. Conversely, once these prerequisites are given, industrialization becomes inevitable. The same reasoning is applied to the consequences of the process. Once industrialization is under way, it has certain inevitable results. In the long run, modernity will drive out tradition and fully industrialized societies will become more and more alike.

The three tenets mentioned here are closely related. Their common basis is the conception of society as a structure arising from a fixed set of preconditions and characterized by mutually reinforcing attributes which make the change of the structure appear as an inevitable modification of interrelated variables. This conception of society is closely related to the theory of social evolution, though that theory is not of direct concern to the present discussion. But the three assumptions of social system, internal differentiation, and developmental inevitability form a coherent approach to the study of industrialization from which the approach to be discussed below will now be distinguished.

A. Against the view that tradition and modernity are mutually exclusive, I wish to maintain that even the two revolutions of the eighteenth century are best understood as culminations of specific European continuities, i.e. that "modern" elements were evident long before the modern era. (By the same token the European tradition, and English society particularly, had distinctive attributes not found in other civilizations.) The point may be illustrated with regard to the bases of social action. Kinship ties, religious beliefs, linguistic affiliations, territorial communalism, and others are typical forms of association in a traditional social order. None of these ties or associations have disappeared even in the most highly industrialized societies; to this day the relative decline of "traditional" and the relative ascendance of "modern" solidarities remain or recur as social and political issues. But some of the old ties or associations were weakened by the ascendance of Christianity, others by the Renaissance and Reformation, and others still in the course of the struggles between absolutist rulers and the estates. It may be recalled that Max Weber's lifework documents the proposition that Christian doctrine and the revival of Roman law militated against familial and communal ties as foci of loyalty which compete effectively with the universal claims of legal procedure and the Christian faith. The ethical universalism of the Puritans and its subsequent secularization were later links in this chain of preconditions. By these prior developments in Western Europe men were freed very gradually for such alternative solidarities as those of the nuclear family, social class and national citizenship. In my view there was indeed a breakthrough to a new historical era, but this was the result of continuities reaching back to classical antiquity, which came to a head in a specific time and place owing to the very particular conditions of English society in the seventeenth and eighteenth centuries. This element of continuity was neglected by men of letters who interpreted the emerging industrial society in terms of a cultural conflict between tradition and modernity. However, in other respects continuity was emphasized.

B. Against the conception of change as intrinsic I wish to

maintain that following the breakthrough in England and France every subsequent process of modernization has combined intrinsic changes with responses to extrinsic stimuli,[71] and has involved government intervention as a prominent feature of that process. The modernization of societies is *not* to be understood primarily as a result of internal changes in which governments play at best a secondary role. The great lacunae of the interpretations here opposed is their failure to account for the diffusion of ideas and techniques, the prominent role of government, and the rising tide of nationalism, all of which have accompanied the process of industrialization throughout.

The point is a general one. All complex societies have an internal structure and an external setting. Likewise, all complex societies possess a formal structure of governmental authority which differs from, and is relatively independent of, the group formations arising from the social and economic organization of society. For analytic purposes it is legitimate to separate these dimensions and to neglect one or another of them, if this seems indicated by the problem under consideration. But in the comparative study of modernization, and especially one that focuses attention on problems of social stratification, such neglect seems inadvisable. The influence of modernization on the means of communication is international in scope, so that we should attend to the external setting of societies, even where our primary focus is on changes internal to their social structures. Moreover, the secondary or dependent role of government resulted from very particular historical circumstances, as noted earlier, and should not be considered a general, theoretical proposition. The facts are that intellectuals have played a major role in helping to transform the social structure of backward societies and have done so more often than not in reference to prior economic and political developments abroad. Likewise, government officials have played a major role in

---

[71]So, of course, did the initial development of England, depending as it did on intense competition with Holland. The point that social structures cannot be understood by exclusive attention to their internal developments is a general one. See Otto Hintze, "Staatsverfassung und Heeresverfassung," in *Staat und Verfassung* (Göttingen: Vandenhoeck & Ruprecht, 1962), pp. 52–83. The essay was published originally in 1906.

the development of economic resources, or have supported and implemented an institutional framework in which such a development became easier. To be sure, these are possibilities, not certainties. But to neglect the rather independent role of intellectuals or governmental officials in the process of modernization is to subscribe to the Marxian view that the international setting, the political structure and the cultural development of a society depend in the long run on its organization of production.

C. Against the concept of industrialization as a largely uniform process of structural change I wish to emphasize the importance of diffusion and of government "intervention" for an understanding of this process. England was the first country to industrialize and in Marx's view she exemplified the "laws of capitalist development." We saw that, in his preface to the first edition of *Capital*, Marx had declared England to be the classic ground of the capitalist mode of production. England was more developed industrially than other countries. As they enter upon the path of industrialization, these other countries will undergo developments comparable to those of England because of the tendencies inherent in the capitalist organization of production. Marx made this prediction on the assumption that the same organization of production generates everywhere the same or similar transformations of social classes and the political structure. As an empirical proposition, this assumption is misleading. Once industrialization had been initiated in England, the technical innovations and the institutions of the economically advanced country were used as a model in order to move ahead more rapidly than England had; and also as a warning so as to mitigate or even avoid the problems encountered by the pioneering country. Marx himself noted this possibility, but did not consider it seriously. He declared that his analysis of the advanced country could only help to "shorten the birthpangs" of similar developments in other countries, for the capitalist mode of production is governed by the same laws or inevitable tendencies wherever it occurs.

Again, the point is a general one. Industrialization itself has intensified the communication of techniques and ideas across national frontiers. Taken out of their original context, these techniques and ideas are adapted so as to satisfy desires and achieve ends in the receiving country. Certainly, such adaptation is affected at every point by the resources and economic structure of the country, but Marx tended to make necessities out of contingencies. He did not give full weight to the historical traditions which affect the social structure of every country and with it the capacity of a people to develop its opportunities. Nor did he consider that this structure is modified materially by the international transmission of techniques and ideas and by attempts to control the process and repercussions of industrialization politically. Against the view that industrialization has the same effects wherever it occurs, I wish to maintain the importance of timing and sequence as crucial variables. Once industrialization has occurred anywhere, this fact alone alters the international environment of all other societies. There is a sense in which it is true to say that because of timing and sequence industrialization cannot occur in the same way twice.

Accordingly, studies of modernization should be guided by two considerations which have been neglected in the past. Although it is true that certain consequences follow from an increasing division of labor, these are embedded in the *particular* transition from a pre-industrial to an industrial structure which distinguishes one society from another. The social structure of a country's "transitional phase" should, therefore, be a primary focus of analysis rather than be dismissed as a survival of the past. In addition. modernization, once it has occurred anywhere, alters the conditions of all subsequent efforts at modernization so that "the late arrivals cannot repeat the earlier sequences of industrial development."[72] Both considerations, the significance of the transition and the demonstration effects of "earlier sequences" preclude an evolutionary interpretation of the process of modernization.

The reorientation I propose considers the industrialization and democratization of Western Europe a singular historic breakthrough, culminating a century-long and specifically European development. But modernization brings about special discontinuities by virtue of its expansive tendencies so that the relation between the intrinsic structure and external setting of societies

[72]See Milton Singer, *op. cit.*, p. 262.

assumes special significance. Thus, the internal, historically developed structure of a country and the emulation induced by economic and political developments abroad affect each country's process of modernization.

Towards a Definition of Modernization

My objective is to define the term so that it refers to change during a specific historical period. I want to show that throughout the designated period the process of change has certain overall characteristics. At the same time I emphasize the distinction between "modernization" and "modernity." Many attributes of modernization like widespread literacy or modern medicine have appeared, or have been adopted, in isolation from the other attributes of a modern society. Hence, modernization in some sphere of life *may* occur without resulting in "modernity." Uncertainty concerning their future existed in the past history of all presently industrialized countries, just as it exists at present in the so-called developing countries. Recognition of this uncertainty provides a better basis for the comparative study of modernization than the alternative assumption that industrialization has the same prerequisites and results wherever it occurs.

In thus preferring uncertainty to a generalizing, systemic analysis we deal in effect with two approaches to the study of social change. The *retrospective* approach employs a "before-and-after" model of society, i.e. some variant of the contrast between tradition and modernity. Such models are indispensable aids in an analysis of social change, which can start from a knowledge of past changes, though with the cautions suggested earlier. The *prospective* approach cannot employ such a model directly, because it seeks to deal with future contingencies. This second approach may still employ the available "before-and-after" models, but its emphasis will be on the diversity of modern societies in the search for clues to the process of transformation. This is the approach I adopt for the remainder of this discussion.

By "modernization" I refer to a type of social change which *originated* in the industrial revolution of England, 1760–1830, and in the political revolution in France, 1789–1794. One can set the inception of the changes here considered differently, and this is in fact advisable for certain purposes. The expansion of Europe, for example, antedated the late eighteenth century; some aspects of modernization like the diffusion of modern weapons can be traced back to the fifteenth century.[73] Also, particular antecedents of modernization can be traced back very far, as in the instance of printing or of representative institutions or ideas of equality, and many others. Nevertheless, there are reasons of scale which make it advisable to separate the transformations of European societies and their world-wide repercussions since the eighteenth century from earlier economic and political changes. Reference was made at the beginning to the massive transformation of agriculture: the changes leading to a declining proportion of the labor force engaged in agricultural production were initiated in the eighteenth century. Similarly, the fundamental elitism of societies prior to the eighteenth century has been replaced, albeit gradually, by a "functional democratization" (Mannheim), and this change may again be traced to beginnings in the eighteenth century. Also, the distinction between rulers and ruled had coincided roughly with the distinction between the literate and the illiterate. That distinction was beginning to break down in the course of the eighteenth century with the slcw spread of both literacy and printed matter.[74] These three transformations of the economic, political, and social order may suffice as an indication that it is useful to treat the eighteenth century as a breakthrough to a new historical era, at any rate in studies of modernization.

The economic and political "breakthrough" which occurred in England and France at the end of the eighteenth century, put every other country of the world into a position of "backwardness." Indeed, the same may be said of the two pioneering countries. The economic transformation of England provided a "model" for France, while the political revolution of France in-

---

[73]Carlo Cipolla, *Guns and Sails in the Early Phase of European Expansion*, 1400–1700 (Longon: Collins, 1965), passim.

[74]The changes in literacy and the availability of printed matter are surveyed for England in Raymond Williams. *The Long Revolution* (London: Chatto and Windus, 1961), pp. 156–72.

stantly became a major focus of political debate in England. Ever since the world has been divided into advanced and follower societies. With reference to the eighteenth and early nineteenth centuries it is appropriate to have this formulation refer to England and France as the "advanced" countries and all others as follower societies, though even then the statement would have omitted earlier pioneering countries such as Holland or Spain. But since that time the process has ramified much further. Follower societies of the past such as Russia or China have become advanced societies, which are taken as models by the satellite dependencies of Eastern Europe or by some African and Asian countries that have won their independence since World War II. Each of the countries that have come to play the role of "pioneer" with regard to some follower society has a history of externally induced changes, though with the success of modernization the emphasis on this extrinsic dimension may become less salient than it was at an earlier time. Accordingly, a basic element in the definition of modernization is that it refers to a type of social change since the eighteenth century, which consists in the economic or political advance of some pioneering society and subsequent changes in follower societies.[75]

This distinction implies a shift in intellectual perspective. The traditional posture of sociological theory conceives of change as slow, gradual, continuous and intrinsic to the societies changing. This view is more or less appropriate as long as we confine ourselves to the enduring characteristics of a social structure which may aid or hinder the modernization of society. As suggested earlier, it is quite appropriate to the interpretation of change in

---

[75]The terms of that distinction do not stay put. Before the "modern" period England was a "follower" society while Holland and Sweden were "advanced," especially in the production of cannons. Cf. Cipolla, *Guns and Sails, op. cit.,* pp. 36–37, 52–54, 87 n. In the twentieth century the Russian revolution, the fascist regimes, and the Chinese revolution have added their own modifications of this distinction. Singer, *op. cit.,* pp. 261–62 refers to the same distinction by speaking of "early" and "late" arrivals, but I wish to emphasize the sense of pioneering or backwardness that has animated people in "advanced" and "follower" societies. These terms refer to the evaluations of the participants rather than to my own assessment of "progress" or "backwardness."

European civilization, and this was the intent of Max Weber's question concerning the combination of circumstances to which the rationalism of Western civilization can be attributed. However, once the two eighteenth century revolutions had occurred, subsequent social changes were characterized by a precipitous increase in the speed and intensity of communication. Ideas and techniques have passed from "advanced" to "follower" societies, and to a lesser extent from "follower" to "advanced" societies. Within a relatively short historical period there are few societies which have remained immune from these external impacts upon their social structures.[76]

Diffusion of ideas and techniques may be a byproduct of expansion by "advanced" societies, but it occurs even in the absence of expansion because of the economic and political breakthrough in eighteenth century Europe. As Gerschenkron has pointed out, leading strata of "follower" societies respond to this breakthrough by introducing the most modern, capital-intensive technology, in order to close the "gap" as rapidly as possible.[77] This tendency is part of a larger context:

> ... one way of defining the degree of backwardwardness is precisely in terms of absence, in a more backward country [or "follower" society as I have termed it here], of factors which in a more advanced country serve as prerequisites of development. Accordingly, one of the ways of approaching the problem is by asking what substitutions and what patterns of substitutions for the lacking factors occurred in the process of industrialization in condition of backwardness.[78]

Such substitutions are believed to represent shortcuts to "modern-

[76]There are those who consider societies closed systems. They would counter this diffusionist argument with the contention that societies are not passive recipients of external stimuli, but select among them in accordance with the dictates of their internal structure. This interpretation is an extension of the equilibrium model and as such a secular version of the original, theological belief in "pre-established harmony." That older view was as compatible with the existence of evil in a divinely created world as the functionalist interpretation is compatible with the existence of conflict and change. Neither view is compatible with the possibility of a self-perpetuating disequilibrium, or cumulative causation as Myrdal has called it.

[77]Gerschenkron, op. cit., pp. 26, 44, and passim.

[78]Ibid., p. 46.

ity." They are part of the effort to avoid the difficulties encountered in the modernization of the "advanced" country. This idea of the "advantages of backwardness" did not originate with Leo Trotsky (as has sometimes been supposed) but was expressed already in the late seventeenth century.[79] All aspects of modernity are up for adoption simultaneously, and it depends upon available resources, the balance of forces in the "follower" society, and the relative ease of transfer which aspects will be given priority. The fact that such items as medication, printed matter, educational innovations, political practices like the franchise are more easily transferred than advanced technology requiring heavy capital investment is another aspect of the divergence of processes of modernization.

Many writers have observed that in this setting of "follower societies" governments play, or attempt to play, a decisive role. The special utility of this perspective for comparative studies of modernization is evident from a recent, comprehensive analysis of English, French, and German industrialization since the eighteenth century. In that context, David Landes states that for the governments of Europe "industrialization was, from the start, a political imperative."[80] Governments may be more or less successful in meeting the imperatives confronting them, and their attempts to do so will be affected throughout by the structural attributes of their societies. Generally speaking, governments attempt to play a larger role in the modernization of relatively backward than of relatively advanced societies. Since this generalization applies to "follower societies" since the eighteenth century, and since most societies of the world are (or have been) in that category, the proposition is perhaps only another aspect of modernization, i.e. of the distinction between the two types of

[79]Cf. the analysis of this complex of ideas in the work of Gottfried Wilhelm von Leibniz (1646-1716), especially the interesting contacts between Leibniz and Peter the Great with regard to the modernization of Russia, in Dieter Groh, *Russland und das Selbstverständniß Europas* (Neuwied: Hermann Luchterhand Verlag, 1961), pp. 32-43.

[80]David Landes, "Technological Change and Development in Western Europe, 1750-1914," in H. J. Habbakuk and M. Postan, eds., *The Cambridge Economic History of Europe; The Industrial Revolution and After* (Cambridge University Press, 1965), Vol. VI, Part I, p. 366.

societies. The difference can be of strategic importance for modernization, since "follower societies" are by definition lacking in some of the elements of modernity found in "advanced societies." Where governments manage to provide "functional equivalents" or "substitutes" for these missing elements, they may succeed in reducing the backwardness of their societies, but this presupposes a relatively effective government which is an attribute of modernity or advance.[81]

Here again a major shift in intellectual perspective is implied. The view that government is an integral part of the social structure, but may have the capacity of altering it significantly, is not in the mainstream of social theory. The opposite view is more common that formal government and its actions are epiphenomena, the product of forces arising from the social and economic structure of society. This view is related to the "emanationist" and "evolutionary" intellectual tradition, and was reinforced as noted earlier, by a particular historical constellation in early nineteenth century Europe. Writers of otherwise incompatible political views agreed that government is an epiphenomenon, and this uncommon agreement still influences modern social thought. Yet in studies of modernization it is more useful to consider social structure and government, or society and the state, as interdependent, but also relatively autonomous, spheres of thought and action.[82]

The gap created between advanced and follower societies and the efforts to close it by a more or less *ad hoc* adoption of items of modernity produce obstacles standing in the way of successful modernization.[83] In his discussion of the "new states" that have come into being since World War II, E. A. Shils has characterized these obstacles as a series of internal, structural cleavages:

[81]Note the frequency with which "political unity" appears as an index of modernity in the several lists of attributes presented in Marius Jansen, ed., *Changing Japanese Attitudes Towards Modernization* (Princeton: Princeton University Press, 1965), pp. 18–19, 20–24, and passim.

[82]For a discussion of this point see above, pp. 15–29.

[83]On the "ad hoc diffusion" of items of modernity cf. the illuminating discussion by Theodore H. von Laue, "Imperial Russia at the Turn of the Century," *Comparative Studies in Society and History*, III (1961), pp. 353–67; and Mary C. Wright, "Revolution from Without?" *Comparative Studies in Society and History*, IV (1962), pp. 247–52.

It is the gap between the few, very rich and the mass of the poor, between the educated and the uneducated, between the townsman and the villager, between the cosmopolitan or national and the local, between the modern and the traditional, between the rulers and the ruled.[84]

Though such tensions exist in "advanced" states as well, they are far more pronounced not only in the "new states" of today but also in the follower societies of the past which can be ranked, albeit roughly, by their degree of backwardness.[85] The analogy between "backward" or "underdeveloped" social structures then and now should not be pressed too much, since the Continental countries possessed many cultural and economic attributes that were relatively favorable to modernization. But it is also true that during the nineteenth century there was a gradient of backwardness within Europe such that the countries to the East paralleled the "gaps" found in the "new states" of today more closely than the countries of Western Europe.[86]

The analogies or parallels noted here are especially close at the cultural level. For the "gap" created by advanced societies puts a premium on ideas and techniques which follower societies may use in order to "come up from behind." Educated minorities are, thereby, placed in a position of strategic importance, while the always existing gulf between the educated and the uneducated widens still further. In a world marked by gradations of backwardness the comparative study of modernization must attend to the "reference society" that becomes the focus of attention in the follower society, especially for the educated minority that seeks to utilize advanced ideas and techniques in order to "catch up."[87] Here one can see at a glance that a focus on the distinction between advanced and follower societies, and on the communications-effects of modernization, necessarily gives prominence to the role of intellectuals and of education, whereas ideas about

[84]Edward A. Shils, "Political Development in the New States," *Comparative Studies in Society and History*, II (1960), p. 281.

[85]Gerschenkron, *op. cit.*, pp. 41–44.

[86]Cf. Landes, *op. cit.*, pp. 354, 358.

[87]The concept "reference society" has been chosen in analogy to Robert Merton's "reference groups." Cf. Robert Merton, *Social Theory and Social Structure* (Glencoe: The Free Press, 1957), pp. 225 ff.

social change focusing on the internal division of labor necessarily made much of standard social classes like workers and capitalists. It is as typical of backward countries to invest heavily in education in order to "bridge the gap," as it is for an intelligentsia to develop and engage in an intensified search for a way out of the backwardness of their country.[88] A typical part of this search consists in the ambivalent job of preserving or strengthening the indigenous character of the native culture while attempting to close the gap created by the advanced development of the "reference society or societies."[89]

Four aspects of the process of modernization have been distinguished in the preceding discussion:

a. Reasons of scale suggest that since the eighteenth century the external setting of societies, and especially the "gap" created by the early industrialization of England and the early democratization of France, have imparted to the "degree of backwardness" the special significance of a "challenge" to modernization.

b. In their endeavor to bridge this "gap" leading strata of follower societies typically search for substitutes to the factors which were conditions of development in the advanced countries. Within the limitations imposed by nature and history all aspects of modernity (as developed abroad) are up for adoption simultaneously, and the problem is which of the adoptable items represents a shortcut to modernity. Since the achievement of "modernity" is not assured, it is part of this process that the adoption of items of modernization may militate against "modernity," or may be irrelevant to it.

c. This common setting of follower societies in turn imparts special importance to government. Typically, governments attempt to play a major role in modernization at the same time that

[88]Cf. the succinct overview of the "intelligentsia" by Hugh Seton-Watson, *Neither War Nor Peace* (New York: Frederick Praeger, 1960), pp. 164–87. See above, pp. 231 ff.

[89]The most sensitive analysis of this bifurcation I have found in the literature is the study by Joseph Levenson, *Modern China and its Confucian Past* (Garden City: Doubleday & Co., 1964), passim. Cf. also Cipolla, *Guns and Sails, op. cit.*, pp. 116–26.

they seek to overcome the sources of their own instability which arise from the special tensions created by backwardness.[90]

d. The division of the world into advanced and follower societies, together with the relative ease of communication, put a premium on education as a means to modernization which is more readily available than the capital required for modern technology. Education and modern communications also encourage the development of an intelligentsia and a cultural product which—as Wilhelm Riehl noted as early as 1850—is in excess of what the country can use or pay for.[91] This recurrent phenomenon is reflected in a mushrooming of efforts to overcome the backwardness of the country by attempts to reconcile the strength evidenced by the advanced society with the values inherent in native traditions.

Comparative Aspects of Social Stratification

This concluding section outlines a program of comparative study dealing with stratification in relation to modernization. In the past that study has contrasted tradition and modernity in "either-or" terms and emphasized changes internal to the society studied and largely determined by the division of labor. The present analysis emphasizes the continuity of social change insofar as the contrast between a social structure then and now is an artifact of conceptualization. But modernization may have a disrupting effect on changing patterns of stratification, due to the hiatus between advanced and follower societies. Governmental intervention is another possible source of discontinuity, since authority structures are relatively autonomous. In other words: although social change is a continuous process, it is often affected by factors conventionally considered extrinsic to the social structure. In a

[90]Cf. the analysis of these tensions by Edward A. Shils, "Political Development in the New States," cited above.

[91]Cf. the chapter on "Die Proletarier der Geistesarbeit" in Wilhelm Riehl, *Die Bürgerliche Gesellschaft* (Stuttgart: J. G. Cottasche Buchhandlung, 1930), esp. pp. 312–13.

process of modernization relations among groups are exposed to such "extrinsic" influences, although other aspects of the social structure (e.g. the family) may be less affected in this manner. Typically, the modernization of societies is accompanied by a nation-wide redefinition of rights and duties. Individuals and groups respond not only to the actions and beliefs of others, but also to the images of such group-relations derived from prior developments in their reference-society. The following discussion attempts to show that these general points bear directly on the study of social stratification.

The simplified contrast between tradition and modernity shows us that medieval society was ruled by a landowning aristocracy and capitalist society by a bourgeoisie owning the means of production. If one conceives of the transition from tradition to modernity as the decline of one set of attributes and the rise of another, one gets the simple picture of a declining aristocracy and a rising bourgeoisie. Possibly Marx has contributed more than anyone else to this conception. His interpretation of the bourgeoisie as the collective, historical agent which "created" the revolutionizing effect of modern industry, has produced a tendency to read a "rising bourgeoisie" back into the last thousand years of European history.[92] The broad effect of this tendency has been to make the merchants of pre-eighteenth-century Europe into direct precursors of nineteenth-century industrial entrepreneurs and to fasten upon them a corresponding degree of striving and social protest, when in fact they fit quite well into the social structure of feudal Europe. The effect is also to antedate the decline of the aristocracy by some centuries in order to provide room for the rising bourgeoisie.[93] But the changes of social stratification in the course of industrialization do not present the simple picture of a declining aristocracy and a rising bourgeoisie. In most European countries the social and political pre-eminence of pre-industrial

[92]For a vigorous critique of this tendency cf. J. H. Hexter, *Reappraisals in History* (New York: Harper & Row, 1963), passim. Note also the cautionary comments regarding the problem of historical continuity in Gerschenkron, *op. cit.*, pp. 37–39.

[93]For a more balanced assessment of the European bourgeoisie, cf. Otto Brunner, *Neue Wege der Sozialgeschichte*, pp. 80–115.

ruling groups continued even when their economic fortunes declined, and the subordinate social and political role of the "middle classes" continued even when their economic fortunes rose. In Europe this pattern applies rather generally to the period of transition to an industrial society. Here is how Joseph Schumpeter puts the case with reference to England, while pointing out that in modified form the same applies elsewhere:

> The aristocratic element continued to rule the roost *right to the end of the period of intact and vital capitalism*. No doubt that element—though nowhere so effectively as in England—currently absorbed the brains from other strata that drifted into politics; it made itself the representative of bourgeois interests and fought the battles of the bourgeoisie; it had to surrender its last legal privileges; but with these qualifications, and for ends no longer its own, it continued to man the political engine, to manage the state, to govern. The economically operative part of the bourgeois strata did not offer much opposition to this. On the whole, that kind of division of labor suited them and they liked it.[94]

In the modernization of Europe, aristocracies retained political dominance long after the economic foundations of their high status had been impaired and after alternative and more productive economic pursuits had brought bourgeois strata to social and economic prominence. The "capacity to rule" obviously varied among the several aristocracies, as did the degree to which other strata of the population tended to accept their own subordinate position. In Europe, these legacies were eroded eventually, but only after the transition to an industrial society was affected by the general pattern to which Schumpeter refers. This pattern of a continued political dominance by traditional ruling groups even under conditions of rapid modernization reflects an earlier condi-

[94]Joseph Schumpeter, *Capitalism, Socialism, and Democracy* (New York: Harper and Bros., 1947), pp. 136–37. See also pp. 12–13 for a more generalized statement. Substantially the same observations were made by Frederick Engels in 1892, but the political primacy of the aristocracy and the secondary role of the bourgeoisie appeared to him only as a "survival" which would disappear eventually. See Frederic Engels, *Socialism, Utopian and Scientific* (Chicago: Charles H. Kerr, 1905), pp. xxxii–xxxiv. For an empirical study cf. W. L. Guttsman, *The British Political Elite* (New York: Basic Books, 1963).

tion of the social structure, when families of high social and economic status had privileged access to official positions while all those below the line of gentility were excluded. Pre-modern European societies were characterized by a vast number of status-differences and clashes of interest of all kinds, but by only "one body of persons capable of concerted action over the whole area of society."[95] That is, a tiny, possessing minority of the well-born was capable of concerted action and hence constituted a class, while the whole mass of unorganized and, under these conditions, unorganizable persons were set apart by their common lack of access to positions of privilege. Accordingly, European societies conformed at one time to a pattern in which class and authority were more or less synonymous terms, but this identity diminished in the course of modernization and was replaced eventually by the principle of separation between office and family status.[96]

This equalization of access to public employment is an aspect of modernization which makes sense of the assumptions we bring to this field of study. In modern sociology government employment is not considered a basis, or an index, of social stratification. Rather, government employment (even in high positions) is seen as a dependent variable, for example when we examine the distribution of public officials by social origin. Yet this perspective presupposes the separation of government office from the claims a family can make by virtue of its social status and economic position. These assumptions were less applicable in an earlier phase of European societies, and today they are less applicable in the follower societies that are economically backward. There, governments play, or attempt to play, a major role in the process of modernization, as we have seen. Under these conditions government employment provides one of the major bases of social mobility, economic security, and relative well-being. In fact, in economically backward countries the government is one of the major economic enterprises. Hence, government officials partake of the

[95]Cf. Peter Laslett, *The World We Have Lost, op. cit.*, p. 22 and passim.
[96]Cf. Ernest Barker, *The Development of Public Services in Western Europe, 1660–1930* (London: Oxford University Press, 1944), pp. 1–6 and passim.

prestige of ruling, even if their positions are humble. And in view of the power at the disposal of government, access to government office and influence upon the exercise of authority are major points of contention—in the personalized sense characteristic of societies in which interaction is kinship-oriented.[97] While this importance of government employment is associated with economic backwardness and the weakness of middle strata in the occupational hierarchy, it can also divert resources from uses which might overcome these conditions. In the absence of viable economic alternatives government employment itself becomes a major basis of social stratification,[98] although these new polities frequently institutionalize plebiscitarian, equalitarian principles in the political sphere. This identification of class with authority differs fundamentally from the elitism of medieval European societies, in which only a privileged minority had access to positions of authority.

The preceding sketch suggests several perspectives for the comparative study of ruling classes in the process of modernization. Within the European context it focuses attention on the continued importance of traditional ruling groups throughout the period of modernization. In this respect, further study would have to differentiate between the relatively accommodating development in England and the much more conflict-ridden development of other, follower societies. At the same time, I have suggested that the modernization of Western societies generally shows a gradual separation between governmental office and family status. The continuity between tradition and modernity remains a characteristic of social change throughout, for even the increasing differentiation between office and family in Western Civilization reveals

[97]Cf. Clifford Geertz, "The Integrative Revolution," in Geertz, ed., *Old Societies and New States* (Glencoe: The Free Press, 1963), pp. 105 ff. Cf. my article "Bureaucracy" in the *International Encyclopedia of the Social Sciences*, 1968 edition.

[98]Cf., for example, the statement that "In Egypt the middle class has been weak in numbers and influence, and civil servants have comprised a large proportion of it." Morroe Berger, *Bureaucracy and Society in Modern Egypt* (Princeton: Princeton University Press, 1957), p. 46.

a variety of historically conditioned patterns. There is no reason to assume that future developments elsewhere will be more uniform. The comparative study of ruling groups in the process of modernization can thus combine the three themes, mentioned above: the continuity of change, the effect of extrinsic influences on the changing role of ruling strata, and the relative separation between government and social structure. The same themes may be combined in the study of other social groups.

The patterns of action and reaction which characterize a society's changing structure come most readily into focus as one moves from the top to the bottom ranks of the social hierarchy. Here one may use the simplified contrast between tradition and modernity as a point of departure, because the rise of political participation by the lower strata is a characteristic feature of modernization. In medieval Europe lower strata fragmented in household enterprises of a patriarchal type existed side by side with a ruling class characterized by wealth, high status and high office. Karl Marx has analyzed this condition effectively with regard to the French peasantry:

> The small peasants form a vast mass, the members of which live in similar conditions, but without entering into maniforld relations with one another. Their mode of production isolates them from one another, instead of bringing them into mutual intercourse. The isolation is increased by France's bad means of communication and by the poverty of the peasants . . . . Each individual peasant family is almost self-sufficient; it itself directly produces the major part of its consumption and thus acquires its means of life more through exchange with nature than in intercourse with society. The small holding, the peasant and his family; alongside them another small holding, another peasant and another family . . . . Insofar as there is merely a local interconnection among these small peasants, and the identity of their interests begets no unity, no national union and no political organization, they do not form a class. They are consequently incapable of enforcing their class interest in their own name, whether through a parliament or through a convention. They cannot represent themselves, they must be represented. Their representative must at the same time appear as their master, as an authority over them, as an unlimited governmental power, that protects them against the other classes and sends them the rain and the sunshine from above. The

political influence of the small peasants, therefore, finds its final expression in the executive power subordinating society to itself.[99]

Probably, Marx would have agreed that this analysis of peasants in nineteenth century France applied *mutatis mutandis* to the small craftsmen of the towns, to the manorial estates as well as to the independent peasant freeholds in medieval Europe. The family-based enterprise fragmented the lower strata into as many units of patriarchal household rule over family, servants, and apprentices. On the other hand, the heads of households would join with others in guilds, exercise authority in official capacities, join in the deliberation of representative assemblies, and thus constitute a "class" or "classes" in the sense of groups capable of concerted action.

In this setting "fundamental democratization" refers to the whole process of class-formation by which the fragmentation of the lower strata is gradually overcome, not only to the extension of the franchise. Geographic mobility increases, literacy rises along with the diffusion of newspapers, patriarchial rule and household enterprises decline as conditions of work lead to an aggregation of large masses of people in economic enterprises providing opportunities for easy communication.[100] As Marx noted, these conditions gave rise to trade unions, political organizations, and a heightened class-consciousness due to repeated conflicts with employers. He was too preoccupied with "industry" to note that other groups than workers and other means of communication than direct contact at the place of work might come into play.[101] He was also too committed to an evolutionary perspective with its emphasis on the eventual decline of the aristocracy to note the importance of the beliefs which upheld the legitimacy of the traditional "ruling class" even in an industrializing society. Large

---

[99] *Karl Marx, The 18th Brumaire of Louis Bonaparte* (New York: International Publishers, n. d.), p. 109

[100] See John Stuart Mill, *Principles of Political Economy* (Boston: Charles C. Little and James Brown, 1848), pp. 322–23.

[101] Cf. the analysis of growing class consciousness among workers in Karl Marx, *The Poverty of Philosophy* (New York: International Publishers, n. d.), pp. 145–46; but note also the evidence adduced by David Mitrany, *Marx against the Peasants* (London: Weidenfeld and Nicolson, 1951), passim.

masses of people at the bottom of the social hierarchy retained their loyalty to the established order, even in the face of the physical and psychological deprivations so suddenly imposed upon them.[102]

This loyalty is evident in the numerous references to the real and imaginary rights enjoyed under the old order. Populist protest based on such references meant, among other things, the demand for equality of citizenship. That equality was proclaimed by the legal order and by the appeals to national solidarity in an era of well-publicized empire-building, but in practice it was denied by the restriction of the franchise, the dominant ideology of class-relations, and the partisan implementation of the law. The rising awareness of the working class in this process of "fundamental democratization" reflects an experience of *political alienation*, a sense of not having a recognized position in the civic community of an emerging industrial society. During the nineteenth century nationalism was so powerful in part because it could appeal directly to this longing of the common people for civic respectability, a longing which was intensified by acute awareness of development in other countries. When this quest was frustrated and as ideas of the rights of labor spread during the nineteenth century, people turned to the socialist alternative of building a new civic community to which they too could belong.[103] This general interpretation of working-class agitation in Europe may be contrasted with the problems encountered today under conditions of greater economic backwardness and greater advance abroad.[104]

[102]To discount such beliefs because they disappeared eventually is no more plausible than to make the aristocracy's role decline in advance of its eventual demise. Cf. the discussion of the "traditionalism of labor" in my book *Work and Authority in Industry* (2nd ed.; Berkeley, University of California Press, 1974), pp. 34 ff.

[103]For a fuller statement of this interpretation see above, pp. 61–74.

[104]As always, the contrast is not absolute. During the nineteenth century, as one went eastwards in Europe, one encountered certain parallels to the "underdeveloped syndrome" of today, namely an increased importance of government and rather weakly developed middle strata. Cf. the illuminating statement by David Landes: "The farther east one goes in Europe, the more the bourgeoisie takes on the appearance of a foreign excrescence on manorial society, a group apart scorned by the nobility and feared or hated by (or unknown to) a peasantry still personally bound to the local *seigneur*." See Landes, *op.cit.*, p. 358.

In employing the English development as the prototype of later developments in other countries, Marx mistook the exception for the rule, a consideration which applies to his analysis of an emerging working class. As English workers attained a level of group-consciousness in the late eighteenth and early nineteenth centuries, they became aware of England's per-eminent position as a worldpower. In follower societies the lower strata rise to an awareness of the relative backwardness of their society. Also, early working-class agitation in England occurred in an anti-mercantilist context which militated against protective legislation during a transitional period of greatly intensified deprivations. In follower societies the greater reliance on government makes social legislation a natural concomitant of early industrialization.[105] In England the work-force in the early factories was separated effectively from the land, and population increase in the countryside as well as the city roughly corresponded to the increasing demand for labor. In many follower societies the work-force retains its familial and economic ties to the land and population increase in city and country is well in advance of the demand for labor.[106]

These contrasts vary with the degree of industrialization achieved locally and the degree of governmental control over internal migration, to mention just two relevant considerations. The permanent separation of workers from their ties to the land obviously facilitates the growth of class consciousness and of political organization in Marx's sense of the word. On the other hand,

---

[105]The debate concerning the deprivations of early English industrialization continues. But whatever its final resolution in terms of the changing standard of living, there is probably less disagreement on the psychological repercussions. The separation of the worker's home from his place of work, the novelty of a discipline which previously had been associated with the pauper's workhouse, the brutalization of work conditions for women and children merely by the shift away from home, and related matters constitute the impressive circumstantial evidence. Note also that the statement in the text makes sense of Germany's pioneering in the field of social legislation as an attribute of an early follower society.

[106]Cf. Landes, *op. cit.*, pp. 344–47 for a summary analysis of the labor supply problem in the English industrial revolution in terms of the current state of research. These findings can be contrasted readily with comparative materials on various follower societies contained in Wilbert Moore and Arnold Feldman, eds., *Labor Commitment and Social Change in Developing Areas, op. cit.*, passim.

a continuation of these ties may result either in a weak commitment to industry (and hence weak group solidarity), and/or in the emergence of segmental peasant-worker alliances in urban and national politics. Where this latter alternative exists, one can begin to appreciate how important it is to consider such phenomena in their own right, rather than treat them as transitions that are expected to disappear with increasing modernization. We do not know after all what forms modernization might take where separation between town and countryside fails to occur, at least for a considerable period of time.[107]

Having considered ruling and lower strata, I wish finally to turn to a brief analysis of education and intellectuals, again using the guidelines of the preceding discussion. In the case of England, education had been a privilege associated with high status until, in the course of religious controversies, several sectarian groups instituted private school systems so as to preserve the integrity of their beliefs. The idea of making education available beyond these narrow circles immediately raised the question of danger to the social order because workers and peasants would learn to read and write. This apprehension is quite understandable when one considers that the basic dividing line between those who officially ranked as "gentlemen" and the vast majority of the people was identical with the division between the literate and the illiterate. Still, the social mobilization of the population due to commerce and industry undermined the old hierarchy of ranks. The effort of ensuring that people would retain their old regard for rank led to the gradual spread of education with a strong emphasis on religion. This spread of education was not unlike the parallel problem of military conscription: both were aspects of a "fundamental democratization" which gave unprecedented political importance to people who could read and—in times of emergency—had guns.[108]

[107]Note that Marx and others with him considered that separation as a prerequisite of capitalist development. Cf. the discussion of the distinctive position of workers in African countries by Lloyd A. Fallers, "Equality, Modernity and Democracy in the New States," in Geertz, ed., *Old Societies and New States, op. cit.*, pp. 187–90. See also Richard D. Lambert, "The Impact of Urban Society upon Village Life" in Roy Turner, ed., *India's Urban Future* (Berkeley: University of California Press, 1962), pp. 117–40.

[108]In these respects there are of course striking differences between France and England which can be considered symptomatic of the radical

These issues are transformed in follower societies which seek to achieve the benefits of an industrial society, but by a speedier and less costly transition than occurred in England. In these societies popular and higher education seem to provide the easiest shortcut to industrialization. By this means the skill level of the population is raised while the highly educated increase their capacity of learning advanced techniques from abroad. For these reasons governments in follower societies usually push education, even though in so doing they also jeopardize their own political stability. They may attempt to avert such dangers through restrictions of the franchise, censorship, control of associations, etc.; one can differentiate between follower societies of the nineteenth and the twentieth centuries in terms of degrees and types of control over a mobilized population.

Such contrasts in the role of education are paralleled by contrasts in the role of intellectuals. Many educated persons engage in intellectual pursuits from time to time, but the term "intellectuals" is usually (if vaguely) restricted to those persons who engage in such pursuits on a full-time basis and as free professionals rather than "hired hands."[109] Intellectual pursuits occur in all complex societies, but "intellectuals" as a distinct social group emerged as a concomitant of modernization. In Western Europe men of letters underwent a process of emancipation from their previous subservience to the Church and to private patrons, because industrialization created a mass public and a market for intellectual prod-

---

and the conservative approach to education and conscription. For a comparative treatment of these issues cf. Ernest Barker, *The Development of Public Services in Western Europe, op. cit.*, Chaps. 2, 5.

[109]The circularity of this statement is unavoidable. In a general sense pursuits engaging the intellect refer to the creation and maintenance (transmission) of cultural values, but each of these terms (cultural values, creation, maintenance, transmission) is the subject of constant debate, and that debate itself is an important intellectual pursuit. Since this debate involves the pejorative as well as appreciative use of these terms, and by that token the endeavor of speakers to "belong" to the positive side of the cultural process (in however marginal a fashion), no one set of defining terms will be wholly satisfactory. In view of this difficulty the most reasonable alternative is to set up a typology of intellectual pursuits and leave the group of persons called "intellectuals" undefined. For one such attempt cf. Theodor Geiger, *Aufgaben und Stellung der Intellegenz in der Gesellschaft* (Stuttgart: Ferdinand Enke Verlag, 1949), pp. 1–24, 81–101.

ucts. The whole process was one of great complexity, but it can be simplified for present purposes. Intellectuals tended to respond to their emancipation by a new cultural elitism, and to the new mass-public by responses which vacillated between a populist identification with the people and a strong apprehension concerning the threat of mass-culture to humanistic values.[110] These responses were quite incongruent with the dominant materialism of advanced industrial societies, so that intellectuals experienced a social and moral isolation. During the nineteenth century the great economic and political successes of advanced European societies reinforced, rather than assuaged, the isolation of those intellectuals who took no direct part in that success and questioned the cultural and personal worth of those who did. To the extent that this estrangement resulted from the emancipation and consequent elitism of intellectuals, as well as from their ambivalent reaction to a mass public, it must be considered a concomitant of modernization.[111]

The response of intellectuals briefly sketched here was largely internal to the most advanced societies of Europe. But the breakthrough achieved by the industrial and political revolutions of England and France made other countries into follower societies. The economic advance of England and the events of the French revolution were witnessed from afar by men who rejected the backwardness and autocracy of their own country. Under these conditions cultural life tends to become polarized between

[110]Cf. the case study of this process in England by Leo Lowenthal and Marjorie Fiske, "The Debate over Art and Popular Culture," in Mirra Komarovsky, ed., *Common Frontiers of the Social Sciences* (Glencoe: The Free Press, 1957), pp. 33–112.

[111]I avoid the term "alienation" because misuse has made it worthless. For a scholarly treatment of this intellectual response to "bourgeois society" in nineteenth-century Europe cf. Karl Loewith, *From Hegel to Nietzsche*, passim. Cf. also the analysis of the social distance between "intellectuals" and "practical men" in Joseph Schumpeter, *op. cit.*, pp. 145–55 as well as the unusual acceptance of that distance by at least one great artist, William Faulkner, who speaks of writers "steadily occupied by trying to do the impossible" while keeping "out of the way of the practical and busy people who carry the burden of America." See Faulkner's speech on the occasion of receiving the National Book Award in *The New York Times Book Review* (February 6, 1955), p. 2.

those who would see their country progress by imitating the "more advanced countries," and those who denounce that advance as alien and evil and emphasize instead the well-springs of strength existing among their own people and in their native culture. Both reactions were typified by the Westernizers and Slavophils of Tsarist Russia, but the general pattern has occurred again and again. It has been a mainspring of nationalism and of movements for national independence. In this setting intellectuals do not remain estranged witnesses of a development carried forward by others; they tend to turn into leaders of the drive towards modernization.[112]

This discussion has endeavored to provide a framework for the comparative study of modernization and inequality. Such studies have been influenced for loo long by a stereotype derived from the Marxian tradition. According to this stereotype, history is divided into epochs, characterized by a predominant mode of production and, based upon it, a class structure consisting of a ruling and an oppressed class. Each epoch is further characterized by a typical sequence of changes in the relations between the two major classes. In the early phase the dominant mode of production is established by a class in its period of revolutionary ascendance. For a time this class is progressive. Its economic interests are identical with technical progress and human welfare, and hence, on the side of liberating ideas and institutions. Eventually however, such an ascending class becomes a ruling class. From a champion of progress in its period of ascendance the class has turned into a champion of reaction in its period of dominance. Increasingly, the ruling class resists changes which would endanger its entrenched position. But meanwhile, within the structure of the old society, a new class has been formed from the ranks of the oppressed, who have no such vested interests and who in due time will overthrow that old structure in order to make way for the material progress which has become technically possible. Within the European context this grandiose simplification ap-

---

[112]See Edward A. Shils, "Intellectuals, Public Opinion and Economic Development," *World Politics*, Vol. 10 (1958), pp. 232-55.

peared to account for the feudal powers of resistance, the progressive, rising bourgeoisie and its gradual transformation into a reactionary ruling class, and finally the class of the oppressed proletariat which has a world to win and nothing to lose but its chains.

It is quite true, of course, that Marx modified this scheme to allow for leads and lags in interpreting the actual historical developments of his time. These modifications may have appeared all the more persuasive because of the passionate moral and intellectual conviction with which Marx adhered to the basic assumptions of the scheme itself. This conviction, I have suggested, was part of the European intellectuals' response to the crisis in human relations brought about by the rise of an industrial society, a response which suggested an "either-or" confrontation between tradition and modernity with its many ramifications.

A critical awareness of this intellectual heritage can assist the reorientation needed in the comparative study of stratification. It prompts us to recognize that the contrast between tradition and modernity is itself part of the evidence we should consider. This intellectual response to the rise of industry has been an aid or hindrance (as the case may be) in each country's modernization, typically marked by the emancipation of men of letters and by the manner in which they assessed their country's backwardness relative to the advances of their reference-societies. Once the unwanted legacies of this intellectual response are discounted, as I have attempted to do in this essay, a rather different approach to the study of modernization emerges.

The division of history into epochs, like the distinction between tradition and modernity, is a construct of definite, but limited utility. These constructs will vary with the purpose of inquiry. While we have found it useful to consider late eighteenth-century Europe as an historical turning point, it is recognized that the process of modernization which reached a crescendo since then, is coextensive with the era of European expansion since the late 15th century, or the "Vasco da Gama era" as Carlo Cipolla has called it. If we want to explain this historical breakthrough in Europe, our emphasis will be on the continuity of intra-societal changes. If we wish to include in our account the worldwide repercussions of this breakthrough and hence the differential process of modernization, our emphasis will be on the confluence of intrinsic and extrinsic changes of social structures. Both emphases are relevant for the comparative study of stratification.

Within this broad context the rise of new social structures as of technical innovations appears as a multifaceted process, not exclusively identifiable with any one social group. Typically, the pioneers of innovation seek the protection of ruling groups rather than defy them, provided of course that such groups exist and can provide protection. The outcome of this process varies with the pressure for innovation and the degree to which given ruling groups themselves participate in innovation or feel jeopardized by it. At any rate, the emphasis upon the continuity of ruling groups in the era of modernization is a first corollary following from the rejection of the "either-or" image of tradition and modernity.

A second corollary involves what Karl Mannheim has called the "fundamental democratization" of modern society. The contrast between the monopoly of rule by a tiny minority of notables and the principle of universal suffrage in modern nation-states is striking and unquestioned. But the growth of citizenship which occurs in the transition from one to the other, involves highly diverse developments in which the relative rights and obligations of social classes are redefined, as the political process interacts (more or less autonomously) with the changing organization of production. In the era of modernization this interaction can be understood best if proper attention is given to the international setting as well as the internal differentiation of social structures.

In the end it may appear—from a mid-twentieth-century viewpoint—that the growth of citizenship and the nation-state is a more significant dimension of modernization than the distributive inequalities underlying the formation of social classes. In that perspective Marx's theory of social classes under capitalism appears as a sweeping projection of certain temporary patterns of early nineteenth-century England. Not the least argument favoring this conclusion is the growth of the welfare state in the industrialized societies of the world, which in one way or another provides a pattern of accommodation among competing social groups as well as a model to be emulated by the political and intellectual leaders of follower societies.[113] My object has been to provide a framework which can encompass these contemporary developments as well as the modernization processes of the past.

[113]Cf. Gaston Rimlinger, *Welfare Policy and Industrialization in Europe, America and Russia* (New York: John Wiley and Sons, 1971).

BIBLIOGRAPHIC ADDENDUM

Nation-Building and Citizenship was written after *Work and Authority in Industry* (1956) and *Max Weber: An Intellectual Portrait* (1960), as well as subsequent to the collaborations with Seymour Martin Lipset on *Social Mobility in Industrial Society* (1959) and the reader *Class, Status and Power* (1953). The early interest in industrialization and ideology can be traced through the articles collected in the two volumes of *Embattled Reason* (1988, 1989). The comparative analysis of historical change[1] begun in *Work and Authority* was a thread that ran through many works, including *Force, Fate and Freedom* (1984) and *Unsettled Affinities* (1993), but *Nation-Building* itself should properly be seen as the precursor to what my father, with some irony, used to say was either his *magnum opus* or the folly of his later years, *Kings or People: Power and the Mandate to Rule* (1978).[2]

---

[1] See the chapter with this title in Tom Burns and S.B. Saul, eds., *Social Theory and Economic Change* (London: Tavistock, 1967), pp. 67–86. A German version is in the *Kölner Zeitschrift für Soziologie* 17:3 (1965), pp. 429–46.

[2] The country cases in *Nation-Building* were discussed in "Public Authority in a Developing Political Community: The Case of India," *European Journal of Sociology* 4:39–85 (1963); "Diskussion über Industrialisierung und Kapitalismus," in Otto Stammer, ed. *Max Weber und die Soziologie heute* (Tübingen: J.C.B. Mohr, 1965), pp. 184–91; "Bemerkungen über die Sozialstruktur der Entwicklungsländer," *Jahrbuch der Universität Frankfurt* (Frankfurt: Klostermann, 1965), pp. 63–73; and in "A Case Study in Cultural and Educational Mobility: Japan and

The concept of nation-building has been widely adopted, particularly by those engaged in studying Asia and Africa. The Library of Congress lists more than 200 books and articles with the term in the title. The following is an indicative rather than comprehensive guide to a few of the longer English-language studies that have appeared, arranged geographically and in reverse chronological order.

Asia

General

Lachman Khubchandani, *Language, Culture and Nation-building: Challenges of Modernization* (New Delhi: Manohar 1991).

Bhuwan Upreti and Ramakant, *Nation-building in South Asia* (New Delhi: South Asian, 1991).

Urmila Phadnis, *Ethnicity and Nation-building in South Asia* (New Delhi: Sage, 1990).

A.K. Kalla and K.S. Singh, *Anthropology, Development and Nation-Building* (New Delhi: Concept, 1987).

Shaukat Ali, *Nation-building Development and Administration: A Third World Perspective* (Lahore: Aziz, 1988; 1979).

India

L.R. Singh, ed., *Nation-building and Development Process* (Jaipur: Rawat, 1994).

N. Radhakrishnan, ed., *Gandhian Perspective of Nation Building for World Peace* (Delhi: Konark, 1992).

Udayon Misra, ed., *Nation-building and Development in Northeast India* (Guwahati: Purbanchal Prakash, 1991).

T. K. Oommen, *State and Society in India: Studies in Nation-Building* (New Delhi: Sage, 1990).

Rabindra Dutt, ed., *Nation-Building in India: Socio-economic Factors* (New Delhi: Lancer International, 1987).

Yogesh Atal, *Building a Nation: Essays on India* (New Delhi: Abhinav, 1981).

the Protestant Ethic," in Neil Smelser and Seymour Martin Lipset, eds., *Social Structure and Mobility in Economic Development* (Chicago, Aldine, 1966), pp. 262–79.

Rajni Kothari, ed., *State and Nation-Building* (Bombay: Allied, 1976).

Jai Narayan, *Nation-building in India* (Varanasi: Navachetna Prakashan, 1975).

Pakistan, Bangladesh, Nepal

Abu Rahman, *Volunteerism and Nation-Building in Bangladesh* (Dhaka: Academic, 1993).

Aftab Kazi, *Ethnicity and Education in Nation-building: The Case of Pakistan* (Lanham: University Press, 1987).

Abdul Hafiz and Abdur Khan, eds., *Nation-building in Bangladesh: Retrospect and Prospect* (Dhaka: Institute of International and Strategic Studies, 1986).

Madhab Poudyal, *Public Administration and Nation-Building in Nepal* (Delhi: NBO, 1984).

Raymond Moore, *Nation-building and the Pakistan Army, 1947–1969* (Lahore: Aziz, 1979).

Thailand, Malaysia, Singapore

Michael Hill and Lian Fee, *The Politics of Nation-building and Citizenship in Singapore* (New York: Routledge, 1995).

Jumbala Prudhisan, *Nation-building and Democratization in Thailand: A Political History* (Bangkok: Chulalornkorn University, 1992).

Michael Howard, *Ethnicity and Nation-Building in the Pacific* (Tokyo: United Nations University, 1989).

Nazrul Islam, *Problems of Nation-building in Developing Countries: The Case of Malaysia* (Dhaka: University of Dhaka, 1988).

James Ongkili, *Nation-building in Malaysia, 1946–1974* (New York: Oxford, 1985).

J. Jayasuriya, *The Dynamics of Nation-Building in Malaysia* (Colombo: Associated Educational, 1983).

Japan, China

Joyce Kallgren, ed., *Building a Nation-state: China after Forty Years* (Berkeley: Institute of East Asian Studies, 1990).

Haruo Nagamine, ed., *Nation-building and Regional Development: the Japanese Experience* (Singapore: Maruzen Asia, 1981).

Arthur Young, *China's Nation-building Effort, 1927–1937: The Financial and Economic Record* (Stanford: Hoover Institution Press, 1971).

AFRICA

General

George Nzongola-Ntalaja, *Nation-building and State Building in Africa* (Harare: Sapes, 1993).

Donald Morrison et al., *Understanding Black Africa: Data and Analysis of Social Change and Nation-Building* (New York: Irvington, 1989).

Henry Okullu, *Church and State in Nation-building and Human Development* (Nairobi: Uyima, 1984).

Ernest Boateng, *Independence and Nation-building in Africa* (Tema: Ghana Publishing, 1973).

John Morrow, ed., *Nation-building in Africa: Problems and Prospects* (New Brunswick: Rutgers, 1969).

Gray Cowan et al., *Education and Nation-Building in Africa* (New York: Praeger, 1965).

West and Central Africa

Gabriel Olusanya, *Attempts at Nation-building in Nigeria: A Study in Poverty of Imagination and Creativity* (Ijebu-Ode: Nire, 1986).

Ndiva Kofele-Kale, ed., *An African Experiment in Nation-building: The Bilingual Cameroon Republic since Reunification* (Boulder: Westview, 1980).

Uma Eleazu, *Federalism and Nation-building: The Nigerian Experience, 1954–1964* (Ilfracombe: A. Stockwell, 1977).

Ladipo Adamolekun, *Sekou Toure's Guinea: An Experiment in Nation-building* (London: Methuen, 1976).

Brian Weinstein, *Gabon: Nation-building on the Ogooue* (Cambridge: MIT, 1966).

East and South Africa

Hermann Giliomee, *From Apartheid to Nation-building* (New York: Oxford, 1989).

Charles Simkins, *The Prisoners of Tradition and the Politics of Nation-Building* (Johannesburg: Institute of Race Relations, 1988).

John Harbeson, *Nation-building in Kenya: The Role of Land Reform* (Evanston: Northwestern, 1973).

Anthony Rweyemamu, ed. *Nation-building in Tanzania: Problems and Issues* (Nairobi: East African, 1970).

Cherry Gertzel et al., *Government and Politics in Kenya: A Nation-building text* (Nairobi: East African, 1969)

MIDDLE EAST

Dov Shinar, *Palestinian Voices: Communication and Nation-Building in the West Bank* (Boulder: Rienner, 1987).

Paula Rayman, *The Kibbutz Community and Nation-building* (Princeton: Princeton, 1981).

Amos Perlmutter, *Military and Politics in Israel: Nation-building and Role Expansion.* (Portland: International Specialized, 1977).

Dorothey Willner, *Nation-building and Community in Israel* (Princeton: Princeton, 1969).

RUSSIA, EASTERN AND CENTRAL EUROPE

Irina Livezeanu, *Cultural Politics in Greater Romania: Regionalism, Nation-building and Ethnic Struggle, 1918–1930* (Ithaca: Cornell, 1995).

Shireen Hunter, *The Transcaucasia in Transition: Nation-building and Conflict* (Washington: Center for Strategic and International Studies, 1994).

Victor Kremenyuk, *Conflicts In and Around Russia: Nation-building in Difficult Times* (Westport: Greenwood 1994).

Hagen Schulze, ed., *Nation-building in Central Europe* (New York: Berg, 1987).

WESTERN EUROPE

Sven Tagil, ed., *Ethnicity and Nation-building in the Nordic World* (Carbondale: Southern Illinois, 1995).

Jeffrey Prager, *Building Democracy in Ireland: Political Order and Cultural Integration in a Newly Independent Nation* (New York: Cambridge, 1986).

John Craig, *Scholarship and Nation-Building: The Universities of Strasbourg and Alsatian Society 1870–1939* (Chicago: University of Chicago, 1984).

Per Torsvik, ed., *Mobilization, Center-Periphery Structures and Nation-Building* (Oslo: Unversitetsforlaget, 1981).

Shmuel Eisenstadt and Stein Rokkan, *Building States and Nations* (Beverly Hills: Sage, 1973).

William Bluhm, *Building an Austrian Nation: The Political Integration of a Western State* (New Haven: Yale, 1973).

NORTH AND SOUTH AMERICA

George Thomas, *Revivalism and Cultural Change: Christianity, Nation-building and the Market in the 19th Century United States* (Chicago: University of Chicago, 1989).

Ann Tickner, *Self-Reliance versus Power Politics: The American and Indian Experience in Building Nation States* (New York: Columbia, 1987).

Francis Wagner, *Nation-building in the United States: The American Idea of Nationhood in Retrospect* (Canter Square: Alpha, 1985).

Cynthia Mahabir, *Crime and Nation-building in the Caribbean* (Boston: Schenkman, 1985).

Stephen Skowronek, *Building a New American State* (New York: Cambridge, 1982).

Rogers Hollingsworth, *Nation and State Building in America* (Boston: Little, Brown, 1971).

NAME INDEX

SUBJECT INDEX